Waltham Forest Libraries

Please return this item by the last date stamped. The loan may be
renewed unless required by another customer.

9|9		MELIA
2 9 OCT 2016		

Need to renew your books? **http://libsonline.walthamforest.gov.uk/** or
Dial 0115 929 3388 for Callpoint – our 24/7 automated telephone renewal
line. You will need your library card number and your PIN. If you do not
know your PIN, contact your local library.

WA   ES

904   D0540574

UNJUSTIFIABLE RISK?

THE STORY OF BRITISH CLIMBING

UNJUSTIFIABLE RISK?

THE STORY OF BRITISH CLIMBING

Simon Thompson

CICERONE

2 POLICE SQUARE, MILNTHORPE, CUMBRIA LA7 7PY

www.cicerone.co.uk

For Fiona

'Kiss the joy as it flies...'

Jim Perrin

Copyright © Simon Thompson 2010

First published 2010

ISBN 978 1 85284 627 5

The author has asserted his right under the Copyright, Designs and Patents Act 1988 to be identified as the author of this work.

A catalogue record for this book is available from the British Library.

Printed by KHL Printing, Singapore.

Front cover: Lenzspitze ridge, Switzerland (John Cleare)
Back cover: Cenotaph Corner, Snowdonia (John Cleare)

CONTENTS

ACKNOWLEDGEMENTS

From the moment I set out to write the story of British climbing, I have been guided along the way by generations of climbers who have written about their own exploits, as well as the many outstanding biographers and historians who have recorded and interpreted the actions of others. All of the authors listed in the Bibliography have contributed something to this book, but I am particularly indebted to Trevor Braham, Ronald Clark, Alan Hankinson, Peter Hansen, Trevor Jones, Arnold Lunn, Jim Perrin, Ted Pyatt, Robert Macfarlane, Kenneth Mason, Geoff Milburn, Jan Morris, Marjorie Nicolson, Simon Schama, Walt Unsworth, Colin Wells and Ken Wilson.

Apart from Colin Wells' excellent 'sampler', *A Brief History of British Mountaineering* (2001), produced for the Mountain Heritage Trust, it is many years since anybody has attempted to compress nearly 200 years of British rock climbing and mountaineering history into a single book. Inevitably, I have included many of the classic lines, for the benefit of those who may be exploring the history of climbing for the first time, but I hope that even the most seasoned veteran of mountain literature will discover one or two new variants here.

Throughout the book I have made extensive use of quotations to try to capture the spirit of the times in which the events I have described took place. I am very grateful to the following publishers and authors for their kind permission to reproduce extracts from the works detailed in the Notes: Bâton Wicks; the estate of Peter Boardman; Canongate Books; Chris Bonington; Constable & Robinson; Dennis Gray; Peter Hansen; Hodder & Stoughton; The Mountaineers Books; Orion Publishing; Jim Perrin; Random House Group; The Scottish Mountaineering Trust; the estate of Joe Tasker; Neil Wilson Publishing; and Walt Unsworth. Unsuccessful attempts were made to trace the copyright holders of a number of the older titles quoted at length. I have also included shorter quotes from a number of other authors, detailed in the Notes, whom I gratefully acknowledge here. Climbing journals and magazines have been an invaluable source of reference and quotes, particularly the *Climbers' Club Journal*, the *Fell and Rock Climbing Club Journal*, the *Himalayan Journal*, the *Rucksack Club Journal*, the *Scottish Mountaineering Club Journal*, *Climber & Rambler*, *Crags*, *High*, *Mountain*, *On The Edge*, *Summit* and, above all, the *Alpine Journal*, now in its 147th year, which remains the greatest record of British mountaineering history.

I am very grateful to the Alpine Club, the Abraham Brothers' Collection, John Beatty, Chris Bonington, John Cleare, Leo Dickinson, the Fell and Rock Climbing Club, Mick Fowler, Jimmy Marshall, Hamish MacInnes, Bernard Newman, Sandra Noel, Ernest Phillips, the Royal Geographical Society, Doug Scott, Gordon Stainforth, the Wayfarers' Club Archive, Ken Wilson and the Wrangham family for permission to use their photographs.

I would like to thank John Cleare, Steve Dean, Anna Lawford, the late Peter Hodgkiss, Tadeusz Hudowski, Gary Mellor and Gordon Stainforth for their help and advice. I am particularly grateful to Livia Gollancz and Sarah Gracie for reading and commenting on early drafts of the book and to Stephen Goodwin, John Porter and Kev Reynolds for their invaluable corrections, comments and thought-provoking suggestions on a much later draft. The climbing world is full of myths, told and retold until they become an established part of the lore. If some myths have crept into this book masquerading as facts, the responsibility is mine.

Finally, I would like to thank Margaret Body for her brilliant editing and fund of extremely funny stories and Jonathan Williams and the team at Cicerone Press for their constant enthusiasm, support and encouragement.

Our poignant adventure, our self-sought perils on a line of unreason to the summit of a superfluous rock, have no rational or moral justification.

Geoffrey Winthrop Young

1

INTRODUCTION

To the impartial observer, Britain does not appear to have any mountains. Yet the British invented the sport of mountain climbing, and for two periods in history, in the second half of the nineteenth century and for a shorter period in the second half of the twentieth century, they led the world. In no other comparably flat country have mountains and climbing played such a significant role in the development of the national psyche, both reflecting and influencing changing attitudes to nature and beauty, heroism and death. This book is about the social, cultural and economic conditions that gave rise to the sport in Britain, and the achievements and motives of the individual scientists and poets, parsons and anarchists, villains and judges, ascetics and drunks who have shaped it over the past 200 years.

Like all sports, climbing is the pursuit of a useless objective – the summit of a mountain or the top of a cliff – for amusement, diversion or fun, and in common with most other sports with a strong amateur tradition the means *are* more important than the end, but not by as much as some climbers like to pretend. Unlike most games, but in common with other field sports, climbing has no written rules. Instead there is an ever-evolving set of unwritten but widely accepted conventions that govern its conduct. The only sanction if you break these 'rules' is the disapproval of your peer group. As Colonel Edward Strutt, Alpine Club grandee and self-appointed guardian of British climbing morality in the 1930s, observed: 'The hand that would drive a piton into British rock would shoot a fox or net a salmon.'[1] In most sports it is easy to define what 'winning' means, but not in climbing. In the early days, success meant reaching the summit of an unclimbed peak, but mountaineering was never simply exploration in high places. People with truly exploratory

1

instincts soon became bored spending months trying to climb a single mountain (even if it was Everest) when the whole of the Himalaya lay around them, untravelled and unknown. The conquest of a virgin peak remains the ultimate ambition for some climbers today, but as the supply of readily accessible unclimbed mountains began to dwindle, winning was gradually redefined. In the mid-1890s, Fred Mummery, the leading climber of the day, wrote that 'the essence of the sport lies not in ascending a peak, but in struggling with and overcoming difficulties'.[2]

Over time, with improving technique and rising standards, it became clear that almost any rock face or ice wall could be climbed, given enough manpower and equipment, and the style of the ascent became paramount. The most dangerous and therefore the 'best' style is to climb a route alone ('solo'), without a rope. The worst is to drill holes in the rock and use expansion bolts to create a line of fixed ropes running from the bottom to the top. Between these two extremes lie an almost infinite variety of styles, the nuances of which confuse all but the most devoted practitioners of the sport. Climbers have always soloed short, easy routes on sunny days. Progressively the same approach was applied to longer, harder climbs, to alpine peaks and finally to the highest peaks of the Himalaya.

As with every sport, a large part of the attraction lies in the uncertainty of the outcome, but in climbing the consequences of failure can be fatal. Bill Shankly, the manager of Liverpool Football Club, once quipped that football 'isn't a matter of life and death, it's more important than that'. For elite climbers, this really is true. Overall, climbing is not a particularly dangerous sport – the risk of harm is more often imagined than real – but the sensation of fear is intensely real and that feeling either attracts or repels. For some it becomes almost an addiction. At the leading edge, the objective of the sport is to take risks that others consider unjustifiable, and within the small community of top climbers everyone knows a dozen or more people who have died in the mountains, and yet they continue to climb. Extreme climbing is the ultimate expression of 'deep play', Jeremy Bentham's term for an activity where the stakes are so high that the potential for loss far outweighs the potential for gain. From a utilitarian standpoint, it is clearly an irrational activity, but climbing is a sport for romantics, not rationalists, and climbers are drawn to risk like moths to a flame. The typical weekend climber eases himself cautiously forwards, pulling back the instant he feels the heat, but the frisson of fear is sufficient to sustain his heroic self-image through another mundane working week. The elite climber flies ever closer to the flame and plays 'this game of ghosts' for real.

Almost regardless of their absolute level of achievement, when climbers operate at their personal limit they experience an emotional intensity, both elation and despondency, that exceeds all but the most ecstatic and traumatic events in ordinary life. During a climb all mental noise, all distractions, are eliminated and the mind focuses solely on the flow of climbing. For a short period of time all of the cares and concerns of the world disappear and all that is left is the climber and the mountain. The experience is so vivid and taut that ordinary life can feel grey and flaccid in comparison. For elite climbers, 'deep play' is rational because a man who is afraid to die is afraid to live.

But there is more to climbing than pure heroics. It is possible to climb in a disused quarry full of rusting cars and stagnant pools or on a specially constructed wall in the middle of an industrial estate, but for the majority of climbers the beauty and grandeur of the surroundings are an intrinsic part of the sport. Mountains have always been regarded as spiritual places, and for the past 200 years they have also been regarded as beautiful, a refuge from the polluted and crowded complexity of the urban environment where most climbers are born and bred. Like ballet or gymnastics, the beauty of climbing also lies in movement. A mountain path is a physical manifestation of the aesthetic urge to see the view from the ridge and the next horizon, and there is beauty in the line of ascent, even individual moves, on the chosen mountain or crag. The most elegant 'classic' lines tend to follow distinctive natural rock features in grand surroundings, with an ever increasing sense of height and exposure as the route is ascended. Classic routes must present a significant climbing challenge and demand a variety of techniques, but they are often the easiest line of ascent of a particular rock face or mountain, so that escape to an easier route is impossible and the choice is either to go up or to retreat. Above all, classic routes have a history. Climbing is a human activity, and a rock without a history is just a rock.

The shared experience of hardship and danger on a climb can be the basis of the strongest friendships, but climbing is essentially a solitary sport and there are few more lonely situations (voluntarily entered into) than leading a long pitch at the absolute limit of your ability. While the activity itself tends to be solitary, the climbing community is gregarious and tribal. Perhaps because of the collective release of nervous tension, climbers are known for their excesses when they return to the valleys and the sport has a well-deserved reputation for wild and reckless behaviour. This strange and contradictory mixture of ingredients – heroic and aesthetic, gregarious and solitary, self-disciplined and reckless, ascetic and debauched – has attracted an equally strange and eclectic mixture of people to the sport. It has also created tensions between those whose motives are primarily heroic – the vigorous pursuit of liberty, adventure and self-fulfilment – and those whose motives are primarily aesthetic – concerned with man's emotional response to the mountain landscape.

Much has changed in the climbing world since its beginnings in the nineteenth century, but even more has remained the same. In many respects British climbers of today would be instantly recognisable to their Victorian predecessors, with their desire for adventure, love of wild places and need to escape from 'civilised' society. But the sport has also evolved, reflecting changes in British society, from a pastime undertaken by an eccentric and privileged minority to a part of the mainstream leisure and tourist industry. Society's attitude to climbing and to climbers has also changed. When British climbers first 'conquered' the Alps in the mid-Victorian era, the sport was regarded with mildly disapproving incomprehension, that men should risk their lives for such a useless ambition. By late Victorian and Edwardian times, as they extended their activities to almost every corner of the globe, climbers came to be seen as plucky heroes whose achievements underscored Britain's right to rule a quarter of the world. In the aftermath of the First World War, the disappearance of Mallory and Irvine, enveloped by clouds as they tried to reach the highest point on earth, had an almost redemptive quality after the mechanised mass slaughter of the trenches. When Hillary and Tenzing finally reached the summit of Everest after the Second World War, even though neither of them was British, they were part of a proudly nationalistic project, marking the end of Empire but heralding the dawn of the New Elizabethan Age. As climbing has progressively become a mass activity in the post-war years, the heroic status of climbers has come under increasing scrutiny. In the secular twenty-first century, the British like their heroes to be banal celebrities or saintly figures who combine benevolence with bravery. Most top climbers are neither banal nor benevolent, but they are brave. They deliberately set out to do things that no-one has attempted to do before: things that most normal, rational people would find quite terrifying. Yet the motives and desires of elite climbers, as they grapple with their icy peaks, are not so very different from those of the 4 million ordinary climbers and hill walkers active in Britain today, and it is partly this sense of recognition and shared experience that makes the lives of these flawed heroes so compelling.

I first started rock climbing in the long, hot summer of 1975. Within a week I seconded an HVS in hiking boots and by the end of the summer I was leading VS (see Appendix I for an explanation of climbing grades and Appendix II for a glossary of climbing terms). I was completely obsessed by the sport and flattered myself that I had the makings of a good climber. By the end of the 1970s, as climbing standards continued to rise inexorably while my own energies and enthusiasms were increasingly directed elsewhere, I concluded that I was probably an average sort of climber. By the mid-1980s it was obvious that even this was an exaggeration. With the benefit of 34 years of experience it is now clear that, in terms of technical difficulty, my rock climbing achievements reached their zenith about 30 years ago while my equally modest mountaineering achievements peaked about 15 years ago. Over the past 34 years many things have changed in my life, but the mountains have remained a constant. I have had good days and bad days at work, but I am hard pressed to think of a single climbing day that I have regretted, at least in retrospect. When I reached the age of 49, mindful of Don Whillans' admonition that 'by the time you're 50, you're completely fucked', I decided to write this book before it was too late. The decision reflects my continuing fascination with this strange sport.

Given my lack of accomplishment as a climber, some readers may question whether I am qualified to write a history of the sport. I would contend that the best climbers do not necessarily make the best historians, since so many of them appear to agree with Winston Churchill that 'history will be kind to me, for I intend to write it'. Donald Robertson, who died in a climbing accident in 1910, observed that a truly honest account of a climbing day has yet to be written, and it remains a truth almost universally acknowledged that there are only two approaches to writing about climbing: exaggeration or understatement. Since the activity necessarily takes place in inaccessible places with few impartial witnesses, the boundary between fact and fiction is often blurred, and climbing history is full of larger-than-life characters around whom myths have grown up that are certainly not literally true, but which may nevertheless provide a true insight into the nature of the climber, their deeds and the times in which they lived.

Gustave Flaubert compared writing history to drinking an ocean and pissing a cupful, and there can be few other sports that have given rise to a body of literature as rich, varied and, above all, extensive as climbing. Having drunk at least part of the ocean, the challenge is to decide what should go into the cup. Inevitably, this particular version of climbing history reflects my own interests and prejudices, and no doubt contains both omissions and inaccuracies. But I hope that it also reflects the true spirit and tradition of the sport which is, first and foremost, about the pure joy of climbing.

2

BEFORE 1854:

IN SEARCH OF THE SUBLIME

Until 1854 the British hardly concerned themselves with climbing except as a means of exploiting the animal and mineral resources of sea cliffs and mountains, or gaining a military advantage. In the 11 years that followed, they climbed almost every major peak in the Alps.

During the 'Golden Age' of alpinism, between 1854 and 1865, 39 major alpine peaks were climbed for the first time, all but eight of them by British parties. During this intense period of activity the British can legitimately claim to have invented the *sport* of climbing, and for the rest of the nineteenth century they remained at the forefront of developments, undertaking ever more difficult routes in the Alps and expanding their exploratory activities throughout the world to Norway, the Caucasus, the Rockies, the Andes and the Himalaya.

What caused this sudden explosion of climbing activity in the second half of the nineteenth century? Developments in science and technology, industrialisation, urbanisation and changing attitudes to the natural world all contributed to the birth of the sport, and Britain led the world in each of these fields. Climbing was both a result of, and a reaction against, a period of unprecedented peace, increasing wealth and leisure, and the ever more complex, artificial and ordered existence of the emerging urban middle class. Just like climbers today, the pioneers were attracted to the sport primarily as an escape from the crowded complexity of life in the city to the vigorous simplicity, beauty and adventure of the mountains.

FROM GLOOM TO GLORY

For most of British history the idea of climbing for pleasure and enjoyment, in other words for sport, was unimaginable. Life for the overwhelming majority of people was a struggle for survival, and man's attitude to the natural world was essentially utilitarian and exploitative. Animals, plants and rocks provided food and shelter, and most people suffered enough hardship meeting these basic needs without undertaking unnecessary activities that might add to their discomfort. The wilderness, and mountains in particular, were literally seen as 'waste land': unproductive and potentially dangerous. In keeping with the classical ideal, beauty was associated with fertility. Fields, orchards, vegetable gardens and fish ponds were beautiful; mountains were not.

Whereas many religions see a natural world inhabited by gods and goddesses, spirits and sprites, the Judeao-Christian tradition is centred on man, made in the image of a single transcendent God, aloof and separate from nature, and commanded in Genesis to 'be fruitful and multiply, and fill the earth and subdue it; and have dominion over the fish of the sea and over the birds of the air and over every living thing that moves upon the earth'. It is not a world view to inspire a love of wild nature, and for most of modern British history man's ascendency over the natural world was the unquestioned object of human endeavour.[1] People took pride in converting wild nature into cultivated land, seeing this as both an economic and a moral imperative. The cultivation of the soil was a symbol of civilisation, and the religious aspiration was to restore the world to the fertility and order of the Garden of Eden before the fall.[2] Even the word 'paradise' is derived from the Persian for a walled enclosure, a man-made garden from which wild nature was excluded.

Most people did not stray far from their homes, and the few who travelled long distances did so for a purpose. Merchants, pilgrims and soldiers went in search of profit, salvation or victory and some may have enjoyed the journey, but travel was a means to an end, not an end in itself. Even young aristocrats setting off on the Grand Tour did so ostensibly for the purpose of education. They studied languages, art, politics or agricultural techniques and collected ornaments for their houses and gardens. Until the late eighteenth century the journey itself, which often took them through the Alps, was generally regarded as dangerous, expensive, time-consuming and uncomfortable.

During the eighteenth and nineteenth centuries, British attitudes to nature and to wilderness fundamentally changed. As the population of Britain and Ireland increased nearly sevenfold from 6 million to 41 million, demand for food expanded and agriculture became larger scale and more systematic, transforming the appearance of the countryside. Six years before the start of the Golden Age of mountaineering, in 1848, John Stuart Mill, the liberal politician, philosopher and campaigner for the preservation of natural landscapes, expressed his fear that Britain was becoming a country with 'nothing left to the spontaneous activity of nature; with every foot of land brought into cultivation, which is capable of growing food for human beings; every flowery waste or natural pasture ploughed up, all quadrupeds or birds which are not domesticated for man's use exterminated as his rivals for food, every hedgerow or superfluous tree rooted out, and scarcely a place left where a wild shrub or flower could grow without being eradicated as a weed in the name of improved agriculture'.[3] Partly due to Mill's influence, some areas of uncultivated common land were preserved for the benefit of urban dwellers who valued it for leisure, but by then vast swathes of the British landscape had been tamed.

As agriculture became more intensive and wilderness became scarce, there was a dawning realisation that beauty lies, at least in part, in *contrast* to the ordinary, and an aesthetic reaction set in. In an increasingly ordered world, the apparent chaos and disorder of wild places came to be identified with beauty, and much of the remaining wilderness was to be found in the mountains. During the late eighteenth and early nineteenth century, mountains, which had previously been dismissed as 'deformities of the earth', 'monstrous excrescences', 'tumors, blisters' and 'warts', became the object of the highest aesthetic

9

admiration.[4] Even parks and gardens were 'landscaped' to make them resemble wild, uncultivated land.

Population growth was accompanied by rapid urbanisation. At the beginning of the eighteenth century just 25 per cent of the British population lived in towns and only 13 per cent lived in 'cities' of more than 5,000 inhabitants. When climbing took off as a sport in the 1850s, more than half of the British population lived in towns (a tipping point that the world as a whole passed only in 2007). By 1900 over three-quarters of the population lived in towns, and over half in cities with more than 50,000 inhabitants. Following the victory over Napoleon at Waterloo in 1815, the population of London swelled to 2 million, the largest city on earth, as it rapidly became the trading and financial capital of the world. At the same time there was a major shift in population from the agricultural south to the industrialising north. Overcrowding, air pollution from coal fires and water pollution from sewage and industrial waste created an ever sharper contrast between the urban and rural environment. In 1854, at the start of the Golden Age of alpine exploration, there was a major outbreak of cholera in London. Four years later the inhabitants were subjected to the 'Great Stink', when the smell from the Thames was so bad that parliament had to halt proceedings. London literally 'consumed' people: the death rate exceeded the birth rate until the start of the nineteenth century, and population growth was driven solely by inward migration from rural areas. But the development of trade and industry resulted in dramatic increases in wealth and prosperity, creating a professional middle class with some education, some capital and much ambition. It was overwhelmingly from this new, urban middle class, rather than the traditional rural aristocracy and landed gentry, that the early converts to climbing were drawn.

During Renaissance times, cities were seen as synonymous with civility, while the countryside was regarded as rustic and boorish. When people thought of heaven, they envisaged it as a city: a 'New Jerusalem'. By the late eighteenth and early nineteenth century, rapid urbanisation and industrialisation brought about a dramatic reversal of attitudes, and the countryside came to be regarded as more beautiful than the urban environment. Mountains were increasingly presented as examples of the virtues of a natural, primitive life, in contrast to the artificial sophistication of life in the cities.[5] Albrecht von Haller's popular epic poem *Die Alpen* (1732), which was translated into all the major European languages, developed the idea of an alpine utopia populated by simple pastoralists, protected from lowland greed, fashion and debauchery. It portrayed a pure, happy and moral existence, despite the evidence of poverty, dirt and cretinism that early travellers to the Alps recorded in their dairies, and helped to establish the idea that mountains are the work of God, while cities are the work of man.

The Romantic movement in the late eighteenth century reflected growing concerns that cities were becoming too large, too overcrowded, and too complex for man's good, and that growing wealth and inequality were leading to vanity and vice. It advocated an escape to an imaginary medieval past of rural simplicity, independence and liberty. In France, the movement had a revolutionary impact. In England it assumed a more conservative aspect, but by the late eighteenth century the romantic idea that mountains are both beautiful and provide an escape, however temporary, from an increasingly urban, materialistic and corrupt society had taken root in British consciousness. It remains strong to this day. As Jean-Jacques Rousseau wrote in 1762: 'Happy is the land, my young friend, where one need not seek peace in the wilderness! But where is that country?'[6]

Rousseau, the founding figure of the Romantic movement, was primarily interested in the social and political implications of rural life rather than the landscape, but he also celebrated mountain beauty. Describing a journey from Lyon to Chambéry in 1732 he wrote: 'I need torrents, rocks, firs, dark woods, mountains, steep roads to climb or descend, abysses beside me to make me afraid.'[7] The attraction of being 'afraid' was new and significant. When Thomas Gray and his friend and fellow Old Etonian Horace Walpole travelled to the Alps in 1739 they too discovered the pleasure of mountain terror. Gray was to become the most widely read English poet of the eighteenth century, while

Walpole was the son of the Whig prime minister Sir Robert Walpole. Walpole took with him to the Alps a King Charles spaniel, 'the prettiest, fattest, dearest creature', called Tory. While they were ascending Mont Cenis, Tory was eaten by a wolf, which caused Gray to observe that Mont Cenis 'carries the permission mountains have of being frightful rather too far'. Gray's record of their journey was the first unequivocally romantic account in English of mountain sublimity; the idea that mountains inspire feelings of wonder and awe. Where earlier travellers had recoiled from mountain terror, Gray and Walpole revelled in it.[8]

Some 18 years later, in 1757, Edmund Burke published his *Philosophical Inquiry into the Origins of Our Ideas of the Sublime and Beautiful*. In the age of the Enlightenment, Burke was the evangelist of darkness, storms, cataracts and precipices. He was interested in the emotional response to 'terrible objects', such as 'gloomy forests and... the howling wilderness',[9] and distinguished between 'beauty', which is light, smooth, delicate and inspires love, and 'the sublime' which is vast, gloomy, rugged, powerful and inspires terror. But Burke believed that the sublime was also capable of producing pleasure, because 'terror is a passion which always produces delight when it does not press too close'. By the late eighteenth century, the emerging urban professional classes in Britain felt sufficiently in control of their own lives and of the environment to make 'terror that does not press too close' a desirable experience, and mountain travel met this new need.

Burke also identified solitude as a sublime experience: 'Temporary solitude...is itself agreeable...[But] an entire life of solitude contradicts the purposes of our being...[D]eath itself is scarcely an idea of more terror.'[10] Many early visitors to the mountains identified solitude as one of the most appealing features of the landscapes they sought out – a reaction to their increasingly overcrowded lives in the cities – and access to open spaces came to be seen as a symbol of human freedom. In 1848 John Stuart Mill wrote that 'solitude in the presence of natural beauty and grandeur is the cradle of thoughts and aspirations which are not only good for the individual, but which society could ill do without'.[11]

In 1769, 30 years after his journey through the Alps with Horace Walpole, Thomas Gray wrote his *Journal of the Lakes,* an account that established the Lake District as the definitively sublime English landscape of 'turbulent chaos' and 'shining purity'. By the 1780s, visitors were pouring into the Lake District and Snowdonia, and the more adventurous began to visit Switzerland and Savoy. Most early visitors, like many tourists today, did not stray far from the roads and were content to admire the views from the valley, but in 1792 Joseph Budworth, a retired army captain who had lost his arm at the siege of Gibraltar, walked some 385km/240 miles through the Lake District, hiring local guides to take him into the high fells. The account of his travels encouraged the development of fell walking as a respectable and fashionable pastime that combined an aesthetic appreciation of the landscape with a distinctly sporting attitude to movement through the mountains. In Britain, an activity may be said to have entered the cultural mainstream when it becomes the object of popular humour. A tour of the Lakes achieved this status in 1811 when it was satirised in William Combe's illustrated poem *The Tour of Doctor Syntax, in Search of the Picturesque.*[12]

In Scotland the original rationale for mountain exploration was primarily military, to extend the network of roads, bridges and forts set up by General Wade after the first Jacobite uprising in 1715, and used to subdue the second in 1745. Captain Birt, a surveyor under Wade's command in the 1720s, used the conventional vocabulary of the time to describe the Scottish mountains as 'monstrous excrescences...rude and offensive to the sight...their huge naked rocks producing the disagreeable appearance of a scabbed head...a dismal gloomy brown drawing upon a dirty purple and most of all disagreeable when the heather is in bloom'.[13] As the security threat receded, the country gradually opened up to more peaceful travel, but perceptions of the landscape were slow to change. In 1773, the committed urbanite Dr Johnson undertook a tour of Scotland during which he observed of the Highlands that 'an eye accustomed to flowery pastures and waving harvests is astonished and repelled by this wide extent of hopeless sterility...[T]his uniformity of barrenness can afford very little amusement to the traveller.'[14] Over the ensuing decades, painters and writers depicting a romantic landscape of shining lochs, gnarled Caledonian pines, craggy mountains and regal stags transformed this uniformity of barrenness into highly desirable real estate for the leisured classes. Today, one of General Wade's military roads forms part of the West Highland Way, along which dozens of travellers may be seen each day trudging through the peat and rain, presumably in the hope and expectation that it will afford some amusement.

The fresh appeal of the mountains was publicised in pictures, plays, poems and novels. Englishmen purchased paintings by Salvator Rosa, Claude Lorrain, Gaspar Poussin and their many eighteenth-century followers, copiers and imitators,[15] and there was a flourishing trade in prints. By the nineteenth century, landscape painting, which was virtually unknown before the seventeenth century, had become the dominant art form, and for many urban visitors to the country the appeal of the landscape lay in its similarity to the pictures they had been taught to admire, hence the expression 'picturesque'. Turner visited the Alps in 1802, producing his Alpine Sketchbook which was later championed by Ruskin in his paean to 'mountain gloom and mountain glory'[16] and helped to define the idea of mountain beauty in the mid-nineteenth century. Like other landscape painters, Turner also sought to capture the moral dimension of the mountains as 'chastisers of human vanity and hubris':[17] it was no coincidence that he painted *Snowstorm: Hannibal and his Army crossing the Alps* in 1812, the year of Napoleon's retreat from Moscow.

The English Romantic poets were also energetic propagandists for the new natural aesthetic. For a time Coleridge and Wordsworth lived some 13 miles apart in the Lake District, in Keswick and Grasmere respectively. Both were prodigious walkers and regularly set out on foot to visit each other, returning the same day. Both of them also went climbing, Wordsworth as a schoolboy in search of birds' eggs, Coleridge in search of sensation. Coleridge's description of descending Broad Stand on Scafell in the Lake District in 1802 is the first literary account

14

of an adrenaline-rush brought about by rock climbing:[18] 'Every Drop increased the Palsy of my Limbs', he wrote of his descent, and when he reached the safety of Mickledore he 'lay in a state of almost prophetic Trance and Delight – and blessed God aloud, for the powers of Reason and the Will, which remaining no danger can overpower us!' In his account, the landscape was merely the backdrop against which he experienced a personal drama of risk and fear.

In the mid-eighteenth century, the idea that mountains are beautiful and worthy of exploration for their aesthetic appeal was revolutionary. By the mid-nineteenth century the idea was commonplace amongst the urban professional classes, but it was still a concept that would have been incomprehensible to the majority of the population at that time, as they struggled to make a living. Leslie Stephen, an early pioneer of alpine climbing, was taken aback when a visiting Swiss guide found the rooftops and chimneys of London far finer than the view from Mont Blanc. Likewise, Cecil Slingsby, the Yorkshire-born 'father of Norwegian mountaineering', once told his guide that he thought the view of the fjord and mountains from his house was very fine. The guide shook his head philosophically: 'Not so fertile,' he replied.[19] To the people who actually lived and worked in the mountains, the romantic ideal was absurd. Amateur mountaineering (as opposed to professional guiding) was overwhelmingly an activity undertaken by rich, well-educated men, and later women, who lived in the towns and cities of the plains, and the appeal of the mountains lay, in large part, in their *contrast* to a comfortable life in town. Even Wordsworth conceded that 'cataracts and mountains are good occasional society, but they will not do for constant companions'.[20]

AESTHETES AND HEROES

Relief from the day-to-day toil of earning a living from the land also enabled the emerging urban middle classes to entertain thoughts of personal liberty and self-fulfilment. Both were an essential part of the Romantic movement. Romantic heroes are vigorous and passionate individualists, with little regard for the social consequences of their actions; love, hate, resentment and jealousy, martial ardour and contempt for cowards are all admired. They are frequently selfish, solitary, violent, anti-social and anarchic.[21] Some climbers clearly conform to this aspect of the romantic tradition, even if they may appear to lack any aesthetic appreciation. Many more are attracted by the mildly anarchic self-image of the sport, and even the most law-abiding climbers appear to take some vicarious pride in the antics of the wilder members of the climbing community. As climbing has developed in Britain over the past 200 years, these twin aspects of the Romantic movement – the aesthetic and the heroic – have developed side by side, sometimes complementary, sometimes in conflict. Aesthetes emphasise the beauty and spiritual appeal of the mountains and man's emotional response to the landscape. The heroic school is more concerned with personal courage and the pursuit of freedom and self-fulfilment. While the aesthetic school is contemplative, the heroic is competitive. The aesthete seeks harmony with nature; the hero seeks to conquer nature. For the vast majority of climbers today and throughout history, the pleasures of mountaineering combine both elements, and the balance between the two often shifts with increasing years: the uncompromising hero dies young, retires or suffers diminishing returns, while the accumulation of reminiscences and personal associations only adds to the allure of the mountains for the ageing aesthete.

The aesthetic tradition may appear to us now to have been stronger for much of the early part of British climbing history, but this probably reflects the literary record more than reality at the time. In general, aesthetically inclined climbers wrote more books than their heroic contemporaries, who were often content just to climb. The strength of the aesthetic influence in the literary record should not obscure the fact that the heroic tradition, of an anarchic, competitive, sometimes criminal and frequently jingoistic pursuit of individual liberty has been a vital part of

British climbing throughout its history, particularly at the leading edge of the sport. After reading Rousseau's *Discourse on Inequality* (1754), which advocated the abandonment of civilisation and a return to the life of the 'natural man', Voltaire wrote 'one longs, in reading your book, to walk on all fours. But as I have lost that habit for more than sixty years, I feel unhappily the impossibility of resuming it.'[22] His thoughts were echoed by a guest staying at the Wasdale Head Inn in the Lake District in the late nineteenth century who described his fellow guests, all of whom were climbers, as 'men struggling to degenerate into apes'.[23] To this day, many climbers are, perhaps unwittingly, pursuing Rousseau's ideal of the 'noble savage' for a few weeks each year.

Pococke and Windham, two Englishmen who visited the Alps in 1741, were in many ways the prototype for subsequent generations of British climbers in the heroic rather than aesthetic mould. They arrived in the Chamonix valley with a party of 11 others and camped in fields near the town. Richard Pococke, who had recently travelled in the East, wore an exotic Arab robe. His companion, 'Boxing' Windham, had a reputation for rowdy athleticism and had been accused of drunkenness, assault and wanton shooting while studying in Geneva. The entire party was heavily armed. As Windham noted: 'One is never the worse for it and oftentimes it helps a Man out of a Scrape.'[24] They climbed up to Montenvers and descended to the glacier which, as a result of Windham's memorable description, is still called the Mer de Glace. Standing on the ice, they uncorked a bottle of wine and drank to the success of British arms. Their expedition contained at least three elements that would reappear throughout the history of British climbing: adventure, alcohol and a belligerent contempt for foreigners.

The motives of Colonel Mark Beaufoy, an Englishman who was the first foreigner to climb Mont Blanc (4,807m/15,770ft) in 1787 (the fourth ascent), remain obscure, but the beauty of the mountain landscape does not appear to have made a lasting impression. He had been moved by 'the desire everyone has to reach the highest places on earth'[25] and recorded that 'he suffered much, thought he had gone blind, got a swelled face and regretted he had undertaken such a thing'.[26] Nevertheless, he was the first Englishman to climb a major alpine peak.

In parallel with the Romantic movement, the growing popularisation of science during the late eighteenth and early nineteenth century provided a further impetus to mountain exploration. The development of printing technology and publishing spread scientific knowledge as subscription libraries sprang up in major towns and cities and natural history became a popular pastime for the educated classes. Geologists and botanists were pioneering explorers of the British hills. The first recorded ascent of Britain's highest mountain, Ben Nevis (1,344m/4,406ft), in 1771, and the first recorded rock climb, on Clogwyn Du'r Arddu in Snowdonia in 1798, were both undertaken in order to collect plant specimens. The idea of mountain climbing purely for sport and pleasure had still not been accepted and, in keeping with the spirit of the age, many early pioneers insisted that their motives were primarily scientific. De Saussure, the Geneva-born founder of 'scientific alpinism' who sponsored the first ascent of Mont Blanc and made the third himself in 1787, wrote: 'I was bound to make the scientific observations and experiments which alone gave value to my venture.'[27] However, as his *Voyages dans les Alpes* (1779–96) makes clear, he was interested in far more than natural history, and his book influenced future generations of British climbers to follow in his footsteps for reasons that were often far from scientific.

James Forbes, one of the founding fathers of British mountaineering, also claimed to be primarily motivated by science. He visited the Pyrenees in 1835 and the Alps in 1839, as well as making extensive journeys on foot across the Scottish Highlands, including the first ascent of Sgurr nan Gillean on Skye in 1836. The son of a wealthy banker, Sir William Forbes, and Williamina Belsches, the first love of Sir Walter Scott, Forbes was elected a Fellow of the Royal Society at the age of 23 and became Professor of Natural Philosophy at Edinburgh one year later. He was particularly fascinated by glaciology, a subject that attracted widespread interest in Britain following the publication of a book by the

Swiss scientist Louis Agassiz in 1840 which suggested that glaciers had once been much more extensive. As evidence accumulated of an 'Ice Age' during which glaciers had scooped out the mountains and scoured the valleys of northern Britain, people travelled to the Alps just for the experience of walking on these rivers of ice. Forbes' book *Travels through the Alps of Savoy,* published in 1843, contained both scientific observations and the first account in the English language of a series of alpine climbs, including the fourth ascent of the Jungfrau (4,158m/13,642ft) in 1841. The book, which was widely read, communicated Forbes' enthusiasm for science and the pure joy of climbing: 'Happy the traveller who...starts on the first day's walk amongst the Alps in the tranquil morning of a long July day, brushing the early morning dew before him and, armed with his staff, makes for the hill-top – begirt with rock or ice as the case may be – whence he sees the field of his summer's campaign spread out before him, its wonders, its beauties, and its difficulties, to be explained, to be admired, and to be overcome.'[28]

Glaciers also had an indirect impact on mountaineering because of the extraordinary popular interest in polar exploration in the first half of the nineteenth century. During the 'Great Peace' following the defeat of Napoleon in 1815, the Royal Navy embarked upon a series of exploratory missions that were the most expensive in history before the United States and Soviet space programmes in the second half of the twentieth century. They set out to fill in the blanks on the map of the Congo, the Sahara and the Sahel, but in the period from 1820 to 1850, expeditions to the Arctic and Antarctic captured the public imagination more than any other. The great polar explorers became household names, including William Parry, who found the entrance to the North-West Passage in 1819; John Franklin, 'the man who ate his boots' during a disastrous overland expedition to Canada's northern coast in 1822; James Ross, who discovered the northern magnetic pole in 1831 and explored the Antarctic in 1839; and the leaders of numerous overland and naval expeditions that set out to search for Franklin when he and his crew disappeared once again in 1847. Accounts of these journeys in the press and in bestselling books formed part of the childhood experience of the generation of Englishmen that set out to conquer the Alps in the 1850s.

These great exploratory expeditions were, from a practical point of view, quite useless. The North-West Passage proved not to be a passage (although global warming has since made it one), the Arctic and Antarctic had no economic or strategic significance, and the leaders of the expeditions were often extraordinarily incompetent. But the public celebrated their failures almost more than their successes. To Victorians, explorers represented the romantic ideal of a quest: a reminder of England's chivalrous and buccaneering past. With its combination of hardship and heroism, polar exploration, in particular, had the effect of making a virtue out of suffering. Franklin appeared alongside Frobisher, Drake, Cook and Nelson in children's books, and a whole generation of young men grew up in the mid-nineteenth century with the ambition to become explorers and to suffer. Most of them never went near the poles, but some found that there was a region of glaciers and snow, accessible by railway in the heart of Europe, where it was possible to become an explorer for a few weeks each summer. Many of the first generation of alpine climbers openly acknowledged the inspiration that polar exploration provided. Edward Whymper, the conqueror of the Matterhorn, wanted to be a polar explorer. Even Leslie Stephen, the great mid-Victorian intellectual, confessed that in the Alps he imagined himself walking across the Arctic wastes to encourage himself to keep going.

The importance of exploration was reflected in the status of the Royal Geographical Society, which was founded in 1830 and to this day occupies 'the best country house in London' on the edge of Hyde Park at Kensington Gore. The link between exploration, suffering and heroism was openly acknowledged. An article in 1881, celebrating the first 50 years of the Society, referred to them as 'the most perilous and therefore the most glorious'.[29] As the Empire expanded, so too did the need for geographers to survey, map and catalogue the resources of the conquered territories, and since high mountain ranges frequently form natural boundaries, exploration in mountainous areas on the edge of the Empire often had a military and strategic, as well as purely geographic, significance. In the Himalaya, in particular, much of the early exploration was motivated by the need to define and defend the boundaries between the British, Russian and Chinese empires. Ambitious and courageous young men were naturally drawn to this 'Great Game', which combined nationalism and heroism in romantic surroundings.

Europeans were late to realise the scale of the Himalaya, and when a reconnaissance expedition by Lieutenant Webb and Captain Raper in 1808 calculated the height of Dhaulagiri at 8,188m/26,862ft they were astonished by the result. Until that time it was widely assumed that the Andes were the highest mountains in the world. In 1848–50 Sir Joseph Hooker, a botanist and protégé of Charles Darwin who had already sailed to Antarctica with Captain James Ross, made a number of journeys into the Himalaya from Darjeeling to Sikkim. He also crossed into eastern Nepal (an area subsequently closed to Europeans for nearly a century), reaching the border of Tibet. When he was arrested and held prisoner by the Raja of Sikkim, the East India Company annexed a portion of southern Sikkim, thereby bringing the British Raj to the foot of Kangchenjunga (8,586m/28,169ft), the third highest peak in the world. The Survey of India started mapping the foothills of the Himalaya in 1846, and the height of Everest (8,848m/29,028ft) was first determined in 1852. Until 1883, when the first purely sporting expedition took place, the main purpose of Himalayan exploration was military and scientific: to map and survey the land and to collect specimens. The remoteness and huge extent of the region made it a scientific curiosity for much longer than the Alps, and British expeditions to the region often tried, usually unsuccessfully, to combine scientific and sporting objectives until the 1930s. As a result of this legacy, and a more recent dispute over ownership of photographs from the 1953 Everest expedition, the Alpine Club and the Royal Geographical Society have a somewhat uneasy relationship to this day.

While scientific and military considerations motivated much early mountain exploration, for John Ruskin the overwhelming attraction was aesthetic. Ruskin was the son of a prosperous sherry merchant in the City of London who bemoaned the fact that his son knew 'the shape of every needle round Mont Blanc, and could not tell you now where Threadneedle Street is'.[30] Like Rousseau, Ruskin was a social critic and reformer, but whereas mountains were merely a backdrop for Rousseau's social and political ideas, Ruskin saw the appreciation and understanding of mountain beauty as an end in itself. He was a gifted public orator, with the ability to speak with absolute conviction on a huge range of topics, and was as popular at working men's clubs as he was at Eton and Oxford.

Ruskin became a convert to and prophet of the cult of mountains after making his first visit to the Alps and reading De Saussure's *Voyage dans les Alpes* in 1833 at the age of 14. He went on to visit the Alps 19 times between 1833 and 1888. A visionary and frequently contradictory thinker and aesthete, he loved mountains and hated mountaineers with almost equal passion. Domineering and protective parents combined with a lack of personal initiative meant that he never climbed himself and, perhaps as a consequence, he despised people who did, regarding almost any intrusion into the high mountain environment as a sacrilege. He identified the heroic tendency in many climbers – 'the real ground for reprehension of Alpine climbing is that with less cause, it excites more vanity than any other athletic skill' – and rejected it forcefully: 'True lovers of natural beauty...would as soon think of climbing the pillars of the choir at Beauvais for a gymnastic exercise, as of making a playground of Alpine snow.'[31] An accomplished artist, he was also profoundly influenced by scientific developments and had ambitions to become president of the Geological Society. He particularly admired the works of Alexander von Humboldt, the great German explorer and scientist, and the pioneering geologists James Hutton and Charles Lyell, who popularised the concept that the present landscape is the key to the past. In *Modern Painters Volume IV: Of Mountain Beauty* (1856), Ruskin set out to open people's eyes to mountain beauty by interpreting its individual components, using a slightly uneasy combination of artistic criticism and scientific analysis, while maintaining an awareness of the aesthetic and spiritual value of the landscape as a whole. The book had a major influence on many early alpinists, including Leslie Stephen, redefining their perception of beauty.

In a typical example of his sometimes contradictory thinking, Ruskin saw the mountains as sacred examples of God's work but, despite his opposition to climbing, he also recognised that they might be a means for men to test and discover themselves. In a letter to his father in 1863 he wrote: 'If you come to a dangerous place, and turn back from it, though it may have been perfectly right and wise to do so, still your *character* has suffered some slight deterioration: you are to that extent weaker, more lifeless, more effeminate, more liable to passion and error in future; whereas if you go through with the danger, though it may have been apparently rash and foolish to encounter it, you come out of the encounter a stronger and better man, fitter for every sort of work or trial, and *nothing but danger* produces this effect.'[32] This was far more than Burke's eighteenth-century idea that terror 'always produces delight when it does not press too close'. By the mid-nineteenth century deliberately seeking out risk and danger had become morally desirable.

Changing attitudes to the moral value of danger reflected the huge influence of the theory of evolution set out by Charles Darwin in *The Origin of Species by Means of Natural Selection* (1859), which was subtitled *The Preservation of Favoured Races in the Struggle for Life*. The biological concept of evolution rapidly became woven into almost every aspect of British thought, providing an apparent justification for imperialism abroad and sharp class divisions at home. But the theory also gave rise to self-doubt, that evolution might be followed by dissolution, and that increasing wealth and comfort were making British society soft and decadent. It was the political philosopher Herbert Spencer, not Darwin, who coined the phrase 'survival of the fittest', and the idea of economic and social Darwinism spurred the British to ever greater efforts to demonstrate their 'fitness' in both their work and leisure pursuits. In Germany, Nietzsche also believed in the moral value of danger and saw in mountaineering the perfect testing ground for his cult of the hero and contempt for weakness: 'The discipline of suffering – of great suffering – know ye not that it is only this discipline that has produced all the elevation of humanity hitherto...This hardness is requisite for every mountain climber.'[33] Nietzsche's philosophy influenced German-speaking climbers, many of whom were students, from the late nineteenth century onwards, and through the writing of German and Austrian mountaineers it had a profound impact on the post-war generation of British climbers in the 1950s and 60s.

Under the influence of eighteenth-century notions of the sublime, mountain travellers had already experienced feelings of awe, terror and exultation once reserved for God. By the mid to late nineteenth century, as urbanisation, industrialisation and scientific developments, including the theory of evolution, progressively undermined the authority of the established church, the experience of walking and climbing in the mountains became at least a partial substitute for traditional religious observance for a growing number of people. At the time of its formation in 1857 more than a quarter of the members of the Alpine Club were clergymen, but many of their books and diaries come close to idolatry. St Augustine warned against confusing the created with the creator, which he regarded as the fundamental sin of paganism. By this standard many of the Victorian reverends who climbed in the Alps were certainly pagans and some were practically animists, ascribing emotions and intentions to the mountains that they climbed. While many saw in the beauty of the mountains confirmation of the existence of God through the perfection of his creation, others lost their religious faith but found a sort of secular pantheism that satisfied their need for spiritual renewal.

In 1825 the first railway in the world was constructed from Stockton to Darlington. Within a few decades all the major centres of population in Britain were connected by rail, and the ability to travel significant distances in relative comfort combined with the growth of the middle class and increasing leisure to create a sports boom. During the 1850s, 62 new race meetings were added to the calendar; the rules of boxing were established in 1857, those of football in 1859 and rugby union in 1871. The first county cricket matches were played in 1873 and the first Wimbledon lawn tennis championship took place in 1877.[34] Soon the railways were advancing beyond the towns and cities into the mountains, opening up once remote parts of the country to visitors from the cities. In 1844, at the age of 74, Wordsworth was indignant at a proposal to extend the railway from Manchester beyond Kendal to Windermere, fearing that the Lakes would be inundated with 'the whole of Lancashire, and no small part of Yorkshire'.[35]

In the Alps, the great passes became accessible to wheeled transport from 1800, initially as a result of Napoleon's military road-building programme. Railways followed from 1847 onwards and contributed to the dramatic growth of tourism. A thousand new inns and hotels were built between 1845 and 1880, many of them above 1,000m. Thomas Cook conducted his first alpine tour to Geneva and Mont Blanc in 1863. The tour in 1864 was extended to include Interlaken and Kandersteg. John Murray's *Handbook for Travellers in Switzerland* in 1838 indicated a journey time by coach from London to Geneva or Basle of 14 days, including two days in Paris, at a cost of £20. By 1852, using railways, the journey time had reduced to three days and the cost to just £2.[36]

Many of the mountain pioneers were aware that the sacred beauty they so admired was under threat from these developments. They saw the damage that was being done to the English countryside and feared that the Alps would go the same way. As the inhabitants of Grindelwald hacked away at their glaciers and exported the ice to Parisian restaurants, and railways headed up once remote and silent valleys, Ruskin thundered: 'You have despised Nature; that is to say, all the deep and sacred sensations of natural scenery. The French revolutionists made stables of the cathedrals of France; you have made racecourses of the cathedrals of the earth. Your *one* conception of pleasure is to drive in railroad carriages round their aisles, and eat off their altars.'[37] But ironically, Ruskin's own writing, painting and photography simply attracted more tourists to the mountains.

By 1850 the stage was set for the development of climbing as a sport. Since 1815, a period of unprecedented peace and prosperity had created a sizeable professional class of ambitious young men who had been taught to regard gloomy forests and icy mountains as objects of glorious beauty. Their heroes were explorers who braved extreme hardships to chart the unknown, the wild and the savage. Their education emphasised the virtues of 'muscular Christianity' and *mens sana in corpore sano* and they had leisure: time in which to seek pleasure, purpose and a contrast to their crowded and complex working lives. They believed, as Blake did, that:

> *Great things are done when men and mountains meet;*
> *This is not done by jostling in the street.*

Even Queen Victoria gave her stamp of approval to the nascent sport by making a somewhat sedate progress to the summit of Lochnagar near Balmoral Castle in 1848. All that was needed to set off the explosion of alpine climbing activity that started in 1854 was publicity. It was Albert Smith, the greatest mountaineering showman of all time, who lit the fuse.

Albert Smith was born in Chertsey in 1816 and studied medicine in Paris for a time before earning a living as a journalist writing for magazines including *Punch*. Since childhood he had harboured the ambition to climb Mont Blanc, and after several attempts he finally succeeded in 1851. He staggered up the mountain dressed in scarlet gaiters and Scotch plaid trousers, with three Oxford undergraduates wearing light boating attire, 16 guides and a score of porters laden with 93 bottles of wine, three bottles of cognac, loaves, cheeses, chocolates, legs of mutton and 46 fowls. Not surprisingly, he fell asleep on the summit.

One of the undergraduates was the nephew of Sir Robert Peel, a former Tory prime minister, who happened to be in Chamonix at the time and greeted their success with a huge party. By coincidence, John Ruskin was also in Chamonix, and it was probably Smith's triumphant return that inspired him to write his famous condemnation of the vulgarisation of the Alps some 15 years later: 'The Alps themselves, which your own poets used to love so reverently, you look upon as soaped poles in a beer-garden, which you set yourselves to climb and slide down again with "shrieks of delight". When you are past shrieking, having no human articulate voice to say you are glad with, you fill the quietude of their valleys with gunpowder blasts, and rush home, red with cutaneous eruption of conceit, and voluble with convulsive hiccough of self-satisfaction.'[38]

If Ruskin was the great prophet of mountain beauty, Smith was the great populariser. Returning to London, he made his ascent of Mont Blanc the subject of an 'entertainment' that ran for six years and featured two chamois, several St Bernard dogs and three pretty barmaids from Chamonix dressed in Bernese costumes. The show made Smith a wealthy man. He wrote *The Story of Mont Blanc* in 1853, and by the summer of 1855 Britain was gripped with 'Mont Blanc mania' according to *The Times*. Special music was composed, including the Chamonix Polka and the Mont Blanc Quadrille; both were hits.

Smith's success was not greeted with unqualified enthusiasm. The *Daily News* wrote: 'De Saussure's observations and reflections on Mont Blanc live in his poetical philosophy; those of Mr. Albert Smith will be most appropriately recorded in a tissue of indifferent puns and stale fast witticisms, with an incessant straining after smartness. The aimless scramble of the four pedestrians to the top of Mont Blanc, with the accompaniment of Sir Robert Peel's orgies at the bottom, will not go far to redeem the somewhat equivocal reputation of the herd of English tourists in Switzerland, for a mindless and rather vulgar redundance of animal spirits.'[39] Another contemporary noted that his initials were only two-thirds of the truth. However, the show was a huge success with the public and Smith was summoned to Osborne for a command performance before Queen Victoria, who evidently enjoyed it because the following year Smith gave a repeat performance at Windsor Castle before the court and King Leopold I of Belgium. Smith went on to become an original member of the Alpine Club, an institution that later gained a well-deserved reputation for exclusive snobbery, but Smith was in fact the first member to have climbed Mont Blanc, and in its early years the Alpine Club welcomed enthusiasts almost regardless of their social background. The arch conservative Douglas Freshfield gave a fair assessment when he said that Smith 'had a genuine passion for Mont Blanc, which fortune or rather his own enthusiasm enabled him to put to profit'.[40]

Smith was the first in a long line of climbers who tried to turn their pastime to profit, including Edward Whymper, Captain John Noel, Frank Smythe and Chris Bonington. All of these were far more competent climbers than Smith, but none of them earned as much as he did from the sport. Thanks in part to the extraordinary publicity generated by Albert Smith, the Golden Age of British climbing was about to begin.

3

1854–65:

A CONSCIOUS DIVINITY

For more than 100 years prior to the battle of Waterloo, Britain had been almost continuously at war. The hundred years that followed from 1815 to 1914 was a period of unprecedented peace and prosperity, the *Pax Britannica*, interrupted by just one war involving other European powers: the costly, inconclusive, but distant Crimean War (1854–56). While much of Europe was convulsed by periodic wars and the revolutions of 1848, a mastery of metallurgy, steam and finance turned Britain into a superpower, with an apparently unassailable lead in trade, industry and military force. By the 1850s, Britain was the workshop of the world, London was the global financial capital and more than half the world's shipping by tonnage was British. The Great Exhibition of 1851 was a celebration of British success, with a Crystal Palace assembled in Hyde Park to show off the science and technology that powered the Empire. It was an age of supreme optimism. After visiting the exhibition, Queen Victoria wrote in her diary: 'We are capable of doing anything', and this sense of unbounded possibilities gave individuals the self-confidence to contemplate things that would previously have been unthinkable.

The early mountaineers were more akin in spirit to the Hudson Bay fur trappers, the Indian nabobs and the other merchant adventurers who built the Empire than they were to the colonial administrators and army officers who later ran it. There was an unconventional, ambitious, romantic fearlessness about the pioneers. Trollope wrote his six 'Barchester' novels between 1855 and 1867, coinciding almost exactly with the Golden Age of mountaineering. The novels describe the lives of clerics, professionals and gentry – exactly the social class from which the early mountaineers emerged – and their popularity stemmed partly from the fact that the main characters were instantly recognisable 'types' to contemporary readers. Trollope describes a society preoccupied with money, property, marriage and status. The idea of climbing the highest peaks in the Alps for pleasure must have seemed far more unconventional to contemporaries of the pioneers than the most outrageous behaviour of modern climbers. The British mountaineering establishment, like the British Empire itself after the Indian Mutiny of 1857, may have become increasingly hidebound, conceited and arrogant, but during the Golden Age it had a spontaneous, joyous heedlessness that must have provided an extraordinary contrast to 'civilised' society and an almost Jekyll and Hyde existence for its adherents. More than any other, it was an age when climbers really did 'escape' from the strictures and conventions of contemporary society.

From the late eighteenth century until the mid-nineteenth century several remarkable ascents of alpine peaks were made by monks, priests, scientists and others living in the alpine countries, some of whom no doubt climbed purely for pleasure and enjoyment. Prior to 1854, nine major alpine peaks had been climbed: Mont Blanc (1786); the Grossglockner (1800); Monte Rosa (whose various peaks were climbed from 1801 onwards, although the highest point of this mountain range was not reached until 1855); the Ortler (1804); Jungfrau (1811); Finsteraarhorn (1829); Wetterhorn (1844); Mont Pelvoux (1848); and Piz Bernina (1850).[1] The British played almost no part in these early developments, but the activities of these adventurous individuals did not coalesce into a recognisable sport, and alpine climbing failed to gain the momentum of a new movement. All of that changed with the arrival of the British in the mid-1850s. During the decade that followed, almost every major mountain in the Alps was climbed in an orgy of peak-bagging that gave birth to the *sport* of mountaineering. Of the 39 major peaks ascended for the first time during this period, 31 were climbed by British parties.

It was a remarkable achievement. There were no maps of the glacier regions, few paths above the alpine meadows and forests, no experienced guides and no mountain huts. Access to the foothills of the Alps was possible by rail, but from the railhead it was necessary to travel by public stage coach and then walk long distances to reach the highest peaks. The early climbers slept out in all weathers and climbed well above the snowline in clothes designed for the English countryside. All of them joked about the fleas that they invariably picked up in their lodgings in the valleys. With no sun-block and inadequate sunglasses, severe sunburn and snow blindness were common. Many climbers wore veils to protect themselves, but when Ruskin wrote of climbers being 'red with cutaneous eruptions' he undoubtedly spoke the truth. Oscar Brown, a schoolmaster at Eton, confessed that 'one became tired of living upon a knapsack, and never being absolutely clean, of seldom sleeping in a decent room or enjoying wholesome food, and when September arrived I began to long for the fleshpots of civilisation'.[2] Offsetting these hardships, labour was cheap and porters carried blankets, fire wood and provisions up to bivouac sites at the foot of the highest peaks. As a consequence, climbs were often noisy, boisterous affairs with large quantities of food and wine consumed before, during and after the ascent.

The ascent of the Wetterhorn in 1854 by Alfred Wills and his four guides signalled the start of the 'Golden Age' of British alpine exploration. The Wetterhorn is clearly visible from Grindelwald, which had already become a popular tourist destination because of its marvellous views of the Bernese Alps and easy access to two glaciers. Although it was probably the fifth or sixth ascent, the decision by a young Englishman, on his honeymoon, to climb the 3,692m/12,137ft snow-covered mountain, wearing elastic-sided boots and cricket flannels, is traditionally taken to mark the beginning of the *sport* of mountaineering. His account of the climb in *Wanderings Amongst the High Alps* (1856) makes passing reference to botany and geology, but it is clear that Wills' primary motive was physical exercise and self-improvement, and there is a strong suggestion

31

that it is the duty of any self-respecting Englishman to undertake such endeavours. The choice of Wills' 1854 ascent to mark the start of the Golden Age was in many ways quite arbitrary. Albert Smith's ascent of Mont Blanc in 1851 has at least an equal claim, but the mid-Victorian historians of the Alpine Club gave Wills the honour, probably because Smith was never quite regarded as respectable.

Alfred Wills epitomised the urban, middle-class, professional background of the climbers who dominated the sport until the First World War. His father was a lawyer and he too went into the law, becoming a high court judge when his predecessor died of a heart attack in a brothel. In 1895 he presided over the trial of Oscar Wilde and sentenced him to two years' imprisonment for gross indecency. Wills visited the Alps almost every year from 1846 to 1896. His son William was an active climber in the 1880s and 1890s, and his grandson Major Edward Norton was leader of the 1924 Everest expedition. A founding member of the Alpine Club when it was formed in 1857, Wills became president in 1864. After *The Times* described members of the Club as men who 'seem to have a special fondness for regions which are suitable only as dwelling-places for eagles', he named his chalet in Sixt 'The Eagle's Nest'.

Where There's a Will There's a Way by Charles Hudson and Edward Kennedy was published in the same year as *Wanderings* and describes the first guideless ascent of Mont Blanc in 1855. Kennedy inherited a fortune at the age of 16 but lost most of it during the course of his life as a result of a series of bad investments. He became something of an expert on the underworld of his day, living for a time with thieves and other low-life in Liverpool and London. For a mid-Victorian gentleman, a journey into the East End of London was probably as great an adventure, with a similar threat of physical harm, as a climb in the Alps, but Kennedy was also a deep thinker, famous for persistently asking the question 'Is it right?' and the author of *Thoughts on Being, suggested by Meditation upon the Infinite, the Immaterial, and the Eternal* (1850). In climbing, he found a purpose in life that satisfied both his thirst for adventure and his quest for meaning, and he set about persuading others to follow. He was a prime mover in the formation of the Alpine Club and its president from 1860–62.

Charles Hudson, the co-author of *Where There's a Will There's a Way*, was an Anglican chaplain during the Crimean War and subsequently became a vicar in Lincolnshire. For him, the mountains offered a reassuring reminder of the mystery and beauty of God's creation. He was 'as simple and noble a character as ever carried out the precepts of muscular Christianity without talking its cant',[3] according to Leslie Stephen. Relaxed, handsome and self-effacing, Hudson was a man of extraordinary stamina and almost reckless courage. At the age of 17, he averaged 43km/27 miles per day on a tour of the Lake District and once walked from Saint-Gervais, near Chamonix, to Geneva and back in a day (a distance of 138km/86 miles). His first ascents in 1855 included the Breithorn (grade F, 4,164m/13,661ft), without guides, and the Dufourspitze (PD, 4,634m/15,203ft), the highest point of the Monte Rosa, with James and Christopher Smyth, who were also parsons, John Birkbeck, a Yorkshire banker, and Edward Stevenson. A fortnight later he climbed Mont Blanc with Edward Kennedy and made the first ascent (solo) of Mont Blanc du Tacul (PD, 4,248m/13,937ft). Hudson continued to climb throughout the Golden Age, making the first ascent of the Moine Ridge on the Aiguille Verte (AD, 4,122m/13,524ft) with Thomas Kennedy (no relation to Edward) in 1865. Thomas Kennedy once rode the Nile cataracts on a log for fun and was also a noted polo player and huntsman: 'No man has ever ridden straighter or harder',[4] Lord Harrington noted approvingly in his obituary.

Several of the pioneers were accomplished sportsmen in other fields, including Charles Barrington who won the Irish Grand National on his horse Sir Robert Peel. During his first and only holiday in the Alps in 1858, Barrington climbed the Jungfrau and then asked some members of the Alpine Club whom he happened to meet which peaks had yet to be climbed. They suggested either the Matterhorn or the Eiger. Barrington chose the Eiger (3,970m/13,025ft) because he could not be bothered to travel to Zermatt and duly completed the first ascent of the mountain, via the West Ridge (AD). As the party approached the summit, Barrington allegedly pulled a pistol from his jacket and informed his guides that if they attempted to reach the summit before him he would blow their brains out. His account of the climb simply noted that 'the two guides kindly gave me the place of first man up'.[5]

Observing the growing popularity of the sport in 1857, the Rev. S. W. King wrote of 'young Cantabs and Oxonians scampering over pass after pass, with often apparently no other object than trying who can venture in the most novel break-neck situations'.[6] These young men were led in their scamperings by local mountain guides, a small minority of whom became outstanding climbers. Melchior Anderegg, born in 1828 near Meiringen in the Bernese Oberland, was one of the best. As a boy he tended cattle, hunted chamois and became an accomplished wood carver. A big, genial man, he made numerous climbs with the Walker family and was the favourite guide of Leslie Stephen and Charles Mathews. His first ascents included the Dent d'Hérens, Zinal Rothorn, the Grandes Jorasses and the Brenva Spur of Mont Blanc (where his cousin, Jakob, led the crucial ice arête). Despite this, it was Anderegg who confounded Leslie Stephen by finding the view of London finer than the view from Mont Blanc. Christian Almer, born two years earlier in 1826 near Grindelwald, had a similar background as a shepherd and cheese-maker and achieved a similar status as a guide. He climbed the Wetterhorn with Alfred Wills and went on to make many of the first ascents of the Golden Age, climbing with Adolphus Moore, Edward Whymper and others. Later he climbed with William Coolidge and lost several toes to frostbite after a winter ascent of the Jungfrau in 1884. He made a golden wedding anniversary ascent of the Wetterhorn with his wife in 1896 when he was 70 and she was 71.

The relationship between *Herr* and guide was a complex one. At the start of the Golden Age, both were equally inexperienced and incompetent. However, over time a small number of outstanding guides emerged, and they were in great demand with the leading climbers of the day. By the end of the Golden Age, the best guides were undoubtedly better climbers than the amateurs, not least because of their greater fitness and experience. 'The guide's skills cannot, in the nature of things, be attained by Englishmen living in England,' pointed out Florence Grove in 1870, 'any more than a Frenchman living in France can become a good cricketer.'[7] The roles of the employer and of the guide were quite distinct. The employer selected the mountain to be climbed and played some role in deciding which route to follow. However, just as British explorers in the tropics used 'natives' to cut the trails and carry the stores, so in the Alps the guide generally cut all the steps on snow and ice and invariably led on rocks. At a slightly later date, Clinton Dent reviewed the respective roles of the gentleman amateur and the professional guide: 'Any guide was immeasurably superior to an amateur in the knack of finding the way...in quickness on rocks the two could hardly be compared. But I had always thought that the amateur excelled in one great requisite – pluck.'[8] In fact, as Dent acknowledged in his account of the first ascent of the Dru, the best guides were often superior in this respect as well. Leslie Stephen observed that 'the true way... to describe all my ascents is that [my guide] succeeded in performing a feat requiring skill, strength and courage, the difficulty of which was much increased by the difficulty of taking with him his knapsack and his employer'.[9] However, guides rarely climbed peaks by themselves and certainly did not make first ascents, since this would deprive them of the bonus that an English gentleman would pay for the conquest of a virgin peak.

Most guides probably regarded climbing as a pointless, hazardous, but well-remunerated job, but among the top guides there was also great professional pride and considerable competition. Stephen noted that his guide, Ulrich Lauener, held strong views on the superiority of guides of the Teutonic, rather than Latin, races which he endeavoured to communicate to some guides from Chamonix. 'As...he could not speak a word of French...he was obliged to convey this sentiment in pantomime, which did not soften its vigour.'[10] Some years later, Fred Mummery recalled an incident when he and his guide, the great Alexander Burgener from the Saas valley, met a party led by a famous Oberland guide who advised them to give up their attempt on the Grépon, because 'I have tried it, and where I have failed no-one else need hope to succeed'. Mummery observed that 'Burgener was greatly moved by this peroration, and I learnt from a torrent of unreportable patois that our fate was sealed and even if we spent the rest of our lives on the mountain (or falling off it) it would, in his opinion, be preferable to returning amid the jeers and taunts of this unbeliever'.[11] On the mountain the relationship between client and guide was often friendly and informal but when they returned to the valley the social divide between gentleman and peasant reasserted itself. While the English gentleman headed to the *table d'hôte* to celebrate his triumph, his guide went to the servants' quarters in the cellar or the attic.

Since the new breed of amateur mountaineer consisted almost exclusively of Englishmen of a certain class, it was inevitable that they should form a club, and the Alpine Club was duly inaugurated on 22 December 1857. It was initially conceived as a dining society at which members could exchange information on alpine climbing. As the first of its kind in the world, its members did not feel the need to attach a prefix, such as 'English'. There were just 29 founding members, but by 1865 their number had grown to over 300. The membership was almost entirely composed of professional men – lawyers, clergymen, academics, civil servants and bankers – educated in English public schools and old universities, who were granted long summer holidays by their employers. Of the 281 members in 1863, just three belonged by birth to the old landed aristocracy.[12] As time went on, they took to signing themselves 'AC' in hotel registers, and a 'murmur of approval would greet their entrance into the dining room'.[13] Anthony Trollope described the Alpine Club Man in his *Travelling Sketches* (1866): 'He does not carry himself quite as another man, and has his nose a little in the air, even when he is not climbing...To be one of a class permitted to face dangers which to us would be suicidal, does give him a conscious divinity of which he is, in his modesty, not quite able to divest himself.'[14] Within a few years of its formation, members of the Alpine Club had become a recognisable 'type' of rich, well-educated, assertive and slightly flippant young men. A quotation from Theocritus, 'one must be doing something while the knee is green', was once proposed as a motto for the Club. As the years went on, membership of the Alpine Club came to be regarded by some ambitious young men as a necessary 'badge of honour'. Courage was a greatly admired virtue in Victorian society and alpinism provided a perfect peacetime means of demonstrating it. Ewart 'Cape-to-Cairo' Grogan, the first man to traverse Africa from south to north and one of the founding fathers of colonial Kenya, never climbed again after joining the Club at the age of 22. To have been elected was sufficient.

The object of the Alpine Club was 'the promotion of good fellowship among mountaineers, of mountain climbing and mountain exploration throughout the world, and of better knowledge of the mountains through literature, science, and art'. The Club did admit a few members purely for their literary and artistic qualifications. Matthew Arnold ('The mountain-tops where is the throne of Truth') was a member and so too was Ruskin which, given his hatred of climbers, seems odd. The Club's aspiration to advance the knowledge of science was derided by Charles Dickens, who noted that 'a society for the scaling of such heights as the Schreckhorn, the Eiger, and the Matterhorn contributed about as much to the advancement of science as would a club of young gentlemen who should undertake to bestride all the weathercocks of all the cathedral spires in the United Kingdom'.[15] Nevertheless, the *Alpine Journal* to this day describes itself as a 'record of mountain adventure and scientific observation', and the Club's early members included a number of distinguished scientists.

John Ball, the first president of the Club, was an Irish politician, who became Under Secretary for the Colonies in Palmerston's administration but was also a respected amateur naturalist. Educated at Cambridge, he travelled widely and published papers on botany and glaciers. An enthusiastic and determined mountain explorer, he published the *Guide to the Western Alps* (1863), *Guide to the Central Alps*

(1864) and *Guide to the Eastern Alps* (1868), which were the standard texts until they were rewritten and reissued by Coolidge at the end of the nineteenth century. He also edited the first volume of *Peaks, Passes and Glaciers* (1859), the forerunner of the *Alpine Journal*, which first appeared in 1863 and is the world's oldest mountaineering periodical.

John Tyndall, another early member of the Club, was also a distinguished scientist. Amongst his many areas of research, he was one of the first to investigate the relationship between water vapour, carbon dioxide and climate change. The son of a sergeant in the newly formed constabulary in County Carlow, Ireland, Tyndall was living proof of the social mobility that could be achieved in Victorian society through a combination of hard work, great intellect and absolute determination. In addition to the Alpine Club, he became a member of the small but influential X Club, together with Thomas Huxley, Joseph Hooker, the botanist and pioneering Arctic and Himalayan explorer, and Herbert Spencer, the political philosopher. The purpose of the club was 'devotion to science, pure and free, untrammelled by religious dogma'.[16] Tyndall was a committed agnostic who argued fiercely and frequently and once offered to fight a man who disagreed with his high opinion of Thomas Carlyle. Elected a Fellow of the Royal Society in 1852, he became a close friend and colleague of Michael Faraday who, unlike Tyndall, never climbed but nevertheless walked from Leukerbad in the Valais over the Gemmi Pass to Thun in the Bernese Oberland, a distance of 70km/44 miles, in ten and a half hours.

As a young man, Tyndall obtained a doctorate at the University of Marburg and appears to have been imbued with some of the more grimly heroic aspects of Teutonic romanticism. He suffered from ill-health and insomnia all his life and focused his attention on the most difficult peaks: a solitary ascent of the Monte Rosa, in 10 hours from the Riffelberg, in 1858; the Weisshorn (AD, 4,506m/14,783m) in 1861; and the Matterhorn (AD, 4,478m/14,690ft), where he got to within a few hundred feet of the top in 1864, the year before Whymper's success, and later made the first traverse from Breuil to Zermatt. Tyndall sought, in climbing, an escape from the stresses and pressures of city life: 'I have returned to [the Alps] each year and found among them refuge and recovery from the work and the worry – which acts with far deadlier corrosion on the brain than real work – of London.'[17] Over time, the beauty and solace that he found in the mountains became almost as important to him as his scientific work. In 1862 he wrote: 'The glaciers and the mountains have an interest for me beyond their scientific ones. They have given me well-springs of life and joy.'[18] He died in 1893 from an overdose of chloral administered by his wife to combat his insomnia.

When Leslie Stephen read a paper at the Alpine Club describing his first ascent of the Zinal Rothorn (AD, 4,221m/13,848ft) in 1862 he included the passage: '"And what philosophical observations did you make?" will be enquired by one of those fanatics who, by a reasoning to me utterly inscrutable, have somehow irrevocably associated Alpine travel and science.'[19] Tyndall was convinced that the word 'fanatic' was directed at him and stormed out of the meeting, resigning from the Alpine Club shortly afterwards. As Stephen observed: 'My first contact with Tyndall was not altogether satisfactory.'[20] In fact, the target of his parody was not Tyndall at all; it was Francis Tuckett, a Bristol Quaker and leather merchant who was with Stephen on the first ascent of the Goûter Route (PD) on Mont Blanc in 1861. Tuckett explored the virtually unknown mountain ranges of Corsica, Greece, Norway, the Pyrenees, Algeria and the Dolomites, but he had the reputation of being slow and ponderous and was obsessed with collecting and recording scientific data. Nevertheless, he amassed a tally of over 40 new peaks and passes between 1856 and 1865, including the Aletschhorn (PD, 4,193m/13,756ft) and the Königspitze (PD, 3,851m/12,634ft).

The three principal centres for the early mountaineers were Chamonix, Grindelwald and Zermatt. Seiler's Hotel in Zermatt, in particular, became a second home for the Alpine Club, where members gathered to plan their routes while the guides sat on the low wall in front of the hotel, waiting for their clients. A conversation outside the hotel recorded by the Rev. J. F. Hardy in August 1861 captures the mood of the early days of alpine exploration:

> 'I say, old fellow, we're all going up the Monte Rosa to-morrow, won't you join us? We shall have capital fun.'
> 'What, is that Hardy? Oh yes, do come, there's a good fellow.'

> Before I had time to answer, a voice, discovered to be J. A. Hudson's was heard to mention the Lyskamm, upon which hint I spake.

> 'Ah, the Lyskamm! That's the thing. Leave Monte Rosa and go in for the Lyskamm; anybody can do the Monte Rosa, now the route's so well known; but the Lyskamm's quite another affair.'
> 'Yes, indeed, I expect it is. Why, Stephen couldn't do it.'
> 'He was only stopped by the bad state of the snow.'
> 'Well, Tuckett failed too.'
> 'He was turned back by the fog.'
> 'So may we be.'
> 'Certainly we may, also we mayn't, and in the present state of the weather the latter's more likely of the two.'[21]

And so a party of eight British climbers, including Hardy and Hudson, and six guides made the first ascent of the Lyskamm (AD, 4,527m/14,852ft) and on the summit they sang the National Anthem.

The Playground of Europe by Leslie Stephen and Scrambles Amongst the Alps by Edward Whymper, both published in 1871, are perhaps the best contemporary accounts of the Golden Age of alpine climbing. Stephen and Whymper epitomised two contrasting approaches to climbing: the former primarily concerned with the aesthetic, almost mystical appeal of the landscape; the latter searching for self-fulfilment and personal achievement.

In later life, Leslie Stephen was an eminent literary critic and biographer who encouraged Thomas Hardy and Robert Louis Stevenson in the early stages of their careers and was knighted for services to literature. His father, Sir James Stephen, was said to have ruled large parts of the Empire as Under Secretary for the Colonies, and was later appointed Regius Professor of Modern History at Cambridge. His first wife was the daughter of William Thackeray, at that time regarded as second only to Charles Dickens as a novelist, and his children included Virginia Woolf, the author, and Vanessa Bell, the painter, who later formed part of the Bloomsbury Group of intellectuals.

Stephen was educated at Eton and Cambridge and taught philosophy at Cambridge until increasing religious doubts forced him to renounce Holy Orders in 1862 and consequently his fellowship. In *The Playground of Europe* he wrote: 'The mountains represent the indomitable force of nature to which we are forced to adapt ourselves; they speak to man of his littleness and his ephemeral existence; they rouse us from the placid content in which we may be lapped when contemplating the fat fields which we have conquered and the rivers which we have forced to run according to our notions of convenience. And, therefore, they should suggest not sheer misanthropy, as they did to Byron, or an outburst of revolutionary passions, as they did to his teacher Rousseau, but that sense of awe-struck humility which befits such petty creatures as ourselves.' Like so many agnostic or atheistic climbers since, he felt a sense of awe and wonder in the Alps that he found difficult to explain in rational terms: 'If I were to invent a new idolatry...I should prostrate myself, not before beast, or ocean, or sun, but before one of these gigantic masses to which, in spite of all reason, it is impossible not to attribute some shadowy personality.'

A man who substituted 'long walks for long prayers',[22] Stephen was proud of the fact that he once covered 80km/50 miles from Cambridge to London in 12 hours in order to attend the Alpine Club annual dinner. In the Alps he made numerous first ascents including the Rimpfischhorn (PD, 4,199m/13,776ft) in 1859, the

Schreckhorn (AD, 4,078m/13,379ft) in 1861, Monte Disgrazia (PD, 3,678m/12,067ft) in 1862 and the Zinal Rothorn in 1864. In common with many early alpinists he did not enjoy climbing in Britain, perhaps because of the absence of guides, and failed to find the way up Pillar Rock in 1863: 'The atmosphere of the English Lakes is apt to be enervating',[23] he observed. However he did put up the first recorded sea cliff climb in Cornwall near his holiday home in St Ives, in 1858. In 1867, at the age of 35, he married and curtailed his climbing activities, later establishing a society called the 'Sunday Tramps', who went on long walks through the English countryside. Their motto was 'High Thinking and Plain Living', and Douglas Freshfield, Martin Conway and Clinton Dent (all three future presidents of the Alpine Club) were members.

Although self-revelation (no doubt selective) was not uncommon, critical comments about the personalities of fellow climbers (but not guides) were largely banished from nineteenth-century mountain literature by the conventions of the time. In many cases companions were simply referred to by an initial. Candid accounts of fellow climbers were not at all common until well after the Second World War, and therefore reliable descriptions of the character and personality of the early climbers by third parties are comparatively rare, barring obsequious, or at least highly coded, obituaries. However, because of his many literary associations, it is possible to obtain several different descriptions of Stephen. In *To the Lighthouse* by Virginia Woolf, the father, Mr Ramsay, is clearly based on Stephen. He is a distant, austere and needy individual, self-centred and insecure. The character of Vernon Whitford, a scholarly, unworldly idealist, in George Meredith's *The Egoist* was also based on Stephen. In later life, he appears to have become a solitary, difficult and demanding man. When a visitor outstayed his welcome he became visibly agitated and muttered, quite audibly, to himself, 'Why can't he go? Why can't he go?' A contemporary described him as 'critical yet deprecating, sarcastic and mournful...not one who ranks either himself or others very high'.[24]

Even allowing for increasing age, it is hard to believe that this is the same man who played cricket in the main square of Zinal in Switzerland 'with a rail for a bat and a granite boulder for a ball. My first performance was a brilliant hit to leg...off Macdonald's bowling. To my horror I sent the ball clean through the western window of the chapel.'[25] Or who, returning from the first ascent of Monte Disgrazia in two carriages with Edward Kennedy and Melchior Anderegg, tried to 'get up an Olympic chariot race' and then sat up drinking champagne until the early hours. His account of climbing in the Golden Age is full of the heedless fun of climbing: 'It was necessary to cut steps as big as soup tureens, for the result of a slip would in all probability have been that the rest of our lives would have been spent sliding down a snow slope and that the employment would not have lasted long enough to become at all monotonous.'[26] The apparent contradiction between the levity, humour and mild anarchism of Stephen the climber and the melancholic austerity of Stephen the father and intellectual perhaps explains the appeal of alpinism for many mid-Victorians.

Stephen was president of the Alpine Club from 1866 to 1868 and Editor of the *Alpine Journal*. Together with John Tyndall, he was in many ways the Club's intellectual mentor in its early years. Elected to the Metaphysical Society, whose diverse membership included William Gladstone, Walter Bagehot, Cardinal Manning, Alfred Tennyson, John Ruskin and Thomas Huxley, Stephen helped to turn the Alps into a ruggedly congenial meeting place for members of the intellectual upper middle class of the mid-Victorian generation, in much the same way as Geoffrey Winthrop Young did for a later generation with his Pen-y-Pass meets in Wales. On a rare visit to the Club towards the end of the century he wrote: 'It was queer enough to go to the old place, and I feel that I was regarded with curiosity like a revived mammoth out of an iceberg.'[27] Safety-conscious, despite his apparently flippant attitude, he was an opponent of guideless climbing but recognised that risk and danger are a vital part of the sport, noting that 'no advertisement of Alpine adventure is so attractive as a clear demonstration that it is totally unjustifiable'. Writing of his first ascent of the Zinal Rothorn, he made two observations that have stood the test of time: 'One, that on the first ascent a mountain, in obedience to some mysterious law, is always more difficult than at any succeeding ascent; secondly, that nothing can be less like a mountain at one time than the same mountain at another.'[28]

If Stephen was the scholarly aesthete of the Golden Age, Edward Whymper was its flawed hero. Stephen called him the Robespierre of mountaineering.[29] The son of a commercial artist, he trained as a wood engraver and always felt a sense of social inferiority, trying hard not to drop his 'aitches'. Throughout his life he was incapable of close relationships or lasting friendships, and from boyhood he exercised a steely self-discipline and pursued the goal 'that I should one day turn out some great person'.[30] His original ambition was to become an Arctic explorer, which would have suited his temperament well, but in 1860 he was commissioned to produce a series of alpine sketches and transferred his ambitions to the mountains. In 1861 he climbed Mont Pelvoux (PD, 3,946m/12,946ft) and was elected to the Alpine Club. He then set his sights on the Weisshorn, 'the noblest [mountain] in Switzerland',[31] but immediately lost interest when he heard that it had been climbed by Tyndall. Thereafter he focused his attention on the Matterhorn which, because of its magnificent shape, commanding position above Zermatt and apparent impregnability, had become the greatest prize in the Alps.

After making unsuccessful attempts on the Matterhorn in 1862 and 1863, Whymper joined forces with Adolphus Moore and Horace Walker in 1864 for a successful 10 day campaign in the Dauphiné Alps, including the first ascent of the Barre des Écrins (PD, 4,101m/13,454ft). He then made three first ascents in the Mont Blanc area before being summoned back to London before the end of the season. Following a winter of detailed planning, over a period of 24 days from 13 June to 7 July 1865, he made four first ascents, including the Grandes Jorasses Pointe Whymper (AD, 4,208m/13,805ft) and the Aiguille Verte by the Whymper Couloir (AD, 4,122m/13,524ft), and crossed 11 passes.

He also climbed the Dent Blanche (AD, 4,356m/14,291ft) in poor weather, apparently believing that Thomas Kennedy had failed to reach the summit in 1862 and unaware that it had also been climbed by another party in 1864. When he saw through a break in the clouds 'about twenty yards off' the outline of a cairn on the summit 'it was needless to proceed further; I jerked the rope...and motioned [to my guide] that we should go back'.[32]

On his ninth attempt, at the age of 25, Whymper finally succeeded in climbing the Matterhorn by the Hörnli Ridge (AD) on 14 July 1865. On the descent disaster struck. Four members of the party fell to their death: Charles Hudson; the young and inexperienced Douglas Hadow; Lord Francis Douglas, the younger brother of the Marquis of Queensberry; and their guide Michel Croz. The death of Hudson was particularly shocking because he was regarded as the best amateur climber of the day. The triumph of reaching the summit of the Matterhorn was the crowning achievement of the Golden Age. The tragedy on the descent marked the end of the era. Whymper effectively abandoned alpine climbing after the accident, although he did return to the Matterhorn in 1874, making the 76th ascent. 'Soon the biggest duffers in Christendom will be able to go up',[33] he wrote in his diary. Today the Zermatt guides claim that they could take a cow to the summit.

The ascent of the Matterhorn was the first climb to receive widespread media coverage, as a result of the accident, and the first to become the focus of competition inspired by nationalism. Both were to become major features of the sport in later years. In the patriotic fervour created by the unification of Italy, the Italian guide Jean Antoine Carrel, who had fought against the Austrians at the battle of Solferino in 1859, was determined that the peak should be climbed by an Italian from the Italian side. When Whymper succeeded in reaching the summit first from the Swiss side, he triumphantly threw rocks down the face to attract the attention of Carrel and his party below. Carrel climbed the Matterhorn by the harder route from Breuil (now called Cervinia) three days later, 'to avenge our country's honour'.[34]

Whymper was the first leading climber apparently motivated solely by the heroic impulse. He found little beauty in the mountains. Seeing for the first time the mountain with which his name would forever become linked, he recorded in his diary: 'Saw of course the Matterhorn repeatedly; what precious stuff Ruskin has written about this, as well as about other things...Grand it is, but beautiful I think it is not.'[35] His writing contains few descriptions other than the act of climbing, and first ascents were his sole preoccupation. He saw himself as fighting and overcoming nature. His interests were not primarily in the mountains, they were in himself: 'We exult over the scenes brought before our eyes... but we value more highly the development of manliness, and the evolution, under combat with difficulties, of those noble qualities of human nature – courage, patience, endurance and fortitude.'[36]

Not surprisingly, opinions on such a figure are divided. Chris Bonington is an admirer: 'His single-minded competitiveness and drive, whilst being very understandable to later generations, was suspect not only to Victorian mountaineers, but to the majority of the British climbing establishment until very recently.'[37] Geoffrey Winthrop Young, the early twentieth-century poet mountaineer, was enthusiastic about Whymper's book *Scrambles Amongst the Alps* but dismissive of its author: 'Whymper founded no school. No one has succeeded in imitating anything but his egoism.'[38] Part of the contemporary antipathy undoubtedly arose because Whymper was amongst the first to commercialise the sport of mountaineering, earning a living as a mountain illustrator, lecturer and writer. But he was also a supremely selfish man. In the preface to Fred Mummery's book *My Climbs in the Alps and Caucasus*, published soon after his disappearance while attempting to climb Nanga Parbat in 1895, Douglas Freshfield wrote that Mummery's death was a grievous loss to the Alpine Club. In the margin of his copy of the book, Whymper wrote: 'I do not agree.'[39] Joe Simpson lamented the decline of climbing ethics in the 1990s in his book *Dark Shadows Falling* (1997) and berated two Japanese climbers who in 1996 failed to assist three dying Indian climbers that they passed on their way to the summit of Everest. Simpson asked the rhetorical question: 'Would Whymper or Mummery have behaved like this?' In the case of Mummery there can be little question that he would not. But with Whymper it is harder to be so categorical. In the close-knit community of British climbing in the 1860s, peer group pressure was just sufficient to keep his ambition and selfishness in check, but in the large, impersonal climbing world of the 1990s perhaps Whymper would have sympathised with one of the Japanese climbers who allegedly said 'above eight thousand metres is not a place where people can afford morality'.[40]

In 1867 Whymper achieved his original ambition of visiting the Arctic when he organised an expedition to Greenland which made some advances in exploration by sledge. In 1880 he travelled to South America, climbed Chimborazo (6,267m/20,561ft), once thought to be the highest mountain in the world, and spent a night on the summit of Cotapaxi (5,897m/19,347ft). He planned the expedition with his usual meticulous attention to detail and made a systematic study of altitude sickness. His account served as a blueprint for future expeditions to remote mountain areas. Mount Whymper in the Canadian Rockies marks a visit to the region in the 1900s, but by then his best climbing days were over. At the age of 66 he married Edith Lewin, aged 21. Women had played no previous part in his life and the marriage was an unhappy one. It broke up four years later. In 1911, feeling unwell during a visit to the Alps, he returned to his hotel and locked the door, refusing any medical help. He died some days later at the age of 71.

Unaware of events unfolding in Zermatt, the day after the Matterhorn tragedy Frank and Horace Walker, George Mathews, Adolphus Moore and their guides Melchior and Jakob Anderegg made an ascent of the Brenva Spur on the Italian side of Mont Blanc which was well ahead of its time. The climb is still graded AD+/D and was the only route up the daunting Brenva Face for the next 62 years. Frank Walker was a prosperous lead merchant from Liverpool who took up climbing at the age of 50 and was 57 at the time of the ascent of the Brenva Face. He climbed the Matterhorn with his daughter Lucy in 1871 at the age of

63, but died the following year. His son Horace Walker climbed his first mountain, Mont Velan, at the age of 16 and his last, Pollux, 51 years later in 1905. He made numerous first ascents in the Alps, with Whymper and others, including reaching Pointe Walker in 1868, the highest point of the Grandes Jorasses, made famous by the magnificent rocky spur to the north. He also climbed Elbrus (5,642m/18,510ft) in the Caucasus in 1874 and was an enthusiastic British rock climber, making the second ascent of North Climb (S, 1892) on Pillar Rock in the Lakes.

Lucy Walker first visited the Alps in 1859 at the age of 28. She climbed only with her family, guided by the Anderegg cousins, but had many notable achievements including climbing the Balmhorn (3,698m/12,133ft) in 1864, the first time that a woman had taken part in the first ascent of a major peak. She was also the first woman to climb the Matterhorn, three days after ascending the Weisshorn. *Punch* celebrated her triumph in verse:

> *No glacier could baffle, no precipice balk her,*
> *No peak rise above her, however sublime.*
> *Give three times three cheers for intrepid Miss Walker,*
> *I say, my boys, doesn't she know how to climb!*

Inclined to plumpness, whilst she was in the mountains she relied on a diet of sponge cake and champagne and, apart from climbing, her only other sporting interest was croquet. The entire Walker family enjoyed a particularly close relationship with their guide Melchior Anderegg, who called Frank Walker 'Papa' and was a life-long companion of Lucy, who never married. As she said, 'I love mountains and Melchior, and Melchior already has a wife'.[41] Lucy Walker became the second president of the Ladies' Alpine Club in 1912 at the age of 76.

Adolphus Moore, who accompanied Frank and Horace Walker on the Brenva Route, was another great Victorian mountaineer with many alpine first ascents to his credit. He went on to visit the Caucasus in 1867 and 1869, climbing Kazbek (5,047m/16,558ft) and the East Summit of

Elbrus. A senior official at the India Office and private secretary to Lord Randolph Churchill, Moore died from exhaustion brought on by over-work at the age of 46.

George Mathews, the final British member of the team, was one of three brothers who played a major role in the development of British climbing. William, Charles and George Mathews took part in many pio-neering climbs during the Golden Age, including first ascents of Grande Casse (3,855m/12,648ft) and Monte Viso (3,841m/12,602ft). The deci-sion to form the Alpine Club was taken at their uncle's home, following a discussion during an ascent of the Finsteraarhorn (4,274m/14,022ft) in the summer of 1857. William subsequently became president in 1869–71 and Charles in 1878–80. Charles went on to play a particularly influential role in the development of Welsh climbing.

The ascent of the Brenva Spur was a great climbing achievement, but it was completely overshadowed by the Matterhorn accident. The news was greeted by the British public with a combination of rage and incomprehension. The Editor of *The Times* wrote: 'What right has [the mountaineer] to throw away the gift of life and ten thousand golden opportunities in an emulation which he only shares with skylarks, apes and squirrels?'[42] The reaction was very different from that which greeted the equally famous loss of Mallory and Irvine on Everest some 60 years later. During the intervening period, increasing coverage of the sport in books and the press had gradually created an understanding of both the risks and rewards of climbing, and Mallory and Irvine were treated as heroes. In 1865, however, the public was totally unprepared for the loss of four young lives, including a lord. The public outcry may at first seem surprising, given that the mid-Victorian generation was so accustomed to premature death. In the mid-1860s there were extremely high levels of child mortality, over six per cent of soldiers sent to imperial outposts died each year from disease alone and the charge of the Light Brigade had taken place just 10 years earlier. Even in sport, members of the middle and upper classes regularly killed or injured themselves in hunting accidents, but hunting was regarded as a worthy occupation because it was a good preparation for military service (even the Indian Civil Service entrance exam included a rigorous riding test). The thing that the public found so shocking about the Matterhorn accident was that three Englishmen should have died undertaking such a *useless* activity. In the decades that followed, the public gradually became accustomed to the idea that *men* might choose to take such risks, but 130 years after the Matterhorn accident, in 1995, some of the same shock and incomprehension resurfaced in the mass media when Alison Hargreaves, a talented climber who was also the mother of two young children, died on K2.

Since those first four fatalities in 1865, over 500 climbers have lost their lives on the Matterhorn, the majority quite recently as the popularity of climbing has soared. Climbing during the Golden Age was in fact remarkably accident-free, bearing in mind the primitive equipment being used and the almost total lack of understanding of ropework, snow and ice conditions, and avalanche risk. But the public vented its anger on the Alpine Club, and for a time it seemed as if the nascent sport of mountaineering might end almost before it had really begun. Alfred Wills, who started the Golden Age with his ascent of the Wetterhorn and was president of the Alpine Club at the time of the Matterhorn tragedy, wrote to Whymper encouraging him to break his self-imposed silence: 'Give your own account, let it be truthful, manly and unflinching – wherever blame is due (if blame there be) let it rest – but do not let people go on conjecturing the worst, when you could silence the greater part of it by your utterance.'[43] Whymper did not provide a thorough public account until *Scrambles Amongst the Alps* was published in 1871. Although climbing continued, it did so discreetly. 'After that frightful catastrophe of July 14, 1865,' Coolidge wrote, '[British climbers], so to speak, climbed on sufferance, enjoying themselves much, it is true, but keeping all expression of that joy to themselves in order not to excite derision.'[44]

The Golden Age had ended.

4

1865–1914:

GENTLEMEN AND GYMNASTS

In climbing history, the period from 1865 to 1914 starts with the death of four climbers on the Matterhorn and ends with the destruction of a generation in the First World War. By the time that Whymper's account of the Matterhorn accident in *Scrambles Amongst the Alps* appeared in 1871 public anger at the incident had already died down. A number of 'penny dreadfuls' involving cut ropes and climbing accidents followed the publication of Whymper's book, presaging the huge popularity of the authentic rope-cutting drama of Joe Simpson's book and film documentary, *Touching the Void*, over a century later. Public interest in the accident also gave a boost to alpine tourism. After the interruption of the Franco-Prussian War in 1870, Thomas Cook tours to Zermatt increased in popularity throughout the decade. Leslie Stephen's elegant portrayal of alpine adventures in *The Playground of Europe*, also published in 1871, further smoothed away opposition to climbing. Slowly but surely the sport was rehabilitated, and climbers emerged from self-imposed obscurity.

At home, the period of peace and prosperity that had started with victory at Waterloo in 1815 continued until the outbreak of the First World War, but the British Empire reached the peak of its economic power and influence in the 1870s. The decades leading up to the outbreak of the war were a period of relative decline and increasing preoccupation with the threat posed by Germany and the United States to Britain's economic and military supremacy. At the time of Queen Victoria's Diamond Jubilee celebrations in 1897, one-quarter of the earth's surface and nearly a quarter of its population was subject to

British rule, but while the Empire continued to expand, the British Isles were becoming increasingly industrialised, urbanised and overcrowded. As the population passed 40 million, and a better educated generation reached maturity, the more adventurous Britons were feeling cramped.

The Empire provided one outlet, with mass emigration to Australia, Canada, New Zealand and British South Africa, as well as to the United States, and opportunities for derring-do in small but frequent colonial wars, generally against rather poorly armed opposition, including Abyssinia (1867), the Ashanti War (1874), the Zulu War (1878), Afghanistan (1879), Egypt (1882) and the Sudan (1896). John Stuart Mill observed that the Empire represented 'a vast system of outdoor relief for the British upper classes',[1] and even those that remained behind in Britain were obsessed by the idea of imperial adventure. Authors such as Robert Louis Stevenson, Joseph Conrad and Rudyard Kipling catered to the public taste for tales of heroism, and explorers such as Richard Burton, John Speke, David Livingstone and Henry Morton Stanley were household names. Young urban professionals in Britain sought out these tales of romance and adventure in part because their day-to-day lives were so unremittingly unromantic. For some, the mountains offered an escape.

The British may have invented the sport of climbing but they did not at first climb in Britain. The sport had been established in the Alps for more than two decades before any real climbing, as opposed to hill walking, took place in the British hills. During the Golden Age of alpine climbing from 1854 to 1865, the unquestioned objective of the sport was to reach the summit of a mountain by the easiest means. In Britain this might involve long, rough walks but, with one or two rare exceptions, it does not require the use of hands. Tyndall, who made the first ascent of the Weisshorn, wrote an account of walking up Helvellyn in a snow storm in the 1850s and climbed Snowdon in December 1860 using a rudimentary ice axe made by a blacksmith in Bethesda. He described the view from the summit as equal to the splendours of the Alps. Leslie Stephen visited the Lakes in the 1860s and spent several hours trying to find the scrambling route to the summit of Pillar Rock, but it was not until the late 1870s that climbers seriously started to examine the sporting potential of the British crags as a preparation for a summer visit to the Alps. Since most of the early alpine climbs were predominantly on snow and ice rather than rock, interest initially focused on the gullies of the highest mountains that tended to hold the greatest accumulations of snow and ice, at Christmas and Easter. Gradually attention shifted from the gullies to the rocky ridges, slabs and walls, and the sport of rock climbing was born. The first ascent of Napes Needle, traditionally taken as the 'birth of British rock climbing', took place in 1886, more than 30 years after the start of the Golden Age of alpine climbing and three years after the first climbing expedition to the Himalaya. The development of rock climbing in Britain coincided with the conquest of the last remaining unclimbed peaks in the Alps and the growing realisation that 'the essence of the sport lies not in ascending a peak, but in struggling with and overcoming difficulties'.[2] Ironically, because of the continuing emphasis on alpine climbing, long after the exploratory phase had come to an end in France and Switzerland there were still many unclimbed mountains at home. The summit of the last major peak in Britain was finally reached in 1896.

Alpine climbing remained largely the preserve of wealthy professionals with long summer holidays until the start of the First World War, but from the outset British rock climbing assumed a more democratic character. Victorian society was obsessed by class, with very precise gradations of status. At the top, there was a tiny but powerful upper class consisting of aristocrats and landed gentry. Some 80 per cent of members of parliament in the 1860s were drawn from this elite group. Very few of them took an interest in climbing, preferring the traditional country pursuits of hunting, shooting and fishing. At the time of its formation, the Alpine Club was dominated by two of the three traditional professions: the church and the law. The third acceptable occupation for a gentleman who was obliged to earn a living was the military. Army officers were frequently posted overseas and played a limited part in the development of climbing in Britain and the Alps, but officers posted to India played a major role in Himalayan climbing. Naval officers with exploratory instincts tended to be drawn to the polar regions rather than the mountains. As the century progressed the newer professions, such as medicine, civil engineering and the civil service, and even people in 'trade' – bankers, merchants, manufacturers and others engaged in business – came to be represented in the membership of the Alpine Club. However, the lower middle class – clerks, commercial travellers, national and local government workers, teachers and other white-collar workers – were almost totally excluded. The pool from which the Alpine Club drew its membership was therefore largely restricted to a professional upper middle class, consisting of perhaps 70,000 people, less than one per cent of the male workforce in 1850.[3] The achievements of the pioneers are even more remarkable, given the tiny segment of the population from which they were drawn.

In the second half of the nineteenth century the professional class grew slightly, but the numbers engaged in lower-middle-class occupations swelled dramatically. In 1850 there were perhaps 130,000 white-collar workers, representing about two per cent of the male workforce. By 1900 this had grown to 500,000 or five per cent. The growth of the middle class reflected the expansion of industry, trade and services and improvements in education. Many of the young people who entered middle-class occupations in the second half of the nineteenth century came from working-class backgrounds and were not necessarily materially better off than well-paid artisans. What distinguished the two was not so much money as the very Victorian concept of 'respectability', the maintenance of which by 'keeping up appearances' placed an additional financial burden on the aspiring middle classes. In the days before the mass production of consumer goods, one way that a young man could signal his membership of the middle classes was to travel. The increasingly fashionable and manly pursuit of mountain climbing provided the perfect status symbol.

In contrast to the alpinists, from the outset many British rock climbers were in 'trade' or lower-middle-class occupations. Especially in the Lake District, the sport came to be dominated by northern manufacturers, shopkeepers and teachers, some of whom came from working-class family backgrounds. As the social base from which climbers were drawn began to broaden, the numbers entering the sport expanded and standards inevitably began to rise. Similar developments were occurring in every other sport. Wherever it was possible to make money (by charging spectators or from gambling), a new form of employment – the professional, and typically working-class, sportsman – was born and standards increased dramatically. Football was the first to professionalise and became overwhelmingly a working-class sport after Blackburn Olympic defeated the Old Etonians in the FA Cup final of 1883. Cricket reached a halfway house with amateur 'gentlemen' and professional 'players' in the same side. Rugby fractured into the professional, and predominantly working-class, rugby league and the amateur, and predominantly middle-class, rugby union. Climbing, like other field sports, did not easily lend itself either to spectators or to gambling. As a result it remained overwhelmingly an amateur sport and participation was restricted to those with some money and leisure. But in Britain, unlike the Alps, it was never exclusively a rich man's sport.

In keeping with the entrepreneurial spirit of the age, a few climbers tried to make money from the sport. Edward Whymper earned a reasonable living producing mountain illustrations and from lecturing and writing. Owen Glynne Jones and the Abraham brothers made money from writing and photography. But climbing remained a minority sport and income from these sources was sufficient to sustain only a small number of 'professional' climbers. Guiding, which played such a significant role in the development of the sport in the alpine countries, did not take off in Britain until the introduction of outdoor education in the 1950s, and it was only after the development of outdoor television broadcasting in the 1960s that climbing became a spectator sport and entered the mainstream.

Improvements in transport played a critical role in the growth of the sport in the second half of the nineteenth century. Often financed and built by the British, railways extended across every continent and shipping lines crossed every ocean. In Britain, as the cost of travel declined, Sunday excursion trains ran from the mill towns of Lancashire and Yorkshire into the surrounding countryside from the 1860s onwards, carrying both young professionals and factory workers, many of whom were first or second generation migrants to the cities and still felt strong ties to the countryside. The Snowdon Mountain Railway was completed in 1896 and a café built on the summit to refresh the tourists who paid to go there. The current Prince of Wales described a recent incarnation of the building as the highest slum in the country. In the Alps too, modern transport began to encroach upon the highest peaks. By 1880 nearly a million people, mainly from England, Germany, America and Russia, visited Switzerland each year, justifying increased investment in infrastructure. The railway reached Grindelwald in 1890, Zermatt in 1891 and Chamonix in 1901. In 1911 engineers tunnelled their way up through the Eiger to reach the Jungfraujoch (3,573m/11,722ft) and would have carried on to the summit of the Jungfrau had better sense, and a weaker economy, not prevailed. However, in both Britain and the Alps, once the railhead was reached, the pace of life returned to that of a man walking or a horse and cart, until the appearance of motor cars at the turn of the century.

Increasing prosperity and shorter working hours also played a significant role. By the 1870s, the most extreme labour abuses had largely been removed but working hours were still long by modern European standards. In the textile industry a ten and a half hour day and a 60 hour week, with Saturday afternoon and Sunday off, was typical. Statutory bank holidays were introduced in the late 1870s, and in the following decade some workers started to receive one week of unpaid leave in the summer. Religious observance remained strong, but gradually leisure activities increased even on the Sabbath. Since the price of food rose relatively slowly, industrial workers benefitted more than agricultural workers from rising wages and some were able to save modest amounts with the newly established Post Office Savings Bank. The union movement, which had 2 million members by 1900, campaigned for shorter hours and better wages, and there were numerous grassroots self-help organisations including the Co-operative Society and the Workers' Educational Association. Industrialisation created a demand for a better educated work force and there was a significant expansion of both secondary and tertiary education, increasing the size of the young middle class that could afford some leisure activities and holidays. The early years of climbing were dominated by men educated at Oxford and Cambridge, but in later years graduates from Manchester University (founded in 1880), Liverpool (1903), Leeds (1904) and Sheffield (1905), all located close to the outcrops and mountains, played a very significant role in the development of the sport.

When Queen Victoria died in 1901, she was succeeded by Edward VII who, at the age of 57, was a polished sporting man of the world. Like the new king, Britain had come to feel somewhat stifled by the pious propriety of the Victorian age, and the style and manner of Edward VII was more in keeping with the emancipated tastes of the opening years of the twentieth century. But the individual flair, heroism and eccentricity that had built the Empire was progressively being replaced by a more ordered and conceited bureaucracy. Like the Empire, the British climbing establishment also became increasingly grandiloquent and chauvinistic, losing its ability to innovate and placing its faith in tradition. While members of the Alpine Club continued to dominate British climbing overseas, advances in Britain were increasingly led by climbers drawn from a broader social background and brought up outside the alpine tradition.

THE ALPS

At the conclusion of the Golden Age in 1865 most of the alpine peaks had been climbed by their easiest routes. During the 'Silver Age' that followed, from 1865 to 1882, the few remaining major peaks were climbed, and the younger members of the climbing community recognised that, with the end of the exploratory phase of alpine development, they were faced with two choices: to go in search of virgin peaks in other parts of the world; or to climb alpine peaks by new and harder routes involving greater risk.

In the Middle Ages several passes over the Alps that are today glaciated were free of snow and ice and were in regular use. The glaciers began to advance from the fifteenth century onwards and by the eighteenth century were far more extensive than they are today. The present retreat began in the nineteenth century and has accelerated in recent years due to the impact of global warming. As a consequence, the appearance and character of many alpine peaks has changed considerably since the pioneers first climbed them in the mid-nineteenth century. Today, the retreating glaciers have exposed extensive areas of moraine, the peaks are rockier in appearance, and many rock faces and ridges are looser because they are not bound together with ice. The pioneers of the Golden Age climbed nearly all the major peaks by following routes that were largely on glaciers and snow fields. Climbers and their guides rapidly developed relatively sophisticated snow and ice climbing techniques but tried, wherever possible, to avoid the rocks. As a result, at the end of the Golden Age in 1865, there were still numerous unclimbed rocky peaks in the Alps that demanded greater rock climbing skills than those possessed by the pioneers.

Clinton Dent elegantly summed up the situation in 1876: 'The older members of the Club (I speak with the utmost veneration) have left us, the youthful aspirants, but little to do in the Alps...We follow them meekly, either by walking up their mountains by new routes, or by climbing some despised outstanding spur of the peaks that they first trod under foot...They have picked out the plums and left us the stones.'[4] His reference to 'walking' delighted the young Turks and infuriated the senior members of the Alpine Club. Dent was an eminent surgeon and one of the leading members of the second generation of alpine pioneers. He was 'inclined to pursue his own line of thought, and had not always the ear of a ready listener'[5] and soon broke with tradition by focusing on rock climbs. Often guided by Alexander Burgener, who came from the Saas valley rather than the traditional and more complacent climbing centres of Zermatt or Chamonix, Dent made the first ascent of the Lenzspitz (PD, 4,294m/14,088ft) in 1870 and the Zinal Rothorn from Zermatt (AD) in 1872, but it is for his ascent of the Grand Dru (AD, 3,754m/12,316ft) in 1878, after 18 attempts over six seasons, that he is chiefly remembered. The Dru, which towers over the town of Chamonix, exemplifies the challenge posed by the slightly lower, but far steeper and rockier subsidiary peaks of the Mont Blanc massif. Its first ascent prompted major celebrations in Chamonix: 'I believe there were fireworks; I rather think some cannon were let off. I am under the impression that a good many bottles were uncorked. Perhaps this last may be connected with a hazy recollection of all that actually took place.'[6] One year earlier Lord Wentworth, the grandson of Lord Byron, succeeded in climbing the Aiguille Noire de Peuterey (AD, 3,772m/12,375ft), another imposing and rocky peak, with the Italian guide Emile Rey. Rey went on to climb the Aiguille Blanche de Peuterey (D, 4,112m/13,491ft), the last and hardest of the major peaks of the Mont Blanc massif to be climbed, with Sir Henry Seymour King, a respected banker and member of parliament, in 1885.

The new generation of climbers also explored the steep and sometimes narrow snow and ice couloirs that had previously been dismissed because of the risk of rock and icefall. The unclimbed ridges of the higher peaks presented an obvious challenge as well. Although relatively free from the objective risk of stone and icefall, they were often technically more difficult and far more exposed than the broad glaciers and snow fields that provided the traditional routes to most summits. As the Silver Age progressed, climbing without guides and winter mountaineering also gained a following, as climbers sought out new ways to maintain the novelty and challenge of the sport.

The end of the Silver Age is usually taken to be the ascent of the twin summits of the Dent du Géant (AD, 4,013m/13,166ft) in 1882. The first summit was ascended by the Sella brothers and their guides, the Macquignaz brothers, of Italy. The second, slightly higher summit was climbed two days later by William Graham, who went on to be the first person to climb in the Himalaya for sport rather than for science. The significance of the ascent of the Dent du Géant lay in the fact that it was the last peak to be climbed that was named and famous *before* it was climbed and the first to be climbed by 'artificial' means, using pitons and fixed ropes. For the British climbing establishment, committed to a 'pure' climbing ethic, the use of pitons signalled the end of the Silver Age and the start of the 'Iron Age'.[7] It was an avowedly romantic view of climbing history. While their contemporaries divided Mankind's progress and development into the Stone Age, the Bronze Age and the Iron Age, British mountain historians saw a regression from the Golden Age, to the Silver Age to the Iron Age. The prevailing mountaineering ethos was a rejection of modernity and a celebration of the primitive, the mysterious and the unknown. But while British views on 'artificial aid' were strongly held, they were never entirely logical or consistent. Cutting a step in ice was acceptable. Cutting a step in rock was unforgiveable. A ladder might be used to cross a crevasse, but to use one on rock was immoral. As Clinton Dent observed in 1878: 'Grapnels, chains, and crampons are the invention of the fiend. Why this should be so is hard to see. Perhaps we should not consider too curiously.'[8] It took a further 90 years before a widely accepted and reasonably consistent framework of climbing ethics was to emerge.

When the sport of climbing started in the Alps only the most prominent peaks had names and these tended to be monotonously descriptive (Mont Blanc, Weisshorn, Schwarzhorn, Aiguille Noire), geographic (Dent d'Hérens) or fearful (Mont Maudit, Schreckhorn). As the lesser peaks were climbed, it became necessary to name them too, and in the years before the First World War 'personal' nomenclature was adopted with a vengeance, including numerous Younggrats and Voies Ryan-Lochmatter, but there were also some humorous names. When Stafford Anderson and his companions reached the summit of the Dent Blanche by a new route along a crumbling ridge, their guide Ulrich Almer summed up the situation by saying, '*Wir sind vier Esel!*' ('We are four asses!'). The ridge became known as the Viereselsgrat. Martin Conway, later Lord Conway, was particularly active in naming peaks: 'The secret of getting a name accepted is to put it about among the guides...as long as no one knows where a name originated no one will object.'[9]

With the trend towards harder routes and guideless climbing, the death toll inevitably began to rise, and the more senior members of the Alpine Club became increasingly concerned about what they regarded as the 'unjustifiable risks' taken by the younger generation. After three serious accidents in 1882, Queen Victoria's private secretary wrote to Gladstone, the prime minister: 'The Queen commands me to ask you if you think she can say anything to mark her disapproval of the dangerous Alpine excursions which this year have occasioned so much loss of life.'[10] Gladstone wisely counselled against it. Swiss Alpine Club records show that during the period 1859–85 there were on average just five fatalities from climbing accidents each year, whereas during the six years from 1886 to 1891 there were 214 deaths.[11] Partly this reflected the increasing numbers of people climbing, but even by the end of the century, there were probably only a thousand or so active climbers. Apart from the British, German students were the other large group that were active in the Alps in the last decades of the nineteenth century, although they tended to confine their activities to the Eastern Alps, which most British climbers regarded as too small to be of interest. In 1887 the Alpine Club had 475 members, not all of whom were active, whereas the Austrian and German Alpine Club (which merged into one in 1874) had 18,020, the French 5,321, the Italian 3,669 and the Swiss 2,607. However the continental clubs were organised along very different lines from the Alpine Club. Deliberately set up as inclusive national clubs, they provided cheap accommodation and their membership included large numbers of mountain walkers. The number of members actively involved in true alpinism remained very small until after the Second World War.

The British climbing establishment was also concerned that in their quest for ever harder technical difficulties the aesthetic aspects of the sport were being ignored. Walter Larden criticised the heroic instincts of rock climbers: 'There are those amongst them who climb for the excitement only; who would sooner spend their day climbing in a gully that affords exciting "pitches", but makes no demand on endurance or mountaineering knowledge...than in gaining the sublime heights of Monte Rosa or in traversing the magnificent Col d'Argentière. Let such recognise frankly that they don't care for the mountains.'[12] The conflict between 'gymnasts' and 'mountaineers', with the latter doubting the ability of the former to appreciate the beauty and spiritual aspects of the mountain landscape, continued until well into the 1930s. Writing in 1904, Cecil Slingsby noted that 'all who are worthy of being termed mountaineers, in contradistinction to climbing acrobats, find that year by year their love of mountains increases, and so too does their respect and veneration',[13] and even in 1935 R. L. G. Irving, the romantic and reactionary mountain historian, still felt obliged to note that rock climbers are 'good cragsmen and indifferent mountaineers, with a somewhat limited and unimaginative way of regarding mountains'.[14] The younger climbers suspected, probably correctly, that their elders used their increasing veneration of the landscape to disguise their declining physical powers.

The Pendlebury brothers, Richard and William, were typical of the second generation of alpinists that began to emerge at the end of the Golden Age. In 1870 they traversed the Wildspitze (3,768m/12,362ft) via the Mittelberg Joch, creating what is now one of the most popular climbs in the Eastern Alps. In 1872 they shocked the climbing world by making the first ascent of the huge East Face of the Monte Rosa from Macugnaga (D+) with the Rev. Charles Taylor and their guide Ferdinand Imseng. The East Face is a steep wall with rocky ribs and couloirs filled with snow and ice. As the sun rises and melts the ice, the couloirs form a natural funnel for rock and icefall. The climb therefore involves a far greater degree of 'objective risk' (risk that is beyond the control of the climber) than would have been acceptable in the early years of alpinism, and both the climbers and their guide were thought by many to have displayed courage bordering on recklessness. The climb was also Imseng's first as chief guide, though he had previously been employed as a porter, an illustration of a recurring theme of major breakthroughs being made by people outside the mainstream of the sport. Nine years later Imseng died in an avalanche attempting to make the third ascent of the same route with his client Marinelli. The Pendlebury brothers went on to make several other first ascents, including the Schreckhorn from the Lauteraarsattel (D+, 1873), which was a remarkable achievement for the time. Richard Pendlebury, who was Senior Wrangler at Cambridge in 1870 and a Fellow of St John's College, was also one of the founders of British rock climbing, ascending Jake's Rake on Pavey Ark and making the Pendlebury Traverse (M, 1872) on Pillar Rock in the Lake District.

The ascent of the Col des Grandes Jorasses in 1874 by Thomas Middlemore, a Birmingham leather merchant, created a similar controversy, particularly regarding the morality of taking professional guides into areas with significant objective risk. Middlemore confessed to being black and blue with bruises caused by falling rocks. Climbing with Henri Cordier, a Parisian student who died in a climbing accident at the age of 21, and John Oakley Maund, a quick-tempered London stockbroker, Middlemore made first ascents of the Aiguille Verte from the Argentière Glacier (D+/TD-), Les Courtes (AD, 3,856m/12,651ft) and Les Droites (AD, 4,000m/13,123ft) all within the space of a week. The Cordier Couloir on the Aiguille Verte once again involved climbing a route that was obviously exposed to frequent rockfall and was not repeated for nearly 50 years. With Cordier, Middlemore also made the first ascent of the beautiful snow and ice arête of the Biancograt on the Piz Bernina (AD, 4,049m/13,284ft), one of the great alpine ridges which, while relatively free from objective risk, is technically more difficult and exposed than many traditional routes. In later life Middlemore bought the Melsetter estate in Orkney which comprised a number of islands including Hoy, whose famous sea stack was to become the setting for a television climbing spectacular in the 1960s.

Middlemore also climbed with James Eccles, who made numerous first ascents on the Mont Blanc massif with the outstanding guide Michel Payot, including the Aiguille de Rochefort (AD, 4,001m/13,127ft) in 1873, the Dôme de Rochefort (AD, 4,015m/13,173ft) in 1881 and, most famously, the upper section of the Peuterey Ridge in 1877, where he camped at the side of the Brouillard Glacier beneath what is now called Pic Eccles and next day crossed the Col Eccles, reached the Frêney Glacier and ascended the ridge. The Peuterey Ridge, which in its entirety still merits a grade of D+, was repeated just twice before the Second World War.

Charles and Lawrence Pilkington, of the glass-making and colliery-owning family, were also active climbers at this time. With their cousin, Frederick Gardiner, a Liverpool ship-owner, and George Hulton, a Manchester businessman, they pioneered guideless climbing in the Alps. They made the first guideless ascents of the Barre des Écrins (PD, 1878), La Meije (AD, 1879) – the last and one of the hardest of the major alpine peaks to be climbed – the Jungfrau from Wengern Alp (PD, 1881) and the Finsteraarhorn (PD, 1881). All four were also active climbers in Britain. The Pilkington brothers climbed Pillar Rock in 1869 when Lawrence was just 14 and were amongst the first to climb on Skye, which at that time was harder to reach than the Alps, making the first ascent of the Inaccessible Pinnacle (M, 1880) on Sgurr Dearg, the only major Scottish peak that requires rock climbing to reach the summit.

One area that remained almost unexplored in the 1870s was the French Dauphiné Alps, and for that reason it attracted the attention of William Coolidge and his formidable aunt Meta Brevoort. Born in 1850 near New York, and brought up by his aunt, Coolidge left the United States at the age of 14 and lived first in France, then England, and finally Switzerland. Since it was possible in those days to travel anywhere in Europe, except Russia and the Balkans, without a passport, Coolidge never obtained one, and at the outbreak of the First World War he found that he was stateless, having lost his US citizenship. Coolidge was introduced to climbing at the age of 15 by Miss Brevoort, a spirited explorer who climbed over 70 major peaks and did not hesitate to beat some mule drivers whom she saw mistreating their animals. They were frequently accompanied by their pet bitch Tschingel – described by a Swiss gentleman who was obliged to share a hut with her as a '*form-loser, watscheliger fettklumpen*' ('a shapeless, waddling fat lump') – who nevertheless succeeded in climbing 66 major peaks. Coolidge too did not possess an athletic physique – a contemporary at Magdalen College where he became a Fellow in 1875 remembered him as a 'tubby, under-sized little man'[15] – but he was tough and resolute. Coolidge was inordinately fond of his aunt, and after her death in 1876 he took Holy Orders and turned his attention to the academic study of the history of alpinism, becoming increasingly obsessive in his pedantry and the vehemence with which he defended his views on the subject. Between 1865 and 1898 he spent 33 seasons in the Alps, amassing a staggering total of 1,700 climbs, including first ascents of Pic Centrale de la Meije (PD) in 1870, Ailefroide (F, 3,953m/12,969ft) in 1870, the Piz Badile (PD, 3,308m/10,853ft) in 1876, and numerous lesser peaks in the Maritime and Cottian Alps. During most of this time he was guided by Christian Almer and later his son of the same name. He made the first winter ascents of the Wetterhorn and Jungfrau in 1874, with Miss Brevoort, and the Schreckhorn in 1879, and is generally regarded as the father of winter mountaineering. He also climbed in the Caucasus with Douglas Freshfield in 1868.

Coolidge wrote numerous books and articles, including the Conway and Coolidge *Climbers' Guides* to the Alps (1881–1910), co-authored with Martin Conway, which were the first practical alpine guidebooks. Coolidge contributed long, pedantic, heavily annotated volumes, while Conway smoothed out the ferocious rows that took place between Coolidge and the publisher. In keeping with Conway's exploratory instincts, the guides were originally conceived as a means of ensuring that pioneering parties *avoided* routes that had previously been climbed. Of course, they were overwhelmingly used for exactly the opposite purpose. The slim volumes gave descriptions of the routes and also named the first ascensionists. Conway noted that even those members of the Alpine Club who abhorred competition and self-advertisement in others were quick to correct any omissions with respect to their own achievements. From 1880 to 1889 Coolidge was also editor of the *Alpine Journal*, a position that brought him into bitter conflict with most of the leading climbers of the day. Famous for his stubbornness, Coolidge 'could do anything with a hatchet but bury it',[16] according to Arnold Lunn, one of his many victims. He resigned from the Alpine Club in 1899, was re-elected as an honorary member in 1904, resigned again in 1910 and was re-elected again in 1923. He is the only member ever to have resigned an honorary membership.

Coolidge's arguments with Whymper, over 'Almer's leap', an illustration in *Scrambles Amongst the Alps* showing Christian Almer apparently making a daring leap during the descent of the Barre des Écrins, were legendary, but towards the end of Whymper's life the two men were reconciled. Coolidge was, in many respects, quite similar to Whymper. Both were fired by single-minded ambition, both had an apparent indifference to the opinion of others, and both appeared completely immune to the beauty of the mountain landscape. Coolidge often regretted that he had not been born earlier so that he might have taken part, with Whymper, in the Golden Age of alpine exploration. His obituary in *The Times* talked of his 'adeptness at the gentle art of making enemies',[17] but without his scholarship much early alpine history would have been lost. Furthermore, Coolidge was a balanced judge of climbing ability. He argued with Fred Mummery, as he did with everyone else, but was appalled when Mummery was blackballed by the Alpine Club in 1880, despite being proposed by Dent and Freshfield. When Mummery finally allowed himself to be put forward for membership again in 1888, Coolidge surreptitiously slipped some of the 'noes' in the ballot box into the 'ayes' to ensure that he was elected.

Fred Mummery was born in Dover in 1855, the son of a tannery owner. He was a sickly child with a deformed back, which prevented him from carrying heavy loads, and was amongst the first in a long line of climbers whose tolerance of huge exposure was attributed to his acute short-sightedness. He spent the first part of his career climbing with Alexander Burgener, and then went on to revolutionise the sport by putting up hard new routes without the use of guides. Even when accompanied by guides, he impressed upon them that his requirement was for another man on the rope, not a leader. Burgener stated that Mummery 'climbs even better than I do',[18] which was high praise from a proud man.

Mummery was a charismatic individual who made many staunch friends in the climbing community, including Norman Collie, Cecil Slingsby, Geoffrey Hastings and Henri Pasteur, as well as some enemies, including Whymper and Edward Davidson. 'Wherein lay his great superiority is a difficult question to answer', wrote Pasteur. 'He was a clumsy walker and no one who had not seen him at work would credit him with his outstanding powers as a climber and a leader. He was a man of will-power and energy tempered with a marvellous patience.'[19]

His first ascents included both unclimbed ridges on the highest mountains and hard rock climbs on the lesser peaks. With Burgener he ascended the Zmutt Ridge (D) on the Matterhorn in 1879. A race developed with William Penhall, a medical student, and the daring guide Ferdinand Imseng. Penhall and Imseng traversed onto the West Face of the mountain, crossing the dangerous Penhall Couloir, and completed a route that has seldom been repeated. Penhall died three years later on the Wetterhorn. Meanwhile, Mummery attempted the fourth unclimbed ridge of the Matterhorn, the Furggengrat (D+/TD), in 1880 but was forced to traverse across the east face to the Hörnli Ridge. The Furggen Ridge was finally climbed in its entirety in 1911. In the Mont Blanc massif, Mummery climbed the Charpoua Face of the Aiguille Verte (D, 1881) and the Grépon (D, 1881). His guideless climbing commenced in 1889 and included the first traverse of the Grépon with Hastings, Collie and Pasteur in 1892; the Dent du Requin (D) and an attempt on the Aiguille du Plan with Slingsby, Collie and Hastings in 1893; and the first guideless ascent of the Brenva Route on Mont Blanc with Collie and Hastings in 1894. The Dent du Requin (the 'Shark's Tooth') was named by Martin Conway and the route was devised by Slingsby, possibly because Mummery could not see it. Nevertheless on this and other ascents, it was Mummery who led the difficult pitches on rock and particularly on ice, where he was probably the best amateur climber of his generation.

Mummery was unusual for his time in that he also climbed with women. He ascended the Täschhorn (4,490m/14,731ft) via the Teufelsgrat (D) with his wife Mary and Burgener in 1887. During the descent, Burgener encouraged Mrs Mummery to lead the way down the steep slope with the words, 'Go ahead; I could hold a cow here!'[20] Mary later wrote that Burgener held 'many strange opinions; he believes in ghosts, he believes also that women can climb'.[21] Mummery also climbed with Miss Lily Bristow (until he was apparently forbidden to do so by his wife). His traverse of the Grépon with Slingsby and Miss Bristow in 1893 gave rise to the observation that all mountains are doomed to pass through three phases: an inaccessible peak; the most difficult climb in the Alps; an easy day for a lady (a phrase invented by Leslie Stephen). Lily Bristow wrote to her parents describing the route as a 'succession of problems, each one of which was a ripping good climb in itself'.[22]

Mummery climbed in the Caucasus in 1888, making the first ascent of Dychtau (5,204m/17,073ft), and was invited by Martin Conway to go to the Karakoram in 1892, but after a visit to the Alps together Mummery declined because it was clear that Conway's priority was exploration whereas his was climbing. Nevertheless, the two remained friends, with Conway describing Mummery as 'the greatest climber of this or any other generation', although he observed that 'he loved danger for its own sake'.[23] Mummery died in 1895 attempting to climb Nanga Parbat in the Himalaya, the first attempt on an 8,000m peak.

The final chapter of his book *My Climbs in the Alps and Caucasus*, which was written shortly before his death, is entitled 'The Pleasures and Penalties of Mountaineering'. It was highly influential in the development of the sport, particularly in France and Germany. He was perhaps the first climber fully to recognise the risks of climbing and to judge those risks worth taking. 'He gains a knowledge of himself, a love of all that is most beautiful in nature, and an outlet such as no other sport affords for the stirring energies of youth; gains for which no price is, perhaps, too high. It is true that great ridges sometimes demand their sacrifice, but the mountaineer would hardly forego his worship though he knew himself to be the destined victim.'[24] This attitude to climbing and to risk was new and revolutionary, and probably accounted for some of the opposition to his membership of the Alpine Club. However, his equally radical views on politics and economics – he was co-author of *Physiology of Industry* (1889) with John Hobson, the left-wing economist whose later critique of imperialism influenced Lenin and Trotsky – and his social background in 'trade' may also have counted against him with some of the more conservative members. His belief that 'the essence of the sport lies, not in ascending a peak, but in struggling with and overcoming difficulties'[25] resonated with continental climbers but did not reflect the mainstream of British climbing until the 1950s. However, in his attitude to the use of artificial aid, he firmly upheld the British approach: 'Someone...mooted the point whether [wooden] wedges were not a sort of bending the knee to Baal, and might not be the first step on those paths of ruin where the art of mountaineering becomes lost in that of the steeplejack. Whereupon we unanimously declared that the Charmoz should be desecrated by no fixed wedges.'[26]

Martin Conway observed that Mummery was 'intellectually rather than aesthetically well endowed',[27] but Mummery always defended himself against the accusation that adventure and aesthetic appreciation are incompatible. 'To the (self-dubbed) mountaineers, the right way up a peak is the easiest way, and all other ways are wrong ways. Thus...if a man goes up the Matterhorn to enjoy the scenery, he will go up the Hörnli route; if he goes by the Zmutt ridge it is, they allege, merely the difficulties of the climb that attract him...To say that this route, with its continuously gorgeous scenery is, from the aesthetic point of view, the wrong way, while the Hörnli route, which is marred by...its paper-besprinkled slopes, is the right, involves total insensibility to the true mountain feeling.'[28] From his writing it is clear that Mummery appreciated both the heroic and the aesthetic aspects of the sport: 'Above, in the clear air and searching sunlight, we are afoot with the quiet gods, and men can know each other and themselves for what they are.'[29]

As well as playing a supporting role to Mummery, his companions Slingsby, Collie and Hastings were outstanding mountaineers in their own right. Cecil Slingsby was a textile manufacturer from an old landed family. Born in 1849, he was 'a thorough Yorkshire dalesman, stalwart, broad-shouldered, full-bearded, with a classic profile, a fine complexion even in age, and shrewd, laughing grey eyes',[30] according to Geoffrey Winthrop Young, who married his daughter Eleanor. As well as climbing in the Alps, Slingsby made 15 visits to Norway from 1872 onwards and was known in both England and Norway as the father of Norwegian mountaineering. During the first ascent in 1876 of the impressive Skagastølstind (2,340m/7,677ft), the third highest mountain in the country, he climbed the final 150m/500ft alone after his companions refused to go any further. He was possibly the first Englishman to learn to ski, helped to establish the sport of ski-mountaineering, and was regarded as an incomparable route-finder across unmapped and difficult terrain. He was also passionate about British rock climbing and pot-holing and put up numerous new routes, including Slingsby's Chimney on Scafell Pinnacle (VD, 1888), climbed with Hastings, Hopkinson and Haskett Smith, which involved a pitch of 33m/110ft – a very long runout in the days when there was no protection for the leader.

Norman Collie was born in Alderley Edge in Cheshire. His family had been the largest cotton importers in Britain, but trade was disrupted by the American Civil War (1861–65) and the family firm went bankrupt while Collie was still at school. He therefore had to work for a living. After studying chemistry at Bristol University and Queen's University, Belfast, he was awarded a doctorate at the University of Würzburg in Germany before taking up a teaching post at Cheltenham Ladies College. His niece recalled that 'he was far from being a ladies' man and probably found that schoolgirls in bulk were rather more than he could stomach'.[31] Collie never married, and after four years at Cheltenham he moved to University College London, where he later became Professor of Organic Chemistry. Collie was involved in the discovery of the noble gases, invented the neon light and took the first x-ray photographs used for medical purposes. He is also credited with inventing the 'Grey Man of Ben Macdui', a ghostly apparition that walked with him to the summit in 1920 and has been seen several times since. An acknowledged aesthete and expert on oriental art, wine, food and cigars, Collie was a distinguished figure in many different fields. When he visited Norway, 'crowds flocked to see him under the impression that he was Sherlock Holmes',[32] but many who knew him well found him cold and disdainful. Geoffrey Winthrop Young wrote: 'When he became interested in a man, his penetrating eyes flashed suddenly into an observant personal sympathy; when he was not, he was incapable of pretence, even of awareness.'[33]

Collie was one of the first British alpinists not to serve an apprenticeship with alpine guides, moving directly to guideless climbing based on experience acquired in the British hills. He pioneered climbs in Scotland and the Lake District, including the first ascent of Moss Ghyll on Scafell (S, 1892) with Hastings and John Robinson, where he chipped the 'Collie Step' in the rock with an ice axe; the first ascent of Tower Ridge (Diff. in summer, grade IV in winter, 1894) on Ben Nevis with Hastings and others; and the first winter ascent of Steep Gill on Scafell which merits a grade V today, a standard of difficulty not widely achieved until the 1950s. Collie also climbed on the remote Isle of Skye with the local guide John Mackenzie, making the first ascent of Sgurr an Lochain (1,004m/3,294ft), the last major peak in Britain to be climbed, with Mackenzie and William Naismith in 1896.

From 1898 to 1911 Collie visited the Canadian Rockies five times, making 21 first ascents and naming more than 30 mountains. Mount Collie in Canada and Sgurr Thormaid (Norman's Peak) on Skye are named after him, and he is buried within sight of his beloved Cuillin in Struan, Skye, next to his guide and life-long friend John Mackenzie. Just before his death in 1942 he was observed at the Sligachan Hotel on Skye by a young RAF officer who was on leave: 'We were alone in the inn, save for an old man who must have returned there to die. His hair was white but his face and bearing were still those of a great mountaineer, though he must have been a great age. He never spoke, but appeared regularly at meals to take his place at the table, tight pressed against the windows, alone with his wine and his memories. We thought him rather fine.'[34]

Shortly before he died, Collie described the climbing companions of his youth: 'Slingsby was a magnificent mountaineer, a perfectly safe man to climb with', he wrote, 'and Mummery was not.'[35] The difference, perhaps, was that Mummery was a climber in the modern idiom, while Slingsby, like Collie, was a traditional mountaineer.

Geoffrey Hastings had a worsted spinning business in Bradford and started climbing with Slingsby in 1885, visiting Norway five times with him between 1889 and 1901. In Britain he put up numerous rock climbs including the first ascent of Needle Ridge on Great Gable (VD, 1887) and North Climb on Pillar Rock (S, 1891) with Slingsby and Haskett Smith. Always the strong man of the team, Hastings was renowned for producing unexpected luxuries from his rucksack at critical moments on a climb. Dorothy Pilley recalled seeing him at the foot of the Dent du Géant in 1920 when he was 60 years old: 'There I spied Mr. Geoffrey Hastings and worshipped. Was he not the doughtiest hero remaining from the Mummery Epoch? He did not let my expectations down. An enormous sack jutted out from between his shoulders. When he lowered it the ground shook and he divulged that he made a practice of filling it with boulders to keep himself in training!'[36]

The standards of mountaineering established by Mummery, Slingsby, Collie and Hastings in the closing years of the nineteenth century were well ahead of other Britons climbing at the time and were at the forefront of amateur climbing worldwide. In the years that followed, leading up to the First World War, the sport continued to expand but, with one or two exceptions, did not advance appreciably. In some ways it even regressed, with a return to guided climbing.

One development that did take place in the closing decades of the nineteenth century was the growing number of women participating in the sport and the appearance of the first all-female climbing parties. Women climbers played a particularly significant role in the development of winter mountaineering, including the first winter ascent of Mont Blanc in 1876 by Isabella Straton, who later married her guide, Jean Charlet, the inventor of abseiling. While male alpinists' participation in the sport helped to reinforce their masculinity and social status, women had to overcome significant prejudice. Climbing was incompatible with traditional concepts of femininity and therefore posed a direct threat to a male-dominated social order. Many of the female pioneers were financially independent and nearly all had a rebellious streak. When Isabella Straton married Jean Charlet she had an income of £4,000 a year, whereas her husband might have expected to earn £25 during the summer season. Mary Mummery, who was clearly a very proficient mountaineer, probably expressed the views of many female climbers when she observed that: 'The masculine mind is, with rare exceptions, imbued with the idea that a woman is not a fit comrade for steep ice or precipitous rock and [believes that] she should be satisfied with watching through a telescope some weedy and invertebrate masher being hauled up a steep peak by a couple of burly guides.'[37] Women also had to overcome the difficulty of climbing in long skirts. As the popularity of the sport increased, a 'convertible skirt' was designed for female mountaineers in 1910: 'By undoing the waist straps and the studs which ran from the waist to the hem the wearer appeared in the smartest of knickerbocker suits...and the discarded skirt became a smart and well-fitting cape. In this way the woman mountaineer could dispense with her skirt when a difficult bit of climbing had to be tackled, and yet be garbed according to the demands of convention when returning to civilisation.'[38] For women, even more than for men, any escape from the demands of 'civilisation' was only temporary.

Lizzie le Blond, née Hawkin-Whitshed, was amongst the first women to practise 'man-less climbing', traversing the Piz Palü (AD, 3,905m/12,812ft) with Lady Evelyn McDonnell in 1900. As a young woman she was part of the social set that revolved around Queen Victoria's playboy son Edward, the Prince of Wales. Sent to the Alps because of her weak health, she immediately took to climbing: 'I owe a supreme debt of gratitude to the mountains for knocking me from the shackles of conventionality.'[39] Her great aunt, Lady Bentinck, was so shocked by her behaviour that she wrote to her mother exhorting her to 'stop her climbing mountains; she is scandalising all London and looks like a Red Indian'.[40] Lizzie le Blond's career is somewhat difficult to follow because she turns up successively as Mrs Burnaby, Mrs Main and Mrs Aubrey le Blond. Her first husband, a colonel in the Royal Horse Guards, was speared by Dervishes at the battle of Abu Klea in the Sudan while seeking to relieve General Gordon at Khartoum. The second died after an adventurous trip to China. Lizzie wrote nine books under her various married names and became the first president of the Ladies' Alpine Club, which was initially formed as a section of the Lyceum, an intellectual ladies' club.

Margaret Jackson had 140 major climbs to her credit, including the first winter ascents of the Lauteraarhorn (4,042m/13,261ft), the Pfaffenstöckli (3,114m/10,217ft), the Gross Fiescherhorn (4,049m/ 13,284ft) and the first winter traverse of the Jungfrau, all in the space of 12 days in 1888. She lost several toes to frostbite after a bivouac on the Jungfrau. Katie Richardson's record was perhaps even more impressive. Described by an admirer as 'resembling a piece of carefully kept Dresden china',[41] her guides took a somewhat different view: 'She does not eat and she walks like the devil.'[42] She began climbing in 1871 and completed 116 major climbs of which six were first ascents and 14 first women's ascents. She made the first traverse of Piz Palü in 1879, became the first woman to climb La Meije in 1885 and made the first traverses from the Bionnassay to the Dôme de Goûter (AD) in 1888 and from the Petit to the Grand Dru (D-) in 1889.

Gertrude Bell was the first woman to be awarded a first class degree in modern history at Oxford. After leaving university she travelled throughout the Middle East, studying languages, archaeology and politics. During the First World War she joined the Arab Bureau and was appointed Oriental Secretary. After the war she settled in current-day Iraq, where she played a key role in the succession of the Hashemites to the throne. She held the most senior position of any woman in the British Empire in the 1920s and was therefore one of the most powerful women in the world:

From Trebizond to Tripoli
She rolls the Pashas flat
And tells them what to think of this
And what to think of that.

Her proudest achievement was the creation of the Baghdad Museum ('like the British Museum only a little smaller'), now sadly looted of many of its treasures, but she was also an exceptional alpinist. With Ulrich Führer as her guide, she completed the first traverse of the Lauteraarhorn–Schreckhorn (AD, 1902) and made an epic attempt on the unclimbed North-East Face of the Finsteraarhorn (now graded ED1 with several pitches of V) lasting 57 hours with a retreat in a blizzard. This climb was well ahead of its time, more appropriate to the bitter Teutonic struggles of the 1930s than an English lady climbing at the turn of the century. Despite these very considerable achievements, women were not admitted to the Alpine Club for over a hundred years, and even then several male members (including Bill Tilman) resigned in protest.

The two leading male alpinists in the years leading up to the First World War were John Ryan, who almost always climbed with the guides Franz and Josef Lochmatter, and Geoffrey Winthrop Young, who often climbed with Josef Knubel. Ryan was an Anglo-Irish landowner. A difficult and charmless man who 'seldom carried rucksack or ice axe, and... never cut a step', he was blackballed by the Alpine Club for 'incivility to some older members'.[43] As Geoffrey Winthrop Young observed: 'The gods who showered on him all worldly gifts, withheld the power of ever appearing happy.'[44] He was, nevertheless, a very able climber. In 1905 he made 25 ascents including the North Face of the Charmoz (D+). In 1906 he climbed the North-West Ridge of the Blaitière (TD), the Ryan–Lochmatter Route on the Plan (D+) and the Cresta di Santa Caterina on Monte Rosa (TD). He also climbed the South-West Face of the Täschhorn with Young, Knubel and the Lochmatters, a huge, loose rock face almost 900m high that was not repeated for 37 years (and then using pitons) and still maintains a serious reputation with a grade of TD+. During the climb Ryan confided in Young that the year before he would not have cared a damn which way it went, live or die, but that year he had married. He did not climb at a similar standard again until 1914, when he put a new route up the Nantillons Face of the Grépon. He was badly injured in the First World War and did not climb again.

Geoffrey Winthrop Young was perhaps the best British alpinist in the early part of the twentieth century and had a profound influence on the development of the sport over the next 40 years. He was proposed for membership of the Alpine Club by Sir Alfred Wills, whose ascent of the Wetterhorn opened the Golden Age in the 1850s, and he knew Joe Brown who played a key role in re-establishing Britain as a leading climbing nation in the 1950s.

Born in 1876, the second son of Sir George Young, although he never exactly fitted the mould of an establishment figure, he was nevertheless part of the British ruling class and saw nothing wrong with using his extensive network of friends and relations to advance his career and various causes. When he was a boy, Sir Leslie Stephen and Lord Alfred Tennyson visited his family home on an island in the Thames near Cliveden. It was a prophetic meeting since in later life Young would gain recognition as both a climber and a poet. His father made the first ascent of the Jungfrau from Wengern Alp in 1865, but all mention of climbing was forbidden in the Young household following the death of Sir George's brother while climbing Mont Blanc in 1866. Despite or perhaps because of this, Young was attracted to climbing while a student at Cambridge, where he wrote *The Roof-Climber's Guide to Trinity* in 1900, in a style parodying early alpine guides: 'In these athletic days of rapid devolution to the Simian practices of our ancestors, climbing of all kinds is naturally assuming an ever more prominent position...'[45]

A climber, poet, educationalist and 'athletic aesthete', Young knew that climbing was just a sport, but was convinced that it had an intellectual and spiritual aspect lacking in other sports. He combined a mystical approach to climbing with practical organisational abilities which he put to use in his Pen-y-Pass meets, as president of the Alpine Club and in the formation of the British Mountaineering Council.

Young was sacked as a teacher at Eton in 1905 and as a school inspector in 1913, in both cases probably because of some homosexual impropriety. When he was not climbing he was drawn to the homosexual clubs and boxing booths of Soho, Paris and Berlin, where the thrill of illicit sex and danger of public exposure seems to have appealed to his risk-taking instincts. His writing combines romanticism with striking homo-erotic imagery, such as his description of a rail journey to the Lake District: 'That first rough hug of the northern hills, where the arms of Shap Fell reached down in welcome about the line, and the eye, bored with the dull fleshiness of plains prostrate and flaccid under their litter of utility, can delight in the starting muscles and shapely bones of strong earth, stripped for a wrestle with the elements – or with the climber!'[46] He also reveals something of his motivation for climbing, and perhaps his sense of guilt at his (then illegal) sexual orientation: 'In return for my guardianship of their integrity [the mountains] offered me a sanctuary for all the higher impulses, all the less sordid hopes and imaginings which visited me anywhere through the years.'[47]

Since most climbers were (not surprisingly) less than forthright about their sexual orientation it is hard to judge how prevalent homosexuality was in climbing circles at this time, but it was probably fairly common. Many leading climbers, both before and after the First World War, went to Cambridge University, where homosexuality was both widespread and generally accepted. On Young's side, at least, part of the attraction in his relationship with George Mallory and Siegfried Herford appears to have been physical. All three climbed naked together on the granite sea cliffs of Cornwall, which must have encouraged a good climbing style. Herford also joined Young on some of his visits to boxing clubs, but whether he went in search of sex or simply the thrill of 'slumming it' is unclear.

After climbing in Wales and the Lakes, Young met Josef Knubel in 1905 and started his alpine career. In 1906 he climbed the South-West Face of the Täschhorn with Ryan. In 1907 he climbed the Breithorn Younggrat (D) and the Weisshorn Younggrat (D). He followed this in 1911 with the Brouillard Ridge of Mont Blanc (AD+), the West Ridge of the Grandes Jorasses (D) and the Mer de Glace Face of the Grépon (D), which he climbed with Ralph Todhunter, who had the strange affectation of climbing in white gloves, and Humphrey Jones. Jones became the youngest Fellow of the Royal Society the following year before dying with his wife and guide while climbing in the Alps on their honeymoon. Todhunter was killed in the Dolomites in 1925. Young's last major route in the Alps was the Rote Zähn Ridge of the Gspaltenhorn (TD- with pitches of V), which he climbed with Siegfried Herford in the last summer before the outbreak of war in 1914.

Young hated the war hysteria that gripped Britain in 1914 and attended a peace demonstration in Trafalgar Square, 'the last protest of those who had grown up in the age of civilised peace'.[48] However, he felt unable to remain inactive when so many of his friends were volunteering and so acted as a war correspondent and subsequently helped to found the Friends Ambulance Unit, 'work...for men who wished to die if need be with their contemporaries but not to fight with them'.[49] A man of extraordinary personal courage, both in the mountains and on the battlefield, he received several decorations, including the Légion d'Honneur. He lost his left leg in Italy in 1917, but his commitment to climbing and love of the mountains remained undiminished:

> *I dream my feet upon the starry ways;*
> *My heart rests in the hill.*
> *I may not grudge the little left undone;*
> *I hold the heights, I keep the dreams I won.*[50]

THE LAKE DISTRICT

The inn at Wasdale Head was the first home of the British climbing community that began to form in the closing decades of the nineteenth century.[51] Originally called the Huntsman's Inn, later the Wastwater Hotel, it was started by Will Ritson, who added a wing to his farmhouse to accommodate visitors and obtained a licence in 1856. Ritson boasted that Wasdale had the highest mountain, the deepest lake, the smallest church and the biggest liar in England. He once won a lying contest outright by declaring that, like George Washington, he could not tell a lie. He was a sportsman, drinker and raconteur: 'Landlord, waiter and customer by turns.'[52] Although he retired in 1879, his spirit lived on in the hotel, which continues to attract fell walkers, climbers and other eccentrics to this day.

The hotel is located at the head of a valley, 12 miles' walk from the nearest railway station. In the early years, women guests rarely, if ever, visited it, and it had a sense of remoteness that allowed a relaxed and convivial atmosphere far removed from the social conventions of Victorian domestic life. It was a place that appealed to those with 'a taste for companionable chaos'[53] where the atmosphere was pervaded by the smell of pipe tobacco and wet tweeds. The climbing world consisted of a small group of enthusiastic amateurs, who would regularly meet each other at Wasdale or in the Alps, but they were remarkably welcoming to newcomers; the cliquiness that characterised so many climbing clubs in later years was notably absent. A book in the hotel recorded the activities of the guests, which included long hard walks and, increasingly, scrambles and climbs.

The *Alpine Journal* first carried an article on fell walking in the Lakes in 1870, and established alpinists, including the Pilkington brothers, Norman Collie, Cecil Slingsby, Geoffrey Hastings, Horace Walker, the Pendlebury brothers and Frederick Gardiner, all visited the district. An increasing number of people also started their climbing in the British hills rather than the Alps. The Rev. James Jackson, self-proclaimed Patriarch of the Pillarites, was an early enthusiast who scrambled up Pillar Rock in 1876 at the age of 80 and died attempting to do the same thing at the age of 83. Walter Haskett Smith was a more conventional figure who also started his climbing career in Britain rather than the Alps. Educated at Eton and Oxford, Haskett Smith excelled at athletics, establishing an unofficial long jump world record of 25 feet in practice. While a student he went on a walking tour of the Pyrenees with Charles Packe, the botanist and pioneering mountain explorer, and visited Snowdonia but did not attempt any scrambling or climbing. In 1881 he was appointed by a group of friends to decide where they should gather for a summer reading party. After studying an Ordnance map of Cumberland he selected an inn in a 'sombre region thronged with portentous shadows'[54] and took rooms at Wasdale Head. His choice was probably influenced by Wordsworth's description of the valley in his *Guide to The Lakes*: 'Wastdale is well worth the notice of the Traveller who is not afraid of fatigue; no part of the country is more distinguished by sublimity.' The group read Plato in the morning and tramped the hills in the afternoon. They also made the acquaintance of Herman Bowring, nearly 40 years their senior, who introduced them to the art of scrambling.

Haskett Smith was a man of private means. He qualified as a barrister but was appalled when a friend offered him a brief. Instead, he devoted his life to philology and climbing, returning to the Lakes each year and progressively moving from scrambling to true rock climbing.

Early climbs included Deep Ghyll on Scafell in 1882. Four years later he made the first ascent of Napes Needle with 'no ropes or illegitimate means',[55] often cited as the birth of British rock climbing. Graded HVD today, Napes Needle was a hard route for the mid-1880s but ironically, like the first routes on Pillar Rock and Scafell Pinnacle, it is truly a summit ascended by the easiest route and therefore, in some respects, more in the tradition of alpine climbing than British rock climbing, where reaching a summit is irrelevant. The real significance of Napes Needle was not so much that it was the 'first British rock climb' but rather that it is a very photogenic piece of rock and publicity surrounding subsequent ascents helped to establish rock climbing in Britain as a sport. Just as the Matterhorn became the symbol of alpine climbing, so Napes Needle became the symbol of British rock climbing (and remains the logo of the Fell and Rock Climbing Club to this day).

Haskett Smith was accompanied on many of his climbs by John Robinson, a successful estate manager born near Cockermouth. Robinson visited the Alps once, in 1898, climbing several mountains, including the Matterhorn, but was not impressed. His first love was always the Lake District. During a visit to the Lakes in about 1900 Geoffrey Winthrop Young recalled being hailed at Keswick station by a stranger, who turned out to be Robinson: 'Hullo, young man, oughtn't you and I to talk? Nailed boots go straight to my heart!' As Young commented (in the 1920s): 'Nails, I fear, are now too common a sight upon the fells to pass for an introduction; so much the mountains have gained in the number of their followers and lost of their one-time fellowship.'[56]

The ascent of Napes Needle by Haskett Smith prompted Cecil Slingsby, who first climbed in the Lakes in 1885 with Geoffrey Hastings, to write an article for the *Alpine Journal* exhorting members of the Club to visit the Lakes: 'Do not let us be beaten on our own fells by outsiders, some of whom consider ice axes and ropes to be "illegitimate". Let us not neglect the Lake District, Wales and Scotland whilst we are the conquerors abroad.'[57] Five years later Godfrey Solly, a pious solicitor who became Mayor of Birkenhead and visited the Alps over 40 times, led Slingsby up Eagle's Nest Ridge Direct, a climb that was well ahead of its time and is still graded mild VS today. As Solly recorded: 'I went first and found it difficult enough to get to the little platform. When there, I sat down to recover my breath with my back to the ridge and a leg dangling on each side. The party below made some uncomplimentary remark as to what I looked like perched up there, and I suggested that I was more like an eagle on its nest. That is, I fear, the very unromantic but truthful origin of the name.'[58]

In an influential article written in 1937, H. M. Kelly and J. H. Doughty distinguished four phases in the development of rock climbing in the Lake District: the easiest way (up to 1880); the gully and chimney period (1880–1900); the ridge and arête (rib) period (1890–1905); and the slab and wall period (1905–present).[59] The dates are necessarily approximate but the overall trend towards more open, exposed and steep climbing is borne out by the record. The gullies and chimneys were climbed first partly because they provided the best winter routes, but also because in their dark and wet confines the climbers felt less exposed to a dizzying sense of height. The transition to more open climbing on slabs and walls involved climbers accepting far greater exposure and also demanded a change of technique from brute strength to balance. Solly and Slingsby's ascent of Eagle's Nest Ridge Direct in 1892 was ahead of its time because it was both hard and exposed.

As awareness of the rock climbing potential in the Lakes began to spread, the sport started to attract climbers from the northern industrial cities of Lancashire and Yorkshire. The Hopkinson brothers typified the social background, ambitions and attitudes of many Lake District climbers in the late Victorian era. A distinguished Manchester family, related to the Slingsby family and close neighbours of the Pilkingtons in Alderley Edge, Cheshire, their father was a self-made man who rose through hard work and ability from mill mechanic to Lord Mayor of Manchester. There were five brothers: John became a Fellow at Cambridge and subsequently improved the management and equipment of lighthouses, designed a lighting system for Manchester, and tram systems for Leeds and Liverpool. Alfred read classics at Oxford and then went into the law, becoming Vice-Chancellor of Manchester University and a member of parliament. He was knighted in 1910. Charles was probably the best climber amongst them and was content to remain with the family firm, although he was active in local government. Edward went to Cambridge and became an electrical engineer, designing the engine for the first electrically driven underground train. He too became an MP. The youngest brother, Albert, studied medicine at Cambridge and became a surgeon in Manchester before returning to Cambridge to lecture in anatomy. As with Leslie Stephen, we gain an insight into the lives of the Hopkinsons because Edward's daughter, Katherine Chorley, wrote a book about her childhood. In *Manchester Made Them* (1950) she portrays her father as a 'vital, unresting man, radiating energy', and his brothers as being 'charged with ambition... they almost worshipped brains and too readily judged a successful life in terms of getting to the top of the tree'.[60] She ascribed their ambition to a strict non-conformist upbringing, believing that they 'tried to contract for the kingdom of heaven by means of the laborious days they lived on earth...Success was a yardstick of hard work and therefore all too easily a sign that you had lived well and frugally in the sight of God.'

The Hopkinson brothers climbed on the East Face of Tryfan in Wales in 1882, four years before Haskett Smith climbed Napes Needle. In 1892 they climbed the North-East Buttress of Ben Nevis (VD) and descended Tower Ridge (Diff.), two of the best known climbs in Britain today. In doing so, they demonstrated a willingness to exit the gullies and accept the increased exposure of climbing on ridges and open faces. Like many of their peers, the Hopkinsons considered 'bragging' to be the worst offence for a climber. They kept few records of their climbs and did not approve of others doing so. As Alfred wrote: 'The labels – Cust's Gully, Westmorland's Climb, Botterill's Slab – convey nothing to my mind. These proprietary brands...are sometimes a little trying to those who like to find out things for themselves.'[61] In 1898 John Hopkinson and three of his children died while climbing near

Arolla in Switzerland. The other brothers never climbed again. Aleister Crowley, the self-styled 'Great Beast 666' (who will re-appear later in this book), appears to have played some part in the accident. Crowley had succeeded in descending a route which the local guides had said was impossible. He recommended it to Hopkinson as being without difficulty or danger for a responsible party and it is possible that they were attempting to find it when they fell. By that time, Crowley had already left the valley. John Hopkinson's two surviving sons were killed in the First World War.

As the popularity of hill walking and rock climbing increased, so too did media interest in the activity, which in turn contributed to the growth of the sport. In 1894 Haskett Smith published *Climbing in the British Isles*, which provided brief details of climbs to be found in Britain, including some outcrops and sea cliffs. Haskett Smith's book suggests that the subsidiary sport of bouldering (climbing small but technically difficult rock faces, without ropes) also had its origins around this time. His description of Bear Rock notes that it is 'a queerly-shaped rock on Great Napes, which in the middle of March, 1889 was gravely attacked by a large party comprising some five or six of the strongest climbers in England. It is difficult to find, especially in seasons when the grass is at all long.'[62] The most influential book on British climbing during this period was undoubtedly *Rock-Climbing in the English Lake District*, a collaboration between Owen Glynne Jones and the Abraham brothers, published in 1897, which contained lively descriptions of climbs and superb photographs. The success of the book ensured that Jones became the most famous rock climber of his generation. Like all successful self-publicists, he also attracted much criticism from his climbing peers.

Jones, like Whymper, was firmly part of the heroic rather than aesthetic school of climbing. He wrote about the challenge and excitement of climbing and rarely referred to the beauty of the mountain landscape. Also like Whymper, he was from a lower social class than many climbers of the day; his father was a Welsh carpenter and builder

1. Leslie Stephen (right) with his guide and lifelong friend Melchior Anderegg, c1870. A man who 'substituted long walks for long prayers', Stephen was the scholarly aesthete of the Alpine Club in its early years. Anderegg was one of the greatest guides during the Golden Age of alpine climbing.

(Alpine Club)

2. Edward Whymper, c1871. The flawed hero of Victorian mountaineering, Edward Whymper's ascent of the Matterhorn in 1865 after eight attempts marked both the crowning achievement and the end of the Golden Age.

(Alpine Club)

3. Frank Walker and Lucy Walker with (behind, left to right) unknown, Melchior Anderegg and Adolphus Moore, c1860. Lucy Walker was the first woman to climb the Matterhorn and to take part in the first ascent of a major alpine peak.

(Alpine Club)

4. William Coolidge with his aunt Meta Brevoort, their guides Christian Almer (left) and Ulrich Almer, and Tschingel (the dog), c1874.
Coolidge's obituary in *The Times* talked of his 'adeptness at the gentle art of making enemies'.

(Alpine Club)

5. (Left to right) Florence Grove, Horace Walker, Adolphus Moore and Frederick Gardiner at Odessa during the Caucasus expedition of 1874.
'English names are in the air wherever danger is to be met or honour won, from the Arctic Pole to the peaks of the Andes. Nowhere is the English name more honoured than in the Central Caucasus.'
(Alpine Club)

6. Fred Mummery, c1890.
The founder of modern alpinism.
'Above, in the clear air and searching sunlight, we are afoot with the quiet gods, and men can know each other and themselves for what they are.'
(Alpine Club)

7. Norman Collie at the Sligachan Inn, Skye. Mountaineer, inventor of the neon light, the first person to use x-ray photographs for medical purposes and an acknowledged expert on oriental art, wine, food and cigars. When Collie visited Norway, 'crowds flocked to see him under the impression that he was Sherlock Holmes'.

(Alpine Club)

8. Martin Conway, 1902. Explorer, art critic, politician, mountain romantic and social climber, who pursued and achieved both a knighthood and a peerage.

(Royal Geographical Society)

9. Owen Glynne Jones, c1895.
The leading British rock climber at the end of the nineteenth century. 'The soul of mountaineering did not appeal to him so much as its physical charms.'

(Abrahams Brothers' Collection/FRCC)

10. First meet of the Fell and Rock Climbing Club at the Wastwater Hotel, Easter 1907. Fred Botterill is sixth from the left.
Wasdale Head was the first home of the Lake District climbing community. It appealed to those with 'a taste for companionable chaos'.

(Abrahams Brothers' Collection/FRCC)

11. Siegfried Herford (left) and George Mallory
at Pen-y-Pass, December 1913.
Herford was 'the untouched child of the heights
and of the sunny morning...coming and going...
with the fresh mystery and spontaneousness of
the wind'. Mallory was 'a Galahad: chivalrous,
indomitable...the splendid personification of
youthful adventure'.

(Alpine Club)

12. (Left to right)
Geoffrey Winthrop
Young, Bishop Evans,
Percy Farrar,
Page Dickinson and
George Mallory at
Pen-y-Pass, 1909.
In later life, members of
Young's climbing parties
at Pen-y-Pass earned three
orders of merit and four
Nobel prizes, five became
cabinet ministers, eight
were made peers and
15 were knighted.
(Alpine Club)

13. Dedication of the Fell and Rock Climbing Club war
memorial on Great Gable, Whit Sunday, 1924.
'We had lost most of the generation who could have set the
standards and goals of our climbing in the nineteen twenties.
It was a diminished and middle-aged world which we inherited.'
(FRCC)

14. Brigadier General Charles Bruce, drinking chang, 1924 Everest expedition. The 14th child of Lord Aberdare, Charlie 'Bruiser' Bruce was respected by his Gurkha troops for his prowess at wrestling and drinking, and his ability to tell bawdy stories in several local dialects.

(Bentley Beetham/Royal Geographical Society)

15. Edward Norton at 28,100ft on Everest, 4 June 1924. Just three days before Mallory and Irvine disappeared, Norton established a new height record on Everest without using supplementary oxygen. The record stood until 1978.

(Noel family/Alpine Club)

who moved to London shortly before Jones was born. Members of the Alpine Club dubbed the new wave of British rock climbers 'gymnasts' or 'chimney sweeps', by which they intended to imply both the intellectual and social inferiority of the sport as compared with alpinism. Jones was unrepentant: 'A line must be drawn somewhere to separate the possible from the impossible, and some try to draw it by their own experience. They constitute what is called the ultra-gymnastic school of climbing. Its members are generally young and irresponsible.'

Born in 1867, Jones showed early promise at school and won a series of prizes and scholarships culminating in a Clothworkers' Scholarship to the Central Institution in Exhibition Road, South Kensington, where in 1890 he obtained a first in experimental physics. He subsequently became a teacher at the City of London School. While a young man he read accounts of the Golden Age of mountaineering, including those by Stephen and Whymper. As C. E. Benson noted at the turn of the century: 'About this time, too, certain striking and somewhat sensational photographs of rock-climbing began to find their way into shop windows, and immediately attracted attention and comment, the latter generally criticizing the intellectual capacity of climbers.'[63] Jones' attention was attracted by just such a photograph in a shop on The Strand and he decided to become a climber. Had he been born just a few years earlier, it is doubtful whether he would ever have considered the sport, but having once discovered it, he was addicted. When unable to get to the mountains, he climbed whatever else was available, including several London church towers, Cleopatra's Needle and a complete traverse of the Common Room at the City of London School.

For Jones, the mountains were simply a stage upon which the climber performed. As a contemporary reviewer of *Rock-Climbing in the English Lake District* (1897) observed: 'The soul of mountaineering did not appeal to him so much as its physical charms.'[64] He had an apparent disregard for height and exposure (allegedly because of his short-sightedness), and days out with Jones had a habit of turning into epics which many partners were loath to repeat. Jones climbed in the Alps, including a guideless traverse of the Zinal Rothorn and the Weisshorn with the Hopkinsons, but it is chiefly for his contribution to British rock climbing that he is remembered. When he died, in a climbing accident on the Dent Blanche, his landlady said: 'I always knew that he must come to this end, and he knew it too. He used to say so and say it was the death he would choose.'[65]

An outstanding gymnast, 'he studied his own physical powers as a chauffeur studies a car and for that reason he talked a great deal about himself',[66] according to Haskett Smith. Although a fearless leader – 'strong, cool and resolute'[67] – he sometimes pre-inspected difficult pitches using a top rope, a technique he adopted on Kern Knotts Crack (VS 4c, 1896). This practice started an ethical debate that has continued in various forms to the present day. In typically acerbic style, Aleister Crowley argued that Jones' reputation 'is founded principally on climbs he did not make at all, in the proper sense of the word. He used to go out with a couple of photographers and have himself lowered up and down climbs repeatedly until he had learnt its peculiarities, and then make the "first ascent" before a crowd of admirers.'[68]

The 'couple of photographers' referred to by Crowley were the Abraham brothers, George and Ashley, who collaborated with Jones on *Rock-Climbing in the English Lake District* and who were amongst the leading rock climbers of their generation. Born in Keswick, they began climbing around 1890, but many of their most famous routes were climbed with Jones from 1896 onwards, including Jones' Route Direct from Lord's Rake (HS, 1898) on Scafell Pinnacle, a route that involved open climbing on steep slabs. After Jones died, the Abraham brothers continued climbing with other partners, completing Crowberry Ridge Direct on Buachaille Etive Mor (S 4a, 1900) with the gritstone specialists Jim Puttrell and Ernest Baker and the North East Climb on Pillar Rock (S, 1912). Ashley also put up numerous routes on Skye with H. Harland, including Cioch Direct (S 4a, 1907). As professional photographers and guide writers, the Abraham brothers were the first people to earn a living from rock climbing as opposed to mountaineering.

Their *British Mountain Climbs*, published in 1908, was particularly successful, remaining in print for 40 years until 1948.

Partly under Jones' influence, rock climbing became more competitive and more rowdy than it had been in the early years. Until surprisingly recently British climbing circles have maintained the pretence that climbing, despite being a sport, is not competitive in the conventional sense of the word. However, the reality is that climbing has always been intensely competitive. Haskett Smith, the 'father of British rock climbing', made numerous gully climbs before and after his famous ascent of Napes Needle. He justified his choice of gullies as follows: 'When A makes a climb, he wants B, C, and D to have the benefit of every single obstacle with which he himself met, while B, C, and D are equally anxious to say that they followed the exact line that Mr A found so difficult, and thought it perfectly easy...If you climb just to amuse yourself you can wander vaguely over a face of rock; but if you want to describe your climb to others, it saves a lot of time if you can say – "There, that is our gully! Stick to it all the way up!"'[69] Despite his later protestations, what Haskett Smith was describing is competition. Jones simply took it one step further by introducing the concept of grading rock climbs according to their difficulty and by publicising his ascents. But for the climbing establishment, competition, grading and publicity were all anathema.

The social atmosphere of the sport was also changing under the influence of the new generation of rock climbers. In the early days, a scholarly atmosphere pervaded meets at Wasdale Head. In many respects the ambience resembled that of an Oxbridge Senior Common Room. From the 1890s until the outbreak of the First World War, more boisterous behaviour became the norm, particularly amongst the younger climbers.[70] While the smoke room remained a place of discussion, where Haskett Smith, Collie and others held court, the younger men indulged in energetic games and disputes in the billiard room. Popular tests of strength and agility included leaping over the billiard table in a single vault and 'the passage of the billiard table leg', passing over and under the table without touching the floor. Inevitably the cloth was torn, and remained so, leading to the development of 'billiard fives' a strenuous and rowdy game that soon resulted in the room resembling a war zone, with pock-marked walls and wire netting to protect the windows. The final of a knock-out doubles competition in 1909 pitted Slingsby and Young, for the Alpine Club, against the Abraham brothers, for the Fell and Rock Climbing Club. The Abrahams won. Billiard fives continued to be played until the 1930s, when the much-abused table was finally removed and the room converted into a lounge. Writing in 1935, Dorothy Pilley remembered: 'Through a cloud of smoke, when the clamour of that extraordinary game, billiard fives (now alas! a thing of the past since the table was mistakenly banished), died down, strained figures could be seen – hands on the edge of the table, feet up on the wall – working their way round it.'[71] The hotel was frequently so overcrowded that the billiard table also functioned as a bed.

In the early years of the twentieth century, Norman Collie, the great late Victorian scientist, aesthete and mountaineer, bemoaned the arrival of the younger generation: 'The glory of the mountains is departing. The progressive, democratical finger of the "New Mountaineer" is laid with...irreverence and mockery.' George Abraham hinted at the coming social revolution, of which Jones was just the beginning, when he wrote: '[Jones'] favourite theory was that all men should climb and that they would be better for it. This was in contradistinction to the somewhat dog-in-a-manger idea which then prevailed, that the joys of the mountain were only for men of liberal education and of the higher walks of life.'[72] Jones' death in the Alps in 1899 did two things: it reduced the speed of development of climbing in Britain and increased the influence of those for whom the beauty and romance of climbing were more important than the standard of difficulty.

By the early 1900s, the motor car was beginning to have an impact on climbing, extending the number of crags that could be reached during one holiday. In the Lakes, where many roads terminate at the ends of major valleys, only the crags in Langdale and Dow Crag, near Coniston, were readily accessible by car from the major towns. In Snowdonia, where the roads cut right across the district, it was possible to access all the major crags relatively easily by car. Partly for this reason, attention started to shift from the Lakes to Wales. The trend accelerated when four climbers fell to their death on Scafell Crag in September 1903.

Despite the primitive equipment and the almost total lack of proper ropework, the early years of rock climbing in the Lakes had been surprisingly free of accidents. Equipment was extremely basic: nailed boots, full weight manila rope and a long ice axe, used for step-cutting in winter and 'gardening' in summer (the removal of vegetation and loose rock). Belaying was initially virtually unknown, with the whole party moving together, as in the Alps. Gradually the concept of the second man being tied to the rock face was developed, and climbers began to experiment with primitive running belays, looping the rope over flakes or untying and running it behind chockstones jammed in cracks. In the 1903 accident, all four climbers were moving together, and when one fell he pulled the others with him. It was the worst accident to afflict British climbing since Whymper's ill-fated ascent of the Matterhorn in 1865 and remained the worst climbing accident in Britain for 50 years. H. V. Reade, a prominent member of the Climbers' Club, had written an article entitled 'Unjustifiable Climbs'[73] just months before, warning of an increasingly irresponsible attitude to risk, and the *Manchester City News* was in no doubt that competition played a role in the tragedy: 'The peculiar danger of the Lakes climbing lies in the natural rivalry that springs up amongst parties at Wasdale Head.'[74] The accident, less than 20 years after the 'birth' of rock climbing, had a traumatising effect on the small and tight-knit climbing community at Wasdale, and the next few years were largely a period of consolidation. The Lake District-based Fell and Rock Climbing Club was founded three years later in November 1906 and immediately made safety a high priority. From the outset the Fell and Rock was far less socially exclusive than the Alpine Club, drawing its membership largely from northern businessmen and admitting women as members. The first president was Ashley Abraham, with John Robinson as vice-president.

Two climbers dominated Lake District climbing in the years leading up to the First World War. Fred Botterill, a school teacher based in Leeds who developed his climbing technique on the gritstone outcrops of Yorkshire, and Siegfried Herford, who started climbing on the gritstone edges of the Peak District. Botterill was probably the best climber since Owen Glynne Jones, but unlike Jones he lacked ambition and never fulfilled his potential. Botterill's Slab (VS 4c, 1903) on Scafell, which he climbed in traditional style with an ice axe, marked the beginning of the modern slab and wall period of climbing and remained unrepeated for nine years until it was climbed by Herford. Botterill's North-West Climb (VS 4b, 1906) on Pillar also maintained a hard reputation well into the inter-war years, but Botterill was poisoned by gas during the war and died in 1920.

As a child, Siegfried Herford appears to have suffered from a form of autism with high intelligence and occasional outbursts of uncontrollable violence. A gifted mathematician, he studied engineering at Manchester University at the same time as Ludwig Wittgenstein and received a postgraduate scholarship to carry out aeronautical research at the Royal Aircraft Factory at Farnborough, which at the time represented the cutting edge of new technology. He started climbing with John Laycock and Stanley Jeffcoat, and in his final year at university in 1912 spent 100 days on the crags – a level of activity almost comparable to many modern 'professional' climbers – while still managing to come top of his year in engineering. At a time when most climbers only spent a week in the British mountains at Christmas and at Easter, this almost obsessive commitment to the sport, coupled with an outstanding physique, enabled Herford to climb at a higher grade than any of his contemporaries.

A withdrawn, solitary and strikingly handsome man, Herford was seen as austere and remote by many, but made a profound impression on his few close friends. He took the idea of a girdle traverse from

Arthur Andrews, who was accustomed to making traverses of Cornish sea cliffs, and applied it first to Castle Naze (VS 4b) in the Peak District and then to Scafell Crag (VS 4c) in the Lakes. In 1912 he led the Direct Route to Hopkinsons' Cairn (S 4a), a longstanding problem considered unjustifiably dangerous after the death of the four climbers in 1903. The route involves a run-out of 40m/130ft which Herford led in stockinged feet because of the greasy dampness of the rock. Just months before the outbreak of war in 1914 Herford made the biggest ever breakthrough in the standard of Lake District climbing when he led Central Buttress (long graded HVS 5b) on Scafell using 'combined tactics' by climbing up George Sansom's body on the crucial Flake Crack. In terms of technical difficulty, 'CB' set a standard that was not exceeded on a major climb for 30 years, until after the Second World War. Unable to obtain a commission, probably because of his German name, Siegfried Herford volunteered as a private and was killed at the Battle of Ypres in 1916.

NORTH WALES

Hard walking and winter climbing started in Snowdonia at roughly the same time as in the Lake District. The Welsh equivalent of the Wasdale Head Inn was the Pen-y-Gwryd Hotel, described by Charles Kingsley, the novelist, as 'the divinest pigsty beneath the canopy'.[75] In 1871 Charles Mathews, a member of a prominent Birmingham family of businessmen and alpinists, formed the Society of Welsh Rabbits, a group of friends who met each Christmas to climb snow and ice gullies in Snowdonia as practice for the Alps. It was the precursor of the Climbers' Club, which was established in 1897 with Charles Mathews as president. The Climbers' Club was officially formed in London, but the Pen-y-Gwryd was its spiritual home: 'In that congenial atmosphere, where conventionalities were not obtrusive, and the bishop or the man of law shared a sofa with the old shepherd and deferred to his opinions, men of different sorts, but united in their deep love of the mountains, grew to know each other, and there the sense of association, the germ of the club, struck its first root.'[76] The club was originally intended to unite all British rock climbers, but rapidly assumed a more regional character as the club for climbers in Wales, following the establishment of the Kyndwr Club (Peak District) and the Fell and Rock Climbing Club (Lake District) in 1899 and 1906 respectively. In his speech at the first annual dinner, Mathews noted that mountaineering 'is a sport that from some mysterious cause appeals mainly to the cultivated intellect. 'Arry or 'Arriet would never climb a hill.'[77] The founders originally expected about 100 applications for membership, but in the event they received almost 200, about one-third of which were from existing members of the Alpine Club. However, the formation of the club did not meet with unanimous approval. Douglas Freshfield, the arch conservative president of the Alpine Club, celebrated C. E. Mathews' new creation in verse:

> *Why is it to the Alpine Club*
> *Our C. E. M. no longer keeps?*
> *Why should he found – himself a hub –*
> *A Climbers' Club for 'chimney sweeps'.*

Charles Mathews, and his brothers William and George, were typical of the generation of climbers that took part in the pioneering climbs of the Golden Age and continued to play an active role in the climbing community until the closing years of the century. A solicitor and close friend of Joseph Chamberlain, the screw manufacturer who became a highly influential Chief of the Colonial Office, Mathews was an active member of Birmingham society where he was a town councillor, justice of the peace, founder of the National Education League, governor of schools and president of numerous societies. 'He looked on the Alps as the means of relief from the strain of a busy professional life, a time to purify mind and body',[78] according to his friend and climbing companion Frederick Morshead. In climbing, he played a similar role to that of Geoffrey Winthrop Young in later years, bringing together enthusiasts and encouraging young climbers. At the turn of the century an aspiring young alpinist asked him for his advice on an outfit for the Alps. 'My boy, what you most need in the Alps is a good drink,' replied Mathews. 'Now if you take six bottles of red wine and three of white, a flask of curaçao, some cognac and chartreuse, two siphons, four lemons, some sugar, and a little spice – and don't forget the ice! – and make your guide carry a large-sized "*Dampfschiff*" to mix it in – well, then, you'll be sure of a sound drink or so on your peak!' The early Climbers' Club dinners were formidable affairs with speeches as numerous as courses, of which there were 11. Despite this, some climbing did take place.

It is almost impossible now to imagine Snowdonia as unexplored country, but in 1873 a February ascent of Glyder Fawr merited a page and half long account in the *Alpine Journal*. A branch line reached Llanberis in 1869, but from there transport was by horse-drawn carts that travelled along the rough mountain tracks at little more than walking pace. Apart from a few farms and quarries, the hills were empty and silent. The Climbers' Club declared its intention of 'fully exploring the Welsh mountains', but most climbers headed for familiar nearby hills where they could be sure of finding their way home over almost pathless country. The first real rock climbing in Snowdonia took place in 1883, when Stocker and Wall put up a route on Lliwedd. Five years later the two explored the Drakensberg Mountains in Natal (now part of South Africa). Progress in Snowdonia followed the same pattern as the Lake District, with crags increasingly climbed for their own sake, rather than as a route to a summit, although in Wales the alpine tradition remained stronger for longer. As a young man, Geoffrey Winthrop Young considered it 'unworthy of a climbing day to fail to go to the summit of the mountain upon which our rock climb had been made',[79] and even in the mid-twentieth century his protégé Wilfrid Noyce was in the habit of doing so, much to the astonishment of Don Whillans.

The great pioneer of Welsh rock climbing was Archer Thomson. A school teacher in Bangor and later Llandudno, he typically left home after work finished at midday on Saturday, walked to Idwal or Lliwedd, did at least one or two climbs and then spent the night at Ogwen Cottage or the Pen-y-Gwryd. After climbing all day on Sunday he walked back to Bangor or Llandudno in the dark. Thomson was introduced to climbing in 1890 when he ascended Deep Ghyll in the Lakes. Often climbing with Arthur Andrews or Oscar Eckenstein – from whom he learnt the technique of balance climbing – he led the development of rock climbing on Lliwedd, creating 14 new routes by 1896. Before Thomson, there had been just 12 routes in the whole of Snowdonia, which was at least a decade behind the Lakes in terms of technical difficulty. Thomson's Black Cleft on Dinas Mot (HVD, 1897) was long thought to be the hardest climb in Wales.

Although many climbers at the turn of the century had visited both the Lakes and Wales, difficulty of transport meant that most tended to concentrate on one or the other, and the two districts developed very different traditions. In contrast to the ebullient Owen Glynne Jones, the leading contemporary climber in the Lakes, Archer Thomson had an aesthetic, almost metaphysical, approach to the mountains. He believed that the relationship between mountain and climber was a purely personal one and that 'the mountains deserve appropriate literary treatment and should not merely act as pegs whereon to hang stories of rollicking adventures'.[80] Always a taciturn man, he once spent a whole day on Snowdon with a friend without uttering a word. When they returned to Pen-y-Pass the friend held out his hand and said 'good-bye'. Thomson shook hands, and smiled. A Swiss man who climbed with Thomson for the day assumed that he was deaf and dumb. In his obituary in the *Climbers' Club Journal* of 1913, his friend Professor Orton described him as a 'sympathetic and stimulating listener, endowed with the faculty of bringing out the conversational powers of others'.[81] Geoffrey Winthrop Young described him as 'trim and dark-clothed, with lion eyes and mane, and supple, silent movements...in closer touch with the crags than with his companions'.[82]

Thomson wrote the original guidebook to Lliwedd with Arthur Andrews in 1909. In the introduction he wrote: 'The qualities of the climbs themselves are not the sole source of their charm; the mystery of the unknown is profoundly felt on Lliwedd, and the element of romance in piercing it is enhanced by the glory and the gloom of the mountain.'[83] Perhaps overcome by mountain gloom, he committed suicide in 1912 by drinking carbolic acid. His successor as guide writer for Lliwedd was Menlove Edwards, who published the 1939 guide. Edwards also committed suicide, in 1958, by drinking prussic acid.

The co-author of the Lliwedd guide could hardly have been a more different character. Arthur Andrews was a man of private means, a scholar and a remarkable all-round athlete who won the one mile race at the European championships and reached the semi-finals of the men's singles at Wimbledon in 1900, subsequently becoming one of the first climbers to use tennis shoes ('rubbers') for rock climbing. At Magdalen College, Oxford, his rooms were directly below those of the Rev. William Coolidge, who was at that time a Fellow at the College. Andrews was a regular at Geoffrey Winthrop Young's Pen-y-Pass meets, where he was famous for his 'solitary and sturdy wanderings in rubbers and audacity, high among the Lliwedd cracks and juts'.[84] Although he was 46 when the First World War broke out, he volunteered and fought in France, surviving unharmed. A pioneer of Cornish climbing, he was co-editor of the Climbers' Guide to Cornwall, published in 1950 when he was 82.

Thomson's other main climbing partner was Oscar Eckenstein, a gymnastic rock climber famous for doing one arm pull-ups, who provoked strong feelings in many of his contemporaries. His father was a prominent socialist who fled Germany in 1848 and moved to England where Eckenstein grew up. Young described him as 'an engineer with the beard and build of our first ancestry',[85] and he inherited many of his father's rebellious tendencies, dressing shabbily and wearing sandals in town. Even in an age when pipe smoking was the norm, his choice of pipe tobacco – Rutter's Mitcham Shag – was considered noxious. Eckenstein was invited to join Martin Conway's expedition to the Karakoram in 1892, but the two men clashed furiously and Eckenstein left the expedition early. During a subsequent expedition to the area with Aleister Crowley he was arrested by the British authorities for spying, allegedly on the instructions of Conway, and was released only after the intervention of Lord Curzon, the viceroy. Aleister Crowley (the 'Great Beast') was an admirer of Eckenstein, which no doubt damaged his reputation further: '[He] had all the civilized qualities and I had all the savage ones...His climbing was invariably clean, orderly and intelligible; mine can hardly be described as human.'[86] Members of the Alpine Club, with whom he conducted a long and bitter feud, regarded him as 'an insufferably arrogant engineer'. Eckenstein is credited with developing the technique of 'balance climbing', using the feet rather than hauling up with the arms. He also invented the 10 point crampon (regarded as cheating by members of the Alpine Club) and short axes for steep ice climbs. Despite being a founding and very active member of the Climbers' Club, his death in 1921 was not even recorded in their journal, probably because of his German origins.

Geoffrey Winthrop Young joined the Climbers' Club in 1898, and over the following decades it came to be dominated by his 'Cambridge Group' of climbers. Election to the Climbers' Club was expected for members of the Cambridge University Mountaineering Club and was automatic for the president and the secretary. While most Lake District climbers at the turn of the century inclined to the heroic school of competitive self-fulfilment, in Wales the aesthetic school had the upper hand, under the influence of Archer Thomson, Geoffrey Winthrop Young and his young protégé George Mallory, who was to become perhaps the greatest romantic hero of British climbing.

As well as being the best British alpinist in the years immediately preceding the First World War, Young was adept at gathering around him mountain enthusiasts drawn from the intellectual world of Cambridge and London. Bill Murray, a Scottish mountain aesthete from a later generation, summed up his approach as follows: '[Young's] principles are simple: that the true joys of mountaineering are spiritual and only to be had when the climber, however high or low his skills, goes to the mountains because he loves and respects them and not just for display of his skills, or to compete for records or first ascents, or the collection of summits. These latter rewards are froth, none of them worth a man's life – or even his time. If the approach is right – for love, not gain – mountains enrich life and are worth all the risks entailed.'[87]

Starting in 1907 and ending in 1947, with breaks during the First and Second World War, Young organised annual meets at the Pen-y-Pass Hotel (now a youth hostel) near the foot of Snowdon. They turned into house parties where climbing was one, but by no means the only, attraction: 'Rhymesters, wits, singers, players on many and unknown instruments...The casual visitor might enter to find Eckenstein hanging upside down by his hands on a rope, H. O. Jones or Miss Bronwen Jones kicking over the matchbox with incomparable finesse, Leslie Shadbolt, Harold Porter, or Miss Sanders swinging easily up on to the window-sill; the children in confederacy perpetrating some general joke upon the company; or Owen himself performing his great feat of climbing round the chair-back – a *geste* which in twenty five years no other succeeded in repeating.'[88] Songs celebrated the personalities that stayed at Pen-y-Pass:

The climber goeth forth to climb on Lliwedd,
And seeketh him a way where man hath trod,
But which of all the thousand routes he doeth
Is known only to Thomson – and God!

The parties before and immediately after the First World War included Ernest Rutherford, who published the first account of splitting the atom in 1919; John Maynard Keynes, the economist; Duncan

Grant, the artist; Robert Graves, the author and poet; Julian Huxley, the biologist; and his brother Aldous, the author. In later life, members of the Pen-y-Pass parties earned three Orders of Merit and four Nobel Prizes. Five became cabinet ministers, eight were made peers and fifteen were knighted. Under Young's guidance, the Welsh climbing community in the early years of the twentieth century came to be intimately linked with the British intellectual and political elite. The contrast with the decades following the Second World War could hardly have been greater.

It was with some consternation that this elite group learnt in 1906 that the Abraham brothers intended to publish a book on climbing in Wales as a sequel to Owen Glynne Jones' *Rock-Climbing in the English Lake District*. The book was lavishly illustrated, and its exciting, tabloid-style prose described the difficulties and dangers of climbing without the burden of British understatement. Young's objection to the book was a firm belief in the tradition of 'romantic reticence',[89] espoused by Archer Thomson and others, coupled with a selfish desire to preserve the solitude and glory of the mountains for a small group of friends. Young's initial opposition to the popularisation of climbing has often been attributed to pure snobbery, but many working-class climbers expressed similar concerns in the 1960s when large numbers of young people were introduced to climbing through outdoor education, a movement which Young helped to found. When Young and the other members of the Climbers' Club finally recognised that they could not prevent the dissemination of information, some of it misleading, they decided to publish their own climbing guides. These publications were intended to communicate and reinforce the aesthetic, amateur approach to mountaineering. Unfortunately, the chosen author for the first guide, Archer Thomson, had a style of writing that inevitably invited ridicule. In describing the Great Gully on Craig yr Ysfa he wrote: 'A novel expedient is to lay the palm of the right hand on the block and, using the arm as a pivot, perform a pirouette to the south; the climber thus lands in a sitting position, with one leg thrust upwards to the roof to maintain the equilibrium...any Gallio, however, will complacently demand a shoulder.'[90]

It is easy now to sense the approaching end of an era in the leisurely atmosphere and effortless superiority of the pre-war Pen-y-Pass meets. Describing a visit in the spring of 1914, Robert Graves remembered that 'we used to take a leisurely breakfast and lie in the sun with a tankard of beer before starting for the precipice on foot in the late morning...In the evening when we got back to the hotel, we lay and stewed in hot baths.'[91] But even before the war destroyed the lives of so many young members of the ruling class, there was an increasing death toll in the mountains. Young described four of the leading climbers of the period: Humphrey Jones was 'a model of elegant movement...[with] the detachment of the philosopher'.[92] Siegfried Herford was 'shapely, powerful...the untouched child of the heights and of the sunny morning...coming and going at our meetings with the fresh mystery and spontaneousness of the wind'. George Mallory was 'a Galahad: chivalrous, indomitable...the splendid personification of youthful adventure'. Hugh Pope was 'the product of cultivated atmospheres, with a typically Etonian and leisurely manner... the soul of romance and poetic adventure'.[93] Within 12 years all four were dead. Pope and Jones died in separate climbing accidents in 1912, Herford was killed at Ypres in 1916. Mallory survived the war but died just six years later on Everest.

SCOTLAND

In Scotland the practice of hard hill walking grew up in the mid-nineteenth century and developed, to some extent, outside the London-based alpine climbing tradition. In 1866 the first domestic climbing club in Britain was established in Scotland. The Cobbler Club of Glasgow was formed for those wishing 'to climb the Cobbler and whatever other worthy hills can be reached in the course of a Saturday expedition from Glasgow' and 'to crown the labour of the day by such an evening of social enjoyment as can be spent by those who have a sniff of fine mountain air during the day'.[94] These splendid aims no doubt reflect the true spirit of British mountaineering, but little real climbing was done. The Cairngorm Club, based in Aberdeen, followed in 1887 and rooted itself firmly in both the romantic and democratic tradition by being open to 'the admission of men and women of heroic spirit, and possessed of souls open to the influences and enjoyment of nature pure and simple as displayed among our loftier mountains'.[95] James Bryce, MP and campaigner for access to the mountains, was elected its first president. The Scottish Mountaineering Club was formed in Edinburgh two years later in 1889 and, like the Alpine Club, remained resolutely all-male. The Scottish Ladies' Climbing Club was formed in 1908, just one year after the London-based Ladies' Alpine Club, becoming the first club in the country for women whose primary activity was climbing in the British hills. It was also the first to undertake an all-female Himalayan expedition when Monica Jackson, Betty Stark and Evelyn Camrass explored the Jugal Himal and made the first ascent of Gyalgen (6,454m/21,175ft) in 1955.

Despite the formation of these clubs, most of the early climbing activists in Scotland were English rather than Scottish. The Pilkingtons, Norman Collie, Cecil Slingsby and others put up numerous routes in Skye during the 1880s. The Hopkinson brothers descended Tower Ridge on Ben Nevis in 1892, and two years later Collie, Hastings and their party made the first winter ascent. From its inception, the Scottish Mountaineering Club concentrated more on winter mountaineering, and while some summer rock climbs were made, there was not the same intensity of activity as in Wales or the Lakes. In part, this was because, unlike south of the border, there were so many mountains to explore that adventurous days out could still be had climbing them by the easiest routes in summer and especially in winter. In the late nineteenth century, the existing guidebooks to Scotland mentioned about 30 mountains. In the first edition of the *Scottish Mountaineering Club Journal*, published in 1890, Joseph Gibson Stott speculated that there might be as many as 300, but nobody knew: 'The field that lies before the Club is therefore a large one; and when our members have climbed all the peaks, and explored all our beautiful glens and passes, we shall still have the excellent advice of Mr Pilkington, a vice president of the Alpine Club, to fall back upon: for he tells us that when we have found all the easy ways up our hills, we must turn our attention to conquering the difficult ways.'[96]

When Sir Hugh Munro published his Table of Scottish Mountains over 3,000ft a year later in 1891 he can have had little idea of the impact that it would have on future generations of hill walkers. Now simply called 'Munros', the term is sometimes even applied, heretically in the view of most Scots, to English and Welsh mountains that exceed the magical but archaic height of 3,000ft (914m). The original tables identified 283 Munros, far more than most people had expected, and this inevitably acted as a stimulus for people to try to climb them all, in general using the easiest route to the summit. The first person to succeed was the Rev. Archie Robertson in 1901 after a 'desultory campaign of ten years'.[97] It was 20 years before his feat was repeated. Robertson went on to become president of both the Scottish Mountaineering Club and the Rights of Way Society.

The definition of a Munro (an independent mountain) as opposed to a 'top' (a subsidiary peak) has always been a bit hazy. As a result, the number of Munros changes from time to time and has recently reduced from 284 to 283 following the demotion of Sgurr nan Ceannaichean in Glen Carron. Assuming a comfortable average of two per day, someone who has climbed all the Munros has probably devoted around five months of his or her life to the task. Moreover, as Dr Samuel Johnson, observed: 'A walk upon ploughed fields in England is a dance upon carpets, compared to the toilsome drudgery of wandering in Skie',[98] and the same could be said of many mainland Munros. In 1935 a contributor to the *Scottish Mountaineering Club Journal* noted that 'to complete the ascent of the...Scottish Munros under modern road and transport conditions is very far from being in the slightest degree a feat'.[99]

Nevertheless, in 1971, some 80 years after the publication of the tables, the number of 'Munroists' (people who have climbed all of the Munros) stood at just 100. Since then over 4,000 more have joined this peculiarly masochistic club, and the number is increasing exponentially as more and more people discover the dubious delights of Munro-bagging.

In the late nineteenth century the social background of the membership of the Scottish Mountaineering Club was similar in many respects to the Alpine Club, and was on average much older than the climbers who were pushing rock climbing standards higher in England and Wales. Lack of transport also played a major role in delaying the development of the sport in Scotland. When the Scottish Mountaineering Club proposed an Easter meet at Fort William in 1895 many members were unaware that there was anything to climb in the district. This was hardly surprising since the journey involved a 60 mile carriage ride over rough roads from the nearest railway station at Tyndrum. However, with the opening of the West Highland Railway in 1896, the SMC started to hold regular climbing meets on Ben Nevis and the surrounding peaks. A few years later the motor car made its first appearance, and members started the systematic exploration of Arran, Glencoe and Lochnagar. In 1903 W. Inglis Clark described a visit by car to Buachaille Etive Mor: 'After much heart searching regarding the reliability of a motor car for mountaineering, we decided to chance it and make primarily for Kingshouse Inn, later moving to Clachaig if the roads seemed practical. But lest any man consider that motor-driving will cause a degenerate race of mountaineers to arise, I would warn them that I have distinctly lost weight as a result of my enterprise.' When his motor car broke down and refused to go up the slightest hill 'a sorry nag was procured, harnessed to the car with ropes, and amid jeers of passers-by I rode into Edinburgh in state'.[100]

The Black Shoot of Stob Maol (S, 1892) in the Central Highlands near Dalmally was amongst the first genuine rock climbs on the Scottish mainland. The party included John Gibson, William Naismith, a founder of the Scottish Mountaineering Club and inventor of Naismith's Rule for timing walks in the mountains (which assumes three miles per hour plus one additional hour for every 2,000ft climbed), and William Douglas. The account of the ascent in the *SMC Journal* was almost apologetic in tone: 'The climb is a pure piece of mountaineering gymnastics, and is a case of seeking out difficulty for its own sake. There are, of course, perfectly easy ways up the mountain by other routes.'[101] Naismith also reconnoitred Crowberry Ridge (S 4a) on Buachaille Etive Mor in 1896 but dismissed it as impossible: 'Any part...could be climbed if it were, say, on a "boulder"...But...a continuous steep climb of 300 feet is at present generally regarded as "impossible", because it would make too great demands on nerve and muscular endurance.'[102] Four years later it was climbed by the Abraham brothers from Keswick with Jim Puttrell and Professor Ernest Baker from Sheffield. The day of the ascent coincided with news of the relief of the siege of Mafeking, a rare British success in the early part of the Boer War, which triggered huge celebrations across the country. Harold Raeburn repeated the route soon afterwards.

Raeburn was a distinguished Scottish climber whose name is particularly associated with Ben Nevis, although he also climbed in many parts of Scotland, the Alps – where he climbed the North Face of the Disgrazia (TD, 1910) and made a solo traverse of the Meije (D, 1919) – and in the Caucasus. Notable Scottish first ascents included Observatory Ridge, solo (VD in summer, IV in winter, 1901) and Green Gully (IV, 1906), both on Ben Nevis. Raeburn believed strongly in the exploration ethic and thought that Scottish winter climbing offered more opportunities for new routes than the Alps, which he considered to have been 'worked out'. Raeburn was appointed climbing leader of the 1922 Everest Expedition at the age of 56, but suffered from ill-health and a bad temper throughout. On his return to Scotland he suffered a complete breakdown and spent the last five years of his life in an institution before dying of 'melancholia'.

Throughout the period leading up to the First World War the exploration of Skye continued; the rough gabbro rock and extraordinary scenery attracting climbers despite the extreme remoteness and appalling weather. The Ordnance Survey map of Skye was said to be the most inaccurate in the country, missing out more than half of the major peaks, including the highest. Despite this, by 1900 all of the Cuillin Ridge had been climbed in parts, much of it by William Naismith, Norman Collie and John Mackenzie, including the direct ascent of Bhasteir Tooth. A detailed SMC Skye guide was published in 1907, which was rendered obsolete almost immediately with the publication of *Rock-Climbing in Skye* by Ashley Abraham, which included many new routes by H. Harland, from the Lake District-based Fell and Rock Climbing Club, including Cioch Direct (S 4a, 1907). In 1911 the complete traverse of the Cuillin Ridge (VD), which is six miles long and involves some 3,000m/10,000ft of ascent, was made by two English climbers, A. C. McLaren and Leslie Shadbolt, a regular at Geoffrey Winthrop Young's Pen-y-Pass gatherings. The ridge was not repeated until Howard Somervell (later of Everest fame) made a solo traverse in 1920.

OUTCROPS

In the nineteenth century the term 'outcrop' was used to describe smaller crags where the rocks outcropped in the sides of valleys as opposed to forming mountains. Hence Lliwedd and Scafell were mountain crags, while the cliffs of Llanberis and Borrowdale were outcrops. More recently the term has been used to denote crags that are remote from the main mountain areas, and that is the sense in which it is used here. Although Haskett Smith is often called the father of British rock climbing for his ascent of Napes Needle in 1886, numerous other people were climbing on outcrops around the country at about the same time. Arthur Andrews and his sister Elsie had started their explorations on the Cornish sea cliffs, later putting up routes such as the 200m/660ft Bosigran Ridge (VD, 1902), used by the Commandos during the Second World War for cliff assault training. Fred Mummery and

Aleister Crowley both climbed at Beachy Head, an area that received little subsequent attention for nearly 100 years until Mick Fowler and others renewed interest in climbing on the white cliffs in the 1980s. John Stogden was also an early proponent of unconventional practice-grounds, noting that 'Hampshire chalk-pits gave fine opportunities for breaking one's neck',[103] but most activity was centred on the southern Pennines. The Yorkshire Ramblers' Club, founded in Leeds in 1892, was the second climbing club to be formed in England, after the Alpine Club. Named with typical Yorkshire understatement, its activities included long hard walks, climbing and potholing. Astutely, they elected the Duke of Devonshire and the Earl of Wharncliffe as honorary members, since both owned large estates where members hoped to pursue their activities, but confrontations between climbers and game-keepers remained a regular feature of the sport until after the Second World War.

Jim Puttrell, born in Sheffield and manager of the silversmiths Mappin & Webb, has a claim to being the inventor of gritstone climbing, an activity that has been at the centre of British climbing ever since, with his early routes on Wharncliffe Edge. Cut off from the mainstream of rock climbing in Wales and the Lakes, he made some remarkable climbs for the time, including Downfall Groove on Kinder Scout (HVS, c1900). By the turn of the century a growing band of followers around Sheffield had formed themselves into the Kyndwr Club, and Puttrell began to climb more regularly outside the Peak District. In many respects, Puttrell was the prototype 'hard man' trained on grit before transferring his athletic climbing style to the bigger crags in the Lakes and Scotland. He took part in first ascents of Crowberry Ridge Direct (S, 1900) on Buachaille Etive Mor and the Chimney of Ben Nuis, Arran (VS, 1901), which was not repeated until 1955, and then only with the aid of pitons. He also made the first winter ascent (solo) of the loose North Face of Mam Tor (III, 1898) in the Peaks. In later life he turned to speleology, pioneering the exploration of cave systems across Britain.

The idea of climbing small outcrops was often ridiculed by the mountaineering establishment as demeaning, reducing the sport to the level of cheap stunts, gymnastics and showmanship. However, outcrop climbing, particularly on the gritstone edges of Derbyshire and Yorkshire, has been extraordinarily influential in the development of climbing techniques and approach over the past 100 years. Gritstone has excellent friction, but there are few in-cut holds, and the climber is forced to rely on a combination of balance and athleticism. Most outcrops are low enough for top-ropes to be used, permitting climbers to push technical difficulties to the limit, and many are also located close to urban areas, allowing regular practice at weekends and even on summer evenings. As a consequence, technical standards on gritstone rapidly exceeded those on the mountain crags. Siegfried Herford, Stanley Jeffcoat, John Laycock and George Sansom, all four of whom often climbed together, started climbing on the gritstone crags of the Peak District. At about the same time, Fred Botterill was developing his skills on the gritstone crags of Yorkshire. In the introduction to his book *Some Shorter Climbs*, written in 1913, Laycock wrote: 'As the climbing is the thing, a day on Castle Naze [in the Peak District] may be better at times than a day on Pillar Rock [in the Lakes]...It is not because I fear comparisons that I say comparisons are odious to both sides. One can respect and adore the Queen of England and still love one's wife.'[104] A true enthusiast, Laycock was once benighted halfway up a 30m/100ft gritstone climb on Hen Cloud in Staffordshire.

In the years before the First World War the most popular crags were Almscliff in Yorkshire, Wharncliffe near Sheffield, Laddow Rocks in the west of the Peak District near Greenfield and Black Rocks near Cromford, in each case because they could be reached relatively easily by walking from major towns. Siegfried Herford also climbed Ilam Rock, a limestone pinnacle in Dovedale in the Peak District, but his hair-raising account deterred climbers from tackling other limestone climbs for many years.

THE GREATER RANGES

At the start of the Golden Age, there was little distinction between mountain climbing and mountain exploration because almost all the major peaks and higher cols were unknown and unclimbed. As the exploratory phase in the Alps progressed, a divergence of views emerged between those who were primarily interested in climbing and those for whom exploration was the attraction. The opposing camps came to be known as the centrists, who based themselves in one place and climbed the nearby peaks, and the excentrists, who travelled from valley to valley, climbing mountains and passes as they went. The archetypal centrist was Sir Edward Davidson, the 'King of the Riffel', who returned to Zermatt year after year and claimed to have made over 250 ascents of the Riffelhorn. A socialite and a snob, 'he would never climb in any but practically certain weather...attended always by the best guides',[105] but over the years he succeeded in putting up numerous new routes. Davidson was intensely jealous of more successful rivals, particularly Mummery, whose initial application for membership of the Alpine Club he probably blackballed. The great champion of the excentrists was Martin Conway, later Lord Conway, art critic, politician, founder of the Imperial War Museum and mountain romantic. Describing his journey from Monte Viso in Italy to the Grossglockner in Austria in 1894, he wrote: 'The mountain hero of my boyhood was a traveller and desired to be an explorer. When he went to the Alps he went to wander about and to rough it.' He contrasted this ambition with 'the systematic climber, the man for whom Alpine climbing takes the place of fishing or shooting. Ceasing to be a traveller he has acquired the habit of settling down for his holiday in a comfortably furnished centre, whence he makes a series of ascents of the high mountains within reach.'[106] Conway wrote an article in the *Alpine Journal* in which he described the ideal climber as a man concerned with mountain exploration, beauty and geographical research, capable of climbing the highest peaks but equally interested in the valleys and passes.[107] The ideal climber bore a striking resemblance to Martin Conway.

In effect, Conway wanted to turn the Alpine Club into the mountaineering section of the Royal Geographical Society, but he lost the argument, the centrists prevailed, and the passage of icy cols that had featured so prominently in the Golden Age ceased to be a major part of alpinism. The excentrists, including Conway, moved on to the greater ranges.

The end of the Golden Age in the Alps roughly coincided with Russia gaining a measure of control over the security situation in the Caucasus in the mid-1860s. For excentrists and others for whom the ascent of virgin peaks was an essential part of the game, the Caucasus appeared to be a bigger and better version of the Alps. In 1868 Douglas Freshfield, Adolphus Moore and Charles Tucker made early forays, including an ascent (probably the second) of the lower peak of Mount Elbrus (5,633m/18,481ft) and the first ascent of Kazbek (5,047m/16,558ft) at the other end of the 700 mile long range.

Freshfield was the son of the managing partner of a firm of London solicitors. A man of private means, educated at Eton and Oxford, in later life he declined a knighthood for services to geography. Temperamentally, he was an explorer rather than a climber. He was appointed President of the Alpine Club in 1895 and informed the members that 'we want here to make mountaineers not acrobats'.[108] During a guideless ascent of the Piz Bernina in Switzerland with E. J. Garwood, Freshfield complained that the rope was hurting him, and Garwood was surprised to discover that he had tied on using a slip-knot. 'Well,' Freshfield remarked, 'you will have a good joke against the president of the Alpine Club; you see, I am accustomed to climb with guides who always rope me up.'[109] In 1899 Freshfield led an expedition that succeeded in making the first complete circuit of Kangchenjunga, the third highest peak in the world on the border of Sikkim and Nepal. He was president of the Royal Geographical Society from 1914 to 1917 and was instrumental in persuading both Oxford and Cambridge to offer degrees in geography. He also persuaded the Royal Geographical Society to recognise mountaineering as a branch of exploration. Geoffrey Winthrop Young recalled meeting Freshfield at an Alpine Club talk in the late 1920s. 'Let's sit at the back,' said Freshfield, 'there's only those bald and white heads to the fore!' As Young observed: 'He himself was well over eighty; but he still revelled in all the intolerant privileges of youth.'[110]

Moore returned to the Caucasus with Florence Grove, Horace Walker and Frederick Gardiner in 1874 and climbed the highest peak of Elbrus. In the 1880s, Mummery, Dent and others followed, climbing Dykh-Tau (5,198m/17,053ft), the second highest peak, and Gestola (4,860m/15,994ft). John Cockin, a Liverpool barrister virtually unknown in alpine circles, also bagged several tough and technical peaks, including Shkhara (5,201m/17,063ft) and the North Summit of Ushba (4,695m/15,404ft), the 'Matterhorn of the Caucasus', in a three week spell in 1888. He died on the Weisshorn in 1900.

When William Donkin and Henry Fox disappeared in the Caucasus in 1888, they were the first English mountaineers to die in the region. *The Times* wrote that 'the disaster is a most melancholy one and will remind all Englishmen of the great catastrophe on the Matterhorn'. But the national attitude to climbing had changed since 1865. *The Times* continued: 'We cannot but sincerely and deeply mourn their loss, though it must be said, nevertheless, that the spirit of research and adventure which occasionally leads to such disasters is one with which Englishmen cannot quarrel and England cannot dispense.'[111] Both Donkin and Fox came from a similar social background to the Matterhorn victims – Donkin was a professor of Chemistry, educated at Eton and Oxford, while Fox's family owned a long established woollen mill in Somerset – but the idea of heroic exploration was now firmly established as an English trait, a symbol of Britain's imperial status and prestige. As a contemporary commentator noted after their deaths: 'English names are in the air wherever danger is to be met or honour won, from the Arctic Pole to the peaks of the Andes. Nowhere is the English name more honoured than in the Central Caucasus.'[112]

Tom Longstaff climbed in the Caucasus in 1903 and 1912, and in 1914 Harold Raeburn led the last British party to the region before the

Russian revolution prevented further exploration. Nearly all the climbs in this era were made in a single day from high camps near the glaciers and demonstrated very considerable strength and stamina. Modern parties frequently take two days, despite the advantage of crampons.

The British were also active in South America. Edward Whymper's expedition to Ecuador in 1880 with Carrel, his rival on the Matterhorn, succeeded in climbing Cayambe (5,786m/18,983ft), the highest point on the equator, and Chimborazo (6,267m/20,561ft), for many years thought to be the highest mountain in the world. Whymper's careful planning of the expedition was a key element in its success. Martin Conway and others later used his account of the expedition as the basis for their subsequent explorations in the Himalaya and the Andes. Edward Fitzgerald, an American who adopted Britain as his home, led an expedition to climb Aconcagua (6,970m/22,867ft), the highest mountain outside the Himalaya, in 1897. Bertrand Russell, who climbed with Fitzgerald in the Alps, described his many accomplishments: 'He was lazy and lackadaisical but had remarkable ability...notably in mathematics. He could tell the year of any reputable wine or cigar. He could eat a spoonful of mixed mustard and Cayenne pepper. He was intimate with Continental brothels. His knowledge of literature was extensive, and while an undergraduate at Cambridge, he acquired a fine library of first editions.'[113] Fitzgerald's guide, Mattias Zurbriggen, reached the summit of Aconcagua alone after Fitzgerald was forced to turn back, suffering from altitude sickness. Zurbriggen also climbed with Conway in the Karakoram and made the first ascent of Mount Tasman (3,947m/11,473ft), the second highest peak in New Zealand, with Fitzgerald. Zurbriggen later shot himself in Geneva.

The boundary between fact and fiction frequently became a little blurred in the early accounts of mountain climbs in the more remote corners of the world, but many felt that Captain Lawson's account of ascending Mount Hercules in New Guinea in 1876 stretched the bounds of credulity too far. He claimed to have climbed from his camp at 600m/2,000ft to a height of 7,716m/25,314ft in one day, reaching the summit at a height of 9,992m/32,783ft the following day, accompanied by a native dwarf named Aboo. The *Alpine Journal* dismissed his account as 'arrant nonsense', but it was widely discussed in other serious journals of the day.

In New Zealand, the Rev. William Spotswood Green, an Irish parson and member of the Alpine Club, and two Oberland guides came within a few hundred feet of the summit of Mount Cook (3,764m/12,349ft) in 1882 but were forced back by the lateness of the hour. The mountain was eventually climbed by a New Zealand party led by Tom Fyfe on Christmas Day 1894, just beating Edward Fitzgerald to the prize. In 1888 the same William Green made the first expedition specifically for climbing purposes to the Canadian Rockies, choosing the Selkirk Range as his objective, because it was close to the newly opened Canadian Pacific Railway. Part of the Selkirks were incorporated into the Glacier National Park in 1886, and with easy access from Europe, via New York, at a cost of £60 first class return they became a favourite summer playground where British climbers joined members of the American Alpine Club, formed in 1902, and the Canadian, formed in 1906. They left behind them a legacy of mountains named after once famous Victorians and Edwardians, including Forbes, Ball, Donkin, Fox and Freshfield. Norman Collie made six expeditions to the Rockies between 1897 and 1911 and assumed an almost proprietorial interest in their development. He was particularly incensed when he heard that Whymper had been invited to pay a visit in 1901 to help advertise the tourist potential of the Canadian Pacific Railway. 'All I can say is damn the man!...Why I am so mad about it is that it is not done for sport at all or because Whymper has any real liking for the hills. From the beginning it is *dollars*.'[114]

Most of the mountain exploration in the United States was carried out by Americans completely independent of the European alpine tradition, although there were a few rare visits by British parties, including James Eccles, who made the first ascent of Wind River Peak and Fremont Peak in Wyoming with F. V. Hayden (who later played a major part in establishing Yellowstone as the first National Park in the world). Eccles claimed that the only time that his guide and life-long friend Michel Payot showed any fear was when he thought he was going to be scalped by Indians during their American tour. Unlike other parts of the world, where mountains were largely explored for sport, in the USA most of the pioneers were trappers, mineral prospectors and railway surveyors. The independent development of climbing in the country was later to have great significance by bringing fresh ideas and approaches to the rest of the world, where climbing had largely grown up in the European alpine tradition.

Even in Japan, which has a long tradition of mountain walking and scrambling, more technical climbing was introduced by the British. The Rev. Walter Weston, a member of the Alpine Club, was sent as British chaplain to Kobe in 1889 and set about introducing the sport. After making an ascent of a peak which Buddhist priests had tried but failed to climb for more than 200 years, he was asked to re-ascend the mountain, build a shrine and become its officiating priest: 'The most novel offer of preferment...I had ever received.'[115] In 1905 he helped to found the Japanese Alpine Club, and in later years the Japanese became a major force, particularly in Himalayan climbing.

In Africa, the highest peak of Mount Kenya, Batian (5,199m/17,060ft), was climbed in 1899 by a British party led by Sir Halford Mackinder. The route is now graded IV, and the second ascent, by Eric Shipton and Percy Wyn Harris, did not take place for over 30 years. Mackinder's party passed through country ravaged by smallpox and famine and suffered attacks by a hostile chief in league with Arab slave traders, who killed two members of the expedition. Mackinder established the School of Geography at Oxford in the same year but missed the start of term. He declared that 'most people would have no use for a geographer who was not an adventurer and an explorer',[116] but he also knew that the great days of exploration were drawing to a close, and that mountains represented the last remnants of unknown and untravelled terrain outside the polar regions. Part of his approach route to Mount Kenya made use of the railway that was then under construction from Mombasa to Uganda.

The greatest prize of all was the Himalaya. When Norman Collie reviewed the state of Himalayan exploration at the start of the twentieth century the scale of the challenge and opportunity was almost unimaginable. 'The sources of the rivers that emerge from these Himalayan Mountains are almost unknown, except in the case of the Ganges... their sources lie in that unknown land north of the so-called main chain. Whether there is a loftier and more magnificent range behind is at present doubtful, but reports of higher mountains further north reach us from time to time.'[117] Moreover, much of the area was relatively accessible for exploration by British climbers because, as a contemporary commentator observed, 'the English are supposed to hold the southern slopes of the Himalaya'. Despite this, as late as 1920, only one European had been within 40 miles of Mount Everest.

Throughout history, mountains have formed natural boundaries, and the world's greatest mountain chain divided three of the world's largest empires: the British in India to the south, the Russians to the north and west, and the Chinese to the north and east. The Royal Navy was more than capable of defending the sea lanes to the south of India, but the British lived in constant fear of an attack by land from the north. While the Chinese Empire was in decline during the nineteenth century, the Russians progressively expanded to the south, building railways as they went. The 'Great Game', made famous by Rudyard Kipling, consisted of probing and testing the ill-defined boundaries of the three empires, and Himalayan exploration therefore had a military and strategic significance in addition to scientific research. In time, purely sporting objectives also emerged.

The Survey of India commenced mapping the foothills of the Himalaya in 1846. The height of Everest was first determined in 1852, and that of K2, the second highest mountain in the world, followed in 1858. Eccentric and courageous Englishmen started to explore the small independent Himalayan kingdoms of Assam, Nepal, Sikkim and

Bhutan that lay along the northern borders of British India and, from 1863, trained local 'pundits' to act as surveyors and spies in areas forbidden to white men. Counting paces on Buddhist rosaries, with compasses hidden in their prayer wheels, the pundits followed the rivers and the ancient trade routes to find out where they went. Pundit No. 9, Hari Ram, succeeded in making the first known circuit of Mount Everest in 1871. Between 1860 and 1865 William Johnson established a large number of survey stations at heights of up to 6,100m/20,000ft while engaged by the Kashmir Survey. He also climbed a number of mountains on his own account, but these sporting activities were not appreciated by the political department of India and, following a reprimand, he left the service and took employment with the Maharaja of Kashmir. His pioneering exploratory work nevertheless earned him a gold watch from the Royal Geographical Society. Around the same time, other officers of the Survey, including Captain Thomas Montgomerie and Colonel Henry Godwin-Austen, were active in the Astor, Gilgit and Skardu districts, reaching the foot of the Muztagh Pass, which Francis Younghusband crossed in 1887, exploring the Baltoro Glacier and establishing the position of the 8,000m peaks of K2, Gasherbrum and Masherbrum. When the Indian Mutiny broke out in 1857 they were instructed to carry on with their survey work to demonstrate the conviction that the British would prevail, which in the end they did. However, control of the territory passed from the British East India Company to the Crown in 1858. A proposal to call K2 'Mount Godwin Austin' was rejected, but the 'Godwin-Austin Glacier' now flows into the Baltoro at Concordia. By the end of the Golden Age of alpine exploration, members of the Indian Survey had already climbed some 37 peaks over 6,100m/20,000ft and five over 6,400m/21,000ft.[118]

In 1883 William Graham, a barrister, travelled to India with his guide Joseph Imboden to undertake the first visit to the Himalaya 'more for sport and adventures than for the advancement of scientific knowledge'.[119] Graham was a highly competent alpine climber (he made the first ascent of the Dent du Géant in 1882) but he had been blackballed by the Alpine Club and was generally mistrusted by the mountaineering establishment. He explored the mountains around Nanda Devi in the Garhwal, before returning to Sikkim and the mountains near Kangchenjunga. He tried, but failed, to force a passage of the Rishi Ganga Gorge, reached around 6,900m/22,700ft on Dunagiri (7,067m/23,187ft) and claimed to have ascended Kabru (7,338m/24,075ft). Graham had little difficulty acclimatising and stated that 'personally I believe that... the air, or want of it, will prove no obstacle to the ascent of the very highest peaks in the world'.[120] While disputing many of his claims, the Alpine Club agreed that lack of oxygen was not a constraint. Charles Mathews, the president of the Club, asserted that 'if the highest peaks of the Himalaya are never climbed, the rarity of the air will not be the cause of failure'.[121] Soon after his visit to the Himalaya, Graham disappeared. At the time it was rumoured that he had lost all his money, emigrated to the USA and become a cowboy. In fact he became British vice-consul in Durango, an obscure Mexican town, before disappearing once again.

In 1892 Martin Conway[122] led an expedition to the Karakoram that included Oscar Eckenstein, Major Charles Bruce, a number of Gurkhas and the Swiss guide Mattias Zurbriggen. Lord Lansdowne, the Viceroy of India, advised Conway to delete the term 'mountaineering party' and substitute 'a party of exploration' on the expedition proposal 'because mountaineering is a sport and couldn't be taken official notice of, at any rate in my case'.[123] Conway took due note of this advice and modelled the expedition on Whymper's travels in the Andes. He carried out detailed survey and scientific work, including the collection of plant and rock specimens, but as an art critic and mountain romantic, Conway was equally concerned with landscape and with self-discovery. For Conway, 'it is not Nature that illuminates the mind, but the mind that glorifies Nature. The beauty that we behold must first arise in ourselves. It is born, for the most part, in suffering.'[124]

A man of private means, when he reached the top of Snowdon as a child, Conway was disappointed to find that he was too small to place a stone on top of the cairn. Happily, a butler was on hand to do so for him. However, he had an expensive lifestyle, and for much of his life he led a rather precarious existence relying upon his American wife's family money, supplemented by his own meagre earnings from books, lectures and speculations in South American rubber and mining stocks. Educated at Cambridge, he became Professor of Art at University College, Liverpool, and subsequently at Cambridge. In 1895 he became the first person to be knighted for services to mountaineering. However, the knighthood had more to do with politics than with peaks, being recommended by Lord Rosebery because he thought it would help Conway to win Bath, where he was standing as the Liberal Party parliamentary candidate. In the event, he lost. His expedition to the Karakoram succeeded in mapping over 5,000 square kilometres of difficult country around the Hispar, Biafo and Baltoro glaciers, as well as ascending to a height of 6,890m/22,606ft, possibly setting a new altitude record. It established his reputation as a climber and explorer, but it was also an almost mystical experience for Conway: 'Romance almost became a reality. The gods were very near at hand. We touched, as it were, the skirts of their garments. Yet even at the culminating moments of these strenuous dream-days there still lingered the sense of incompleteness, of something lacking. The secret was almost disclosed, but never quite, the veil never entirely withdrawn.'[125] After giving 10 lectures on the expedition in 1893, 21 in 1894 and 24 in 1895 the subject had lost some of its allure, and he became heartily sick of the Himalaya. He never returned.

In 1894 he traversed the Alps from Monte Viso to Grossglockner, with two Gurkhas and Edward Fitzgerald. In 1896–97 he explored the interior of Spitsbergen, and in 1898 he went to the Bolivian Andes, climbing Sorata (6,553m/21,499ft) and Illimani (6,461m/21,198ft). He subsequently made the third ascent of Aconcagua, although he turned back just short of the summit for reasons that remain obscure, and explored Terra del Fuego. In the end, he found the technicalities of climbing and long expeditions conflicted with the basic appeal of the landscape: 'Mountains had called me as things of beauty and wonder, terrible and sublime, and instead of glorying in their splendour, here I was spending months in outlining the vagrant plan of them on a piece of paper. That realisation ended my mountain career.'[126] Although he gave up serious climbing in his mid-40s, he continued to take an interest in climbing history and exploration.

Conway was an ambitious dilettante who dabbled in many things but mastered just one: the art of making useful friends and relations. 'For all of us there are many kinds of joy as yet unexperienced, many activities untried, many fields of knowledge unexplored. We must not spend too large a fraction of life over one or the next will escape us. It is life, after all, that is the greatest field of exploration.'[127] Conway was elected as the Unionist Member of Parliament for the Combined Universities from 1918 to 1931 and pursued and achieved a barony in addition to his knighthood, becoming the first member of the peerage to incorporate an ice axe into his coat of arms. When his peerage was announced *Punch* carried a cartoon with the somewhat ambiguous title of 'The Climber'.

Conway's large scale expedition to the Karakoram and Graham's lightweight self-sufficient travels formed the models for two contrasting approaches to climbing in the Himalaya that have persisted ever since. The establishment, particularly the Royal Geographical Society and the Alpine Club, favoured Conway's approach. But the lightweight 'alpine style' pioneered by Graham came to inspire future generations of climbers. Mummery's 1895 expedition to Nanga Parbat (8,125m/26,657ft) was very much in the alpine style. It consisted of three friends – Mummery, Hastings and Collie – supported by Major Charles Bruce and two Gurkhas, Raghobir and Goman Singh, and was purely a sporting affair. With no knowledge of the effect of altitude they were wildly ambitious in their objectives. On practically their first day in the Rupal valley, below Nanga Parbat, after travelling continuously for 27 days from London, Mummery and Hastings set out from their camp site at 3,700m/12,150ft to climb a 6,245m/20,490ft peak in order to get a better view of the mountain. By lunchtime, after crossing a glacier and floundering through deep snow, they had reached 4,877m/16,000ft and agreed to give up their attempt. 'We were hopelessly out of condition,' wrote Collie.[128] In fact their performance, including at one point climbing non-stop for 31 hours, was extraordinary, but despite their best efforts they failed to make significant progress on the mountain. Mummery, Raghobir and Goman Singh disappeared while crossing a high pass to see whether there was a better route to the summit. They were the first casualties of the sport in the Himalaya and the first of 31 men to die on Nanga Parbat before Hermann Buhl finally crawled to the summit, alone, in 1953.

The death of Mummery, probably the best amateur climber in the world at that time, had a major impact on Himalayan climbing for the next half century because the climbing establishment concluded, quite wrongly, that small expeditions were inherently dangerous and that there was safety in numbers. The Duke of Abruzzi's 1909 expedition to K2 (8,611m/28,251ft), the second highest mountain in the world, consisted of 11 lead climbers, with 13,000lbs of baggage and over 500 porters. Drawing on his previous experience of successful expeditions to Alaska and the Ruwenzori, it was well organised and, although it failed to climb this very difficult mountain, it set the mould for most subsequent British expeditions to big peaks until the 1970s.

Seven years prior to the Abruzzi expedition, Oscar Eckenstein had also attempted to climb K2. The party included Aleister Crowley, a Swiss doctor called Jacot-Guillarmod and a young engineer called Guy Knowles. The party reached 6,532m/21,430ft on the North-East Ridge despite Eckenstein being arrested as a spy and a violent argument which ended with Crowley chasing Knowles off the mountain at gunpoint. Aleister Crowley, the self-styled 'wickedest man in the world', was one of the more colourful characters of the early years of mountaineering. Dabbler in black arts, hallucinogenic drugs and obscene sexual rituals, Crowley was the son of a prosperous and pious member of the Plymouth Brethren. As a boy he was attracted to things that were thought to be difficult or impossible, so when he heard that a cat had nine lives he determined to kill one: 'Having administered a large dose of arsenic I chloroformed it, hanged it above the gas jet, stabbed it, cut its throat, smashed its skull, and, when it had been pretty thoroughly burnt, drowned it and threw it out of the window that the fall might remove its ninth life...All the time I was genuinely sorry for the animal; I simply forced myself to carry out the experiment in the interests of pure science.'[129] Crowley was educated at Cambridge where he soon gained a reputation for outrageous behaviour. In his early years he was also a climber of distinction, leading new routes on Napes Needle and on the Devil's Chimney, a chalk stack at Beachy Head that collapsed in 2001. He also got two-thirds of the way up a route now called Crowley's Crack at Beachy Head before having to be rescued by coastguards. The route was completed by Mick Fowler in 1980 and is graded Extremely Severe.

Crowley visited the Alps each year from 1894 to 1898 with Eckenstein (one of the few friends he did not betray) and climbed with Tom Longstaff and others. He was proposed for membership of the Alpine Club by Norman Collie and Martin Conway. Collie was known for his mischievous sense of humour but Conway's support is inexplicable, and Crowley's name mysteriously disappeared from the ballot papers before the elections took place. In 1900 he climbed Popocatepetl (5,452m/17,887ft) in Mexico and two years later joined Eckenstein on the ill-fated K2 expedition. In 1904 Dr Jacot-Guillarmod, fellow member of the K2 expedition, visited Crowley's estate in Scotland, keen to distinguish himself as a hunter. Crowley regaled him with stories about the 'haggis', a dangerous rogue ram that roamed the hills, and two days later one of Crowley's men burst in with the news: 'There's a haggis on the hill, my Lord.' They immediately rushed out into the pouring rain and Crowley led Jacot-Guillarmod on a long and uncomfortable stalk before encouraging him to blast the neighbouring farmer's prize ram to pieces with an elephant gun.

In 1905 Crowley returned to the Himalaya and, never lacking in ambition, this time attempted Kangchenjunga (8,586m/28,169ft), the third highest mountain in the world. The ill-assorted party once again included Dr Jacot-Guillarmod who, according to Crowley, 'knew as little of mountaineering as he did of medicine', and a hotel keeper from Darjeeling called de Righi ('I blame myself for not foreseeing that his pin brain would entirely give way as soon as he got out of the world of waiters'[130]). Crowley explained his choice of companions by noting that 'thanks to the Alpine Club, there are no Englishmen of mountaineering ability and experience available'.[131] Inevitably there was a violent argument late one afternoon and several members of the party decided to descend. Crowley warned them of the avalanche risk but they nevertheless set off. Three were killed but Jacot-Guillarmod and de Righi survived. Despite their cries for help, Crowley remained sipping tea in his bed commenting that 'a mountain "accident" of this sort is one of the things for which I have no sympathy whatsoever'.[132] The expedition marked the end of his climbing career.

Crowley is one of only two climbers whose portrait was on display in the National Portrait Gallery in 2008 (the other was Sir Leslie Stephen). Depicted in profile, he was painted wearing nothing but a flowing red gown, open to the waist. He also found his way onto the cover of the Beatles' *Sgt. Pepper's Lonely Hearts Club Band,* and many of the wilder members of the climbing community in the late 1960s and 70s, including Al Harris and Al Rouse, thought that they recognised a kindred spirit in Crowley as they sought to outrage the establishment.

Tom Longstaff, another mountain explorer in the lightweight 'alpine' tradition, made three expeditions to the Himalaya. In 1905, following in Graham's footsteps, he visited the Indian Garhwal, explored the Nanda Devi Sanctuary, and made an attempt on Nanda Devi East, before embarking on 'a walk of some thousand miles across and around the Himalaya'[133] to forbidden Tibet. The six month expedition cost less than £100. In 1907, the Jubilee year of the Alpine Club, he originally intended to carry out a reconnaissance of Everest with Arnold Mumm and Charles Bruce, but politics intervened. Instead they went back to the Garhwal, where they failed to force a way through the Rishi Ganga Gorge into the Nanda Devi Sanctuary, but Longstaff succeeded in climbing

Trisul (7,120m/23,360ft) with the Brocherel brothers from Courmayeur and Gurkha Karbir. Trisul was the highest summit yet climbed, a record that stood for 21 years. In 1909, he was invited to join Captain Scott's expedition to the South Pole. Longstaff's father had helped to finance an earlier expedition and had been an early supporter and sponsor of Ernest Shackleton, but Longstaff was determined to return to the Himalaya and went instead to the Karakoram, journeying out with the Duke of Abruzzi who was on his way to attempt K2 with his huge and well-organised party. In contrast, Longstaff was joined by Morris Slingsby, the nephew of Cecil Slingsby, who was a subaltern in the 56th Rifles, Frontier Force, and two Pathan riflemen. While Scott perished in the Antarctic, Longstaff and Slingsby crossed the Saltoro Pass and discovered the Siachen Glacier, the largest on earth outside the polar regions.

Longstaff went on to make five visits to the Arctic, as well as climbing in the Rockies and the Selkirks. He was a member of the 1922 Everest expedition led by Charles Bruce, and although he 'had no liking for all the hurly-burly of a big expedition...the real inducement [was to] enjoy at leisure every moment of the journey'.[134] Longstaff summarised his philosophy of travel in his book *This My Voyage*: 'Since happiness is most often found by those who have learned to live in every moment of the present, none has such prodigal opportunities of attaining that art as the traveller...Attainment of a set objective is but a secondary matter; the traveller should not anticipate the journey's end. So long as he loses consciousness of self, and is aware in all his senses of the present scene, almost any part of the world is as good as another...We shall have realised ourselves as being a tiny portion of the universe; not lords of it.' Upon his return to civilisation after one of his extended journeys, Longstaff recognized an old school friend and went up to introduce himself. His fellow Old Etonian was so shocked by Longstaff's appearance that his monocle popped out of his eye and smashed on the floor.

Alexander Kellas also explored the Himalaya in the years before and immediately after the First World War. A Scottish scientist who worked with Norman Collie at University College, London, for a time before transferring to the Middlesex Hospital, he carried out some important early research on high-altitude physiology. His conclusions, reached in 1920, were that: 'Mount Everest could be ascended by a man of excellent physical and mental constitution in first-rate training, without adventitious aids [supplementary oxygen] if the physical difficulties of the mountain are not too great.'[135] He was finally proved right in 1978. According to George Mallory, Kellas was 'beyond description Scotch and uncouth in his speech...slight in build, short, thin, stooping and narrow chested; his head...made grotesque by veritable gig-lamps of spectacles and a long pointed moustache'.[136] He explored the Kangchenjunga area and the Garhwal several times between 1907 and 1921, climbing some outlying peaks, including Pauhunri (7,065m/23,179ft) in 1911, and making an attempt on Kamet (7,755m/25,446ft) in 1920 and Kabru (7,338m/24,075ft) in 1921. He broke with tradition by using Sherpas for the first time in preference to the traditional Swiss guides. In 1922 he had the dubious distinction of becoming the first person to die while attempting to climb Everest.

Like every other aspect of British life, exploration in the greater ranges was brought to an abrupt halt by the outbreak of the First World War in August 1914. When the war finally ended in November 1918, the world was a very different place.

5

1914–39:

ORGANISED COWARDICE

As Geoffrey Winthrop Young observed: 'The war came; and it eliminated much of the more leisured class, and destroyed the balance between work and cultivated leisure. It altered the conditions of mountaineering no less than all our other circumstances, and it shuffled the social elements from which climbers were drawn.'[1]

Rock climbs that were scratched and polished by nails in 1914 were covered with grass and moss by the spring of 1919 when most troops were demobilised. Of the 68 members of the Fell and Rock Climbing Club who served in the war, 19 were killed and many more injured. When the war finally ended, some found solace in the mountains, but for many the memories of rain, mud, vermin and death were too vivid to make climbing seem attractive. For over two decades British climbers struggled to exceed the standard set in the immediate pre-war years. 'We had lost most of the generation who could have set the standards and goals of our climbing in the nineteen twenties,' Sir Jack Longland recalled. 'It was a diminished and middle-aged world which we inherited.'[2]

A few pioneering women continued to climb in Britain during the war. In 1915 the novelist Emily Daniell (née Young) led the first rock climb in Britain created by a woman – the classic Hope (VD) on the Idwal Slabs. Mrs Daniell recalled that 'people on the road near Ogwen would walk backwards for quite a long way in astonishment and mirth at the sight of my sister and me in our corduroy breeches'.[3] The 'hope' referred to in the name was that a route would be found through the steeper wall above the slabs. A way was eventually found in 1918 when

Ivor Richards led Dorothy Pilley (whom he later married) and Charles Holland up the Original Route (S 4a) on Holly Tree Wall.

Something of the atmosphere of the post-war years is captured in Dorothy Pilley's autobiography, *Climbing Days*. Herford, the greatest pre-war rock climber, was dead. Charles Holland, his partner on Central Buttress on Scafell, the hardest rock climb before the war, was a 'white-faced invalid fresh from hospital',[4] his arm shattered by a shell fragment. Before the war, Holland, who was a preparatory school teacher, had fallen while roping down Scafell Crag and landed by pure chance on a knob of rock. 'It will always be a proud memory that my ejaculation during this unexpected performance was "God save the King"', he wrote. 'There are so many things one might have said and regretted it.'[5] After the war he suffered another fall, while his arm was still in plaster, and sat, fully composed, calmly smoking his pipe while 'every muscle in his body began to shake and shiver'.[6] Described by a friend as 'a short, stocky, sharp featured man, with a grin that reminded one of a famous gargoyle on Notre Dame and a laugh that became more and more Rabelaisian after the second or third pint',[7] like many of his generation his experiences in the trenches gave Holland a fatalistic approach to life: 'You may be killed, but what if you are? The only sane way of viewing life is as one step of a series in an upward progression and not as an end in itself, and that what matters is not the manner or the time of its end, but the spirit with which we have faced its difficulties.'[8]

Pilley described climbing Scafell Pike for the peace celebrations on 19 July 1919: 'We started for Scafell at 7 pm, the lens-like air and the strange hour stripping all films of familiarity from the accustomed path, so that the stone-walled meadows, the gorse clumps, the high iron stiles, the hawthorn bushes, the teeth-clipped grass under the reddening, falling sun were phantasmagoria through which we phantoms also passed.' After a cold bivouac near the summit they made coffee on Mickledore and watched the peaceful dawn hoping it was an omen 'that the days of war were at an end'.[9]

Before the war, climbing in Britain had been overwhelmingly a middle-class pursuit, and it was this 'officer class' that suffered a disproportionate number of casualties. In Germany and elsewhere in Europe, where the sport was more democratic and broad-based, standards rose rapidly in the years immediately following the war, in some cases motivated by a sense of injured national pride at the post-war settlement. The hard new routes in the Eastern Alps, put up by German and Austrian climbers, were often achieved using pitons for both protection and direct aid. This approach was largely rejected by British climbers, reflecting the relative scarcity of rock faces in Britain and the need to preserve both the environment and the challenge of climbing. Partly as a consequence, the standards of difficulty achieved by leading climbers in Britain progressively fell behind those attained in the Alps. Rock climbing standards in eastern Germany, Czechoslovakia and Poland were also higher than in Britain, although few British climbers were aware of this at the time.

The brutality and violence of the war shattered British society and culture as well as its economy and international status as a superpower. In its wake, society was divided between those who hoped for a return to 'normality', a largely imaginary past of security and effortless superiority, and those who were determined to build a better new world out of the ruins of the old. Both were to be disappointed. The climbing establishment fell largely into the former category, taking comfort from the pre-war achievements of British climbers and adopting an ever more reactionary attitude to new developments, particularly those emanating from Germany. However, a better-educated and more self-confident younger generation was increasingly prepared to challenge the establishment. The traumatising effect of the war is reflected in the fact that few serious books about it emerged before the late 1920s. The first reaction for many returning soldiers was a rather forced frivolity and self-indulgence. The recently popularised works of Freud on sex and inhibitions were seized upon as a justification for abandoning self-restraint. The novels of Aldous Huxley, a regular guest at Pen-y-Pass, reflected and supported the trend. There was also a studied rejection of the past. Lytton Strachey, a reluctant visitor to the 'imbecile mountains' but an ardent admirer of George Mallory, was one of several intellectuals who attacked the idols of Victorian England with his book *Eminent Victorians*.

After the war, the British Empire continued to expand as Germany ceded its territories in Africa and the Pacific and a new sphere of influence was established in the Middle East in the remains of the Ottoman Empire. But British self-confidence, swank and martial ardour had been destroyed on the battlefields of Europe, and during the 1920s and 30s an increasing number of people started to question the purpose and morality of the Empire. While popular support for the Empire may have declined, the lure of the open spaces it provided remained strong, as urban sprawl and ribbon development pushed ever farther into the British countryside. When the British Empire Exhibition at Wembley opened in 1924 *The Times* wrote: 'Many a young man of our cities will find it difficult to walk past the overseas pavilions with their suggestion of adventure, and space, and a happy life under the open skies of the bush, the prairie and the veld.' Travel (and crime) books replaced ripping imperial yarns as the characteristic literary genre of the inter-war years. The discovery of Tutankhamen's tomb, complete with ancient curses, caused a sensation in 1922, and the disappearance of Mallory and Irvine near the summit of Everest two years later generated a similar level of public interest. The 1924 British Empire Exhibition included a huge scale model of Mount Everest showing the routes followed by the 1921 and 1922 expeditions. When news of Mallory and Irvine's disappearance reached London a wreath of bay leaves was laid upon it.

In 1922, Lieutenant-General Robert Baden-Powell, hero of the siege of Mafeking during the Boer War and author of *Scouting for Boys* (1908), commissioned Geoffrey Winthrop Young to write a 2,000-word piece on climbing as an educative activity for Boy Scouts. This was probably the first attempt in Britain to codify the benefits of outdoor education. During the 1930s, Young continued to develop his ideas in this area through his work with the Rockefeller Foundation, particularly in Germany, where he met Kurt Hahn, a Jewish educationalist who shared similar views. When Hahn was arrested by the Nazis, Young was influential in bringing him to Britain and helped him to establish Gordonstoun School, where the Duke of Edinburgh and Prince Charles were subsequently educated. Young was chairman of the governors for many years and encouraged Hahn to establish the Outward Bound movement. The Duke of Edinburgh later sponsored the eponymous awards, which celebrate achievements in outdoor pursuits, physical fitness and community service. Participants in the scheme – normally wet and bedraggled youths – and their anxious adult overseers are a common sight in the British countryside to this day.

When Ramsay Macdonald, the son of a Scots farm labourer, became the first Labour prime minister in 1924, King George V recorded in his diary: 'Today 23 years ago dear Grandmamma died. I wonder what she would have thought of a Labour Government!' A Labour activist recorded that 'bishops, financiers, lawyers, and all the polite spongers upon the working-classes know that this is the beginning of the end'.[10] His statement rather accurately described the membership of the Alpine Club at the time. In 1926, just nine years after the Russian revolution, the only General Strike in British history started with the coal miners and rapidly spread to almost every branch of industry. For nine days it looked as if this really might be 'the beginning of the end', but British public opinion swung against direct action, and parliamentary democracy emerged from the crisis with renewed strength. However, the class struggle continued to express itself in industrial unrest in the cities and in the increasingly acrimonious battle for access to private land in the country, particularly on the Pennine moors that lie between the industrial conurbations of Lancashire and Yorkshire.

The Wall Street crash of 1929, and the ensuing rise of protectionism and decline of world trade, had a disproportionate effect on people living in the industrial cities in the north of England, south Wales and Scotland. Unemployment in Britain increased from around 1 million in 1929 to nearly 4 million in 1932. Young men, in particular, tended to be sacked at the end of their apprenticeships, when their wages would otherwise have gone up, leading to the bitterness of long-term youth unemployment. For the first time large numbers of young people at both ends of the social spectrum found that they had ample leisure but, at the lower end, virtually no money. In the depressed industrial towns numerous clubs sprang up, including gyms, cycling, running and rambling clubs, providing low-cost activities for the unemployed. Church attendance declined throughout the period, and for many households a Sunday walk became the secular equivalent of religious worship. As hill walking and climbing gradually became mass activities, public transport responded to the demand by running cheap rail and bus excursions into the hills and mountains. The growth of private motorised transport also dramatically increased mobility, allowing climbers to be active in more than one area. In 1920 there were 1 million motor vehicles. By 1930 the number had climbed to 2.5 million, and hitch-hiking started to become a viable means of travel to the hills for those with more time than money.

The 1930s saw a vast increase in the number of university students taking up hill walking and climbing, particularly in the north of England. The Manchester University Mountaineering Club was formed in 1928, Imperial College London followed in 1929, Liverpool in 1930 and Sheffield in 1933. The Youth Hostel Association was established in 1930 and by 1939 had 83,000 members. Based on the German *Landheime*, it gave young people access to accommodation in areas of the country that had previously been beyond the means of most workers and students. Dinner, bed and breakfast in a youth hostel cost 3 shillings (15 pence), while a hotel cost 10 shillings (50 pence) or more. Early hostels were opened near some of the most popular climbing crags in Britain, including Idwal in Wales (1931), Black Sail in the Lakes (1933) and a purpose-built hostel in Glenbrittle on Skye (1939). Experienced climbers often gave aspiring youngsters staying with the YHA their first taste of climbing. Alastair Borthwick, writing in the late 1930s, described youth hostels as 'a young world, governed by the young. I was twenty at the time and most of the people I met were my own age; people who, like myself, had only recently discovered that they could leave city, class, and the orthodoxy of their elders behind them at week-ends and create their own lives for a day and a half a week...they were the greatest library of ideas and human experience in Scotland.'[11] Barns, caves and bothies provided accommodation for climbers and hill walkers who were even more impecunious.

The combination of easier transport and cheap accommodation allowed climbers to visit the British hills far more often. Before the First World War most climbers spent Christmas and Easter in the British mountains and the summer in the Alps, but did very little climbing in between. By the 1930s, a large number of climbers were visiting the British mountains and outcrops almost every weekend, achieving a far higher level of strength, fitness and habituation to exposure.

Lively political discussions and spontaneous 'sing-songs' were a feature of the outdoor movement, with occasional dances after the day's activities. 'Song is so common in the hostels that it seldom interrupts the business of the day. One goes on with one's job, singing but not pausing,' observed Borthwick. As the economic crisis of the early 1930s gradually receded, it was replaced by increasing international tensions and growing militarism in Germany, Italy and Japan. Throughout this period the outdoor movement in Britain was overwhelmingly left wing and pacifist in its leanings, and there was a radical tone to much of the debate and many of the songs, such as 'The Manchester Rambler' by Ewan MacColl:

> I'm a rambler, I'm a rambler from Manchester way,
> I get all my pleasure the hard, moorland way,
> I may be a wage slave on Monday
> But I am a free man on Sunday.

As early as 1924 the social changes in the climbing community were being felt. H. M. Kelly and J. H. Doughty wrote in the *Fell and Rock Climbing*

Club Journal: 'In former days we had among climbers a preponderance of the more fortunate people endowed with a certain limited degree of means and leisure. Never what would be called a rich man's sport, it was not a poor man's either. Nowadays all that has largely changed.'[12] Informal working-class climbing clubs started to spring up around the country, including the Sheffield Mountaineering Club and the Creagh Dhu Mountaineering Club in Glasgow, which rose to prominence after the Second World War. The purpose of these new clubs differed markedly from the more established climbing clubs. The traditional clubs were primarily social in character, providing opportunities for men of similar backgrounds to enjoy meetings and meals in relatively comfortable surroundings. The new clubs provided information, shared transport, low-cost lodging and a unique social and political education for their younger members, as well as introducing them to climbing. Writing in 1939, E. A. M. Wedderburn, a member of the conservative Scottish Mountaineering Club, speculated that a typical conversation in the new clubs that sprang up in the 1930s might include 'Jimmy's exploits of last weekend or perhaps dialectical materialism'.[13] His comments suggest that he did not hold many conversations with members of the Creagh Dhu. Whereas the older clubs based themselves at comfortable country hotels, the new clubs began to establish rudimentary climbing huts in the mountains, or based themselves in hostels, barns or camping fields. This highly individualistic approach was in marked contrast to the continental model, where a unitary national climbing club was divided into local sections for administrative purposes. This perhaps partly explains why the climbing movement in Germany and Italy was relatively easily co-opted to the cause of fascism and militarism, while the British outdoor movement, outside the small and exclusive traditional clubs, remained resolutely independent, anti-establishment and overwhelmingly pacifist.

In *The Long Weekend*, a social history of the 1920s and 30s published in 1940, Robert Graves and Alan Hodge included a chapter entitled 'Pacifism, Nudism, Hiking', all three being regarded as libertarian ideas, intended to promote longevity, health and fitness. The word 'hiking' was an import from the United States and started to appear in Britain from 1927 onwards. It was a more ambitious form of rambling, often extending over a week or more. Rambling also remained extremely popular. When a journalist suggested a moonlight walk over the South Downs in July 1931 he expected 30 or 40 people. Instead nearly 1,500 people turned up and four special excursion trains had to be laid on. Nude bathing was the norm on both climbing and hiking expeditions. Even the all-female Pinnacle Club engaged in mass naked swims, much to the consternation of new members, but in other respects it was a curiously prim organisation, inclined to celebrate major events with home-made cake and a glass of sherry. When both sexes sought to swim naked at the same time the convention was that women stayed at one end of the lake and men at the other. As Sir Jack Longland observed, 'there were usually some pretty well-known homosexuals in the swimming party – or at least fashionable bisexuals – but that wasn't the point of the exercise'.[14]

Climbing equipment remained rudimentary. A pair of walking boots cost £2, with a set of clinker or tricouni nails 5 shillings (25 pence) extra. Rope cost 16 shillings (80 pence) for 100 feet of full weight manila. The orthodox used Alpine Club Rope (with a red thread) while others diced with death by using rope without red thread. Some people used plimsolls, or 'rubbers', but many agreed with Lord Chorley that this was cheating because 'it didn't give the rocks a chance'.[15] It was understood that it was poor form to use rubbers on a V. Diff.[16] Ropework improved, with the second man customarily belayed to the rock face, but running belays were still relatively uncommon, depending on looping the rope over flakes or using occasional slings. During the late 1920s and 30s some specialised climbing equipment, including windproof clothing, started to become available, often as a result of developments for Himalayan and Arctic exploration, but in general most people simply used old work clothes and cut-down macs, often liberally patched. One area where major improvements were made was in camping. At the turn of the century, tents typically weighed 100lbs or more, and needed porters or pack animals to carry them. By the 1930s, lightweight tents weighing just 10lbs became generally available, but most did not have sewn-in groundsheets.

The outdoor movement gave rise to a growing awareness of the importance of wilderness as a place of sanctuary and recreation. In 1924 Ernest Baker, who climbed with Jim Puttrell before the First World War, wrote *The Forbidden Land*, a plea for public access to mountains, moors and other waste lands in Great Britain. He noted: 'One unlucky day, grouse-shooting became a pastime with the idle rich, and the policy of shutting up the open wild gradually began. Nobody was yet alive enough to the charm of these vast solitudes to raise objection. Only in the last few decades have the public realised the seriousness of their loss. Now, however, it is becoming at length an obvious fact, and we wonder how our fathers could have failed to appreciate it, that the open spaces of the Pennine are the back garden, the recreation ground, for the crowded millions of workers in the adjoining towns.'[17]

There was nothing new about demands for access. Disputes between the ruling classes and rural commoners about access to royal game reserves and other private land date back to medieval times. But by the late nineteenth and early twentieth century the main protagonists were not rural peasants but town-dwellers, accustomed to pursuing their ends by political means and, as the movement became increasingly politicised, by mass protests. Nearly all the mountainous areas of Britain are privately owned. Without the right of access they are theoretically as private as a suburban back garden. In Wales and the Lake District access was rarely a problem, because the land was considered to be of limited value, but in Scotland and the Peak District many landowners restricted access because of deer stalking and grouse shooting.

In 1865 the radical liberal John Stuart Mill formed the Commons Preservation Society, which campaigned to preserve open spaces around London such as Epping Forest and Wimbledon Common. Some 20 years later the Access to Mountains (Scotland) Bill was introduced into the House of Commons by James Bryce, later Viscount Bryce, but rejected by the majority of MPs. Bryce was an outstanding mountaineer who had climbed in the Alps, Pyrenees, Norway, Caucasus, Andes, Rockies and the Himalaya and, as British ambassador to Washington from 1907 to 1913, urged the Americans to exclude motor cars from the newly formed Yellowstone National Park. His 1884 bill foreshadowed the arguments over access to mountainous areas that continued to grow as the popularity of climbing and hill walking increased. It proposed to grant a right of access to the Scottish mountains and moorlands to any person 'walking or being on such land for the purposes of recreation or scientific or artistic study'. In Scotland large areas were closed to mountaineers from June to October during the stalking season. Prior to the First World War, there was little opposition because there were relatively few climbers and walkers, and most of them were drawn from the same social class as the landowners, which allowed informal, friendly access arrangements to be made. Moreover, since many climbers spent the summer in the Alps and climbed in Scotland only at Christmas and Easter, they were largely unaffected by the stalking season. The Edinburgh-based Scottish Mountaineering Club reflected the view of many climbers before the First World War in supporting private ownership as a means of preserving the landscape, but the Aberdeen-based Cairngorm Club (of which Bryce was the first president) was more active in fighting for access and rights of way, in part because many of its members were less affluent than those of the Scottish Mountaineering Club and could not afford to go to the Alps in the summer.

In the Lake District, the National Trust, formed in 1895 by Octavia Hill, Canon Hardwicke Rawnsley and Robert Hunter, was inspired by a desire to protect the landscape eulogised by Wordsworth but carried with it the clear aim of ensuring access for all. One of the first beauty spots the National Trust acquired was Gowbarrow Park on Ullswater, site of the daffodils that inspired Wordsworth's most famous poem. After the First World War, two large tracts of land were acquired by the National Trust. Lord Leconfield donated Scafell Pike above the 3,000ft contour as a war memorial, while Herbert Walker sold 3,000 acres above the 1,500ft contour line around Wasdale Head for £400.

From the late nineteenth century onwards, the Peak District became the main flashpoint as ever larger numbers of ramblers and climbers from the industrial cities that surround the district came into conflict with game-keepers employed by landowners to protect the grouse-shooting moors. Various attempts were made to resurrect the substance of James Bryce's bill, including private member's bills in 1908, 1924 and 1927. All of them failed. Against the background of the national strike in 1926 and rising unemployment in the 1930s, the issue became increasingly radicalised, with many walkers and climbers asserting a right to *their* land, long denied to them by royalty, rich landowners, the military and other representatives of the ruling classes. The British Workers' Sports Federation started to organise open air meetings and camps in the north of England, particularly around Manchester, at Disley, Marple and Hayfield. As many as 5,000 people attended annual rallies in the Winnats Pass near Castleton in Derbyshire to campaign for free access. There were also a number of mass walks across the grouse moors around the northern industrial cities, culminating in the mass trespass on Kinder Scout and Abbey Brook in April 1932. Five trespassers were sent to prison, the sentences handed down by a jury consisting of two brigadier-generals, three colonels, two majors, three captains and two aldermen.[18] The original trespass involved just 400 demonstrators, but a subsequent protest at the injustice of the prison sentences, held in the Winnats Pass in June 1932, attracted a crowd of over 10,000 and it became obvious to the political establishment that concessions had to be made. The 1939 Access to Mountains Bill was finally passed by both houses but was denounced by campaigners as a 'landowners' protection bill', and no access orders were issued prior to the outbreak of war. After the war, a fresh start was made and the National Parks and Access to Countryside Act was finally passed in 1949. The 'right to roam' was further extended by the Countryside and Rights of Way Act of 2000.

Jim Perrin described climbing in the mid-1930s as having 'all the freshness, enthusiastic endeavour and bright optimism...when the balance between romance, risk and achievement was so perfectly held'.[19] Sir Jack Longland called it 'organised cowardice'.[20] Both are accurate descriptions of the sport in the inter-war years. Before the 1930s, 'vertical' or 'absolutely perpendicular' in a route description usually meant about 70 degrees. By the time the Second World War broke out, climbers had the physical and psychological strength to undertake pitches at 90 degrees as well as tackling shorter sections of overhanging rock. With today's equipment, any reasonably fit and determined person can climb at a Very Severe standard, but in the 1930s there were huge psychological barriers to overcome. In most cases the leader was effectively soloing and the golden rule was that 'the leader must not fall'. The climbing community was small and close-knit, and when fatal accidents did occur the repercussions were felt throughout the sport. Pinnacle Face on Scafell was hardly ever climbed because of its reputation for seriousness after the 1903 accident in which four climbers died. When Colin Kirkus and Alan Hargreaves repeated Herford's Direct Route to Hopkinsons' Cairn in 1929, a vice president of the Fell and Rock Climbing Club was horrified: 'You silly young buggers,' he said, 'you'll cause another fatal accident.'[21] But the younger generation persisted, climbing longer and more exposed routes in what would today be regarded as a very pure style, with almost no use of pitons for aid or protection. Many of the routes put up in the 1930s remain classics because they follow bold natural lines, while more recent, harder climbs often had to seek out less distinctive lines on the remaining unclimbed rock.

Despite these advances, the hardest new routes in Britain during the entire inter-war period did not exceed the technical grade (5b) set by Herford's Central Buttress in 1914, and overall standards of climbing fell behind those achieved in Germany, Austria and Italy. In the Alps, the increasingly chauvinistic, snobbish and reactionary attitudes of the establishment held back the development of British alpinism until the 'great proletarian climbing revolution' after the Second World War brought an entirely new approach and re-established Britain at the forefront of the sport.

THE LAKE DISTRICT

After several years of Welsh ascendancy, the Lake District had become the leading British climbing centre immediately before the start of the First World War with the 1914 ascent of Central Buttress. This position was reinforced in the immediate post-war years by the publication of a series of new guidebooks to the district between 1922 and 1926. The first guide, written by George Bower, to Doe Crags [*sic*] and Coniston, contained a number of hard new climbs, including Joe Roper's Great Central Route (HVS 5b, 1919), which equalled but did not surpass Central Buttress for technical difficulty, and Bert Gross' Eliminate B (HVS 5a, 1922). Roper and Gross were both members of the Yewdale Vagabonds, an active group of climbers based in Barrow-in-Furness who came close to re-establishing pre-war climbing standards in the Lakes at a time when climbing elsewhere in the country was in steep decline. Roper was a graduate of Ruskin College and a committed socialist who lectured for the Workers' Educational Association. By his own admission, he was afflicted with a 'divine discontent...a search for an escape from the drab and troubled world and a need for a freer more personal and self expressive activity than the world at the time allowed'.[22] Gross worked at the Vickers shipyard in Barrow and was also a troubled individual, who committed suicide in 1943. George Bower, the author of the first post-war guidebook, maintained the pre-war tradition of eccentric prose ('the panting climber thus arrives on the Band Stand, but the time for a paean of praise from the instruments of brass is not yet'[23]), but subsequent Lake District guides established a tradition of brevity and contained a list of routes in ascending order of difficulty which caused endless debate and encouraged the competitive spirit. In contrast, Welsh guidebooks continued to be more descriptive and literary in style.

The nomenclature of British rock climbs came under scrutiny in an article in the 1934 edition of the *Fell and Rock Climbing Club Journal*, which identified four categories of names in use up to that time: personal (Jones' Route); alphabetical or numerical (Route I); topographical

(South East Gully); and descriptive or imaginative (Grooved Arête). The personal category was mainly a Lake District tradition before the First World War, reflecting the heroic rather than aesthetic traditions of Lake District climbing. It later became more common in Wales and the Peak District (Kelly's Shelf, Longland's Climb, Kirkus' Route, Nea). In the years following the 1930s, alphabetic and numerical names rapidly became impractical as the number of climbs, often in between existing climbs, increased, but a few, such as Route 1.5 and Point Five Gully, were added. Topographical names also declined in popularity as all the main features were climbed and routes increasingly followed relatively undistinguished expanses of rock. As a result, from the 1930s through to the present day, descriptive, imaginative, esoteric and increasingly bizarre names have become the norm. Today it is often possible to guess the vintage of a first ascent from the style or the cultural references contained in the name. Leeds University and the Cioch Club were particularly well known in the 1960s for leaving behind them a trail of Depravity, Lust, Necrophilia, Bestiality and Debauchery.[24] There is an understandable preoccupation with death, including Rigor Mortis ('a stiff problem'), Post Mortem, Cemetery Gates and Ivy Sepulchre leading, perhaps, to Valhalla. Deliberately provoking the natives is a well-established tradition. When Whillans grabbed a coveted line in Glencoe he called it Sassenach, the Carlisle-based climber Peter Whillance put up Culloden on Creag an Dubh Loch, while Ben Moon named two sought-after routes in France Maginot Line and Agincourt. After completing a new route on a Cornish sea cliff, Ron Fawcett was berated by the owner of the property, novelist John le Carré, who accused him of trespassing. Fawcett decided to call the route Twat in a Clifftop Cottage. Meanwhile Borstal Buttress inevitably appeared next to Oxford and Cambridge Buttress on Bowfell.

On some crags, themes have emerged, such as the Nelson theme on Birchens in the Peak District, started by Byne and Moyer (Trafalgar Crack, Top Sail, Powder Monkey Parade, Emma's Dilemma, Porthole Buttress) or the 'knots' and 'nots' of White Ghyll in the Lakes (Gordian Knot, Slip Knot, Laugh Not, Haste Not, Do Not, Why Knot). The best names are often humorous and slightly obscure: Kirkus climbed Lot's Groove without looking back. Kipling Groove was ruddy 'ard. An even harder nearby climb, which required a lot of artificial aid, was called If. When the birch tree was accidentally pulled out of Birch Tree Wall the next climb was called Bring Back the Birch. Communist Convert gradually moves from left to right, and when Sid Cross and his wife-to-be Alice Nelson put up two adjacent climbs they called them Double Cross and Half Nelson. Pilgrim's Progress was 'interesting, but tough', as Huckleberry Finn observed of Bunyan's book, and when a censorious guidebook editor refused to publish a proposed name it became Asterisk.

With so many of the pre-1914 generation of climbers gone, Harry Kelly became the leading light of Lakeland climbing in the post-war years, frequently climbing with Charles Holland, the indefatigable veteran of the first ascent of Central Buttress. Kelly was an enigmatic man. An agnostic, socialist Mancunian, he was described by Ivan Waller as being rather like a sergeant-major, and yet he somehow avoided military service during the war and no-one ever knew what, if anything, he did for a living. Kelly wrote and edited several guidebooks and added several hard climbs including Moss Ghyll Grooves on Scafell (VS 4b, 1926), but it was the volume and quality of his new routes, rather than their technical difficulty, that marked him out. His wife, Pat Kelly, was also an accomplished climber who founded the Pinnacle Club for women in 1922. Eleanor Young (always known as Len), the daughter of Cecil Slingsby and wife of Geoffrey Winthrop Young, was the first president. Pat Kelly died on Tryfan just one year later, tripping on some newly fitted nails while descending easy ground.

Harry Kelly trained on the gritstone outcrops in the Peak District during the war and repeated Cave Arête Indirect on Laddow (E1 5a, 1916), immediately after Ivar Berg, an extremely talented Norwegian, had made the first ascent. Using proper rope belaying techniques, Kelly often climbed in plimsolls and further developed the balance-climbing approach pioneered by Eckenstein, Herford and others before the war. However he never managed to repeat Herford's greatest route, Central

Buttress. He descended almost every climb that he ascended, which allowed the investigation of new climbs with the safety of a rope from above. He also climbed with Eric Shipton in Zermatt in 1928, but was unimpressed by the ice and loose rock, preferring pure rock climbing in the UK – an almost heretical idea at the time.

Bentley Beetham was also active in the Lake District, putting up over 50 new routes, often on newly discovered crags, including numerous popular climbs such as Little Chamonix (VD, 1946) on Shepherd's Crag in Borrowdale. Beetham seconded Claude Frankland on the second ascent of Central Buttress in 1921 and was invited to join the 1924 Everest expedition after a successful alpine season with Howard Somervell, when they racked up 35 routes in six weeks. He remained a prolific but not high standard climber until well after the Second World War. Despite teaching natural history at Barnard Castle, Beetham frequently attacked overgrown crags with an axe and was strongly suspected of starting the huge fire that engulfed Great End Crag in Borrowdale in 1940 and several smaller fires in Langdale in the 1950s.

The first female ascent of Central Buttress was made by Dr Mabel Barker in 1925, climbing with Claude Frankland once again. Frankland, a Leeds school teacher who trained on Almscliff, putting up Green Crack (VS 4c, 1919) and other routes, was regarded as one of the best rock climbers in the Lakes at this time but died shortly afterwards in a fall from Chantry Buttress, a simple but loose V. Diff. on Great Gable. Mabel Barker went on to become the first woman to make a complete traverse of the Cuillin Ridge. After studying at Oxford and London universities, she was awarded a doctorate by the University of Montpellier, writing a thesis setting out her advanced views on education. In the Lake District she established a small school in Caldbeck and introduced scores of children to the joys of outdoor education. A striking, gypsy-like figure, she apparently subsisted on a diet of cigarettes and strong tea.

Graham Macphee was a caustically witty Scot and reputedly the most expensive dentist in the north of England, with surgeries in Shrewsbury and Liverpool. During the war he served with the Royal

Flying Corps, was shot down and became a prisoner of war. He was regarded as the 'greatest second' of the 1920s and 30s, with a remarkable record of supporting the leading climbers in the Lakes and elsewhere as they put up some of the best routes of the day, including Hiatus on Gimmer Crag (VS 4b, 1927) led by George Bower; Gimmer Crack (VS 4c, 1928) led by Arthur Reynolds (who normally climbed in bare feet); and Deer Bield Crack (HVS 5a, 1930) led by Albert Hargreaves, one of the hardest climbs in the Lakes at that time. Hargreaves was a founder member of the Manchester University Climbing Club with Maurice Linnell and put up numerous hard climbs in the Peak District including Black Slab (Hargreaves' Original) on Stanage (VS 4c, 1928) before moving to Barrow-in-Furness, where he lived in the same street as George Bower. He married a granddaughter of Cecil Slingsby and led half of the new VS routes (several of which are now graded HVS) recorded in the Lakes between 1930 and 1938. He died in a skiing accident in 1952.

During the early 1930s, with leading climbers such as Colin Kirkus, Maurice Linnell and Menlove Edwards mainly active in Snowdonia, the Lake District was once again eclipsed by Wales, although periodic visits produced some outstanding climbs, such as Linnell's Overhanging Wall (HVS 5a, 1933) on Scafell. By the end of the decade, however, the gap was once again closed with Jim Birkett's May Day Climb (HVS 5b, 1938), which was as hard, if not harder, than anything in Wales at the time.

Jim Birkett, a Langdale quarryman, and Bill Peascod, a Workington coal miner, were the vanguard of an emerging group of talented working-class climbers in the Lake District. Like many working men of his generation, Peascod had lived within 15 miles of the Lake District all of his life but had never even considered visiting it. In *Journey After Dawn* he described the day that changed his life: 'I had been on night shift. When I came out of the pit, up into God's real air, the morning was so beautiful I couldn't bear to go to bed...I set out – towards the sun. On that day I discovered Lakeland...it was a revelation.' Peascod went on to climb numerous hard new routes, particularly in Buttermere. Limited contact with the mainstream climbing community meant that Peascod and Birkett were less constrained by conventional ideas on difficulty and ethics. On his first ascent of Eagle Front, a new VS route in 1940, Peascod guessed the grade based on the fact that it was harder than a V. Diff. – the hardest previously recorded climb that he had done. Birkett used three pitons for protection on May Day Climb. The climbing establishment was predictably appalled, and Bentley Beetham felt moved to write: 'Peep around the corner of our most famous crag, look on what I have heard referred to as the gentleman's side of Scafell, and you will not see one piton, but three within almost as many yards of each other.'[25] The implication was clear: a gentleman would never hammer a piton into Lakeland rock. It was the only time that Birkett used pitons. For the rest of his career he continued to climb at the highest level, using minimal protection, and he never fell off: 'If you ever got into a situation where you were going to fall, you just didn't...Apart from being curtains, there was the indignity of it. It meant you weren't climbing right and it would be a real blot on your copy book.'[26] Birkett established something of a climbing dynasty. His son, Bill, put up a number of hard new climbs in the Lakes in the 1970s and 80s, including Centrefold (E6 6b, 1984) on Raven Crag in Langdale, and the third generation is represented by Dave Birkett, Bill's nephew, who climbed the first E9 in the Lakes with If Six was Nine (E9 6c, 1992) on Iron Crag, Thirlmere.

Sid Cross and Alice Nelson, both employees of K Shoes in Kendal, were also putting up hard new routes at about this time. Nelson was the first woman to lead Central Buttress and also repeated Collie's Steep Gill, a grade V ice route on Scafell, with Cross and Albert Hargreaves, making her probably the best all-round female climber of the inter-war years. Nelson and Cross also climbed Bowfell Buttress in full winter conditions, which merits a grade VI in the current guidebook. After the war they took over the Old Dungeon Ghyll Hotel in Langdale and encouraged a younger generation of rock climbers who drank in the climbers' bar and often slept in the Wall End Barn nearby. Sid Cross always denied that there were any social barriers to working-class climbers in the Lakes before the war, other than those created by the young climbers themselves. 'We were scruffy and ignorant – and we were often rude about [older, middle-class climbers] calling them the "Pilgrim bloody Fathers" and things like that. But they made a bit of a fuss of us – encouraged us, gave us useful tips, bought us shandies. It's the mountains – that's what mountains do.'[27]

NORTH WALES

The social atmosphere in Wales was rather different. At the insistence of his young wife, Len, Geoffrey Winthrop Young restarted the Pen-y-Pass meets in 1919. Despite the loss of so many friends during the war, they filled the hotel and the Easter weather was perfect. Young tested his new artificial leg by climbing Gashed Crag (VD) on Tryfan, and enjoyed a triumphant holiday. However, Welsh climbing in general went into steep decline after the war and consideration was even given to winding up the Climbers' Club. George Mallory was appointed President in 1923 and immediately set up a 'Demoribundisation Sub-Committee'. The *Journal* became a vital propaganda tool in the efforts of the few remaining active members to revive the club. 'In writing the account of a Club meet at which only one member had turned up it needed a certain amount of *suppressio veri* and *suggestio falsi* to convey the notion that the affair had been a howling success.'[28] In one issue, Maurice Guinness wrote a letter on grading under the *nom de plume* 'Moderate Climber', to which he then wrote a sneering reply signed 'Mountaineer'. An elderly member was so incensed by the rudeness of the reply he demanded that 'Mountaineer' be identified and expelled. The club also set about producing a new series of guides covering the relatively unexplored cliffs of the Llanberis Pass and Clogwyn Du'r Arddu. The acquisition of a club hut near Tryfan in 1925 marked the turning point and 'Helyg' rapidly became the hub of Welsh climbing activity.[29] Nearly 30 years later, in 1953, James (later Jan) Morris, *The Times* correspondent attached to the

Everest expedition, noted that the climbers talked 'a good deal about the doings of climbers, a subject which always seemed to get back, sooner or later, to something called "the Climbers' Club Hut at Helyg"...After two or three months in their company...I developed a passionate dislike for the Climbers' Club Hut at Helyg.'[30]

Geoffrey Winthrop Young was living in Cambridge by this time, and partly under his influence a number of talented climbers emerged from the Cambridge University Mountaineering Club. Jack Longland recalled that the Youngs' house 'was the centre for all the most active, ambitious and no doubt insufferable young Cambridge climbers',[31] including Wyn Harris, Noel Odell, Lawrence Wager, Ivan Waller, Charles Warren and Freddy Spencer Chapman, many of whom joined the Climbers' Club. Although Helyg was a miserable hovel, according to its habitués, meets had much of the gaiety and abandon of the Jazz Age. When Ivan Waller climbed Belle Vue Bastion (VS, 1927), a steep and spectacular route on Tryfan, the party carried a gramophone to the large ledge at the foot of the climb which they played during the ascent. Many of the young climbers were also keen motorists and soon established the tradition of combining hard climbing with reckless driving. Waller went on to compete as a racing driver. He won the 1932 Irish Grand Prix and would have won the Monte Carlo Rally had his car not been disqualified during the final hill climb. The Rucksack Club also opened a hut at Tal-y-Braich, not far from Helyg, which attracted a new generation of Manchester-based climbers to Snowdonia, including Fred Pigott and Morley Wood.

Pigott's Climb (VS 5a, 1924) and Longland's Climb (VS 4c, 1926) on Clogwyn Du'r Arddu opened up the finest cliff in England and Wales and set new standards for exposure on steep ground.[32] The two routes marked the beginning of Welsh ascendancy in rock climbing after a long period of Lakeland dominance. Pigott's Climb, the first on the East Buttress, was more serious and strenuous than several subsequent routes, while Longland's, which was climbed by a combined group from the Climber's Club (Jack Longland and Frank Smythe) and the

Rucksack Club (Fred Pigott and Bill Eversden), was slightly less hard, but delicate and exposed. Longland recalled that 'a leader is simply powerless against a man like Pigott: he is pursued upwards by winged words of encouragement, and any voicing of hesitation is greeted with the briefest expressions of incredulity'.[33] Both Pigott and Longland showed a willingness to use jammed chockstones and the occasional piton, but karabiners were still a rarity. Since karabiners have a moving part they were regarded as mechanical devices, and therefore utterly rejected by the climbing establishment. As R. L. G. Irving noted in 1935, the word *karabiner* is German: 'There is no English word for it. It is, in fact, decidedly un-English in name and in nature...In so far as an aesthetic or moral value is attached to the ascent, the use of mechanical devices cannot help us, and it may hinder us.'[34] When Longland eventually acquired a karabiner and proudly clipped it onto his belt, an elderly Lakeland climber spluttered: 'It's people like you who are the real vandals in the climbing world.'[35]

Fred Pigott was a Stockport sugar merchant. Educated at Manchester Grammar School, he served as a sniper during the First World War and his hand was permanently deformed by a war wound that became gangrenous. Pigott and Morley Wood were known as 'the inseparables', and while Pigott did most of the leading, Morley Wood, who volunteered as a private at the start of the First World War and ended up commanding a battalion, was able to follow him anywhere. He also led the gritstone test piece Kelly's Overhang (HVS 5b, 1926) on Stanage, which continues to repel its fair share of aspiring hard men today. As founding members of an *ad hoc* group of climbers called the Black and Tans, Pigott and Morley Wood put up new routes all over the Peak District before turning their attention to the mountain crags where Pigott established his reputation by making the third ascent of Central Buttress in 1923.

Sir Jack Longland, climber, educator and BBC broadcaster, lectured at Durham University after leaving Cambridge and was Director of Education for Derbyshire for 23 years, where he was responsible for establishing the White Hall Outdoor Centre near Buxton in 1951, the first of its kind in England. Although very much part of the climbing establishment in his later years (he was President of the British Mountaineering Council from 1962 to 1965), in his youth he was ambitious and rebellious. 'It is difficult to over-emphasise the frustration felt by young climbers in the mid-1930s, believing, as they did, that the conduct of the Alpine Club and of Everest affairs was largely in the hands of people who had not been near a serious climb for years.'[36] Javelin Blade (E1 5b) on Holly Tree Wall, Idwal, led by Longland in 1930, was 'an outstanding lead that stood as the most difficult piece of Welsh climbing for many years, though few were aware of it'.[37] Longland recalled the climb: 'I remember the pull-out onto the actual blade of the javelin was very strenuous; though not dangerous – I had a belay about 40 feet below me.' Longland was invited to join the 1933 Everest expedition, where he helped to establish the highest camp (camp VI) at 8,230m/27,000ft with Wyn Harris, Lawrence Wager and eight Sherpas. He then descended with the Sherpas in white-out conditions, bringing all to safety after a 36 hour epic.

The Climbers' Club and Rucksack Club, and established climbers such as Alan Hargreaves and Alf Bridge, encouraged a younger generation of climbers from Liverpool and Manchester, including Colin Kirkus, Maurice Linnell and Menlove Edwards, who revolutionised Welsh climbing in the 1930s. Kirkus was regarded as the best climber in Wales in the early 1930s and later introduced many newcomers to the sport through his book *Let's Go Climbing* (1941), which perfectly expressed his simple, unaffected love of the sport. While Pigott's Climb and Longland's Climb opened up Clogwyn Du'r Arddu, it soon became known as 'Colin's Cliff' after a series of new routes during the 1930s, which were unparalleled until the arrival of Joe Brown in the 1950s.

Kirkus was born in 1910 and brought up in a solidly middle-class Edwardian family. After leaving school he took a job as a clerk in an insurance company in Liverpool, where he remained until joining the RAF at the start of the Second World War. Wilfrid Noyce, a future member of the successful 1953 Everest expedition, was his cousin, and the

Noyce and Kirkus families went on holiday together in Wales when they were children. However, Wilfrid was the son of Sir Frank Noyce, a member of the Viceroy's Council in India, and went on to study at Cambridge. While Kirkus was respected for his outstanding climbing ability, it was Noyce who was invited to Geoffrey Winthrop Young's Easter parties at Pen-y-Pass because Kirkus was 'just a little boring, too quiet and rather lacking in conversation'.[38] Although Kirkus had a respectable white-collar job, he was by no means rich, often doing without mid-week lunches in order to save enough for a weekend trip to Wales.

After a period of solo exploration, Kirkus started climbing regularly with members of the Liverpool-based Wayfarers' Club, and was introduced to Alan Hargreaves by a member of the Climbers' Club. Hargreaves recalled: 'The Climbers' Club people seemed to think that [Colin] was a bit mad and our introduction was on that basis – possibly they thought I was too – anyway we were promptly dubbed "The Suicide Club".'[39] Kirkus developed strength and technique by training on the small sandstone outcrops at Helsby, overlooking the River Mersey, putting up several test pieces including Jericho Wall (HVS 5b, 1929), which was probably as hard as any outcrop climb in the country at that time. He also started climbing with Maurice Linnell and Alf Bridge, two Manchester-based climbers who had established a reputation for bold new climbs on gritstone. Alf Bridge[40] acquired his great strength working as a steeplejack and was reputed to wear out the tops of his plimsolls before the soles, dragging his feet behind him like useless appendages. He was also a famously truculent defender of the rights of ordinary climbers against the 'mandarins' of the climbing establishment, a trait that caused him to resign, at various times, from the Rucksack Club the Climbers' Club (twice), the Karabiner Club and the Alpine Club.

Over the next five years, climbing with Bridge, Linnell, Hargreaves and the ubiquitous 'greatest second' Graham Macphee, Kirkus put up numerous outstanding climbs, including Lot's Groove (VS 4c, 1929) on Glyder Fach; Great Slab (VS 4c, 1930) on Clogwyn Du'r Arddu; Direct Route (VS 4c, 1936) on Dinas Mot, which was not equalled for delicacy until Birtwistle's Diagonal Route (HVS 5a, 1938); and Mickledore Grooves on Scafell (VS 4c, 1930), where Wilfrid Noyce had a serious fall while climbing with Menlove Edwards in 1937. 'Every precious moment was squeezed out of our weekends – youth, vigour, ambition and the joy of living in our mountains meant so much to us,'[41] recalled Alf Bridge. Like so many office workers since, Colin Kirkus would daydream through the working week, longing for the weekend: 'On a photograph of some cliff I would have all the known routes marked with dotted lines. The black spaces in between fascinated me...I used to sit, pretending to work, with the drawer slightly open, so that I could see the photo inside.'[42]

Maurice Linnell, born in Stockport and a founder member of the Manchester University Mountaineering Club, was the perfect foil to Kirkus. Prior to the late 1920s the leading climbers of the day often climbed with seconds that were strong and reliable but not themselves capable of leading at the same standard. From the 1930s onwards, the major advances were often made by partnerships where both climbers were equally capable of leading; the knowledge that the second could take over perhaps driving the leader on when discretion might have prevailed in a less competitive atmosphere. Where Kirkus was strong and steady, Linnell was bold and mercurial. As Jack Longland said: 'Quite frankly, Maurice used to frighten the life out of me sometimes.'[43] Geoffrey Winthrop Young mused that 'Linnell's amazing ascents had something fatalistic in their character.'[44]

Linnell was also unorthodox: on Overhanging Wall on Scafell (HVS 5a, 1933) he used a piton for aid – 'I offer no apologies; those who prefer to climb the place unaided are cordially invited to remove the piton and do so'[45] – and made the first ascent of both the lay-back pitch of Curving Crack (VS 4c) on Clogwyn Du'r Arddu and the Bayonet-Shaped Crack (HVS 5b) at the top of Central Buttress on Scafell, climbing solo. Narrow Slab (HVS 4c) on Clogwyn Du'r Arddu involved a leap to a small grass-covered ledge on an almost vertical face. Linnell was killed in an avalanche in 1934 while climbing with Kirkus on the Castle, Ben Nevis. Kirkus was seriously injured and never fully recovered his eyesight. The accident ended a great climbing partnership and brought to a close the most creative period of Kirkus' climbing career.

Kirkus' main contribution to British rock climbing was a willingness to accept long run-outs on exposed and serious rock, far above belays. Unlike Owen Glynne Jones, Siegfried Herford and Harry Kelly, both Kirkus and Linnell were prepared to make hard first ascents 'on sight', without prior inspection or preparation, starting from the ground with very little knowledge of the difficulties above. His technique was based on delicate footwork, balance and finger strength developed through regular outcrop climbing. Previously, hard moves more than 30 feet above a belay were regarded as extremely serious (which they were). Kirkus had the concentration and focus to cope with the psychological demands of huge exposure while climbing at the limit of his ability. The first ascent of Great Slab on Clogwyn Du'r Arddu (VS 4c, 1930), on sight, with retreat exceedingly difficult and rescue from above impossible, epitomised the style and established Kirkus as the leading British climber of the day. 'To take out 130 feet of line on this entirely virgin face up a steep, loose and grassy wall, tremendously exposed, with no knowledge of what difficulties lay in the 600 odd feet above, was surely mountaineering courage of the highest order,' according to Alan Hargreaves.[46]

Kirkus climbed in the Alps, but not with any great distinction. Although it was now possible for non-university-educated climbers in clerical jobs to reach the highest standard on British rock by climbing at weekends and in the evenings, short holidays and lack of money meant that most failed to gain significant alpine experience. Based on his outstanding UK record, Kirkus hoped to be chosen for the 1933 Everest expedition, but he was overlooked. Instead he was invited to join Marco Pallis' Gangotri expedition to the Indian Garhwal where he made a pioneering alpine-style ascent of Satopanth II (now Bhagirathi III) (6,724m/22,060ft) with Charles Warren in 1933. Tom Longstaff, who was President of the Climbers' Club at the time, encouraged them to pursue a lightweight approach that was ahead of its time but received little publicity. Warren, a

Cambridge-educated doctor, later joined the 1935, 1936 and 1938 Everest expeditions, but Kirkus was again left out. Although Kirkus continued to climb after the accident in 1934, it was generally at a lower standard, and he spent an increasing amount of his time teaching beginners. He died in 1942, shot down during a RAF bombing raid on Bremen.

Kirkus' successor as the leading Welsh climber in the mid-1930s was the complex and troubled John Menlove Edwards. Inevitably their styles were compared. Geoffrey Winthrop Young wrote: 'Seeing Kirkus as slow and inevitable as the hands of a clock upon a holdless slab and Menlove Edwards, serpentine and powerful as an Anaconda coiling up loose or wet overhangs, I had the conviction that human adhesiveness in movement could go no further.'[47] Nearly all Kirkus' routes have that indefinable characteristic of greatness – exposed, in fine positions, with distinctive rock architecture. In contrast Edwards was a connoisseur of loose rock, vegetation and overhangs. This willingness to accept 'bad rock' enabled him to open up vast new areas of rock climbing that had previously been dismissed, most notably the Three Cliffs of the Llanberis Pass: Dinas Cromlech, Carreg Wastad and Clogwyn y Grochan. The dank and crumbling rocks of the Devil's Kitchen in Idwal also became something of an obsession.

Edwards was born in Lancashire, the fourth child of an impoverished vicar, and was educated at Fettes College in Edinburgh and Liverpool University, where he studied medicine and became a psychiatrist. He was also a poet and writer whose work was frequently autobiographical and self-analytical: 'There was once a man who desired glory more than he desired any other thing...A sport called rock-climbing promised him all the glory that he desired, and though requiring great energy it was very immediate and certainly much easier in this sense than anything he had yet come across. It was an impersonal struggle making personal relationships much easier.'[48] Brought up in the north of England tradition of Christian socialism, Edwards was a homosexual who always felt himself to be an outsider and who became increasingly introverted and isolated over time.

A powerful but erratic climber, with his training as a psychiatrist he recognised that beyond a certain point, climbing is more about mind than body. He had little respect for reputations or tradition, and when he was climbing well he was willing to accept risks that others considered unjustifiable. He was responsible for hundreds of new routes, including many of the most popular climbs in north Wales today.

Like Kirkus, Edwards trained at Helsby Crag in Cheshire where he put up numerous short, hard climbs including Eliminate 1 (E1 5b, 1928). His early self-belief was amply demonstrated when he made the first free ascent (without using combined tactics) of Central Buttress (HVS 5b) on Scafell at the age of 21. His lead was particularly impressive since he had just watched Alf Bridge, seconded by Maurice Linnell and Alan Hargreaves (at that time regarded as three of the strongest climbers in the country), fall from the crucial Flake Crack. Chimney Route (VS 4c, 1931), climbed with Kirkus, and Bow Shaped Slab (HVS 5a, 1941), on Clogwyn Du'r Arddu, Brant and Slape (both VS 4c, 1940) on Clogwyn y Grochan, and many others followed.

Edwards was involved in an incident in 1936 that demonstrated the strength of feeling that existed in Britain at that time against the use of pitons. A party of Bavarian climbers had been invited to Britain as guests of the Workers' Travel Association. They easily climbed all the hardest Welsh routes in wet conditions but appalled their hosts by using pitons to make the first ascent of the Munich Climb (VS 4c) on Tryfan. Edwards, with Noyce, was dispatched to remove the offending iron-mongery. As Noyce recalled: 'A German party had earlier in the year attacked the steep dark north wall of the South Buttress and, with that second nature of theirs, had thought fit to hook themselves to it with iron pegs. The pegs were left, defacing Welsh rock. They needed to be removed.'[49] The pitons were returned to the Germans with a courteous note explaining that they were not wanted in British rock.

In addition to climbing, Edwards also undertook a number of dangerous boating and swimming exploits, including swimming through the Linn of Dee near Braemar and rowing from Gairloch to the Isle of

Harris and back, alone, in winter; a distance of 80 miles. In his account of the journey he wrote: 'I'm not frightened of being alone, but I do not like not being anything else ever...I can do with very little appreciation as for affection, and I had long since realised that if one cannot do without what one wants of that sort, one had better go hang.'[50] Although he was invited to Geoffrey Winthrop Young's gatherings at Pen-y-Pass, it was largely because of his relationship with the handsome and graceful Wilfrid Noyce, who formed a schoolboy infatuation for the older man and was the only openly acknowledged love of Edwards' life. Edwards always felt ill at ease and, according to Noyce, believed that northerners and southerners saw the hills in fundamentally different ways: 'The North, he claimed, has at the back of its mind the idea that mountains are lumps of rock or grass or snow. The Southerner, more steeped in the Victorian tradition, speaks of the "Queenly Weisshorn", of Mont Blanc or Snowdon "lording it" over surrounding peaks...It was no mere pose that made Menlove forbear ever to use such expressions. He simply did not feel that way.'[51]

A conscientious objector during the Second World War, living in a remote Welsh cottage that he rented from Colin Kirkus, Edwards became increasingly withdrawn and obsessed by his attempts to find a unifying theory of the mind. After the war he suffered a complete breakdown and made several attempts to commit suicide, finally succeeding in poisoning himself with cyanide in 1958. Nea Morin, a leading female alpinist and rock climber, invited him to Cornwall in 1953 when he was already very ill. She later wrote: 'Often I have wished that he had gone like so many others when climbing in the splendour of his strength.'[52]

SCOTLAND

'In the 1920s climbing in Scotland had to all appearances died',[53] according to Bill Murray. With its proud military tradition and relatively small population, Scotland suffered higher casualties *per capita* than any other country in the First World War, and the young men who survived had little appetite for the hardship and discomfort that climbing in Scotland necessarily involves much of the time. Even by the 1930s, climbing standards had advanced little since the turn of the century. As a result of this unnatural generation gap, the Scottish Mountaineering Club became old, cliquey and moribund, and most of the new climbs put up in Scotland in the immediate post-war years were by English parties. The Crack of Doom (HS, 1918) on Skye, climbed by David Pye and Leslie Shadbolt, and Noel Odell's Chasm (VS, 1920), a tremendous 425m/1,400ft gully that cleaves the side of Buachaille Etive Mor and which had previously been explored by Harold Raeburn, were among the most notable routes of this period.

The formation of the Junior Mountaineering Club of Scotland (JMCS) in 1925 marked a turning point in affairs. Any man over 17 could join, no climbing experience was required, and within a few years its contribution to climbing in Scotland was probably greater than its parent's. Unlike the Scottish Mountaineering Club, founded in the self-confident Edinburgh of the 1880s, the inspiration for the JMCS came during a visit by a group of friends to the still war-scarred battlefields of the Somme in 1924. Rising unemployment in the 1930s, particularly amongst the foundry and shipyard workers on Clydeside, also resulted in an increasing number of working-class young men going into the countryside, sleeping rough in howffs and bothies. There were meeting places like Craigallion Loch, where the fire reputedly never went out because there was always someone there to feed it, and 'the unemployed, people tired of city life, dreamers, poachers, hikers and revolutionaries...gathered to swap tales, sing and spend the night in the open'.[54] Many of these 'weekenders' soon graduated from hill walking to climbing and began to form clubs of their own. The Ptarmigan, founded by Jock Nimlin in 1929, and the Creagh Dhu, founded by Andy Sanders in 1930, were two such clubs in Glasgow, but similar clubs sprang up in industrial towns across Scotland. Together Nimlin and Sanders put up numerous new routes on the Cobbler, and Nimlin pointed the way to developments after the Second World War by climbing Raven's Gully on Buachaille Etive Mor (VS 4c), one of the hardest climbs in Scotland, in 1937. In England, some progress had been made in assimilating young, working-class climbers into the established northern climbing clubs, but in Scotland the traditional clubs remained overwhelmingly middle-aged and middle-class. The new clubs brought 'an element, hitherto not prominent, of youth and relative poverty', and the young climbers found themselves 'not so much as heirs to a tradition as the discoverers of a secret hitherto kept from their class'.[55]

Improvements in the roads and more numerous and reliable cars increased the frequency with which climbers could visit the Highlands, and the Charles Inglis Clark (CIC) Memorial Hut, which opened in 1929, transformed the logistics of climbing on Ben Nevis, particularly during the short winter days, and led to a rapid increase in activity. Route I on Carn Dearg (S, 1931), climbed by Albert Hargreaves with the 'greatest second' Graham Macphee, and Rubicon Wall (VS, 1933) on Ben Nevis also led by Hargreaves, led to the development of a new style of open climbing. The Scottish climbing establishment predictably regarded these new routes as 'unjustifiable' or, worse still, 'Germanic', while Bill Murray, a member of the younger generation, described the feeling of exposure as 'an abandonment to Providence'.[56] The Scottish establishment may have protested, but people like Macphee and Murray were hardly wild revolutionaries compared to the Scottish climbers that would emerge after the Second World War. Murray worked in a bank, and when Macphee was invited to give a talk to the Junior Mountaineering Club of Scotland he arrived in his Bentley, immaculately dressed in a pinstripe suit and creamy spats.

The new road across Rannoch Moor to Glencoe was opened in 1935, further improving access to Ben Nevis and the Western Isles. Climbers heading for Skye would often stop off at Glencoe or Ben Nevis on the way, and a few parties even ventured further north to the almost unexplored regions of Wester Ross and Sutherland. An influx of tourists was also attracted to the eastern end of the Great Glen following the providential sighting of a monster in Loch Ness in 1933. Operating from his base in Liverpool, Graham Macphee edited a guidebook to

Ben Nevis and put up 11 new routes in 1936, something that would have been inconceivable before the advent of better roads and more reliable cars. Dr Jim Bell, who was editor of the *Scottish Mountaineering Club Journal* at the same time, was also active on Ben Nevis and conducted a long-running feud with Macphee through the medium of the CIC Hut climbing logbook, each man taking it in turns to write derogatory remarks about the other's activities.

Jim Bell put up over 70 new routes, most notably the 425m/1,400ft Long Climb (S, 1940) on the Orion Face of Ben Nevis. As a practical chemist, Bell insisted that food was simply fuel and that separation into courses was an 'auld wife's nicety'. Accordingly, a typical Bell breakfast in the CIC Hut consisted of porridge, sausage and kippers all stirred into one pot. During one of several summer seasons that he spent in the Alps with Frank Smythe his preferred lunch consisted of sardine and honey sandwiches. Bell was passionate about exploratory climbing in Scotland, maintaining that 'any fool can climb good rock...but it takes craft and cunning to get up vegetatious schist and granite',[57] and unlike most of his contemporaries he was not averse to using pitons, not least because he knew it would infuriate Macphee. Bill Murray recalled Bell using two pitons on the first ascent of Parallel Buttress on Lochnagar in 1939: 'Bell dug into his rucksack and produced – I wish that one could write in a whisper – two pitons. Their use is frowned upon by many British mountaineers. Like the queen of Spain's legs, a piton not only ought never to be seen, but must not be supposed to even exist.'[58]

Murray was a leading Scottish climber in the years immediately before and after the Second World War. His classic book *Mountaineering in Scotland* (1947) was written on toilet paper whilst he was a prisoner of war in Italy. When the allied forces invaded Sicily, Murray was moved first to Germany and then to Czechoslovakia, where the Gestapo destroyed the nearly complete manuscript. He immediately began again. It is a rather beautiful book: part climbing guide, part recollection of lost youth and part mystical treatise. When Geoffrey Winthrop Young read it, he immediately wrote to Murray: 'Oh thank heaven at last – for someone who can write!' A deeply spiritual man, Murray contemplated becoming a monk, but decided that he needed the freedom to pursue truth wherever it led, and could not accept the strictures of the Catholic Church. 'I have learned the truth, that in fact there is beauty in everything; and that one is not always apt in seeing it...In mountain days, one may win fleeting glimpses of that beauty which all men who have known it have been compelled to call truth. Such, for me, has become the end of mountaineering to which the sport is a means.'

Like Martin Conway, the pre-war explorer of the Karakoram, Murray always felt that the immediate appeal of the mountain landscape was just a hint of some underlying essential beauty. 'We had set out in search of adventure; and we had found beauty...What more can we fairly ask of mountains? None the less, I came down from the summit filled with the acute awareness of an imminent revelation lost; a shadow that stalked at my side ever more openly in the hills. Something underlying the world as we saw it had been withheld. The very skies had trembled with presentiment of the last reality; and we had not been worthy.'

Murray's approach to winter climbing signalled a new attitude to risk. With the exception of the three classic ridges of Ben Nevis, all the Scottish winter routes put up before the 1930s were gully climbs. Murray, together with Macphee, Bell and others, started to climb buttresses, ridges and faces, particularly around Glencoe, which brought a new variety to the climbing. As Alastair Borthwick noted: 'For the maximum and minimum pleasure in the open air, winter mountaineering in Scotland is pre-eminent.'[59] Murray and his companions were prepared to accept less than perfect climbing conditions and often set off on a route knowing that they would not complete it before nightfall. This considerably increased the amount of climbing that they actually accomplished and led to a steady rise in standards. Garrick's Shelf (grade IV), on Crowberry Ridge, Buachaille Etive Mor, climbed by Murray and W. M. Mackenzie in 1937, was in many respects the prototype of modern ice climbing. Other notable routes included Deep Cut Chimney on Stob Coire Nam Beith (IV, 1939) and the 500m/1,700ft Clachaig Gully (S, 1938).

Murray was deputy leader to Eric Shipton on the Everest reconnaissance in 1951, with Michael Ward, Tom Bourdillon, Ed Hillary and Earle Riddiford. Many mountaineers felt a sense of regret when Everest was eventually climbed in 1953, but Murray's reaction was more pronounced. Given his strong views on mountain aesthetics he saw the success, and the outpouring of national pride, as 'damaging to mountains and to real mountaineering'. In 1962 he was commissioned by the National Trust for Scotland to undertake a survey of the Scottish Highlands to identify areas of outstanding natural beauty. In his report *Highland Landscape* his criterion for inclusion of a landscape was that it should be 'the perfect expression of that ideal form to which everything that is perfect of its kind approaches'.[60] As a definition of beauty, this is not without difficulty, but his selection of areas and descriptive justification for their inclusion played a major role in heightening awareness of Scotland's natural beauty and strengthened the resolve of the conservation movement at a time when hydro-electric and forestry projects threatened many of the most spectacular Highland glens.

In the more cynical and hedonistic world of the 1950s and 60s, Murray became something of a standing joke. Jimmy Marshall recalled that during the regular confrontations that took place between young Edinburgh climbers and the park wardens at Salisbury Crags, where climbing was illegal, when names were demanded the most frequently offered was Bill Murray (who was then in his late 40s). Today, his preoccupation with aesthetics, ethics and the mountain environment seems more in keeping with current concerns. The last words of his last book were simply: 'I have known beauty.'[61]

OUTCROPS

Climbing in Yorkshire and the Peak District did not share the upper middle-class origins of the sport elsewhere in Britain. With a few exceptions, such as Cecil Slingsby, members of the Alpine Club showed no interest in outcrop climbing and regarded even the Lake District or Welsh crags primarily as practice grounds for the Alps. As a consequence, the students and working men who climbed on these gritstone crags grew up outside the alpine tradition and probably benefitted from having fewer preconceived ideas on what constituted acceptable style and justifiable risk. In this, they had something in common with the workers in Germany, Austria and Italy who were beginning to climb in the Eastern Alps.

The Peak District and Yorkshire gritstone crags became a forcing ground during the inter-war years, with standards on the outcrops often significantly higher than on the larger cliffs in Wales or the Lakes. Cave Arête Indirect (E1 5a, 1916) at Laddow was the first route in Britain that still merits an E1 grade today. Harry Kelly, Fred Pigott, Alf Bridge, Maurice Linnell, Albert Hargreaves, Jack Longland and Arthur Birtwistle all started on gritstone and went on to advance standards elsewhere in the inter-war years. Colin Kirkus and Menlove Edwards both trained on the sandstone of Helsby in Cheshire. During the 1930s a new type of climber also began to emerge who, for reasons of poverty or simply personal taste, only climbed on outcrops and never 'graduated' to the mountain crags. The 1930s therefore signalled the final break when rock climbing definitively became a separate sport and ceased to be merely a preparation for mountaineering.

Some of the remoter Peak District crags, such as Laddow, may actually have been more popular in the 1930s than they are now because of their mountain atmosphere and relatively easy access (by public transport and walking, as opposed to driving) from Manchester. But then, as now, Stanage Edge was probably the most popular crag, and climbs such as Wall End Slab Direct (E2 5b, 1930), put up by Sheffield climbers Harry Dover, Frank Elliott, Gilbert Ellis and Clifford Moyer, set a high standard of difficulty. In common with many climbers of their class and generation, they remained gritstone specialists, largely because of lack of money during the depression. Elliott also pioneered limestone climbing in the Peaks with Aurora (VS 4c, 1923) at Stoney

Middleton. Dover, Elliott and Ellis eventually abandoned the dole queues of Sheffield and found work at the newly opened Ford factory at Dagenham near London, thereby bringing their gritstone climbing careers to an end, but Elliott continued to climb on the sandstone outcrops of Kent and Sussex.

New crags were discovered and developed throughout the period, and outcrop climbing even attracted its own historian, Eric Byne, who charted its development in the High Peak.[62] Arthur Andrews, who climbed with Thomson, Young and others in Wales but lived in Zennor, continued his exploration of the Cornish sea cliffs, and developments at Bosigran and elsewhere in West Penwith accelerated after the opening of the Count House as a Climbers' Club hut in 1938, only the seventh climbing hut to open in Britain.

THE ALPS

By 1914 most of the obvious routes in the Alps had been climbed, but there remained three outstanding challenges to overcome: the great North Faces of the Matterhorn, the Grandes Jorasses and the Eiger. All three were climbed between the wars, but not by British parties. The North Face of the Matterhorn (ED1) was climbed in 1931, the Croz Spur of the Grandes Jorasses (ED1) was ascended in 1935 and the harder and more elegant Walker Spur (ED1) in 1938. The North Face of the Eiger (ED2) also finally succumbed in 1938. The first British ascents took place in 1961, 1959 and 1962 respectively, more than two decades after the first ascents. This is one measure of how far behind continental standards British alpinism had fallen in the inter-war years.

The stagnation that characterised the British domestic climbing scene after the First World War was even more pronounced in the Alps. As Eric Shipton noted: 'The British, who can be said with some justice to have started the sport of mountaineering and who had the field almost to themselves during the Golden Age of the mid-nineteenth century, played almost no part in the developments of this great era in the Alps.'[63] Some new routes were climbed by British parties in the 1920s, but they were less difficult than the standard achieved by Young and others prior to 1914, and were often climbed with guides. S. L. Courtauld and E. G. Oliver climbed the Innominata Ridge of Mont Blanc (D+) in 1919 with the guides Henri and Adolphe Rey and Adolf Aufdenblatten. George Finch led a guideless party up a devious route on the North Face of the Dent d'Hérens (D) in 1923. Professor Ivor Richards and Dorothy Pilley made the first ascent of the North-North-West Ridge of the Dent Blanche (D+) in 1928, guided by Joseph Georges. But the only British climbers to make a significant contribution to alpine climbing during this period were Graham Brown and Frank Smythe.

Frank Smythe sprang to prominence when he made the second ascent (21 years after the first) of the Ryan-Lochmatter route (D+) on the Aiguille du Plan with Jim Bell. Graham Brown took up climbing at the age of 42. He was not in the same class as Smythe as an alpinist, but he had a remarkable eye for a good line and had identified several possibilities on the Brenva Face of Mont Blanc. Together they made the first ascent of Sentinelle Route (D+) in 1927. It was a magnificent achievement, the first breach in the daunting Brenva Wall, but both Brown and Smythe were strong-willed and quick to take offence. When Smythe suggested (probably correctly) that Brown could not have climbed the route without him, the two men argued bitterly and went their separate ways. Against their better judgement, they teamed up again in 1928 and climbed the Route Major (TD-), the finest route on the Brenva Face, after which they were barely on speaking terms for the rest of their lives. Route Major was not repeated by another party for nine years, although Brown climbed it again with two guides in 1933, perhaps to prove to Smythe that he could. Brown went on to create a third new route on the Face, Pear Buttress (TD) in 1933.

Frank Smythe's father died when he was very young. After a lonely childhood, during which he suffered from frequent ill-health, he studied electrical engineering in Austria and Switzerland and briefly joined the RAF, where he was invalided out because of a heart murmur, before finding his vocation as a professional climber. Smythe formed a close relationship with Sir Francis Younghusband, the imperial adventurer, with whom he shared a common interest in mountains and mysticism. Younghusband selected Smythe to be his biographer, a task which he described as 'a religious duty',[64] and Smythe had an affair with, and subsequently married, Lady Younghusband's nurse Nona, who was practically an adopted member of the Younghusband household. Like Younghusband, Smythe was a prolific writer, producing 27 books in 20 years. Inevitably his reputation suffered amongst his peers. Raymond Greene, brother of Graham Greene the novelist, who had been at school with Smythe and later climbed with him on Kamet and Everest, observed that 'physically on the mountains, intellectually in his books, Frank always tried to reach heights which were just a little beyond his powers, great though those were'.[65] Eric Shipton regarded him as 'an agreeable companion...but not a stimulating one, for he lacked originality and tended to talk and think in clichés'.[66] Nevertheless, his books were very popular. With their romantic, almost languid style they provided the perfect escape from the economic and political crises of the 1930s.

Smythe was a member of the party that put up Longland's Climb on Clogwyn Du'r Arddu in 1928, but he was not a natural rock climber and in any event he disliked 'those horrid northern climbers'.[67] As a mountaineer he was sound rather than brilliant, and he owed his success to his remarkable stamina and determination, particularly on the highest peaks. Smythe often preferred to climb solo, and throughout his life he had a reputation for irritability, but his temper was said to improve with altitude as he became increasingly hypoxic. According to Greene: 'Above 20,000 feet...he became easy to deal with, and quite unquarrelsome.' Smythe was a member of the unsuccessful 1930 international expedition to Kangchenjunga led by Professor Gunter Dyhrenfurth, but succeeded in climbing Jongsong Peak (7,473m/24,510ft). He made his reputation by leading the successful 1931 Kamet expedition (7,700m/25,263ft), the first 25,000ft mountain to be climbed. On the 1933 Everest expedition, Smythe equalled Edward Norton's height record, reaching 8,580m/28,126ft. He was also a member of the 1936 and 1938 Everest expeditions. His feud with Graham Brown continued after the war, and in 1949 Brown sent him a letter as he was organising an expedition to India: 'I hope you perish', it concluded. Smythe was taken ill and died a few days later.

Graham Brown was professor of Physiology at the University of Wales. After being elected a Fellow of the Royal Society at a relatively young age he took no further interest in his subject, and the university spent many years trying to remove him from his post. As well as climbing in the Alps, he visited the Himalaya twice, going to Nanda Devi at the age of 54 on the 1936 Anglo-American expedition with Bill Tilman, Noel Odell and Charles Houston, and to Masherbrum two years later. He reached heights well above 6,100m/20,000ft on both occasions. Brown was a supporter of Colonel Edward Strutt, the great defender of Alpine Club tradition, but clashed with almost everybody else, including the more progressive Geoffrey Winthrop Young, who described him as a vicious lunatic. He was the only editor of the *Alpine Journal* ever to be sacked, because of the vendetta that he waged against certain individuals through its pages and his unbusinesslike methods which led to endless delays in its publication. He retired to his native Scotland where, slightly mellowed by age, he became an active and apparently popular honorary president of the Edinburgh University Mountaineering Club, renting out part of his large and ramshackle flat to a series of young climbers.

The only other notable achievement by a British climber in the Alps during the inter-war years was by Eustace Thomas, who became the first Briton to climb all 83 peaks over 4,000m. Remarkably, he accomplished this in just six years, starting at the age of 54. A contemporary of Owen Glynne Jones at Finsbury Technical College, Thomas moved to Manchester in 1900 and established an engineering company. After setting numerous endurance records for bog-trotting in the Pennines and fell-running in the Lakes, he took up mountaineering and climbed 24 major peaks during his first alpine season, including the Jungfrau, Mönch and Gross Fiescherhorn in a single day.

Apart from these isolated achievements, British climbing became so insular that most climbers were probably not even aware of rising standards in the Alps. The field was left clear for the German and Austrian members of the 'Munich School', the Italians and, increasingly, the French members of the Groupe de Haute Montagne to pursue their 'obsession for the mentally deranged' as Colonel Strutt called their attempts to climb the great North Faces.

In reality, attempts during the 1930s to climb the North Faces of the Matterhorn, Grandes Jorasses and Eiger developed naturally from climbs made before the First World War. The ascent of the East Face of the Monte Rosa, by the Pendlebury brothers in 1872, the West Face of the Matterhorn, climbed by Penhall in 1879, and the East Face of the Grépon, climbed by Young in 1911, all involved significant and unavoidable objective risk. Mummery's attempt on the North Face of the Plan in 1892 and Gertrude Bell's attempt on the North-East Face of the Finsteraarhorn in 1902, a 57 hour epic involving loose rock, stonefall and a retreat in a blizzard, had all the ingredients of a *Nordwand* epic, except that they survived. French alpinists in the 1920s and 30s openly acknowledged their debt to Mummery in defining a style and approach to climbing, which they called *élégant*.

The fundamental difference between British and continental climbers in the 1930s revolved around what constituted justifiable risk. The view of the British establishment (represented by the Alpine Club) was that climbers should follow routes that avoided places where rockfall or avalanches were inevitable. The continental view was summed up by the great Italian climber Ricardo Cassin: 'The perfect line is that taken by a stone dropped from the summit.'[68] Climbers from Italy, Germany, Austria and France increasingly believed that the perfect line must be attempted, taking all precautions but accepting that some risk was inevitable.

These differing approaches to risk did not arise overnight. Together with the British, German students were the other large group of climbers active in the Alps in the late nineteenth and early twentieth century. In 1905 Sir Martin Conway remarked on the crowds of people from the 'lower middle-classes of south-German towns' in the Tirol: 'The activities of the German and Austrian Alpine Clubs have no doubt opened the mountains to a number of persons who otherwise would not have visited them, and who profit greatly by the exercise, the fine air, the noble views, that Nature provides for all alike...But in doing so it has made parts of the country unpleasant to travel in.'[69] Many of the student climbers had read the works of Nietzsche, the great German romantic philosopher, whose cult of the hero and contempt for weakness influenced both public and private life in the country. The German climbing tradition tended to emphasise the 'heroic school', and some climbers adopted an almost fatalistic approach, deliberately choosing to climb solo, in bad weather, at night, or on faces notorious for stonefall. This ethic can be traced from the late nineteenth century to the 1930s, when it was exploited by the Nazis for political purposes, and beyond to Hermann Buhl's writing in the 1950s, which had a profound influence during the renaissance of British alpinism in the post-war years. Early exponents of the purist school, such as Guido Lammer, also rejected the use of artificial aid, believing that as little as possible should come between the climber and the mountain environment. Lammer advocated the removal of all man-made structures above the tree line, including club huts. In this he differed little from many members of the Alpine Club who opposed the vulgarisation of the Alps and wanted to preserve the environment for people like themselves. Where Lammer did differ from the British climbing tradition was in his belief in strength through will, his reckless pursuit of danger and his almost morbid fascination with pain. Ironically, Lammer died of old age, in 1945, at the age of 83.[70]

Inevitably, given the rise of fascism in Germany during the 1930s, the difference of approach became tied up with German and British nationalism. In Britain, outside the Alpine Club and the Scottish Mountaineering Club, both of which had always been small and exclusive, the prevailing attitude of climbers tended to be libertarian, mildly anarchic and anti-establishment. In contrast, the organisation of climbing in Germany and Austria was highly centralised. The German and Austrian Alpine Clubs had thousands of members, organised into regional branches for administrative purposes. The clubs ran training for young members and, unlike in Britain where overt competition was frowned upon, a competitive atmosphere prevailed. Many ex-soldiers felt a sense of humiliation at the post-war settlement and the economic chaos that followed, and the self-styled *Bergkameraden* sought to restore the honour of Germany through increasingly dangerous and heroic feats in the mountains. When the Nazis recognised the propaganda value of climbing exploits and started to provide funding to alpinists, many of whom were very poor, they found that it was easy to co-opt the climbing community to the cause of German nationalism. Paul Bauer, prime mover behind the German Kangchenjunga expeditions in 1929 and 1931, was typical of his generation. Inspired by a fierce romantic nationalism, he described the members of the 1929 expedition as being 'filled with unquenchable pride in their own invincible courage...Like some desperate band they held the lists for Germany, which at that time was lightly valued even at home... They were a band pledged together for life or death...proud, determined, self-confident men, united in fanatical devotion.'[71] When Hitler became Chancellor of Germany in 1933 Bauer was put in charge of the Hiking, Mountaineering and Camping section of the new German Reich League for Physical Exercises, and the German Alpine Club soon fell into line with National Socialist doctrine.

In Italy, the link between climbing and militarism was even more explicit, reflecting the fact that all its land boundaries are protected by mountains. The *Revista del Centro Alpinisto Italiano* included the following paean to the cult of danger: 'A climber has fallen. Let a hundred others arise for the morrow. Let other youths strew edelweiss and alpenrose upon the body of the fallen comrade; and lay it with trembling emotion face upturned under the soft turf. Then up, once more to the assault of the rocks and of the summit, to commemorate the fallen one in the highest and most difficult of victories! The medal for valour in sport, the highest distinction accorded by the Duce to exceptional athletes who break world records or are victors in international contests, will be awarded to climbers who vanquish mountains by new ascents of the sixth standard. All Italians ought to know how to live in mountainous country. All our wars will always take place in the mountains, and the cult of mountaineering passionately pursued, and spreading more and more among our young men, will contribute to the military preparedness of the young generation.'[72]

The practice of using climbing as a propaganda tool for totalitarian regimes continued long after the war. The Chinese celebrated their first ascent of Everest in 1960 with an analysis of the reasons for their success: 'Summing up our conquest on Everest, we must in the first place attribute our victory to the leadership of the communist party and the unrivalled superiority of the socialist system of our country... The victory is also due to the fact that we followed the strategic thinking of Mao Tze-Tung, that is to scorn difficulties strategically, while paying full attention to them tactically.'[73]

Most British climbers were scornful of this competitive, nationalistic approach, conveniently forgetting that competition and jingoism had long been a feature of British climbing. Meanwhile, the real reason for the relative decline in British alpine climbing standards was isolation. While leading British climbers concentrated on the greater ranges on the fringes of the British Empire, an extraordinary increase in standards was taking place in Europe, particularly in the Eastern Alps and, apart from the growing nationalism and militarism, there was much to admire. The German and Austrian Alpine Clubs welcomed climbers from all social backgrounds, and the sheer number of active climbers, combined with a willingness to innovate with new equipment and techniques, ensured that standards rose. The karabiner, the ice peg, modern crampons and fixed ropes were all invented by German and Austrian climbers in the Eastern Alps. As the French climber Lucien Devies observed: 'The capital of the mountaineering world has shifted from London to Munich, where youth is ambitious and innovation encouraged.'[74] This news was not welcomed at the headquarters of the Alpine Club in Mayfair.

The Schmidt brothers' ascent of the North Face of the Matterhorn in 1931, undertaken after cycling to Zermatt from their home in Munich, set a new standard for boldness and commitment. It also attracted unprecedented media attention because of the familiarity of the peak and the notoriety of its first ascent. For the first time the mass media around Europe started to take an interest in events in the Alps, and some climbers began to see publicity as a means of attracting celebrity and money. All of this was, of course, anathema to the British climbing establishment. Just 10 years earlier Arthur Hinks, the honorary secretary of the Everest Committee, had proudly recorded that 'the [first Everest] expedition has got away without any interviews and photographs in the press, which so often discredits the start.'[75] No doubt he would have shuddered at the steps taken by future British Everest expeditions to court the media.

The Croz Spur of the Grandes Jorasses was climbed by two Germans, Peters and Maier, in 1935. The Walker Spur was climbed by the Italians Cassin, Esposito and Tizzoni in 1938. The North Face of the Eiger finally fell to two Germans, Heckmair and Vorg, and two Austrians, Harrer and Kasparek, in 1938. 'We, the sons of the older Reich, united with our countrymen of the Eastern Border to march together in victory',[76] as Heckmair put it at the time, although he later denied being a Nazi sympathiser.

Before their final success, Colonel Strutt, then president of the Alpine Club, had observed that 'the Eigerwand – still unscaled – continues to be an obsession for the mentally-deranged of almost every nation. He who first succeeds may rest assured that he has accomplished the most imbecile variant since mountaineering first began.'[77] The 1938 route must have a claim to being the greatest mountaineering route of all time. The rock architecture of this huge face is instantly recognisable. The route is hard throughout, but follows the easiest line up the face, weaving its way between even greater difficulties. As the pioneers found to their cost, escape is difficult. The position, overlooking the green meadows of the Kleine Scheidegg, is extraordinary and the history of the route unsurpassed. It has been the ambition and inspiration of generations of climbers. To describe it as 'an imbecile variant' shows just how far out of touch the British had become.

Edward Strutt came from a Derbyshire family of cotton spinners who had collaborated with Arkwright at the start of the industrial revolution. His grandfather was created Lord Belper in 1856. His father died when he was a child. After being educated at the universities of Innsbruck and Oxford, he joined the army and served in the Boer War and throughout the First World War, receiving numerous decorations. In 1918 he rescued the Austrian royal family from a revolutionary mob and conducted them to safety in Switzerland. Whenever the train stopped he mounted guard on one side of the carriage with his revolver drawn, while his batman stood with a rifle on the other. Strutt was second-in-command of the 1922 Everest expedition, editor of the *Alpine Journal* from 1927 to 1937 and president of the Alpine Club from 1935 to 1937. He was a brave and decent man, but in fighting a stubborn rearguard action against crampons, pitons, oxygen, ski-mountaineering and any other innovation since the end of the nineteenth century he 'probably did more than any other man to convince the advance guard of Continental climbers that the Alpine Club was hopelessly out of touch',[78] and under his editorship the *Alpine Journal* 'too often appeared in the role of a shocked and censorious aunt'.[79]

Opposition to the more conservative elements in the Alpine Club was in the hands of a younger generation of climbers led by Douglas Busk, Jack Longland and Frank Smythe, with covert support from Geoffrey Winthrop Young who thrived on intrigue. This rebel group called themselves the 'Young Shavers', in contrast to their bearded elders. The fashion for beards appears to have re-emerged as a result of the Crimean War (1853–56), during the course of which even officers and gentlemen found it inconvenient to shave every day. The war coincided with the Golden Age of mountaineering, and amongst ex-climbers of a certain age the fashion persisted into the 1930s. Colonel Strutt was invited to join a meeting of the Young Shavers in a pub near the Alpine Club. Douglas Busk recalled that 'he was flattered by the invitation to share a new outlook and surroundings, however essentially repugnant they remained to him'.[80]

Ironically, Strutt's views were both behind and ahead of their time. While he undoubtedly saw himself as upholding the traditions of the past, many of his views on artificial aid and climbing ethics would not be out of place in Britain today. What he failed to understand was that young ambitious climbers, confronted with an unclimbed face, will use any means at their disposal to overcome the challenge. For the sport to progress, it had to pass through an 'Iron Age' of pitons and artificial aid before there could be a return to purer ethics in the late twentieth century.

The first Winter Olympic Games, which took place in Chamonix in 1924, included medals for achievement in mountaineering. Given his views on competition and nationalism in climbing, Strutt must have felt some qualms as he collected the Olympic gold medal in recognition of the achievements of the 1922 Everest expedition, of which he was climbing leader. In 1932 the gold medal went to the Schmidt brothers for their ascent of the North Face of the Matterhorn. The 1936 medal was awarded to Professor Gunter Dyhrenfurth for his 1930 expedition to Kangchenjunga and explorations of the Baltoro region in 1934. The practice of awarding medals for climbing was dropped by the Olympic Committee after the overtly nationalistic 1936 Berlin Olympics. The Winter Olympics built upon the success of the international ski championships, the first of which was also held in Chamonix in 1908, and the popularity of other winter sports that grew in parallel with the development of alpine resorts as sanatoria for people suffering from respiratory diseases. Strongly encouraged by the alpine tourist industry as a means of extending the holiday season, winter sports soon became the main source of income for many hoteliers and mountain guides as the popularity of guideless climbing increased. To a far greater extent than climbing, the development of winter sports as a mass activity has had a profound impact on the mountain landscape, particularly since the Second World War, as ski lifts, lodges and bulldozed ski runs have increasingly disfigured any valley with reasonable terrain and reliable snow conditions.

THE GREATER RANGES

As interest in Himalayan exploration started to rekindle in the years following the First World War, attention inevitably turned to Everest. In his 1920 presidential address to the Royal Geographical Society, Francis Younghusband gave his full support: 'If I am asked, "What is the use of climbing this highest mountain?" I reply, "No use at all." It will not put a pound in anybody's pocket. It will take a good many pounds out of people's pockets...But if there is no use, there is unquestionably much *good* in climbing Mount Everest. The accomplishment of such a feat will elevate the human spirit.'[81] From the start, climbing Everest was far more than a sporting enterprise. As a semi-official project, with the support of the Royal Geographical Society, the Alpine Club and the India Office, it rapidly became a question of national prestige. It was entirely fitting that the successful conclusion of the 32 year campaign should coincide with the coronation of Queen Elizabeth II in 1953, but perhaps unfortunate that a Briton did not actually reach the summit until 1975, more than half a century after the first attempt.

Lieutenant-Colonel Sir Francis Younghusband was a soldier, spy and imperial adventurer who once held the world record for the 300 yard dash. In 1887 he travelled from Peking across the Gobi Desert to the edge of the Tien Shan mountains, passed through Kashgar and made the first crossing of the Muztagh Pass, near K2, to reach Askoli in Baltistan. The journey took 20 months. Always an active promoter of the 'Great Game', some five years later in 1904 he succeeded, in conspiracy with Lord Curzon, the Viceroy of India, in converting an irrelevant border incident into a brutal invasion of Tibet in order to avert an imaginary Russian threat. It was, perhaps, the last great imperial adventure and was very badly received by the authorities in London, still smarting from the humiliation of the Boer War and fearful of antagonising Russia. British troops were soon withdrawn from Tibet and the Chinese quietly reasserted suzerainty over the territory.

Younghusband combined fervent nationalism (the music for 'Jerusalem' was written as the anthem for his Fight for Right movement during the First World War) with bizarre mysticism, including a belief in the existence of an extra-terrestrial unisex leader who lived on the Planet Altair. He was also profoundly influenced by the Hindu and Buddhist tradition of sacred mountains. He saw the ascent of Everest both as an extension of the Great Game, involving personal adventure and national prestige in a romantic setting, and as an almost sacred quest. 'I sometimes think of this expedition as a fraud from beginning to end', wrote George Mallory in 1921. 'Invented by the wild enthusiasm of one man, Younghusband; puffed up by the would-be wisdom of certain pundits in the AC; and imposed upon the youthful ardour of your humble servant.'[82]

In 1920 a joint committee was set up by the Royal Geographical Society and the Alpine Club with the aim of climbing Everest. From the outset there was bitter rivalry between the two institutions, but it was agreed that there should first be a reconnaissance expedition to determine the approaches to the mountain, about which nothing was known, followed the next year by a determined effort to climb it. As the richer and more senior of the two partners in the enterprise, the Royal Geographical Society appointed the honorary secretary: the academically brilliant but acerbic Arthur Hinks, who ruled the Everest Committee until 1945 and was disliked by everyone. John Farrar, the president of the Alpine Club, offended the Royal Geographical Society by proposing that the great Swiss cartographer and climber Marcel Kurz should accompany the expedition. The suggestion was flatly rejected. When Freshfield, an active member and future president of the Royal Geographical Society, proposed Alexander Kellas as leader of the expedition, Farrar naturally dismissed the idea saying that he had 'only walked about on steep snow with a lot of coolies, and the only time they got on a very steep place they all tumbled down and ought to have been killed!'[83] In the end General Charles Bruce was chosen as a compromise leader.

The fourteenth child of Lord Aberdare, the great south Wales coal owner and former president of the Royal Geographical Society, Charlie 'Bruiser' Bruce was commissioned to the 5th Gurkha Rifles in 1889. He trained his Gurkha troops in mountain warfare and they acquitted themselves with distinction in numerous border wars on the North-West Frontier as well as accompanying a number of climbing expeditions. As a young officer, Bruce joined Conway's Karakoram expedition in 1892. He was with Younghusband in Chitral in 1893 (where they discussed the ascent of Everest together on the polo field) and with Mummery, Collie and Hastings on Nanga Parbat in 1895 (although he left early as a result of contracting mumps). In 1898 he joined Longstaff and Mumm in the Nanda Devi area, when Longstaff climbed Trisul and they reconnoitred Kamet.

Bruce was respected by his Gurkha troops for his wrestling, his prowess at drinking and his ability to tell bawdy stories in several local dialects. He could also swear continuously for minutes on end in English without repeating himself, an accomplishment which had Tom Longstaff 'transfixed with envy'.[84] The British establishment in India admired him for his understanding of the 'native mind', and he appears to have had a particularly marked predilection for female 'natives'. During the First World War he commanded the Gurkhas at Gallipoli, where their extraordinary bravery and loyalty was such that when Bruce was seriously wounded and evacuated, the Staff believed that the brigade had suffered a loss equivalent to a battalion.

Bruce's other duties prevented him from taking over leadership of the Everest campaign immediately. In his absence, Lieutenant-Colonel Charles Howard-Bury DSO, an Anglo-Irish landowner, war hero and big game hunter, who had never climbed a mountain, was selected to lead the reconnaissance expedition. Educated at Eton and

Sandhurst, Howard-Bury's family had owned an estate in the Austrian Tirol before the First World War, where he went chamois hunting as a young man. As the writer of his obituary in the *Alpine Journal* politely noted: 'If, therefore, he was not a mountaineer in the strict sense, he had the feel of the mountains in him from an early age.'[85] During one of his many hunting trips, Howard-Bury captured a small bear in Kazakhstan in 1913 and took it back to his estate in Ireland. The bear grew to be over seven foot tall and wrestling with it was said to be his favourite pastime. After the expedition, he became a Tory member of parliament and lived with Rex Beaumont, an actor, who inherited the estate in Ireland when Howard-Bury died.

Harold Raeburn, the distinguished but, at 54, rather old Scottish mountaineer, was chosen as climbing leader of a team consisting of Alexander Kellas, George Mallory and Guy Bullock. The India Office eventually deigned to support the expedition, and at their request the government of Tibet issued a permit. Younghusband wrote to the Dalai Lama to thank him. Presumably his letter made no reference to his invasion of Tibet some 18 years earlier. The Indian Survey seconded two experienced mountaineers, Major Henry Morshead and Major Oliver Wheeler. Alexander Wollaston, the doctor, was also a climber. Each member of the team was given just £50 towards their personal equipment and clothing. As a consequence, the expedition looked 'like a picnic party in Connemara surprised by a snowstorm',[86] as George Bernard Shaw observed. Kellas died of a heart attack during the approach march and Raeburn also became seriously ill and was sent back to India. As a result George Mallory took over as climbing leader.

Mallory was a well-known figure in the climbing community, having been an active participant in Geoffrey Winthrop Young's Pen-y-Pass gatherings since before the war. Born in Cheshire, the son of a reasonably prosperous rector, Mallory was educated at Winchester and Cambridge. Together with Guy Bullock, who also joined the 1921 expedition, he was introduced to alpine climbing by R. L. G. Irving, a teacher at Winchester who later became a noted mountain historian. He started climbing in Britain in 1906 while he was still at Cambridge.

During and after his time at Cambridge, Mallory was on the fringes of the Bloomsbury set, a loose group of intellectual friends and relations including Sir Leslie Stephen's two daughters Virginia Woolf and Vanessa Bell, Lytton Strachey, Aldous Huxley, John Maynard Keynes, Duncan Grant, E. M. Forster and others. Several of the male members of the group were homosexual and admired George Mallory, as Geoffrey Winthrop Young did, for his exceptional physical beauty. The character of 'George' in *A Room with a View*, published by Forster in 1908 – a healthy, muscular Fabian with a taste for the outdoors and nude bathing – was probably based on Mallory. Lytton Strachey was also an admirer: 'Mon dieu! – George Mallory! – When that's been written, what more need be said? My hand trembles, my heart palpitates, my whole being swoons away at the words...desire was lost in wonder...For the rest he's going to be a schoolmaster, and his intelligence is not remarkable. What's the need?'[87]

Mallory was happy to accept the admiration. He posed for a series of nude photographs taken by Duncan Grant, and a picture taken on the walk in to Everest in 1922 also shows him naked apart from a small rucksack and a trilby hat. As Strachey foretold, Mallory became a teacher at Charterhouse, where he introduced the poet Robert Graves to climbing. He served as a gunner during the First World War and returned to Charterhouse in 1919. But his association with the glittering world of the Bloomsbury set and the Pen-y-Pass gatherings made him discontented with life as a school teacher.

Under Young's influence, Mallory became a committed mountain romantic. In an essay entitled 'The Mountaineer as Artist', published in the *Climbers' Club Journal* in March 1914, Mallory endeavoured to answer the question: 'To what part of the artistic sense of man does mountaineering belong? To the part that causes him to be moved by music or painting, or to the part that makes him enjoy a game?' His answer summarised the aesthetic school's creed of mountaineering: 'It seemed perfectly natural to compare a day in the Alps with a symphony.

For mountaineers of my sort mountaineering is rightfully so comparable; but no sportsman could or would make the same claim for cricket or hunting, or whatever his particular sport might be. He recognises the existence of the sublime in great Art, and knows, even if he cannot feel, that its manner of stirring the heart is altogether different and vaster. But mountaineers do not admit this difference in the emotional plane of mountaineering and Art. They claim that something sublime is the essence of mountaineering. They can compare the call of the hills to the melody of wonderful music, and the comparison is not ridiculous.' Geoffrey Winthrop Young called Mallory 'Galahad'. He was the perfect choice to undertake the quest to climb Mount Everest.

The success of the 1921 reconnaissance expedition in finding an apparently feasible route to the summit via the North Col owed much to Mallory's dogged determination and persistence, despite initially overlooking the crucial entrance to the East Rongbuk Glacier and, characteristically, failing to take numerous critical photographs because he inserted the film plates the wrong way round.

Mallory and Morshead returned in 1922 together with 13 other climbers led by General Bruce, with Colonel Strutt as climbing leader. The party included Tom Longstaff; Major Edward Norton, the grandson of Alfred Wills; Major Geoffrey Bruce, the general's nephew; Captain John Noel; the experienced Australian climber George Finch, who had been excluded from the previous expedition on medical grounds; and Dr Howard Somervell, a London surgeon with a double first from Cambridge, who was a talented artist and musician as well as being a very strong climber. Bruce described Somervell as 'a wonderful goer and climber. He takes a size 22 hat. That is his only drawback.'[88] The expedition took oxygen equipment, despite opposition from some members of the team on both ethical and practical grounds.

Captain John Noel described the military siege tactics adopted by General Bruce, which provided the blueprint for major Himalayan expeditions for the next half century: 'Each advance, each depot built, must be considered as ground won from the mountain. It must be consolidated and held, and no man must ever abandon an inch of ground won, or turn his back on the mountain once he has started the attack. A retreat has a disastrous moral effect.'[89] Although it was referred to as the 'Polar method', in reality this was trench warfare translated to the mountains.

On the return from the first attempt on the peak, after reaching 8,168m/26,800ft, Mallory narrowly averted tragedy when Morshead slipped, dragging Somervell and Norton with him. Mallory managed to hold all three on an ice axe belay. The second attempt, by Finch and Geoffrey Bruce, reached 8,321m/27,300ft using oxygen, thereby setting a new height record. As General Bruce remarked, the gas offensive had begun. Astonishingly, Everest was Geoffrey Bruce's first experience of climbing. Although he was a very fit young officer with the Gurkhas, to reach over 8,300m (the previous record was 7,503m/24,615ft set on Chogolisa during the Duke of Abruzzi's K2 expedition in 1909) was an extraordinary achievement, particularly given the lack of knowledge of the effects of altitude. On the summit attempt their intended meal of Heinz spaghetti in tomato sauce froze solid in the tin, and the party suffered from almost permanent dehydration because their inefficient stoves took too long to melt snow. On the third and final summit attempt, led by Mallory, seven Sherpas were swept away by an avalanche. It was the end of the expedition.

Another expedition followed in 1924 with Major Edward Norton appointed leader after General Bruce suffered a bout of malaria during the approach march. The party included Mallory, who prophetically wrote to Geoffrey Keynes: 'This is going to be more like war than mountaineering. I don't expect to come back.'[90] Howard Somervell, Geoffrey Bruce and John Noel from the 1922 expedition were joined by Bentley Beetham, John de Vere Hazard, Noel Odell and Sandy Irvine.

Harry Kelly, the socialist Mancunian and leading climber of the day, was rejected. Finch was also dropped, despite establishing the height record in 1922 and putting up a difficult route without guides on the North Face of the Dent d'Hérens in 1923. He was deeply unpopular with the climbing establishment, allegedly because of his Australian unorthodoxy: 'Cleans his teeth on 1 February and has a bath the same day if the water is very hot,' wrote General Bruce, 'otherwise puts it off until the next year.'[91] However, the real problem was not his personal hygiene, but rather that he was too clever and too outspoken. Although born in Australia, he was educated at the Ecole de Médicine in Paris, the Eidgenossische Technische Hochschule in Zurich and the University of Geneva, and went on to become Professor of Applied Physical Chemistry at Imperial College, London, and a Fellow of the Royal Society. John Farrar, the Alpine Club representative on the Everest Committee, was a supporter (perhaps because he too had received a technical education in Germany and Switzerland), but for his fellow climbers, brought up in the English public school, classical tradition, his rigorous, scientific approach and strong opinions were anathema. Unlike some of the British members of the party, Finch was also extremely fit, regarded people who climbed with guides in the Alps with contempt and, after studying the question in detail, was convinced that Everest would not be climbed without supplementary oxygen. He appears to have been blissfully unaware of how unpopular his dogmatic approach was with the other members of the party. In his book *The Making of a Mountaineer* he describes the oxygen drills that he insisted upon as being 'deservedly popular, being held, as a rule, each evening at the end of a long day's walk, when everybody was feeling particularly fit and vigorous'. A poem composed by another member of the party suggests otherwise:

> *But Hark? What is that? It's six bells without doubt*
> *And soon all our holiday's gone up the spout,*
> *For whether we're resting, or reading or ill*
> *We're ruthlessly summoned to Oxygen Drill.*

> *Have you theories precise on the subject of gas?*
> *Respiration, and so on and action in mass? –*
> *The exactest of thought will appear rude and boorish*
> *Compared with the latest in science from Zurich.*

Do you think you know about altitudes high,
And what kind of glass keeps the sun from your eye?
On such questions your ignorance really is crass,
But you'll soon be made wise when George Finch starts to gas.[92]

Finch was rejected for the 1924 expedition even though it was acknowledged that he was the strongest climber on Everest in 1922. This approach, of selecting people based on their social background and manners rather than their climbing ability, was to dog British expeditions to Everest until the 1970s, and throughout the history of the sport people at both ends of the social spectrum have used 'the ability to get on with the team' as a justification for exercising their personal prejudices.

The 1924 expedition started off with a series of near-disasters, but a top camp was eventually established at 8,169m/26,800ft, from which Norton and Somervell made a determined bid for the summit without using oxygen. Somervell had to turn back and nearly died when his frostbitten larynx choked him. Norton reached 8,580m/28,126ft, but also turned back when it was clear that he could not reach the summit and return safely. The new height record was not exceeded for 30 years and remained the highest point reached without oxygen until 1978. Norton retired from climbing after the expedition, eventually becoming military governor of Hong Kong. Somervell devoted much of the rest of his life to treating the poor in India.

Mallory and Irvine made a second attempt using oxygen. Noel Odell reported seeing them ascending one of the major steps on the ridge and going strongly for the top before the clouds rolled in and obscured his view. They were not seen again. Odell returned to the highest camp to see whether there was any trace of them. 'I glanced at the mighty summit above me...It seemed to look down with cold indifference...and howl derision in wind-gust at my petition to yield up its secret – this mystery of my friends...There seemed to be something alluring in that towering presence. I was almost fascinated. I realized that...he who approaches close must ever be led on, and oblivious of all obstacles seek to reach that sacred and highest place of all. It seems that my friends must have been enchanted also.'[93]

Sir Francis Younghusband, with characteristic zeal, wrote: 'Of the two alternatives, to turn back...or to die, the latter was for Mallory probably easier. The agony of the first would be more than he as a man, as a mountaineer, and as an artist, could endure.'[94] Mallory's choice of Irvine rather than the more experienced Odell as his companion for the summit bid has been endlessly debated. Duncan Grant, a member of the Bloomsbury set, suggested that Mallory chose the handsome young Oxford rowing blue purely on aesthetic grounds. A more prosaic explanation is that Mallory, who was notoriously inept with mechanical equipment, needed Irvine to ensure that the oxygen equipment functioned. Or perhaps Mallory chose Irvine precisely because he was young and inexperienced. Had Odell reached the summit with him, the glory would have been more evenly divided.

Mallory's body was found in 1999 at 8,155m/26,750ft on the North Face of Everest. Two cameras that he had apparently carried with him were not discovered. Nor was a photograph of his wife, which he had intended to leave on the summit. His snow goggles were in his pocket, suggesting that it was dark when he died. In all probability he did not reach the summit. The second step at 8,600m/28,200ft is graded V and was not free climbed until 1985. Nevertheless, in the manner of his death, enveloped by clouds with his handsome young companion, going for the top of the highest mountain on earth, Mallory became the quintessential romantic hero. The expedition had an almost redemptive quality about it. After the mechanised mass slaughter of the First World War, the deaths of Mallory and Irvine restored the idea that the British were capable of individual, noble acts of heroism. The fact that their bodies were not recovered had a particular poignancy for the many parents who had lost their sons in the trenches. In sharp contrast to its criticism of the Matterhorn accident some 60 years earlier, *The Times* called Mallory and Irvine 'the glorious dead', and Everest became 'the finest cenotaph in the world'.

But was Mallory a hero? Not according to Chris Bonington: 'It is crass nonsense to say that Mallory's attempt was noble! He was utterly and completely selfish!'[95] After the first expedition Mallory was certainly not motivated by the aesthetic appeal of the mountain. He described Everest as 'an infernal mountain, cold and treacherous...It sounds more like war than sport – and perhaps it is.'[96] But he knew very well the transformation that success on Everest would make to his life as a school teacher, and for that chance of fame and glory he was pre-pared to leave behind a wife, who had already suffered the enforced sep-aration of the First World War, and three young children. For George Mallory, Everest had become an obsession.

Captain John Noel was also obsessed by the mountain. In 1913 he made an illegal journey in disguise to Tibet, getting to within 40 miles of Everest before having to turn back after a skirmish with Tibetan troops. Returning to his regiment in Calcutta, he was two months over-due. When his colonel demanded an explanation, Noel told him that he had lost his calendar during a river crossing. The Colonel advised him to take two calendars on future trips.

Noel was attached to the 1922 expedition as official photographer, and in 1924 he purchased the film rights for the huge sum of £8,000, which effectively paid for the expedition. Despite the use of the most modern camera technology, including long distance shots of climbers through a telephoto lens, much of the film consisted of a rather dull travelogue through Tibet and men with beards standing around in base camp. Without the culmination of a successful ascent, turning it into a commercial success was always going to be a challenge. Perhaps inspired by Albert Smith, the great Victorian mountain showman, Noel decided to import a troupe of Tibetan lamas to liven up performances of the film by conducting religious rites and dances, accompanied by cym-bals and horns. The Dalai Lama and the Indian Office were sufficiently incensed by this that an expedition planned for 1926 was banned from entering Tibet. Meanwhile, Noel's film company went bankrupt, leav-ing the lamas stranded with no money in Ceylon on their way back to

Tibet. An interlude of nine years followed before the assault on Everest could be resumed.

The successful ascent of Kamet (7,756m/25,447ft) by a British party in 1931 – at that time the highest mountain climbed – compensated for the lack of achievement on Everest and in the Alps. The expedition was led by Frank Smythe and included Eric Shipton. It represented the culmination of a long campaign. Tom Longstaff explored the approaches in 1907; Charles Meade was there in 1910, 1912 and 1913, reaching 7,138m/23,420ft; and Kellas also attempted the peak in 1911 and 1914. Describing his team selection, Smythe wrote: 'The ideal team is one that includes different interests, paradoxical though this may sound...I cannot conceive of a team of mountaineers composed exclusively of doctors, barristers, or politicians.'[97] No doubt, a team composed exclusively of Manchester plumbers would have been even more inconceivable, but Smythe was himself a victim of class prejudice when his obvious qualifications to lead the 1933 Everest expedition were overlooked because of his criticism of the Everest Committee in the 1920s and his professionalism. The objection was not that he made money from writing about his mountaineering experiences – many members of the climbing establishment now did that – Smythe's sin was that he relied upon those earnings for his livelihood. In the end, to everyone's amazement including his own, the Everest Committee selected Hugh Ruttledge, a 48-year-old who had travelled extensively in the Himalaya with his wife and had a pronounced limp from a pig-sticking accident.

Permission to mount the 1933 Everest expedition was granted by the Dalai Lama after discreet pressure from the Indian Office, reflecting concerns that the Germans, who had already mounted expeditions to Kangchenjunga and Nanga Parbat, might stake a claim on Everest. The Dalai Lama's permission included a codicil that all members of the expedition must be British, which was almost certainly inserted by the British political officer in Lhasa. After a gap of nine years, most of the climbers with previous Everest experience were

16. Colin Kirkus, c1934. A Liverpool insurance clerk, Kirkus was the best British rock climber in the early 1930s, but some members of the establishment considered him to be 'just a little boring, too quiet and rather lacking in conversation' and he was not invited to Everest.

(Wayfarers' Club Archive)

17. Geoffrey Winthrop Young, 1934. Climber, poet, educationalist and 'athletic aesthete', Young lost a leg in the First World War but continued to play an active role in the climbing world, including campaigning for the formation of the British Mountaineering Council in 1944.

(Alpine Club)

18. Eric Shipton, Everest expedition, 1935. Shipton was a mountain romantic who was involved in every Everest expedition from 1933 to 1951. He was unceremoniously sacked as leader of the 1953 expedition for failing to recognise that success had become a matter of national prestige.

(Royal Geographical Society)

19. Bill Tilman, Everest expedition, 1935. Soldier, explorer, mountaineer and sailor, Tilman was utterly self-reliant, taciturn, intolerant and perhaps the funniest mountain writer of all time.

(Royal Geographical Society)

20. Frank Smythe on the summit of Mount Hardesty, Canadian Rockies, mid-1940s. Climber and prolific popular writer: 'Physically on the mountains, intellectually in his books, Frank always tried to reach heights which were just a little beyond his powers, great though those were.'

(Alpine Club)

21. Joe Brown making the first ascent of The Right Unconquerable on Stanage, April 1949. In the late 1940s rumours started to circulate about a young Manchester builder who climbed routes with apparent ease that had defeated generations of climbers. Brown was climbing's supreme craftsman, instinctively seeing the best way to move on steep rock.

(Ernest Phillips/ Gordon Stainforth)

22. John Streetly on the first ascent of Bloody Slab, Clogwyn du'r Arddu, 10 June 1952. '...it is difficult to recall how the next thirty feet were managed at all...the previous move being apparently impossible to reverse, left no alternative but to go on...' Streetly's companions were unable to follow him so he unroped and climbed solo to the top.

(Wrangham family/Gordon Stainforth)

23. John Hunt and Geoffrey Winthrop Young, 1953. Young lived long enough to see Hunt lead the ascent of Everest in 1953. A proudly nationalistic project, it was fitting that news of the success coincided with the coronation of Queen Elizabeth II, but unfortunate that British climbers did not reach the summit for another 22 years.

(Alpine Club)

24. Members of the Rock and Ice Club in Chamonix, 1954.
(Left to right) Back row: unknown, Ray Greenall, Don Whillans.
Sitting: Joe Brown, Fred Ashton, Nat Allen, Ron Moseley.

In the 1950s members of the Rock and Ice raised British alpine standards to the same level as those of continental climbers for the first time since 1914.

(Alpine Club)

25. (Opposite) Rusty Baillie leading Cenotaph Corner, Dinas Cromlech, Llanberis Pass, 1965.
First climbed in 1952, like many Brown and Whillans routes Cenotaph Corner retained an aura of difficulty long after its technical standard had been surpassed.

(John Cleare)

26. Robin Smith, c1958.
Philosophy graduate and hell-raiser, Smith was the most promising of his generation of Scottish climbers. He died in the Pamirs at the age of 24.

(Jimmy Marshall)

27. (Left to right) Don Whillans, Les Brown, Robin Smith, Gunn Clarke and John Streetly in Courmayeur after climbing the Walker Spur, 1959.
Smith and Clarke made the first British ascent. Whillans, Brown, Streetly and Hamish MacInnes climbed the same route one day later. As Whillans remarked: 'If I'd known, I wouldn't have bothered.'

(Hamish MacInnes)

28. Dougal Haston, 1967. An enigmatic mixture of self-indulgence and impenetrable asceticism. Like many youth icons of the 1960s, part of the attraction of Haston was that he seemed destined for an early grave.

(John Cleare)

29. Don Whillans on Heptonstall Moor, 1972.
With his flat cap, frequent fights, slow Lancashire drawl and direct, uncompromising stare, Whillans was the definitive hard man.

(John Cleare)

too old and a number of proficient young climbers had emerged in Britain, but the Everest Committee was still dominated by men such as Norman Collie, Tom Longstaff and Francis Younghusband whose outlook was firmly rooted in the past. Not being a climber himself, Ruttledge knew almost no-one in the climbing community, but this did not prevent him from holding strong views on team selection: 'I am coming more and more to the opinion that we must beware of the north British school of rock-climbers if we are to succeed on Everest. Individually they are probably good men, but they are a close corporation, with, it seems to me, a contempt for every one outside their own clan.' Ruttledge duly failed to select Colin Kirkus, Maurice Linnell or Alf Bridge, each of whom appeared to be well qualified.

The core of the team was formed from the successful Kamet expedition, including Shipton and Smythe, and the rest of the party consisted of army officers and ex-Cambridge University climbers, including Percy Wyn Harris, Jack Longland and Lawrence Wager. Wyn Harris and Wager made the first attempt on the summit, equalling Norton's height record and discovering an ice axe that was long believed to be Mallory's, but was probably Irvine's. Smythe and Shipton made a second attempt, with Smythe reaching roughly the same height as Wyn Harris and Wager, but both had been too high for too long and had to give up.

The 1933 expedition helped to shape Eric Shipton's dislike for large scale expeditions: 'In violent contrast to the simplicity of this ancient land came our massive caravan of 350 pack-animals carrying all the civilised amenities thought necessary for our welfare. Among the more unlikely items of equipment was a set of boxing gloves used for the promotion of bouts between various members of our retinue.'[98] Shipton was born in Ceylon in 1906. His father died when he was three, and his stepfather was killed during the First World War when he was ten. He was educated in England and climbed in the Alps as a young man, meeting several leading climbers including Nea Barnard (later Morin), Harry Kelly, Jack Longland and Graham Macphee. In 1928 he moved to Kenya as a coffee grower. He climbed Nelion, a peak of Mount Kenya, by the 'normal' route (IV-) in 1929 with Percy Wyn Harris, who was then a district commissioner. A year later he traversed the mountain, climbing the West Ridge (V-) and descending by the normal route, with Bill Tilman, who had moved to Kenya after the war. It was their first climb together and the start of a remarkable partnership.

Major Harold William Tilman CBE, DSO, MC and Bar[99] was nine years older than Shipton. Soldier, explorer, mountaineer and sailor, he was also perhaps the funniest and most self-deprecating of all mountain writers. The son of a prosperous sugar merchant, he was educated at Berkhamsted School and volunteered for the army at the age of 17. He spent his 18th birthday in 1916 in a dug-out on the Somme. He fought throughout the First World War, leading one of the first artillery units to cross into Germany in 1918. Thirty years later, he wrote 'after the war, when one took stock, shame mingled with satisfaction at finding oneself alive. One felt a bit like the Ancient Mariner; so many better men, a few of them friends, were dead: "And a thousand thousand slimy things lived on; and so did I".'[100]

The war made Tilman self-reliant, taciturn and intolerant of whiners and malingerers. He was fond of quoting Frederick the Great, who said 'the more I see of humanity, the more I love my dog', and once said, only partly in jest, that 'there is a good case for dropping bombs on civilians because so very few of them can be described as inoffensive'.[101] In contrast, Shipton, who had been too young to fight in the war, was mercurial, talkative and gregarious. It is tempting to think that in Shipton, Tilman saw something of his lost youth, while for Shipton, Tilman was an unlikely father figure.

In 1931 Shipton joined the successful Kamet expedition, and in 1933 he was invited to join Ruttledge's Everest expedition. Meanwhile, Tilman sold his farm in Kenya and, after spending some time prospecting for gold, bought a bicycle for £6 and cycled 3,000 miles across Africa, passing through Uganda, the Belgian Congo and French Cameroon, in order to catch a ship to England. When he got back he wrote to the manufacturer of the bicycle hoping that they would reward his unsolicited testimonial by giving him a new bike. However, 'they managed to contain their enthusiasm within due bounds...all I received was a kind little note expressing the pleasure it gave the firm to hear of what had been no doubt an agreeable and satisfactory journey'.[102]

Back in England for the first time since the war, Tilman contacted Shipton and proposed a fortnight's holiday in the Lake District. Shipton suggested a seven month exploratory climbing expedition to the Himalaya instead, and Tilman readily agreed. They went to the Garhwal, an area previously explored by Graham and Longstaff, and succeeded in finding a route through the Rishi Ganga Gorge to the Nanda Devi sanctuary. It was a famously frugal expedition, during which they were even forced to share a pipe after Tilman dropped his into the gorge. Shipton recalled that 'as we had done in Africa, we continued to address one another as "Tilman" and "Shipton"; and when, after seven months continuously together I suggested it was time he called me "Eric", he became acutely embarrassed, hung his head and muttered, "It sounds so damn silly."'[103]

In 1935, the Everest Committee offered Shipton the leadership of a small reconnaissance expedition to Everest, consisting of six climbers. Somewhat reluctantly, Tilman agreed to join him. 'Though he did not say so, I suspected that the root of the objection was that, while he had been forced to accept the stark necessity of my company, the prospect of having five companions was scarcely tolerable.'[104] Astonishingly, Shipton's contract as leader contained a clause forbidding an attempt on the summit. As Shipton recorded: 'My dislike of massive mountaineering expeditions had become something of an obsession, and I was anxious for the opportunity to demonstrate that, for one tenth of the former cost and with a fraction of the bother and disruption of the local countryside, a party could be placed on the North Col, adequately equipped to make a strong attempt on the summit.'[105] The expedition was a typically Spartan Shipton–Tilman affair, and the other expedition members were reduced to foraging for delicacies left behind by the 1933 expedition. After reaching the North Col, and forbidden to go any further, the team set off on an orgy of peak-bagging, exploring a large area of new country and climbing 26 peaks over 6,100m/20,000ft, at a cost of £1,500.

Had Shipton ignored the clause in his contract and succeeded in climbing Everest in 1935 the future course of Himalayan climbing might have been very different. As it was, he was back on Everest in 1936, this time as part of a large expedition once again led by Ruttledge, including numerous experienced climbers such as Smythe and Wyn Harris. The monsoon arrived early and they failed even to reach the North Col. George Finch, no doubt still harbouring a grudge after being sacked in 1922, wrote a newspaper article criticising the Everest Committee: 'We are beginning to look ridiculous!'[106] he concluded.

Tilman, who had acclimatised badly in 1935, was not included in the 1936 expedition and instead joined Noel Odell (another Everest reject), Graham Brown and a group of American climbers from Harvard, including Charles Houston, on a small and harmonious Anglo-American expedition that succeeded in climbing Nanda Devi (7,816m/25,643ft), the highest peak in the British Empire and the highest in the world to be climbed before the Second World War. When Tilman reached the summit with Odell he recorded that: 'I believe we so far forgot ourselves as to shake hands on it.' Characteristically, his telegram to Tom Longstaff simply recorded that 'two reached the top 29 August'; no names were mentioned. But reaching the summit brought no lasting satisfaction: 'After the first joy in victory came a feeling of sadness that the mountain had succumbed, that the proud head of the goddess was bowed.'[107]

Tilman was particularly pleased that no mechanical aids – oxygen equipment, pitons, crampons or snow shoes – were used. The ages of the participants, from 22 to over 50, and the way in which people from two nations had co-operated was also a source of pride. However, there was one disaster as Charlie Houston recorded: 'When the entire supply of tea fell down a steep snow slope...the Brits were devastated. There was serious talk of going home.'[108] Tilman's success on Nanda Devi also had one further unexpected consequence. It was apparently the inspiration for W. E. Bowman's *The Ascent of*

Rum Doodle, a brilliant parody of early British Himalayan expeditions. Rum Doodle peaks have subsequently appeared on the maps of Antarctica, New Zealand and the United States.

After the disappointment and frustration of another large Everest expedition, Shipton was delighted to set off in 1937 on a lightweight exploratory expedition with Tilman, Michael Spender and John Auden (both of whom were brothers of famous poets). The four month expedition explored a large blank on the map of the Karakoram, but by this stage Tilman's interest lay mainly with climbing, while Shipton was happier exploring.

After his success on Nanda Devi, Tilman was invited to lead the 1938 Everest expedition. He 'took comfort from the thought that, with men like Shipton, Smythe and Odell amongst the party, it would be my part to sit listening with becoming gravity to their words, waking up occasionally to give an approving nod'.[109] Tilman regarded the 1921 reconnaissance expedition and Shipton's lightweight expedition of 1935 as the model, and deliberately planned a small expedition. His determination was reinforced when news arrived of Freddy Spencer Chapman's extraordinary ascent of Chomolhari (7,314m/23,996ft) in 1937.

Spencer Chapman shared many characteristics with Tilman and Shipton. Born in 1907, his mother died shortly after his birth and his father was killed in the battle of the Somme. He was educated at Sedbergh School, where he developed a deep love of wild places, and Cambridge University, where he came under the influence of Geoffrey Winthrop Young. After a season in the Alps in 1928 when he climbed with Jack Longland, he joined Gino Watkins on two Greenland expeditions in 1930 and 1932, during the second of which Watkins was drowned. Following a spell of teaching in Britain, Spencer Chapman joined Marco Pallis on an expedition to Sikkim in 1936, and subsequently travelled to Tibet as private secretary to the British political agent for Sikkim, Bhutan and Tibet. On the return journey he made his remarkable alpine-style ascent of Chomolhari on the border of Tibet and Bhutan, reaching the summit with Sherpa Pasang after seven days of climbing, followed by a desperate retreat lasting five days with almost no food. The climb was accomplished with equipment borrowed from the Himalayan Club and the entire expedition cost him less than £20.

During the Second World War, Spencer Chapman was training the Ski Battalion of the Scots Guards in Chamonix when the Germans invaded France. Transferred to Singapore, he arrived just in time for the Japanese invasion and was parachuted behind enemy lines where he spent three years in the jungle, often alone, attacking Japanese supply lines. After the war, he took various educational jobs in Germany, Britain and South Africa, becoming secretary of the Outward Bound Trust for a time. He wrote seven autobiographical books during his life, of which *The Jungle is Neutral*, an account of his covert war in Malaya, became a bestseller. Increasingly plagued by ill-health, he shot himself in 1971.

Following Spencer Chapman's success on Chomolhari, provisioning on Tilman's 1938 Everest expedition was, if anything, even more frugal than Shipton's 1935 reconnaissance, consisting of 'badly cooked porridge [and] an inferior brand of pemmican',[110] according to Odell. Tilman conceded that 'for a man accustomed to a choice of three or four kinds of marmalade for breakfast it comes as a disagreeable surprise to find none at all'. But he was unrepentant: 'The supply of candles may have been short, but we were not reduced to eating them.'[111] The other members of the team were once again reduced to pillaging supplies left behind by the 1936 expedition in search of rare luxuries such as jam, pickles and liver extract (of which there were several cases).

Tilman reached 8,290m/ 27,200ft without oxygen, but once again the expedition failed to reach the summit. Tilman took comfort from the fact that whilst they had failed, they had at least failed cheaply. In his book *Everest 1938* he wrote: 'Some day, no doubt, someone will have the enviable task of adding the last chapter, in which the mountain is climbed...That book, we may hope, will be the last about Mount Everest.' This was to prove a forlorn hope.

In 1939, the Everest Committee demonstrated its grasp of current affairs by seeking permission for expeditions in 1940, 1941 and

1942. Meanwhile, Tilman explored the remote Assam Himalaya with three Sherpa companions. All four contracted malaria and one of the Sherpas died. Despite having hardly lived in England since he was a schoolboy, Tilman was concerned about travelling at a time when he felt war in Europe was inevitable. 'I was not so abandoned yet as to consider being beyond recall an advantage...Moreover, the War Office, after twenty years of deep thought, had just remembered they had a Reserve of Officers, of which I was one.'[112] Tilman's attitude to the war, like so much else, remains obscure. He apparently had little affection for England, and yet he returned and volunteered again. During the Second World War, Tilman saw action in Dunkirk, Iraq, Persia and in the Western Desert before being parachuted behind enemy lines to fight with partisans in Albania and Italy. His account of the war is punctuated with detailed descriptions of mountain climbs snatched during odd days of leave, which seem strangely irrelevant against the backdrop of the great events unfolding elsewhere. But these days, enjoying the freedom of hills, clearly provided a great comfort to him. In contrast, Shipton was content to become H. M. Consul in Kashgar and to pass the early part of the war in Central Asia, before moving to Persia, where he may have played some role in military intelligence.

Climbing together or separately, Shipton and Tilman had spent almost the whole of the 1930s in the Himalaya and been involved in every expedition to Everest from 1933 to 1938. 'How I hated Tilman in the early morning,' Shipton observed. 'He never slept like an ordinary person. Whatever time we agreed to awake, long before (how long I never knew) he would slide from his sleeping bag and start stirring his silly porridge over the Primus stove. I used gradually to become aware of this irritating noise and would bury my head in silent rage against the preposterous injustice of being wakened half an hour too soon. When his filthy brew was ready he would say "Show a leg", or some such imbecile remark.'[113]

Shipton's involvement with Everest continued after the war, but Tilman, who was nine years older, increasingly turned to the sea, where his reputation for sailing a succession of small Bristol cutters to remote corners of the Arctic and the Antarctic Oceans soon came to rival his reputation as a climber. He disappeared, sailing from Rio de Janeiro to the Falkland Islands, in 1977 at the age of 80.

The Shipton–Tilman partnership represented a return to the light-weight 'alpine-style' expeditions undertaken by Graham, Mummery and Longstaff at the turn of the century, but subsequently abandoned in favour of large, military-style operations. Tilman openly acknowledged the inspiration Longstaff and others had provided: 'Anything beyond what is needed for efficiency and safety is worse than useless. In 1905 Dr Longstaff and the two Brocherel brothers, with no tent and one piece of chocolate, very nearly climbed Gurla Mandhata, 25,355ft high, a practical illustration of the application of that important mountaineering principle, the economy of force – an imperfect example, perhaps, because one might argue that with a tent and two pieces of chocolate they would have succeeded.'[114] Tilman's rule that an expedition that cannot organise itself on a single sheet of notepaper is bound to suffer from the effects of too much organisation, and his 'ideal to be kept in mind...of two or three men carrying their food with them as in the Alps',[115] were largely ignored for the next 30 years, but came to inspire the outstanding generation of British climbers that emerged in the mid-1970s.

6

1939–70: HARD MEN
IN AN AFFLUENT SOCIETY

After the First World War, British climbing standards stagnated for nearly two decades. In contrast, after the Second World War they shot up almost immediately, despite food and petrol rationing. By 1939 the number of people participating in the sport had increased substantially and a lower proportion were killed or wounded during the hostilities than was the case in the First World War. Climbing also continued during the Second World War to a far greater extent than during the earlier conflict as climbers in the armed services visited the hills during periods of leave, and the services themselves trained soldiers to undertake mountain and snow warfare and cliff assaults. Significant advances in clothing and equipment also took place to meet military requirements. As a consequence, when the war finally came to an end, a new generation of climbers was ready to head into the mountains.

In 1943 the Mountain and Snow Warfare School was set up at Braemar in Scotland. Frank Smythe was appointed commandant. Major John Hunt, who later led the successful 1953 Everest expedition, was chief instructor. Perhaps understandably, a distinctly jingoistic tone crept into Smythe's 1942 book *British Mountaineers*, the dust jacket of which observed that 'mountaineering is a sport which makes a particular appeal to our national temperament. It...calls forth the qualities of high courage and daring that are inherent in our race.' Hunt also organised 'toughening up' exercises for an armoured unit of the Kings Royal Rifles at Helyg, the Climbers' Club hut in Snowdonia. The instructors included Alf Bridge and Wilfrid Noyce. A soldier on leave who visited the hut in 1943 noted that 'you are not likely to suffer long from peaceful illusions there for your morning sleep is frequently broken by the irritating spatter of machine guns'.[1]

When the Mountain and Snow Warfare School moved to north Wales, the emphasis shifted to rock climbing and cliff assaults, in preparation for the D-Day landings. The Commandos also started their own cliff assault unit at St Ives in Cornwall, which continued to operate until 1949. The 52nd Division, which had been specially trained in mountain warfare, was finally deployed in 1944 on Walcheren Island in Holland, which lies just slightly below sea level. Many of the instructors in the armed services climbed independently, particularly in the closing months of the war. David Cox and Jock Campbell climbed Sheaf on Clogwyn Du'r Arddu (HVS 4c, 1945) and Chris Preston led the impressive Suicide Wall in Idwal (E2 5c, 1945), which had defeated Kirkus and Edwards and represented the first major technical advance in British rock climbing since Central Buttress (technical grade 5b) was climbed by Siegfried Herford in 1914. At the insistence of David Cox, who was his commanding officer, Preston inspected the route by top-rope before leading it and Cox ensured that he was elsewhere when Preston led it, so that he could not be held responsible for the consequences. Suicide Wall remained the hardest climb in Britain for nearly a decade and was not repeated until Joe Brown climbed it, in rain, in 1952. Preston was so exuberant after his lead that he crashed his motorbike on the way back to Llanberis.

The RAF Mountain Rescue Service, established in 1943, was originally intended to retrieve wounded pilots who had crashed in mountainous areas but was considerably expanded after the war to deal with civilian climbing accidents. The British Mountaineering Council was established one year later in 1944. The idea had originally been mooted by Geoffrey Winthrop Young as early as 1907, but the need to provide advice and assistance to the armed services during the war finally provided the impetus for its formation. At the time of its inauguration, the BMC spoke for 40 clubs with a combined membership of 12,000 (perhaps 6,000 individuals, taking into account multiple memberships). Today it has around 65,000 individual and climbing club members and also represents the interests of an estimated 4 million hill walkers. Unlike on the continent, where national clubs were the norm, there was considerable opposition in Britain to the bureaucratic centralisation of a sport whose participants took pride in being individualistic and independent.

Despite the activities of the armed services, the war years inevitably marked a hiatus, and many climbers entering the sport in the immediate post-war years did so with little knowledge of climbing in the 1930s. It was, in many respects, a fresh start, with the attitudes, preconceptions and prejudices of the pre-war years erased or at least muted. The war had a marked levelling effect on society, with shared experiences of service, rationing, air raids and evacuation blurring some of the class distinctions that had existed in the 1930s and creating pressure for a more egalitarian society. In contrast to the end of the First World War, there was little nostalgia for the past. For most people the 1930s were associated with economic crises, unemployment and loss of national prestige. With the Second World War finally over, there was an overwhelming desire to build a different and better future. The need for change was reflected in the landslide victory of the Labour Party in the 1945 elections, the first held for nearly 10 years. Rationing continued well into the 1950s, taxation remained high to support the programme of social and economic reconstruction, and a chronic balance of payments deficit led to restrictions on foreign exchange which limited overseas travel. However, full employment and increasing investment and productivity gains resulted in higher standards of living, and the majority of the population had more money and more leisure than at any time in the past. As the Tory prime minister Harold Macmillan remarked in 1957, 'most of our people have never had it so good'.

In *The Affluent Society* (1958), J. K. Galbraith wrote: 'To have failed to solve the problem of producing goods would have been to continue man in his oldest and most grievous misfortune. But to fail to see that we have solved it and fail to proceed thence to the next task would be fully as tragic.' The next task, in Galbraith's mind, was investment in man, rather than investment in things. In the years following the war there was a significant expansion of public education. The Butler Act of 1944 raised the school leaving age to 15 and substantially expanded university education. The percentage of children staying at school until the age of 18 doubled between 1938 and 1956. These reforms ultimately gave rise to the 'classless', often university-educated, climbers that came to dominate the sport in the 1960s and 70s, and the development of climbing as a mass activity in the post-war years was perhaps one manifestation of the concerns and aspirations expressed by Galbraith. As the industrial world became increasingly wealthy and obsessed with production and materialism, and traditional religious beliefs continued to decline, many young people sought an alternative to the consumer society. The aim of most consumer products is to make life easier and more comfortable. In principle, the aim of climbing is the reverse, but in practice climbers have become voracious consumers of climbing products. Perhaps there was also an element of nihilism from the 1960s onwards, particularly in the university clubs, with some young climbers drawn to the sport by its anarchic self-image and the fact that so many of its leading exponents, like other pop icons of the era, died before they got old.

Before the expansion of tertiary education took effect, the most dramatic change in the 1950s was the emergence of working-class climbers as a potent force for change in the sport. Much has been made of the impact of working-class climbers in the post-war years, but throughout the history of the sport the great innovators have tended to come from outside the establishment of their day. Tyndall was the son of a policeman, Whymper was a commercial artist and O. G. Jones was the son of a builder and carpenter. In the inter-war years Smythe, Shipton and Tilman all acquired their skills outside the senior clubs. In the immediate post-war years, the greatest breakthroughs came from working-class climbers, but as they progressively became part of the climbing establishment in the 1960s and 70s, the next wave of innovation was led by the university clubs and individuals, like Peter Livesey, who were never members of any club.

In the post-war years, higher wages and shorter working hours played a critical part in freeing workers to participate in the sport, but better nutrition and improved physique also had a role. At the beginning of the twentieth century, life expectancy in the country generally was 51 years, but for the working-class in Manchester and many other industrial towns, it was less than 30 years. When conscription was introduced in 1916 so many men from the industrial cities failed to reach the minimum height requirement of five foot four inches that special Light Infantry Divisions, the 'Bantam Battalions', were formed for men between five foot and five foot three inches tall. During the Great Depression in the 1930s, the average daily per capita calorie intake of the poorest 10 per cent of the population was less than 2,000 per day.[2] The adult, usually male, breadwinner took the lion's share, women and children often received much less, and during periods of unemployment everyone went hungry. In depressed areas rickets and anaemia were commonplace. One of the most dramatic impacts of rising living standards in the post-war years was that young working-class men and women developed far better physiques (before the onset of widespread obesity) and for the first time had energy to burn.

The children of the Affluent Society were better fed, better clothed and better educated than any previous generation. They were also more numerous. Contrary to all predictions, the birth rate went up in the 1950s and early 60s. Changing social attitudes and increasing disposable income gave rise to a youth culture which found expression in climbing as in so many other aspects of society. Although the younger generation of climbers would certainly not have described themselves as 'romantics', it was precisely the romantic aspects of the sport that appealed. In keeping with the spirit of the age, the emphasis was on the heroic rather than the aesthetic – the pursuit of personal liberty and self-fulfilment rather than the search for beauty – not least because the aesthetic school was irredeemably linked with the class prejudices and establishment attitudes of older climbers. But in many respects the new generation of working-class climbing heroes, with their vigorous individualism, lack of regard for the social consequences of their actions, resentment and jealousy, contempt for weakness and propensity for violence, mirrored the attitudes of the romantic heroes of the past.

The term 'hard man' was in common usage in the nineteenth century, meaning a 'good goer' in the Alps. In the 1950s and 60s it came to signify an attitude of mind and social manner as much as the ability to climb hard routes. Beneath the blunt, uncompromising, antisocial exterior, perhaps the new generation of hard men continued to be deeply moved by the beauty and mysticism of the mountain landscape, as Jim Perrin suggested in his description of Stanage Edge: 'Such as I was, you see today in odd places: the young boys, awkward and painful often, unconsciously loving a place.'[3] But any outward expression of that love was severely constrained by the social conventions of the time. The number of climbs in the 1960s named after characters or places from Tolkien suggests a continuing appetite for the mythical and the mystical amongst the climbing fraternity, but when Don Whillans was caught reading a copy of *The Lord of the Rings* and asked for his opinion, his response was unequivocally that of a hard man: 'Fuckin' fairies' was his verdict.[4]

Dennis Gray, who became secretary of the British Mountaineering Council, described the climbing community in the early 1950s: 'The new-wave climbers of the immediate post-war years would not have been happy amidst the stuffiness and formality of traditional clubs, so they formed associations of their own making, with few rules, a small intimate membership and no social qualifications.'[5] In the margins of the copy of his book in the Alpine Club library, someone has written: 'Obviously they had: An aristocrat was disqualified.' The rejection of authority and hierarchy in the new clubs extended only to those forms that were imposed by the older generation or by the middle class. There was a very definite hierarchy within the working-class clubs themselves, where a system akin to an industrial apprenticeship prevailed. In the Glasgow-based Creagh Dhu, potential new recruits were called 'Black Boys' and had to serve their time collecting water, brewing tea and carrying gear for the more senior members of the club. In the Rock and

Ice, Dennis Gray himself was 'Gentleman's Gentleman' to Joe 'Baron' Brown; a humorous title, no doubt, but one that still entailed Gray carrying the rope and making the tea. Furthermore, the 'great proletarian climbing revolution' did not extend to women. Before the war, middle-class women had climbed with the leading climbers and the best guides of the day, albeit generally as seconds rather than leaders. In the 1950s and 60s as the climbing scene was increasingly dominated by the heroic, macho culture of the working-class hard men and their middle-class imitators, women were reduced to the role of camp followers. At the time, there was an assumption that 'birds' were simply not physically capable of climbing at the new standards of difficulty. Subsequent events have shown this to be wrong. Airlie Anderson, an Essex girl who rose to prominence in the 1990s with new routes such as the 15-pitch Venus Envy (E4 6a, 2001) (climbed with Lucy Creamer) in Greenland, once famously accused Al Burgess, a gritty northern climber in the working-class hard-man tradition, of being a 'wuss' for only ever having taken a single leader fall. It is hard to imagine a similar conversation taking place in the 1950s and 60s. The rather limited achievements of British female climbers during these decades appear to have been almost entirely due to social conditioning.

The social and attitudinal generation gap between pre- and post-war climbers was underlined by an ever widening gulf in the difficulty of the climbs undertaken. The dramatic rise in the standards of achievement in the post-war years arose for a wide variety of reasons, but perhaps the most important were better information, more competition, increased leisure and mobility, improved technology and greater specialisation.

The climbing community in the immediate post-war years was still very small compared with today. There were just three shops in the country specialising in climbing equipment: Robert Lawrie in London, Ellis Brigham in Manchester and Blacks of Greenock. Other than the journals of the traditional climbing clubs and pre-war books (some of which did not appear until after the war – Tilman's *Everest 1938* was finally published in 1948) the only means of getting information on climbing developments was by word of mouth from other climbers. Not surprisingly, this oral tradition gave rise to numerous myths and legends about the new working-class climbers, many of which have subsequently appeared in books (including this one) about the immediate post-war era.

Climbing in Britain, written by John Barford, the first secretary of the British Mountaineering Council, with editorial help from Geoffrey Winthrop Young, was the first authoritative new book on climbing to appear after the war. Published in paperback by Penguin in 1947 it sold over 120,000 copies. Barford died the same year in the Dauphiné Alps while climbing with Bill Murray and Michael Ward. *Climbing in Britain* played a major role in revitalising the sport, and its success encouraged other publishers to enter the field, creating a virtuous circle of increasing publicity and increasing demand. The first national climbing magazines appeared in the 1960s, and gradually the regional affiliations of climbers, with their distinctive identities, traditions, loyalties and mythologies, started to merge into one under the influence of mass media and greater mobility. As the popularity of the sport grew, the mainstream media also took an interest, with frequent articles and photographs in the new 'colour supplements' that were added to Sunday newspapers in the 1960s. The invention of relatively lightweight television cameras also made live outdoor broadcasts possible, turning climbing into a spectator sport for the first time. Climbs were broadcast live from Clogwyn Du'r Arddu, the Cheddar Gorge and, most famously, the Old Man of Hoy during the 1960s. Rock climbing's emerging place in British popular culture was confirmed when the *Monty Python* team made the first ascent of the North Face of the Uxbridge Road in the early 1970s.

The changes were not limited just to the national scene. Through better coverage in the press, and translations of specialist books and magazine articles, British climbers became increasingly aware of climbing developments around the world, and the 1950s were an exciting time for world climbing. In the Alps, Walter Bonatti was putting up extraordinary routes on the Dru and elsewhere. In the USA, The Nose of El Capitan in Yosemite received its first ascent. In the Himalaya the 8,000m barrier was finally broken with the first ascent of Annapurna by a French team and Hermann Buhl's remarkable solo ascent of Nanga Parbat: both had a major impact on young British climbers. As information became more widely available, the isolationism of the inter-war years came to an end and British climbers discovered how much they had to learn about new techniques and approaches, and how far they had fallen behind leading continental climbers.

Increased leisure time also played a vital role in driving standards higher. The five-day week was progressively introduced after the Second World War, and keen climbers naturally migrated to the trades and professions where it was introduced first. The luxury of a two-day weekend allowed working climbers to spend more time climbing and to travel outside their immediate area. The rapidly growing economy, with virtually full employment and higher wages, also enabled climbers to reject the apparent security of a job for life in the expectation that they would be able to fund their climbing activities with *ad hoc* work when they wanted. National Service ended in 1960, and with the expansion of tertiary education increasing numbers of young climbers started to go to university, in many cases attracted more by the opportunity to live away from home, long holidays and generous student grants than by a love of academia. For the first time, large numbers of young people without private incomes had three or four years of extended leisure, and keen climbers naturally selected universities located close to the mountains. The growth of the education system also created numerous new positions for teachers and lecturers with long summer holidays. Not surprisingly, university-educated climbers often chose to work in this sector.

Increasing mobility gave climbers more frequent access to the rock. Immediately after the war, even before the removal of rationing, people started to return to the hills using the comprehensive public transport that then existed, or private buses organised by walking and climbing clubs. Although it was illegal for private bus companies to compete with public transport by advertising their routes, a highly effective 'travelling climbers' grapevine' ensured that London-based climbers congregated outside the Park Lane Hotel on a Friday night, where a bus would miraculously appear to transport them overnight to a farm at the foot of Tryfan. The same bus collected climbers on Sunday night, transported them across the border to an English pub (since pubs in Wales were shut on Sundays) and then returned them, suitably refreshed, to Euston station. Many slept in the waiting room before heading straight to work.

Petrol rationing was finally removed at Whitsuntide in 1950. The impact on the climbing scene was immediate, with many climbers buying motorbikes and a few buying cars. Many smaller clubs, where the communal hiring of buses was the main *raison d'être*, simply ceased to exist, while more informal groupings, such as the Bradford Lads, began to form. The 1964 decision to spend more on roads, particularly motorways, made weekend trips to the Peaks, the Lake District or Snowdonia feasible, even for climbers based in the south of England. The journey to and from the crag became an integral part of the climbing experience, with numerous spectacular crashes and miraculous escapes. 'A climber might spend a third of his weekend on the road', Tony Smythe observed in 1966. 'The first requirement then is for his vehicle to be fast.'[6] The record from Marble Arch to the Pen-y-Gwryd stood at 2 hours 57 minutes, representing an average speed of 76 miles/122km per hour *before* the M1 and the M6 motorways were built. Dennis Gray recorded the inevitable consequences: 'Five weekends running I accepted lifts to the Lakes, to end each hitch-hiking home or in hospital after a crash. On the fifth weekend of the series, a party of [the Bradford] Lads were riding in a convoy of six motor-cycles. Without warning we came to a sharp bend...Some farm-hands scything grass behind the fence must have thought they were hearing the biggest pile up in motoring history – grinding gears, screaming engines, squealing brakes, shouts, curses, rending metal – an impression no doubt heightened when two bodies, hurtling as if shot from a cannon, landed in their midst.'[7] Paul Nunn recalled 'Barry Ingle...momentarily silhouetted in sparks as his motorbike hit the first Betsw bend, but we still did the Cromlech Girdle'.[8]

Apart from making cars and motorbikes go faster, technology also played a major role in advancing climbing standards after the Second World War. In the immediate post-war years, surplus War Department clothing was ubiquitous: hooded fawn-coloured cotton smocks with four pockets, camouflaged trousers, white sea-boot stockings, balaclavas or bobble hats and military rucksacks. Steel karabiners could be bought relatively cheaply, but the army surplus ones tended to open under strain and top climbers preferred foreign imports. Nylon rope, developed during the war for towing gliders, was much stronger and lighter than hemp rope and stretched by as much as 66 per cent under strain, absorbing the energy of the fall gradually rather than communicating it directly to the belayer. Rubber-soled Vibram boots also began to appear in the 1940s and progressively replaced nails during the 1950s and 60s.

There was a significant increase in the use of natural flakes, chockstones and the occasional piton for running belays. In general the climbing community was still opposed to pitons, for protection or for aid, but their use was condoned on the hardest new climbs. Joe Brown had a self-imposed limit of two pitons per pitch, and climbers who used more were often criticised. The general attitude was: 'If you can't do it without excessive use of pitons, leave it to a better man.' While the occasional use of slings or pitons for aid was accepted on the hardest new routes, subsequent climbers endeavoured to eliminate such aid and climb the routes free. In the 1950s climbers also started to carry pebbles or knotted slings that they wedged into cracks. By the mid-1960s ready-threaded chocks, initially using drilled-out machine nuts, started to appear, and by the end of the 1960s a range of specially manufactured chocks became available. Improved protection had a marked impact on climbers' willingness to take on longer and harder pitches, and better equipment also gave climbers the confidence to tackle hard climbs even in bad conditions. Given the vagaries of the British weather, a willingness to climb in the rain dramatically increased the amount of time actually spent climbing. By the early 1970s protection had improved to such an extent that many leading climbers felt that the element of adventure had been removed from the sport and some started to undertake hard solo climbs.

Before the First World War and even during the inter-war years, most leading climbers were middle-class men for whom climbing was an enjoyable pastime but by no means their sole leisure activity. After the Second World War, in common with many other sports, the amateur tradition gradually declined. It became increasingly difficult for climbers to operate at the top levels of the sport, and particularly to spend long periods in the Alps or the greater ranges, without effectively devoting their lives to climbing. This did not necessarily mean becoming a 'professional' climber, but it did mean subordinating many other aspects of life to climbing. Increasing specialisation made the climbing world a less varied and perhaps a less interesting place in some respects, but it undoubtedly contributed to rising standards. One of the ironies of the rise of the 'working-class' climber was that the best of them actually did less work than the idle rich they replaced.

The steady influx of new climbers also produced further changes in the social ambience of the sport. Accommodation was rudimentary, both as a result of money constraints and personal preferences. Many climbers opted for the basic accommodation but convivial atmosphere of a barn or camp site rather than submit to the rules and regulations of a youth hostel or climbing hut. As one climber observed of the Climbers' Club in 1966: 'Can any member who has not done military service possibly take seriously the huge lists of rules to be found in the entrances to the huts?'[9] In contrast, the Wall End barn in Langdale, Williams' barn in Idwal, the road mender's hut in Llanberis and Cameron's barn in Glencoe all became legendary climbers' haunts. No doubt there is a certain amount of misty-eyed 'happy but poor' nostalgia for the post-war years, but clearly something has been lost in the modern era where most climbers transport themselves to the mountains by car, climb in small, self-contained groups, cocooned by expensive equipment, and return safely and predictably to their homes by nightfall. The experience of hitch-hiking (with its complex gamesmanship to avoid the Biblical injunction that 'the last shall be first'), of club buses with their songs and distinctive smell of wet clothes and cigarettes, and of sleeping rough in barns and caves was as important for many climbers as the climbing itself: 'For many a sixteen year old, it was in Cameron's barn that real education began...Here the middle-class student met the shipyard worker, the conservative met the radical and the timid the bold...Some gave up jobs and devoted themselves to climbing... others who had failed in the school system met those who were more successful and...gained the confidence to try again.'[10] The radical tradition of the 1930s continued amongst most climbers in the 1950s. 'Sing-songs were likely to include Scottish melodies, socialist, communist and Wobbly anthems (sometimes in comic parody), dust bowl, hill-billy and blues lyrics...the poetry of the poor.'[11]

From contemporary accounts, it seems that in the immediate post-war years the climbing community was in many respects remarkably conventional and abstemious. Because of the housing shortage, most climbers continued to live at home until they married, when most gave up the sport. Smoking was certainly common, but the most popular brew was tea, and while there were occasional brushes with authority they tended to be of a minor nature. During the 1960s, with the increased independence brought about by rising living standards, high spirits and youthful exuberance more frequently gave way to outright lawlessness, particularly in the Alps. Shoplifting was endemic among British climbers in the 1960s and 70s and became almost a competitive sport in its own right. French supermarkets were a particular target, closely followed by climbing equipment stores, where gear was often stolen to order, but climbers also stole from hotels, restaurants, mountain huts and even vegetable gardens. 'Any crime was defensible if it provided an opportunity for the next hard climb.'[12] Some of the immediate post-war generation of climbers, including Joe Brown, Nat Allen and others, who came from far more deprived backgrounds than the shoplifters, were appalled. It particularly irked them when the 'little crooks' claimed to be impoverished students and gave philosophical and political justifications for their actions. Relations between British and continental climbers also deteriorated as alcohol-fuelled battles erupted in various alpine resorts. As a visiting American climber observed: 'Basically in Chamonix the scene centres round two bars: the "Nash", or Bar National, and Le Drug Store. Only the English hang out in the Nash. At Le Drug Store you find all nationalities. That's where the English go when they're looking for a fight.'[13]

All of this took the older members of the climbing community somewhat by surprise. Having politely tolerated the foibles of their elders, and having often served their country during the war, they in turn expected to be treated with a degree of respect as they took up positions of responsibility and, in theory, authority in climbing clubs around the country. Instead, many perceived that the younger generation of climbers treated them with a surly or sneering attitude, frequently accompanied by flagrant breaches of club rules.

Alcohol has played a major role in British climbing since Albert Smith's ascent of Mont Blanc with 93 bottles of wine and three bottles of cognac. Mummery, the founding father of modern mountaineering, consumed an invigorating combination of red wine, Marsala, bottled beer and cognac during his bivouac with Burgener before the first ascent of the Zmutt Ridge on the Matterhorn in 1879, and refreshed himself at regular intervals during his ascents with bottles of Bouvier. The risk-taking and thrill-seeking urge has also ensured that climbing and drugs have often gone together, from opium-addicted Coleridge's first account of a climbing-induced adrenaline-rush in 1802. However, the alcohol- and drug-induced bacchanalia of the 1960s and 70s do appear to have been of a different order of magnitude. Jim Perrin recorded one of the more extreme escapades in 'Street Illegal' (1977),[14] an account of soloing Coronation Street (E1 5b) in the Cheddar Gorge, primed with a combination of cocaine and amphetamines. Trips to Yosemite in the United States broadened the drug-taking experience of many climbers, while Himalayan expeditions provided a good opportunity to sample the marijuana that grows wild by the side of many trails or the opium that was both cheap and, in the 1960s, perfectly legal.

Perversely, just as the morals of the climbing community were descending to new lows, the idea of outdoor education became popular. As Paul Nunn, himself a university lecturer, commented: 'It is good to see the young on the crags, though what the climbing community will do to their characters I shudder to anticipate.'[15] Adrian Burgess, one of the notorious Burgess twins and a somewhat unconventional role model for the younger generation, taught outdoor education at a tough school in Ellesmere Port for a while. 'I doubt it changed many lives', he noted. 'It might have made them safer while robbing tall buildings.'[16]

The purported character-building benefits of outdoor education have their origins in the romantic idea of the moral superiority of the simple, rural life as compared with the corruption to be found in the cities. As the popularity of mountaineering spread, many people who perhaps should have known better started to believe that taking young people from the inner cities to the mountains for a few days would somehow reform their characters. The French novelist François Mauriac believed that 'above a certain height it is impossible to nourish evil thoughts...on the peaks a coarse creature becomes less coarse and a noble being may sometimes meet God'.[17] Writing in the bitter aftermath of the Second World War, his compatriot Claire Elaine Engel disagreed, noting that the most obvious proof that climbing is not beneficial to the character is the fact that in the 1930s the Germans were the world's best climbers. Geoffrey Winthrop Young, however, was an enthusiastic supporter, and found in Kurt Hahn a charismatic champion of the character-building benefits of mountaineering and small boat sailing.

Hahn, who established Gordonstoun School in Scotland, took up the challenge issued by William James in 1906 to find in peacetime 'the moral equivalent of war', an ambition that today seems somewhat suspect. His open admiration for the Hitler Youth Movement (despite being Jewish) might also have given pause for thought. However, the idea gained ground during the war that training in the mountains built both the character and the team. The Central Council of Physical Recreation acquired Glenmore Lodge in the Cairngorms soon after the war and

Plas y Brenin in Snowdonia in 1955. When Jack Longland, a friend and protégé of Geoffrey Winthrop Young, became Director of Education for Derbyshire he established the first Local Education Authority Outdoor Education Centre at White Hall, near Buxton, in 1951. For a time, Joe Brown, Harold Drasdo and other leading climbers were instructors. Numerous other local authorities followed, and thousands of school children and students were exposed to the joys of hill walking and climbing.

The belief in the benefit of outdoor education seems to stem from the confusion of cause and effect. It is certainly true that many successful climbers from relatively deprived backgrounds have used the same drive, determination and self-discipline that made them good climbers to become highly successful in other walks of life. But the idea that dangling a feckless youth from the end of a rope for an afternoon will transform his life chances is clearly ridiculous. If there is anything 'character-building' about climbing it is the need to take individual responsibility in a situation where the outcome is uncertain and potentially life-threatening. Not surprisingly, this is unacceptable in a situation where adults are responsible for the safety of other people's children. As in any other branch of education, there are gifted instructors who help their students to discover the value of self-discipline and individual responsibility, but most outdoor education is ersatz adventure. It may be fun, but it is unlikely to build anybody's character.

The objections of the climbing community to outdoor education were not, however, based on the efficacy of the training. Instead, they simply disliked the increasing popularisation and bureaucratisation of 'their' sport and worried about the impact of ever increasing numbers on the mountain experience. Despite the dramatic change in the social composition of the sport, many of their arguments would have sounded familiar to nineteenth-century members of the Alpine Club, with their concerns about the vulgarisation of the Alps, or the intellectual Pen-y-Pass set in the years before the First World War, with their preference for romantic reticence. However, these principled objections did not prevent individual climbers from taking full advantage of the

opportunities that outdoor education created. One unintended consequence was the creation of a whole new class of 'professional climbers'
– instructors and managers – responsible for introducing thousands of
children to the sport. In the past, climbers were forced to choose between
a life of adventure or a secure career. Now they could theoretically have
both. At Glenmore Lodge and Plas y Brenin pay was on National Union
of Teachers scales, complete with generous equipment allowances, long
holidays and an index-linked pension. Not surprisingly, competition
for the posts was intense, and many of the top climbers of the 1960s and
1970s spent time teaching at one or other institution.

As climbing was progressively transformed into a mass activity
during the 1960s, the regional differences that had characterised the
sport since the 1860s diminished under the influence of greater mobility and the increasingly national and international climbing media.
However, in the immediate post-war years regional differences were,
if anything, reinforced by petrol rationing and a shortage of transport.

NORTH WALES

In Wales, Menlove Edwards, Wilfrid Noyce, Arthur Birtwistle and others were still active after the war, but their achievements were soon
eclipsed by a new generation of climbers led by Peter Harding and Tony
Moulam, with routes such as Spectre (HVS 5a, 1947) and Kaisergebirge
Wall (HVS 5b, 1948). Harding's achievements were particularly impressive given the combined restrictions of short holidays and petrol rationing. In 1947 he spent just five weekends and a week's holiday in Wales.

Harding and Moulam both started climbing in the Peak District
and together founded the Stonnis Climbing Club. The inaugural meeting took place at the Navigation Hotel in Derby, during the course of
which a billiard table was set on fire. Harding put up some fine climbs
on gritstone including Goliath's Groove at Stanage (HVS 5a, 1947) and
Demon Rib at Black Rocks (E3 5c unaided, 1949), which was probably

the hardest route on grit at the time, although Harding did use a shoulder for aid at the start. As Harding and Moulam transferred their activities to Wales some members of the older generation of climbers, particularly Alf Bridge, encouraged the younger men, despite pressure from the old guard not to dilute the Oxbridge character of the Climbers' Club. Wilfrid Noyce was also a supporter, but when Harding wrote the *Climbers' Club Guide to the Llanberis Pass* in 1951 it contained so many references to pitons that Noyce, who edited the guide and who had helped to remove the German pitons from the Munich Climb in 1936, felt obliged to note that: 'It is the duty of a Guide to record, not to pass judgement.'[18] The Llanberis guide was also the first to recognise that the limits of the Very Severe grade had been reached and to introduce the new Extremely Severe grade.

Both the Cambridge and Oxford University Mountaineering Clubs produced some strong climbers in the late 1940s and early 1950s, such as Tom Bourdillon and Michael Ward, who made several new routes and variants in Wales before turning their attention to the Alps and Himalaya. For a while it seemed as if Welsh climbing might revert to the same pattern as the 1930s, but in the late 1940s rumours started to circulate about the activities of a young Manchester builder called Joe Brown. Gritstone problems that had defeated generations of top-roped climbers were being led, on sight, with apparent ease. The rumours went quiet for a couple of years, and many assumed that Brown was just another flash in the pan. In fact, he was in Singapore doing his national service. When he returned in 1951, Brown set about transforming Welsh climbing.

During three sunny days in 1949 Brown repeated all 13 of the major routes on Clogwyn Du'r Arddu, then regarded as amongst the hardest in the country. In 1952 alone, he climbed six new routes on the same crag. Until 1959, Brown and other members of the Manchester-based Rock and Ice Club put up all the major new routes on Clogwyn Du'r Arddu with the exception of Bloody Slab. Prior to 1955 not one of these new routes had even been *repeated* by a non-member of the club.

In the mid-1950s, it was probably harder, psychologically, to make a second ascent of a Rock and Ice route than it was to put up a new route of comparable grade, such was their aura of difficulty.

The one exception to this monopoly of new routes on Clogwyn Du'r Arddu was John Streetly's extraordinary ascent of Bloody Slab (E2 5b, 1952). No-one else was able to follow Streetly up the first pitch, so he untied and soloed the rest of the route. Streetly started climbing while he was at Cambridge but soon returned to Trinidad, where his family lived, reappearing in Europe at irregular intervals to climb the hardest routes with remarkable ease. During a brief vacation in the Alps in 1959 he made the third British ascent of the Walker Spur on the Grandes Jorasses, just one day after the first British ascent. It was his first alpine route. Joe Brown was so impressed by Bloody Slab that he made the second, third and fourth ascents.

The Rock and Ice was the most celebrated climbing club of the post-war era. Formed in 1951, its members included Joe Brown (the 'Baron'), Don Whillans (the 'Villain'), Ron Moseley, Nat Allen and Joe ('Morty') Smith. The club never had more than 30 members, but between them they were responsible for setting new standards in British rock climbing, particularly on the gritstone edges of the Peak District, in the Llanberis Pass and on Clogwyn Du'r Arddu in Wales. The club foundered in 1958 when several members got married. It was re-established in 1959, but it is for its achievements during its first seven years that it is chiefly remembered.

Perhaps the nearest equivalent in British sporting history was middle-distance running in the 1980s when Steve Ovett, Sebastian Coe and Steve Cram, three exceptionally gifted athletes, all reached their peak at the same time, and competition drove each individual to achieve performances that they would almost certainly not have achieved in isolation. In the Rock and Ice there were three exceptional climbers – Joe Brown, Don Whillans and Ron Moseley – and several other very competent ones who would have been regarded as outstanding in less august company. Competition was fierce both on and off the rock, with regular trials of strength and endurance. Remarkably, there were no serious climbing accidents during the seven year life of the club.

Joe Brown is regarded by many as the finest British climber of the twentieth century. The seventh child of a poor Catholic family, he was brought up in Ardwick, Manchester. His father died when he was eight months old and his mother took in washing to make ends meet. He left school at 14 and joined a local builder. His first major new route on grit was Brown's Eliminate on Froggatt Edge in Derbyshire (E2 5b, 1948), which he led at the age of 18, followed soon after by the Right Unconquerable (HVS 5a, 1949), the last of Stanage's great cracks to be climbed. Jim Perrin described it as 'not so much a test of technique as one of approach, an initiation into the attitude of the harder climbs'.[19] Two years later, he climbed Right Eliminate on Curbar (E3 5c, 1951), probably the hardest route in the country at that time. In all, Brown has created some 600 new routes during a climbing career spanning over 50 years.

Cemetery Gates (E1 5b, 1951) on Dinas Cromlech in the Llanberis Pass was the first significant new route of the Brown–Whillans partnership: 'The position on the face was very sensational and frightening. I brought up Don and he was flabbergasted. "Christ, this is a gripping place," he muttered hoarsely.'[20] It did not represent a major technical increase of standards but it was unremittingly steep and on poor rock. John Allen later quipped that the route should be graded E5 1b, but when Nat Allen sent an account of the climb to the Climbers' Club he received a polite reply from one of the club's officials noting that, interesting as these routes were, they were only 'fillers in of detail'. The official suggested that the Rock and Ice might be better employed applying their talents to something more serious.[21]

The ascent of Cenotaph Corner (E1 5b, 1952) in the Llanberis Pass, although not technically more difficult, was a major psychological breakthrough. The corner presents an obvious challenge, and numerous climbers had tried and failed to climb it. 'The climb required the leader to undertake technical and strenuous climbing many feet above protection for sustained periods. To climb it, he had to be both good and strong – and to have a cool head.'[22] Like many Brown routes, it retained an aura of seriousness long after its technical difficulties had been surpassed. Peter Crew recalled that 'even in 1959, the golden year when the youth of the next generation cut their teeth on Brown's myth, it was still possible, sitting by the camp fire in the Grochan field, to enumerate the ascents [of Cenotaph Corner] and the names of those who had made them'.[23] Brown and Whillans also created many new routes in the Lake District and Scotland, including Dovedale Groove (E1 5b, 1953) on Dove Crag, which was not repeated for 10 years, and Sassenach (E1 5b, 1954) in Glencoe.

Joe Brown's reputation will always be linked with Clogwyn Du'r Arddu and routes such as Vember (E1 5b, 1951), Octo (E1 5b, 1952), Llithrig (E1 5c, 1952) and Shrike (E2 5c, 1958). As the potential for new routes at Clogwyn Du'r Arddu diminished, he developed a series of climbs at 'new' Welsh crags such as Tremadog, including Vector (E2 5c, 1960), which immediately gained a reputation for difficulty: 'Leader after leader plummeted from the crack of the top pitch; an inscrutable, smiling crack slipping across the lip of the overhangs, it established a dev-astating psychological advantage; of having a strenuous crux right at the top after a great deal of hard technical climbing...a climb of great beauty, of scintillating movement and exquisite situation.'[24] Subsequently Brown explored the sea cliffs at Gogarth on Anglesey, often climbing with Peter Crew, where they were each responsible for nearly 50 new routes, domi-nating the development of the cliffs until the end of the 1960s. Brown's routes included Mousetrap (E2 5a, 1966) and Red Wall (E2 5b, 1966).

Not obviously possessing an outstanding physique and apparently rather laid back in his approach to training and fitness, Brown was rock climbing's supreme craftsman, instinctively seeing the easiest way to ascend steep rock. He was extremely supple, and his balance and poise were so well developed that it was often impossible to tell whether the route he was climbing was easy or verging on impossible. Dennis Gray recalled watching Brown climbing Vector during a televised ascent:

'Standing on minute footholds, Joe puffed at a cigarette and carried on a conversation with the commentator below through a tiny microphone hung round his neck...Completely relaxed, he rested in a position where I and most other climbers would barely have been able to stay on the rock...Why should he smoke a cigarette? Force of habit? Perhaps, but I think not. Despite his modesty...Joe is only human. He knows his worth and place in British climbing history...Smoking a cigarette in a position where others can barely stay in contact is part of the role.'[25] Despite his relaxed manner, Brown was extremely competitive. 'Basically, he's a tricky little fucker,' according to Jim Perrin, 'playful, inventive, wiley and watchful as a cat.'[26]

If Joe Brown was the greatest climber, Don Whillans was certainly the greatest climbing icon of the last century, a man around whom more stories and myths have grown up than any other. With his flat cap and uncompromising expression, a cigarette in his mouth and a pint of beer in his hand, his motorbike and frequent fights (often with foreign climbers), Whillans was the definitive hard man. In the end, he became almost a self-parody. Colin Wells called him 'a kind of Mancunian Popeye'; he was 'a cross between Andy Capp and Hermann Buhl', according to Jack Soper. When Whillans was invited to address the Alpine Club following his ascent of the West Face of the Blaitière in 1954 he started his speech with the words: 'Never before have I lectured to such an old...', and then paused, causing the organisers of the event to squirm in agony, before continuing '...and venerable club as the Alpine Club.'[27] His reputation as a lecturer and raconteur was established and continued until his death.

In the mid-1970s Whillans and Brown were both recommended by the British Mountaineering Council for an honour in recognition of their contribution to British climbing. Unfortunately, as the recommendation was passing through official channels, Whillans became embroiled in a contretemps on his way home from a pub in Rawtenstall which resulted in five injured policemen, a damaged panda car and headlines that read 'Everest Climber in Jail'. When the Honours List appeared Brown received an MBE while Whillans' name was missing. But the 'Rough-up with the Rawtenstall Rozzers', as the event soon came to be known in climbing circles, helped to cement Whillans' position as the most celebrated climber of his generation.

Don Whillans was three years younger than Brown. Born in Salford, he followed a similar path, leaving school at 14 and joining a local company that repaired boilers. Small, strong and agile, 'by the time he was eighteen he had the physique and temperament of a pocket-sized Hercules'.[28] He started climbing in 1950 and was soon leading the hardest climbs of the day. He first climbed with Joe Brown in 1951 at the Roaches in Staffordshire. Their last new climb together was Taurus (E3 5b) on Clogwyn Du'r Arddu in 1956. During that five year period they formed one of the most formidable partnerships in the history of the sport and restored Britain to the first rank of alpine climbing. However, like many post-war climbing partners at the leading edge of the sport, they were not friends. Whillans' relations with the other members of the Rock and Ice were also occasionally strained, particularly when Ron Moseley 'stole' White Slab on Clogwyn Du'r Arddu the day before Whillans intended to climb the route.

Many of Brown's best routes are subtle, almost devious. In contrast, Whillans' routes tend to be direct, hard and uncompromising. Whillans was undoubtedly one of the most naturally gifted climbers of all time, but he was by no means a risk-taker. As he said: 'The mountains will always be there. The trick is for you to be there as well.'[29] Like George Best, his exceptional ability meant that he never had to exercise the same self-discipline as other less gifted climbers and this, combined with his slightly cautious approach, probably meant that he did not fulfil his extraordinary potential. Chris Bonington described him as being 'shrewd, cautious...rarely, if ever, swayed by emotion', while beneath it all lay 'a brooding belligerence...he doesn't argue or discuss; he states a view or decision and does not budge'.[30] According to Dougal Haston, 'Whillans did not have a romantic thought in his head. To him, you get the job, you are sent out to do it, and you do it the best you can.' If there is just a hint of romance in his autobiography, it concerns his first visit to Clogwyn Du'r Arddu: 'I went on up the track and then on to Maer du'r Arddu and stopped there ages just looking at Cloggy. It was a forbidding sight and one that I'll never forget. Everything was still and quiet, the wind had dropped, the sky was that middle stage between light and dark. Cloggy stood there huge and solid. This was it. I don't remember exactly what I thought as I looked at it, but I know I was impressed.'[31] An earlier generation might have described his thoughts as wonder and awe.

Ron Moseley was perhaps the only other member of the Rock and Ice who could match Brown and Whillans for pure climbing ability, but he often felt that his own achievements were eclipsed by their reputation. An erratic but occasionally brilliant climber, he made numerous second ascents of their routes as well as putting up a number of outstanding routes of his own including White Slab (E2 5c, 1956) on Clogwyn Du'r Arddu, regarded as one of the finest climbs in Britain, and Left Wall on Dinas Cromlech (E2 5c, 1956). Unlike Brown and Whillans, who both had physically demanding manual jobs, Moseley was a commercial artist and had to work hard to maintain his fitness. In the end he lost interest, describing his short but brilliant climbing career as 'five wasted years'.[32] Nat Allen was the peacemaker in the volatile and competitive world of the Rock and Ice. He had an encyclopaedic knowledge of climbing history and became an influential founder member of the Alpine Climbing Group, but his abilities as a climber were often underestimated because of the illustrious company that he kept.

What was it that distinguished Brown and Whillans from the rest? Most of their routes did not represent a significant technical advance on Preston's Suicide Wall (E2 5c, 1945), and several other climbers were capable of climbing at a similar standard on short, outcrop climbs. But the sheer quantity of high quality hard routes created by them was staggering, and whereas many other climbs of equivalent grade were short, single-pitch test pieces, their routes often sustained a high level of difficulty over hundreds of feet of climbing.

Advances in the use of running belays played a role; many Brown–Whillans routes probably would not have been led, on sight, without the reassurance of better protection. But perhaps the biggest difference was their physical and psychological strength, built up over many hours of hard climbing, which gave them the composure to work out the solution to the next problem while hanging onto small holds in positions of extreme exposure. The standards set by Brown and Whillans in crack climbing in particular (where today's climbers, trained on climbing walls, have less of an advantage) remain high to this day, and many modern hard men still struggle with the wide crack on Goliath (E4 6a, 1958), Whillans' classic test piece on Burbage. There was also the fortuitous conjunction of two exceptional climbers and an exceptional crag. The standard of climbing they achieved opened up numerous opportunities for new routes on Clogwyn Du'r Arddu that were just beyond the abilities of their contemporaries, and for a five year period they enjoyed a virtual monopoly on the finest crag in England and Wales, creating a legacy of classic routes that will probably never be surpassed in Britain.

Whillans gave up British rock climbing in the early 1960s. By then, the gap between Brown, Whillans and the rest had started to close. Once again, better equipment played a role. Specialist rock climbing boots, called PAs after their French inventor Pierre Allain, started to appear in 1956 and were relatively common among leading climbers by 1958. With high friction rubber soles, they were light and laterally rigid, for 'edging' on small positive footholds, while being relatively flexible lengthways for 'smearing' on rounded or sloping holds. Most climbers believed that PAs made one grade difference, and their appearance coincided with a general rise in the highest standards from E1 5b to E2 5c. The long hot summer of 1959 was the decisive year when the Brown–Whillans myth was finally broken. A group of younger climbers including Hugh Banner and the informal Alpha Club, consisting of Martin Boysen, Peter Crew, Barry Ingle, Paul Nunn and others, started to repeat their hardest climbs on Clogwyn Du'r Arddu and elsewhere. Almost overnight, many became almost popular as the aura of difficulty

213

that had surrounded them was dispelled. Hugh Banner even put up two new routes on Clogwyn Du'r Arddu, until then considered almost the personal preserve of Joe Brown.

Many saw the first ascent of Great Wall in 1962 as the end of Brown's reign as unquestionably the best rock climber in Britain. Great Wall follows a thin crack up a steep and blank part of Clogwyn Du'r Arddu called Master's Wall in deference to Brown, who had made several attempts to climb it but had stopped when he reached his self-imposed limit of two pitons per pitch. Its ascent represented a challenge that had become as well known as Cenotaph Corner had been when Brown climbed it 10 years earlier. Among all the young pretenders, it was Peter Crew who finally succeeded in leading the route, perhaps because, unlike the others, he really believed that he was better than Brown. Born in the coal mining town of Elsecar near Barnsley in Yorkshire in 1942, Crew won a scholarship to read mathematics at Oxford but left after the first term. With his mop of blond hair and thick black-rimmed glasses, he became rock climbing's first pop icon as a result of articles by Al Alvarez and Ken Wilson and photographs by John Cleare. 'He was loud, arrogant, confident, brash, dismissive...He'd psyche himself up behind those myopic specs, and blast off.'[33] Crew had the power and audacity to lead the hardest climbs, and for a time he was the best rock climber in Britain, perhaps the best in the world, but then he burnt out. In later life he regarded his climbing career as barren, wasted years. Ironically, despite being 12 years older, Joe Brown was still climbing at the highest standard long after Crew had given up.

After Great Wall, just as Crew had aspired to topple Brown so a generation of younger climbers started to target Crew, including Ed Drummond, a student at Bangor who had trained on the limestone cliffs in the Avon Gorge. He decided to take on Crew directly by inviting him to climb The Equator (E2 5b), a huge girdle traverse of the Main Wall at Avon which Drummond had painstakingly pieced together over several weeks. Crew blasted across in a couple of hours. The return match took place on Clogwyn Du'r Arddu, where

Drummond made an early repeat of Great Wall on a cold day despite Crew's constant jibes and taunts from below. He followed that up with the second ascent of The Boldest (now E4 5c without aid, 1963), another Crew test piece. Crew finally won the psychological battle on Gogarth when he got bored waiting for Drummond to lead a new route, took over and produced Mammoth (now E5 6b without aid, 1967). But it was Crew's last major route as a leader.

Drummond was always something of an outsider, putting up some superb routes but invariably attracting controversy. Whereas Crew drank hard, smoked and never trained, Drummond was an ascetic, who trained hard, watched his diet and drank little. At the cottage that Crew rented with Barry Ingle near Llanberis, the morning routine consisted of cigarette, tea, turn on the record player: 'From that moment the Beatles...sing with vigour until an unpredictable hour the following morning, except for the interval when everybody is out climbing.'[34] In contrast, Drummond wrote and performed poetry, creating perhaps the best name for a rock climb in Britain – A Dream of White Horses – immortalised by Leo Dickenson's photograph of a huge spume of water almost touching the feet of Drummond and his partner as they tiptoed high above the waves at Anglesey on the first ascent in 1968. Drummond was also one of the first 'social climbers', ascending Nelson's Column in London to protest against the apartheid regime in South Africa. In the tribal world of Welsh climbing, the crowded, smoky bar of the Padarn Lake Hotel in Llanberis had long replaced the Pen-y-Gwryd and Pen-y-Pass Hotels as the spiritual home of Welsh climbing. It was a place where climbers got drunk, played darts and sniped at each other. Drummond was not popular at the Padarn.

Martin Boysen, the other climbing prodigy of the early 1960s, also outlasted Crew and is still climbing at a very high standard, often in the company of former Creagh Dhu climber Rab Carrington. Boysen was born in Germany in 1942 to a German father and English mother. As a teenager he lived in the south of England and became a local expert on the sandstone outcrops of Harrisons, where Boysen's

Arête merits a technical grade of 6a. He studied biology at Manchester University in order to be close to the rock and developed an elegant, languid style of climbing, gliding apparently effortlessly up steep rock. Don Whillans was impressed and had no doubt about Boysen's place in the climbing hierarchy: 'After me, it's Martin.' Perhaps his best route in Wales was The Skull (E4 6a unaided, 1966) on Cwm Glas which Boysen led using five points of aid. He was also active in the early development of the sea cliffs of Anglesey, putting up Gogarth (E1 5b) with Bas Ingle in 1964. In the late 1960s and early 1970s he turned his attention to the Alps and the greater ranges, before returning to his first love of rock climbing.

Like many keen sportsmen and women, climbers can become slightly obsessive about their activity, and reading guidebooks forms an important part of the obsession. Climbers read and re-read these small books with their detailed descriptions, line drawings and histories, ticking off the routes they have done and mulling over the routes they would like to do, their palms sweating with anticipatory fear. Nobody knows how many routes there are in the UK – certainly tens of thousands – but if you read the guidebook description of a relatively well-known route to a group of climbers, the chances are that someone will be able to name the route, even if they have not climbed it. Despite this, many climbers still contrive to get lost on the route itself. The 1963 guidebook to Clogwyn Du'r Arddu, edited by Crew and Banner, with its plastic cover, terse descriptions and absence of unnecessary comment, was the 'manifesto of the modern climber'.[35] When it was published the crag was strangely silent as climbers sat in cafés, absorbing the new route descriptions, making plans, and wondering whether they had the courage to carry them out.

The rejection of artificial aid remained the accepted ethic. When Crew placed a bolt on The Boldest it was grudgingly accepted by the Welsh climbing fraternity because of Crew's reputation. When Rowland Edwards used three bolts on Fibrin, a traverse of the West Buttress (subsequently climbed free at E4 6a, 1966), there was an outcry. Edwards

continued to challenge the accepted orthodoxy throughout his exceptionally long and productive climbing career, using pitons and bolts
with relative impunity as he led the development of the virtually unexplored limestone cliffs of the Great and Little Orme in North Wales in
the 1970s, but attracting the ire of the climbing community for doing
the same thing, together with his son Mark, on the more established
Cornish sea cliffs in the 1980s. Mark Edwards went on to become a
leading south west climber, putting up numerous hard new routes,
including Rewind (E10 7a, 1999) at Carn Vellan.

During the 1960s a number of climbers started to move to Llanberis,
soon establishing a 'climbers' ghetto' in the post-industrial landscape of
this bleak former slate-mining town on the edge of Snowdonia. Some
worked, like Joe Brown who opened a climbing shop, but many survived
on odd jobs and unemployment benefit. Whilst much hard climbing
was done, particularly as the great sea cliffs of Anglesey were first opened
up, there was also a fair amount of crime and dissipation. At the centre
of much of the mayhem was Al Harris. 'Prankster, maniac, hero, saint
and fool...We climb together sometimes...He's better than me – better
than almost everyone, in fact – but for the most part couldn't give a fuck
whether he does it or not...If it wasn't an instinctive, joyful outpouring
of energy it wasn't really for him.'[36] Tales abound of jousting with JCB
excavators and cars driven over cliffs in the style of James Dean in *Rebel
Without a Cause*. Harris once kissed his girlfriend while she was driving her car along a twisting country lane at 60 mph. He was riding his
motorbike at the time. Harris' cottage near Llanberis was the centre of
activities: 'Music blasted constantly and all the paraphernalia of hedon-
ism was close at hand...[Harris] was...the darer, the rebel...whose activities always managed to tinge the scene with colourings of high farce. He
had the uncanny ability to trigger other people's pent-up wildness.'[37] Not
all of the climbing community was impressed: 'In the psychiatrist's paradise of Llanberis...the consumption of beer rose in bars now commandeered and degraded by unruly climbers...the scene...was thoroughly
squalid. Drugs were circulating and the police were making inquiries

about a multitude of misdemeanours.'[38] Harris' lifestyle was sustained by alcohol, drugs and adrenaline. His death, in a car crash in 1981, had a certain tragic inevitability. After his funeral, 'the Harris record collection had been set up in the Padarn and we all partied with a vengeance during the day and into the night...Next morning we straightened out with mushroom tea made by Alex MacIntyre.'[39]

In 1958, just one year before his death, Geoffrey Winthrop Young noted with sadness the shift of focus from the mountain to the mountaineer. In his beloved Snowdonia, the contrast between the Pen-y-Pass meets, attended by four future Nobel laureates, and Al Harris' orgies could hardly have been greater. The heroic school of climbing had triumphed over the aesthetic: 'In the growing emphasis we place upon the pleasures of self-realization, even our Welsh mountains, their greatness and adventure, are vanishing in the background, behind the assertive brilliance of the climbing hero's halo.'[40]

THE LAKE DISTRICT

In the Lake District, the post-war revival was led by Bill Peascod and Jim Birkett, both of whom had been active before the war, with climbs such as Harlot Face (E1 5b, 1949) on Castle Rock of Triermain. Soon they were joined by Arthur Dolphin and later Peter Greenwood, Harold Drasdo and the other members of the Bradford Lads. Arthur Dolphin, a metallurgist at Leeds University, 'looked like a wraith, tall and gangling, with white hair and an albino complexion'.[41] He began climbing as a schoolboy at Almscliff in Yorkshire in 1939 and made some notable ascents on Yorkshire grit, including Great Western (HVS 5a, 1943) and Birdlime Traverse (HVS 5a, 1946), before turning his attention to the Lakes with routes such as Kipling Groove (HVS 5a, 1948) on Gimmer Crag and Deer Bield Buttress (E1 5b, 1951). A leading caver and cross country runner, he did not smoke or drink, and according to Harold Drasdo there was a lonely, puritanical side to his character.[42] He adopted a strict ethical approach to climbing, particularly on outcrops, where he followed a fixed sequence of top-roping in rubbers, top-roping in boots and then leading in rubbers. He did not consider that a climb had been fully developed until it had been led in nailed boots. Dolphin died in the Alps in 1953 at the age of 28 after a solo ascent of the Dent du Géant. Soon after his death, Paul Ross, the 'climbing teddy boy', recalled setting off to solo Kipling Groove in Langdale, a route that was regarded at the time as one of the hardest in the Lakes. He was called back by his companion Peter Greenwood: '"Come back down" he said.... "What's up?" I said. "That's Arthur's route and if you solo it, you'll ruin it." So that was that. He had a tremendous respect for Dolphin.'[43] Greenwood was also furious when he discovered that Joe Brown had put a peg into Kipling Groove on the third ascent, an ethical crime that would cause a storm of protest if it happened today.

Peter Greenwood was 'short, compact, powerful, almost Latin in appearance and volatility...He ran into problems with policemen, licensees, hostel wardens, girls, other climbers. A Berserker spirit ruled his nature.'[44] His philosophy of life was to give way to no man, and once he set out he completed the climb whatever the conditions. He climbed at the highest level from 1952 to 1956, with first ascents such as Hell's Groove (E1 5b, 1952) on Scafell, and then sold his gear to Don Whillans and became a successful businessman. Harold Drasdo, a fellow member of the Bradford Lads, was a more contemplative, even poetic figure. He led North Crag Eliminate (E1 5b, 1952) on Castle Rock of Triermain where he was seconded by a young Dennis Gray 'in appearance an underfed, streetwise fourteen-year-old; ready to go anywhere, do anything'.[45]

Allan 'Tubby' Austin, whose Billy Bunter appearance belied great strength and ability, started climbing in Yorkshire in the mid-1950s. According to Drasdo, he 'arrived in Ilkley Quarry where he was a beginner for two or three days and then the local expert'.[46] He put up numerous hard new routes on Yorkshire grit, including Western Front (E3 5c, 1957) and Wall of Horrors (E3 6a, 1961) on Almscliff, before transferring to the Lakes, especially Langdale, where he played a dominant role from the mid-1950s to the mid-1970s, with new routes such as Astra (E2 5b, 1960) and Haste Not Direct (E2 5c, 1971). He also made the first free ascent of Scorpio (HVS 5a, 1959) at Malham Cove, which pointed the way for the future development of hard free climbing on Yorkshire limestone. Austin was the 'spiritual head of the Yorkshire purist movement'.[47] He rarely used aid himself and sometimes refused to include climbs that needed aid in the guidebooks he wrote and edited. When Peter Crew placed a bolt in The Boldest in Wales, 'Allan Austin nearly choked on his Yorkshire Pudding',[48] according to Dennis Gray, and he became even more determined to preserve the pure ethical code in the Lakes.

In contrast, Paul Ross was happy to accept the role of the bad boy of Lakeland climbing, combining a reputation for drinking and fighting with hard climbs that sometimes involved considerable use of aid. Ross climbed with Don Whillans for a while, and the two of them even went to the Alps together. However, they were both strong-willed individualists and were soon barely on speaking terms. On the question of aid, Ross self-righteously objected to the 'po-faced purists', but according to Paul Nunn 'his tastes and preferences placed him nearer to Al Harris than to righteousness'.[49] Ross was a forestry worker who lived in Keswick and climbed mainly in Borrowdale. However, he did make occasional forays into Langdale, the home ground of the Yorkshire purists, where he climbed If in 1960, close to Kipling Groove on Gimmer, using several pitons. Ross admitted that he put up the route partly to annoy Allan Austin, and in this he was particularly successful. The row rumbled on for years, and in a 1974 interview Ross admitted that 'if you'd thought that in twenty years time Ken Wilson [the editor of *Mountain*] was going to play hell with you, you wouldn't have done some routes with pegs'.[50] But Ross also put up many fine routes, including Thirlmere Eliminate (E1 5b, 1955) on Castle Rock with Peter Greenwood and Post Mortem (E2 5c, 1955) on Eagle Crag in Borrowdale, which was probably the hardest route in the Lakes at that time and the first significant technical advance in the district since Central Buttress in 1914. Ross later moved to the USA and continues to climb at a high standard.

Les Brown, Peter Crew, Paul Nunn, Jack Soper and the other members of the informal Alpha Club (whose only rule was: 'If you ask to join, you can't') were active in both Wales and the Lakes in the late 1950s and early 1960s. Largely composed of graduates from Sheffield and Manchester Universities, members of the Alpha Club were all trained on grit and generally adopted a pure ethical approach to climbing. Les Brown, a physicist who worked for a time at the Windscale nuclear power plant in Cumbria, was the first member of the group to make a major impact in the Lakes and went on to have a distinguished mountaineering career, making the second British ascent of the Walker Spur with Don Whillans in 1959 and climbing Nuptse with a youthful Chris Bonington in 1960. Gormenghast (E1 5b, 1960) on Heron Crag and Praying Mantis (E1 5b, 1965) on Goat Crag in Borrowdale were two of Les Brown's finest routes in the Lakes. Peter Crew stole the magnificent Central Pillar (E2 5b, 1962) on Esk Buttress by the simple expedient of getting up earlier than Jack Soper and Allan Austin who had planned the first ascent. The Alpha Club was active throughout the 1960s, but from 1965 onwards attention shifted to Wales, where the great sea cliffs of Anglesey were being explored, and new developments in the Lakes were relatively subdued until the 1970s.

SCOTLAND

Writing in the 1970s, Ken Wilson, the mountaineering journalist and publisher, described the advent of working-class climbers in Scotland as being 'rather as if a group of East Enders had suddenly decided to take up grouse-shooting or polo'.[51] Times have changed since the 1970s. When City traders from the East End of London go grouse shooting now, no-one bats an eyelid. But to the class-conscious Scottish society of the 1950s, and particularly the staid and solidly middle-class Scottish

Mountaineering Club, the standards of both climbing and behaviour of the new working-class Scottish climbers seemed truly shocking.

The Scottish view of life after the 'great proletarian climbing revolution' of the post-war years was distinctly unromantic: 'When on the hills you take with you the baggage of problems and tensions that drive you to seek their solace. And you find, not a rural Utopia, but another set of social relations with their own problems, conflicts and ugliness – and strengths. Nature is...not an escape from, but a reflection of, wider social issues and concerns.'[52] As in England, the heyday of the truly 'working-class' climber was relatively short-lived, before the arrival of a new generation of classless, university-educated climbers in the 1960 and 70s, but it shaped many of the social attitudes of the Scottish climbing community for far longer.

The Creagh Dhu Mountaineering Club of Glasgow was in many ways similar in outlook to the Rock and Ice in Manchester or the Bradford Lads in Yorkshire, but it was also imbued with Glasgow's long tradition of gangs, street fights and sectarian violence. Founded in 1930 by Andy Sanders, it gained prominence and notoriety in the post-war years by producing some great climbers, including John Cunningham, Bill Smith, Pat Walsh, John McLean and Mick Noon, as well as a minor crime wave across the Highlands of Scotland. The foundations of the club in the 1930s are chronicled in *Always a Little Further* by Alastair Borthwick. Read today, and knowing the subsequent development of the club, the book has a rather innocent charm, but at the time it had an impact similar to Jack Kerouac's *On the Road*, signalling the liberation to be found by rejecting conventional society and taking to the highways and byways of Scotland. In the post-war years, much of that innocence was lost. Many of the fringe members of the Creagh Dhu were not even particularly interested in climbing, preferring punch-ups, poaching and petty crime. Bill Murray recalled entering the Ben Alder bothy late one night to find a Creagh Dhu sing-song in progress. As he opened the door, the notes died abruptly and a dozen young scruffs looked at him 'like a band of robbers'.[53] In a shed behind the bothy he found a stag hanging from the rafters. Tom Patey recalled two individuals turning up at the Charles Inglis Clark (CIC) Hut near Ben Nevis one February weekend in 1957 'whose characteristic patois, coupled with a distinct air of authority, stamped them as members of the Creagh Dhu'.[54] They were, in fact, John Cunningham and Mick Noon, intent on climbing Zero Gully. Jacksonville, the club's notoriously dank, unlit hovel in Glencoe, was built on National Trust land without planning permission. It was never locked; the Creagh Dhu's reputation was sufficient to deter all unwanted visitors.

Many of the stories of pub brawls instigated by the Creagh Dhu may well have been exaggerated – a celebrated pitched battle against the Swiss guides in Zermatt, in particular, appears to have received some embellishment over the years[55] – but there is no doubt that many members of the Creagh Dhu were not averse to a good fight. Membership was strictly by invitation, and candidates had to have a touch of evil: 'If you were obnoxious you stood a good chance of getting in',[56] according to George Shields, who made the second ascent of Arthur Dolphin's Kipling Groove during a Creagh Dhu raid on Langdale in the early 1950s. Although nearly all the members were working-class and from Glasgow, there were some exceptions. Jimmy Marshall, the Club's only honorary member, was an architect from Edinburgh, while Rab Carrington even had the misfortune to be born in England. Hamish MacInnes was closely associated with the club but never became a member. The strict selection process led the Creagh Dhu to the edge of extinction on a number of occasions. Jimmy Marshall recalls turning up to an annual meeting in 1988 to find just three members present. Emigration also depleted their ranks. The same thirst for adventure and search for a better life led many members to move from Clydeside to Canada or New Zealand.

Part of the success of the Creagh Dhu climbing club, and others like it, was due to the fact that it rejected all orthodoxy and was prepared to think the unthinkable. At a time when convention demanded that Himalayan expeditions should consist of at least 10 lead climbers, supported by hundreds of porters, the Creagh Dhu Everest expedition in 1953 consisted of John Cunningham, Hamish MacInnes and two 65kg rucksacks. They hoped to live off supplies left behind by the 1952 Swiss expedition. Cunningham was concerned about his lack of high-altitude training, but MacInnes brushed this aside: 'You've done Ben Nevis, so the next logical step is Everest.'[57] Despite this iconoclastic approach, they accepted traditional ethical standards when climbing in Scotland. It would have been very easy for the young rebels of the Creagh Dhu to have adopted the same approach as Continental climbers, but while pitons were used on winter routes, their use on summer rock climbs was strictly rationed.

John Cunningham was probably the most gifted climber in the Creagh Dhu, with first ascents including Gallows Route (E2 5b, 1947), Glencoe's first extreme, and Carnivore (E2 5c, 1958), which he 'stole' from Whillans. He was born on Clydeside and served an apprenticeship in the dockyards. Later he became a professional climber, working as an instructor at Glenmore Lodge and elsewhere. From 1942 to 1966 he climbed mainly with Bill Smith, forming the Scottish counterpart of the Brown–Whillans partnership in England. Like many climbing partners, they did not greatly enjoy each other's company off the crag. Cunningham climbed in the Alps, and made three visits to the Himalaya and a number of first ascents in the Antarctic and on South Georgia while serving with the British Antarctic Survey. But his major contributions were in Scotland, where he raised rock climbing standards to a level comparable with England and Wales and was an early adopter of new ice climbing techniques that revolutionised snow and ice climbing in the 1970s. That he failed to fulfil his potential in the greater ranges was partly due to a mean streak and a constant need to demonstrate who was boss. As a consequence, other climbers, particularly from south of the border, were reluctant to invite him to join major expeditions. He drowned in 1980, trying to rescue a young climber on South Stack in Anglesey.

While the Creagh Dhu dominated the Glasgow climbing scene, some equally strong, and in some cases unfashionably middle-class, climbers were beginning to emerge in other parts of the country. Tom Patey, a doctor from Aberdeen, Jimmy Marshall, an architect from Edinburgh, and Robin Smith, an ex-public schoolboy and philosophy student also from Edinburgh, were amongst them. At the same time, Dougal Haston, whose social origins and attitudes were closer to the Creagh Dhu, started his career as perhaps the most iconic Scottish mountaineer of the era.

The ex-public schoolboy Robin Smith was a 'thick set, medium height figure with incredibly bowed legs',[58] according to Dougal Haston. Highly intelligent and capable of great personal charm, he was also profoundly self-centred and perfectly capable of turning up to a climbing meet with neither food nor sleeping bag, taking it for granted that others would feed and shelter him. His behaviour was often wild, sometimes boorish and occasionally criminal, particularly in the Alps, which aroused the ire of older, less privileged, climbers. At university he obtained a first class degree in philosophy, but climbing dominated his life. Like many great climbers, he had an extraordinary sense of balance. One of his university tutors once observed him sitting on the floor at a gathering before 'rising from the lotus with a supple simian grace in one fluid motion, no upper body movement, nor hand nor arm assists, to slouch with studied gawkiness...toward the canapés and tea, returning bearing his supplies, then again his sinuous genie-glide, now in controlled descent, despite the well-filled cup on wobbly saucer, to resume his gnomic version of the teatime Buddha. A few repeats...sufficed to foster dawning appreciation.'[59]

Dougal Haston came from a considerably less privileged background. Born and brought up in Currie near Edinburgh, he was intense, lean and wild-eyed. He started climbing with John Stenhouse and John Eley Moriarty, the 'Currie Boys', and was later introduced to Robin Smith by Jimmy Marshall, who was some 10 years older than both of them. Smith and Haston climbed together for the next three years, putting up numerous hard climbs, including The Bat (E2 5b, 1959) on Carnmore Crag, but they were frequently barely on speaking terms.

Jimmy Marshall recalled that 'though only sixteen or seventeen, the Currie Boys were "worldly wise", they frequently drank themselves legless, bopped, jived and chased the lassies. They accepted no one at face value and distrusted authority, especially if it wore an old face. Robin [Smith], no doubt analysing this phenomenon, delighted in their company.'[60] But he also noted that 'Smith retained some vestige of respect for the establishment [while] Dougal set out to test by transgression every canon prevailing in climbing society.'[61] The visiting English climber Allan Austin described an ascent of Bill Murray's classic Clachaig Gully in a typical Scottish downpour in the early 1960s with a group of unnamed but recognisable local experts including 'one called the Old Man [Marshall], who seemed to be in charge...a dark, black-visaged giant [Moriaty]...a thin faced youth with shifty eyes who seemed incapable of telling the truth [Haston]...and a stocky, short-legged one with strange, round eyes who giggled a lot [Smith]'.[62]

Haston climbed with the Creagh Dhu crowd but was never a member, coming from Edinburgh not Glasgow. Smith's relationship with the Creagh Dhu was more complex. Initially disdainful of soft Edinburgh students, the Creagh Dhu soon learnt to respect, even like, Robin Smith. Smith returned the compliment in typical style. He led a magnificent route on the Slime Wall of Buachaille Etive Mor, an area of rock the Creagh Dhu regarded as their own domain, and called it Shibboleth (E2 5b, 1958), a word which he probably picked up from reading Bertrand Russell rather than the Bible, which means a 'word or custom or principle regarded as testing a person's nationality or social class or orthodoxy, the criterion or password of a group'.[63] It remains a testing climb. Martin Boysen described the fourth pitch: 'No runners relieved the tension of the climbing...as the rope runs out in a single sweep, the sense of exposure increases terrifyingly...Relief follows. Then admiration; such a pitch will never, thank God, be made easy by nuts or wires; it will always remain a test of nerve.'[64]

With Marshall's help, Haston and Smith joined the Scottish Mountaineering Club in the late 1950s. It was not an easy relationship.

Haston, in particular, thought that the SMC did not give due recognition to the achievements of climbers such as Marshall. The SMC in turn had difficulty coming to terms with breaking and entering, fighting, vandalism, theft and drunkenness, and Haston drank a lot even by the heavy drinking standards of the Scottish climbing scene. The Scottish Mountaineering Club rooms on the first floor of 369 High Street in the heart of Edinburgh's Old Town rapidly became the social focus for young climbers in the city, commandeered for 'unwholesome parties',[65] with the windows thrown open and music blasting onto the street below. Potential gate-crashers were held at bay at the top of the narrow twisting stairs while the climbers circulated between beer in the kitchen, girls and dancing in the main room and fighting on the stairs.

Robin Smith had four seasons in the Alps. In 1958 he completed the second full ascent of the West Face of the Blaitière (ED2), climbed by Whillans and Brown some four years earlier. At the bivouac, his partner Trevor Jones put on his down jacket and asked Smith where his was. 'Och, it's Haston's week for it',[66] Smith replied. He also climbed the West Face of the Petit Dru (TD+) with Joe 'Morty' Smith of the Rock and Ice. The introduction was made by Dennis Gray, who met the young Scotsman with a bandage round his head after he had fallen off an alpine path. In 1959 he left London on 19 July and completed the first British ascent of the Walker Spur (ED1) with Gunn Clark on 22 July. Some 20 years after its first ascent, this was still a major milestone in British alpine history. Don Whillans, John Streetly, Hamish MacInnes and Les Brown just missed out on the prize when they climbed the same route one day later. They feared the worst when they found an empty packet of Smarties halfway up. As Don Whillans remarked: 'If I'd known, I wouldn't have bothered.'[67] The following year Smith made the first British ascent of the North Rib of the Fiescherwand (TD+) with 'unpremeditated bivouacs before, during and after'[68] the climb.

After this spectacular alpine debut, Robin Smith was invited to join the 1962 Anglo-Russian expedition to the Pamirs. The British party was led by John Hunt, leader of the successful 1953 Everest expedition and perhaps the most respected member of the British climbing establishment. During a pre-expedition meet at the CIC Hut on Ben Nevis, as Brigadier Sir John Hunt was tidying the hut and sweeping the floor, he became conscious of Smith watching him with an appraising eye while he lounged in his sleeping bag.

During the expedition, Robin Smith and Wilfrid Noyce died while descending Pic Garmo. Their deaths affected every part of the climbing community. Smith, the youngest member of the expedition at 24, was the most promising of the new generation of Scottish climbers. Noyce, at 45, was reaching the end of his climbing career and was described (inaccurately) as the last of the poet mountaineers. Their two lives spanned perhaps the widest generation gap in British climbing history from Noyce's gilded youth in the 1930s to the beginning of the swinging sixties.

Noyce's father was a member of the Viceroy's Council in India. As a boy Noyce remembered 'sitting happily and watching the General [Charles Bruce] in his pyjamas, with the sun on his large chest at breakfast time..."The Himalaya," [Bruce] said; "the biggest thing, that's what you want...go all out for it. Rocks are practice"; and he exploded in fury at the "rocknasts".[69] Noyce later played a significant role in making Charlie 'Bruiser' Bruce's dream of climbing Everest a reality by forcing the route to the South Col in 1953, thereby enabling Hillary and Tenzing to make their summit bid. When he was 17, Noyce met and formed a schoolboy infatuation with Menlove Edwards. He also got to know Geoffrey Winthrop Young and later co-authored a book with him. At Cambridge he was awarded a double first in classics and modern languages, and climbed in the Alps with the best guides of the day, including Armand Charlet in 1937–38, with whom he completed the Mer de Glace Face of the Grépon in three and a quarter hours and the Old Brenva Route in three and a half hours. During the war he learnt Japanese, served as an intelligence officer in India and later joined John Hunt in Britain. After the war he taught modern languages at Malvern and Charterhouse and was able to deliver lectures on the 1953

Everest expedition in fluent French, German and Italian. On the 1957 Machapuchare (6,993m/22,943ft) expedition, Noyce and others were forced to retreat by avalanche risk when within 45m/150ft of the summit. No further expeditions have been allowed to this most graceful and sacred of Himalayan peaks. Roger Chorley contracted polio during the expedition. David Cox subsequently had a severe attack of polio after climbing with Noyce in the Alps in 1958, and Don Whillans also appeared to suffer a mild attack on the Trivor expedition with Noyce in 1960. It has been speculated that Noyce may have been an unwitting carrier of the disease.

In the Pamirs, Robin Smith and Wilfrid Noyce were roped together and descending relatively easy ground when one of them slipped and both fell 1,200m/4,000ft to their deaths. The climbers who saw them fall agreed never to reveal who had slipped. Noyce had suffered a number of serious accidents during his life in 1937, 1939 and 1946, before the fatal one in 1962. Jack Longland believed that he was 'accident-prone' while Edwards, who knew him so well, was also fearful: 'Probably you tried to force it...Your damnable courage coming in: which I hate so much.'[70] But Robin Smith could also be careless. Joe Brown, who had climbed with him in Scotland, observed that he was quick and careful on difficult ground but completely reckless on easy terrain.

The Pamir expedition had been conceived in the same spirit as the increasingly fashionable idea of outdoor education. John Hunt's underlying assumption was that by bringing together people of different nationalities in a mountain setting, international understanding would be enhanced and Cold War tensions relieved. Chris Bonington even suggested that Don Whillans should be included in the party which, given his record of fighting foreign climbers, would certainly have put the theory to a severe test. The fact that Hunt sincerely believed that international (as opposed to personal) relations might be improved through the interactions of single-minded, strong-willed and, in some cases, mildly criminal climbers betrays a somewhat naive and outdated view of the climbing world in the 1960s. But ironically, it was the older climbers on the Pamirs expedition who behaved badly. Nationalistic clashes *within* the British party, between members of the Scottish Mountaineering Club and the London-based Alpine Club, nearly derailed the expedition before it had begun, and the first draft of Malcolm Slesser's book *Red Peak* allegedly resulted in a flurry of solicitors' letters from other team members. The 'yobbish' Robin Smith appears to have been not only the fittest member of the team, but also the most adaptable and popular with their Russian hosts.

Robin Smith's short climbing career is remarkable for the first British ascent of the Walker Spur, but especially for his legacy of outstanding Scottish climbs in summer and winter. Like those of Joe Brown and Don Whillans, many of Smith's climbs have become classics because of his willingness to attempt bold, natural lines and tolerate huge exposure. In contrast, very few of Dougal Haston's routes in Scotland have become classics, and his reputation is based largely on climbs undertaken in the Alps and the Himalaya in the years following Smith's death in 1962. Three years later, in 1965, after an all-day drinking session, Haston crashed a transit van into three hikers near the Clachaig Inn in Glencoe. One of the hikers died, and Haston fled from the scene. He gave himself up to the police the next day and was convicted and imprisoned for 60 days. There is no mention of this incident in his autobiography, and opinions are divided on the extent to which it impacted his personality and future career, but it does appear to have made him even more withdrawn and focused on climbing. It almost certainly played a role in his decision to leave Scotland and move to the Alps, where he soon established a reputation as the finest Scottish mountaineer of his generation.

In parallel with improvements in summer rock climbing standards, there were also major advances in Scottish winter climbing in the post-war years. Tom Patey led the breakthrough in standards when he made the first ascent of the Douglas-Gibson Gully (V, 1950) on Lochnagar at the age of 18. One of the greatest amateur climbers of the post-war era,

Tom Patey was born in Aberdeen, the son of an episcopalian minister. He studied medicine at Aberdeen University, qualified as a doctor and after national service with the Royal Marines became a GP in Ullapool. Over the years he put up hundreds of new routes in the Cairngorms, on Ben Nevis and in the rest of Scotland, including the first winter traverse of the Cuillin Ridge with Hamish MacInnes and others in 1965.

Patey made the first ascent of the Old Man of Hoy (HVS 5a) in 1966 with Chris Bonington and the Rhodesian climber Rusty Baillie. He repeated the route one year later when he orchestrated the most famous TV rock climbing spectacular, watched by 15 million viewers, starring Chris Bonington, Joe Brown, Peter Crew, Dougal Haston and Ian McNaught-Davis, with Rusty Baillie, John Cleare, Ian Clough and Hamish MacInnes as climbing cameramen, 50 or so camera technicians, a dozen climbing 'Sherpas' and a platoon of the Scots Guards. It made compelling viewing. Broadcast live to give it 'a touch of the Coliseum', the programme revealed the climbers' differing personalities: the whimsical Patey contrasting with the stiff and formal Bonington; McNaught-Davis playing the fool; Joe Brown, understated, leisurely smoking a cigarette in an impossibly exposed position; and the two monosyllabic hard men, Haston and Crew. This concentration of talent was in stark contrast to normal life in Ullapool, where a lack of climbing companions forced Patey to climb solo, something which he increasingly enjoyed for its own sake. According to Chris Bonington, 'it all too often became a race in which I was trying to catch him, to persuade him to put on a rope before we reached the top of the climb'.[71] The Crab Crawl (IV, 1969), a much sought-after 2,400m/7,900ft winter girdle traverse of Creagh Meaghaidh, was certainly his greatest solo. Several climbers had predicted that it would take days to complete the route. Patey finished it in four hours.

Patey climbed in the Alps during the 1950s and 60s, putting up a number of new routes with Bonington and others. He was considered for the 1953 Everest expedition but rejected because of his youth. In 1956 he took part in the first ascent of Muztagh Tower (7,273m/23,862ft) in the Karakoram with John Hartog, Joe Brown and Ian McNaught-Davis and in 1958 he made the first ascent of Rakaposhi (7,788m/25,551ft) with Mike Banks. A highly effective, but by no means elegant climber, he made frequent use of his knees, in defiance of climbing convention, and wrote an article entitled 'Apes or Ballerinas' defending a fast, energetic and direct approach to climbing. 'The most impressive thing was not his style, which was fierce and ungainly, but his speed and his judgement of a line',[72] according to Chris Brasher.

Patey was a satirist, humorous essayist, songwriter and raconteur who was hugely popular amongst his peers both within the climbing counter-culture and the establishment. Much of his life was characterised by spontaneous, manic outpourings of energy, a wild, devil-may-care gaiety, but in the years leading up to his death on the Maiden sea stack in 1970, there were also signs of depression in the long gaps between the intense experience of extreme climbing. After his death, Tom Weir wrote: 'His happiest days were his early ones, exploring the Cairngorms in summer and winter with like-minded friends. With rapid sophistication and organisation in the sixties he thought something simple and joyous had been lost.'[73]

Together with Patey's early explorations in the Cairngorms, Hamish MacInnes' winter lead of Raven's Gully (V) on Buachaille Etive Mor with Chris Bonington in 1953 marked the beginning of hard Scottish ice climbing. He used an unusual combination of footwear consisting of crampons on the icy sections and stockinged feet on the wet rock. The route was quickly repeated by John Cunningham of the Creagh Dhu and Jimmy Marshall as competition for the plum lines increased. MacInnes was one of the most active and innovative of the Scottish climbers of the post-war generation. During national service in Austria he learnt continental pegging techniques in the Kaisergebirge and was instantly nicknamed 'MacPiton' when he returned to Scotland. MacInnes climbed in the Alps, New Zealand, the Caucasus, Venezuela and the Himalaya, including the celebrated Creagh Dhu Everest expedition with John Cunningham in 1953. He founded the Glencoe School of Mountaineering with Ian Clough and was a successful equipment designer and manufacturer, producing the first all-metal ice axe with an inclined pick, which had a major influence on modern ice technique. Bonington recalled a conversation that took place in Glencoe during the 1950s when another climber recognised MacInnes and asked whether he had been in Chamonix the previous summer with his head bandaged and a leg in plaster. 'Aye, that'd be me', replied MacInnes. 'I had a bit of trouble on the Charmoz. I was doing the traverse solo and abseiled from some old slings on the way down; the buggers broke on me and I fell about fifty feet. I was lucky to get away with it – landed on a ledge. But I only cracked my skull on that. We got pissed the same night and I tried to climb the church tower. The drain pipe came away when I was half way up. That's where I broke my leg. What did you do last summer?'[74]

The CIC Hut on Ben Nevis provided the perfect base for winter climbing in Scotland, with attention increasingly focused on Zero Gully and Point Five Gully, both of which had been reconnoitred before the war and dismissed as unjustifiable. Competition was fierce. On one weekend in February 1957 a dozen climbers from Glasgow and Aberdeen, including John Cunningham, Hamish MacInnes, Graeme Nicol and Tom Patey, converged on the hut, intent on climbing one or other gully. In the end, Zero Gully (grade V) fell to MacInnes, Nicol and Patey. It was MacInnes' seventh attempt. The first four pitches consisted of unrelenting high-angled ice with minimal protection, regularly swept by avalanches of spindrift. With Zero Gully climbed, the competition for the first ascent of Point Five Gully became even more intense. Joe Brown fell from the second pitch and a strong party from the Creagh Dhu was repulsed on the third. The route was finally climbed in 1959 by Ian Clough after a 40 hour, five day siege using 275m/900ft of fixed rope and 60 rock and ice pegs. The second ascent, one year later, by Robin Smith and Jimmy Marshall, took just seven hours. Characteristically, Bill Murray wrote to Robin Smith: 'My congratulations on Point 5. To my mind, that is the first ascent.'[75] The route is graded V today. During the same week of perfect winter weather Marshall and Smith also put up the 500m/1,600ft Orion Face Direct (grade V), which was not repeated for a decade and then only after there had been a significant advance in equipment and technique. Jimmy Marshall and Dougal Haston also climbed Minus Two Gully (grade V) on Ben Nevis in 1959, which did not receive a second ascent for 12 years. These ice climbs were as hard as any in the world until the development of revolutionary new ice axes in the 1970s.

OUTCROPS

Yvon Chouinard, the leading American climber and founder of Patagonia, the outdoor clothing manufacturer, once remarked that all climbers are the product of their first few climbs. For most British climbers their first few climbs are on gritstone: a steep, abrasive, rounded rock where a slab, a corner, a crack and an overhang may be compressed into 10m of beautifully sculpted rock face. As a consequence, the small gritstone outcrops of Derbyshire and Yorkshire have helped to define the British approach to climbing throughout the world.

The vast granite cliffs of Yosemite in the United States, where a single monotonous crack may rise for 100m, almost demand the psychological support of artificial aids. In contrast, using a piton on a 10m outcrop feels like cowardice and, having proved that it is possible to climb slabs, corners, cracks and overhangs without artificial aid on a 10m cliff, why should it be impossible on a 100m cliff? Before the introduction of climbing walls in the 1970s, outcrops were the training grounds where climbers learnt technique, developed strength and, most importantly, acquired the confidence that would allow them to transfer those techniques to the bigger crags and mountains of the world.

British isolationism and rejection of pitons for *protection* may have held back standards in the inter-war years, but the rejection of pitons for artificial aid probably helped to engender higher standards of free climbing. In the post-war years the British became increasingly comfortable free climbing steep, hard rock, while many continental climbers continued to rely on aid. Artificial climbing is slow, repetitive and tiring. Free climbing, by comparison, can be much faster, and speed is important on big mountains where the routes are long and weather conditions changeable. It was the application of techniques learnt on the small outcrops of Derbyshire and Yorkshire that enabled British climbers to leap-frog continental climbers in the 1950s and 60s and re-establish Britain at the leading edge of alpinism after a gap of nearly half a century.

As the popularity of climbing increased, new crags were explored that were often outside the traditional mountain regions, thereby allowing more people to go climbing at weekends and in the evenings, as well as extending the climbing season. Sea cliff climbing in Cornwall was developed by the Royal Marines and the Climbers' Club from their base at Bosigran with routes such as Bishop's Rib on Chair Ladder (E1 5b, 1956), climbed by 'Zeke' Deacon, and Suicide Wall on Bosigran (E1 5c, 1955), climbed by Trevor Peck and the Biven brothers. Peter Biven went on to develop hundreds of new routes throughout the south west of England and on Lundy, attracted by the romance of 'the rising and falling tides and the ever-changing background of the sea...the caverns, creeks and crystals...the sea and time-worn rocks'.[76]

In north Wales, attention turned to Tremadog (initially explored by Tony Moulam, Trevor Jones and others) and the sea cliffs of Anglesey. Disused quarries were explored in Lancashire and elsewhere. In the south of England, where geology dictates that there are few cliffs, there was intensive development of the few natural or quarried rock faces that do exist in Avon Gorge and Cheddar. For London-based climbers, the small sandstone outcrops near Tunbridge Wells are the only natural rocks within easy reach, except for those with a taste for crumbling sea cliffs. As a consequence, climbs at Harrison's Rocks and the other outcrops reached a high standard of difficulty and became a nursery for numerous outstanding climbers. Their potential was recognised by Nea

Morin, who had climbed on similar outcrops at Fontainebleau near Paris, and early pioneers included Eric Shipton and Menlove Edwards. In the post-war years Chris Bonington, Martin Boysen and others cut their climbing teeth on southern sandstone. When he was 17, Boysen spent a day climbing on Harrison's with two young Edinburgh students called Robin Smith and Gunn Clark, who were picking peas in Kent to earn money before going to the Alps. Nea Morin invited all three to her Georgian house in Tunbridge Wells for an elegant tea of toast and climbing gossip. Morin had just flown over the Alps and told them that the Grandes Jorasses looked free of snow and in very good condition. Her comments led to the first British ascent of the Walker Spur.

During the 1950s, harking back to the days when British rock climbs were seen as preparation for the Alps, limestone outcrops and quarries in the Peak District and Yorkshire were used to practise pegging in preparation for artificial climbing in the Dolomites and the Western Alps. Kilnsey Main Overhang (A3, 1957), climbed by Ron Moseley of the Rock and Ice, was an outstanding product of this era. Peter Biven and Trevor Peck waged a war of attrition with the Central Wall at Malham Cove, where the first pitch took over 22 hours, and also developed Millstone Edge, a steep gritstone quarry in Derbyshire, as a major artificial climbing venue. As standards continued to rise, many artificial routes were climbed free, including Biven's spectacular Quietus at Stanage which Joe Brown climbed without aid (E2 5c, 1954).

In the 1960s, as the new-route potential of gritstone appeared to be drying up, a number of climbers turned their attention to the free climbing potential of the limestone crags of Derbyshire and Yorkshire. In the Peak District, Stoney Middleton became the focus of activity because it was easily accessible from Sheffield by public transport and benefitted from both a café (now an Indian restaurant) and The Moon pub almost at the foot of the crag. Competition was fierce, and the steamy atmosphere in the café was 'edgy, mistrustful and very male'.[77] Tom Proctor and Jack Street, among others, were responsible for putting up numerous extremely hard new limestone climbs, including Our Father (E4 6b,

1969), which became as big a draw as the traditional gritstone routes. Proctor was equally proficient on gritstone, climbing Green Death (E5 5c, 1969) on Millstone Edge which featured in the BBC television series *Rock Face* in 1974.

THE ALPS

Eric Shipton observed that 'it is often the case that a man with fewer inhibitions is better equipped to tackle [an unsolved problem] than one with greater experience'.[78] In alpine climbing, even more than the domestic scene, the enforced gap of the Second World War allowed a fresh start, with new climbers and new approaches, uninhibited by experience. The immediate post-war years were dominated by climbers from the Oxford and Cambridge university mountaineering clubs and the traditional senior clubs, but after graduating from the gritstone outcrops to the mountain crags of Wales and the Lakes, the new generation of working-class climbers began to make their mark in the Alps in the mid-1950s.

Notable climbers from Oxford included Alan Blackshaw, Tom Bourdillon, Hamish Nicol and Michael Westmacott, while Cambridge climbers included Roger Chorley, John Streetly and Michael Ward. Bourdillon, whose father was a founding member of the Oxford University Mountaineering Club in 1909, was a leading spirit in the post-war alpine climbing revival. His ascent, with Nicol, of the North Face of the Petit Dru (TD) – one of the six classic north faces of the Alps – in 1950 was the first by a British party of a modern *grande course*. Nicol went on to climb the West Face of Pointe Albert with Blackshaw in 1953, a relatively short route but the first *Extrêmement Difficile* route climbed by a British party in the Western Alps. Invited to give a talk to the Alpine Club about his ascent of the Grand Capucin (TD+), Bourdillon described a passage of artificial climbing on the overhanging face by saying 'for the next hour we were hardly in contact with the rocks'. Several older members of the Club openly wondered why he had bothered to go to the mountains.

Rather than try to reform the Alpine Club, which most young climbers regarded as beyond redemption, they decided to form the Alpine Climbing Group (ACG) in 1952, with Bourdillon as its first president. The ACG was modelled on the Groupe de Haute Montagne, the elite French climbing group. It had three categories of member: active, retired and deceased. Members moved from the first to the second category if the committee determined that they had not climbed anything serious in the last year. As a result, an increasing number ended up in the third category. The ACG was associated with the Alpine Club for administrative purposes but maintained a strictly separate identity. The Alpine Club was in imminent danger of becoming extinct at this time. At the start of each meeting, in addition to the usual announcements, the president read out a list of members who had died since the last meeting, most of them from old age. Members were then invited to say a few words about their former friends. Dennis Gray, one of the great raconteurs of the climbing world, claims to have been present during one such meeting in the mid-1960s when an octogenarian struggled to his feet and declared in a high-pitched, reedy voice: 'I never climbed with old Bunty Smith, but my brother did, and he said he was a bounder!' Muffled 'tut-tuts' were audible round the room because good manners dictated that one should only be rude about fellow members while they were still alive.[79]

The Alpine Climbing Group included a number of talented young Oxbridge climbers, who might previously have expected to join the Alpine Club, but it also included several members of the Rock and Ice, who would certainly not, such as Don Whillans (who was appointed to the committee) and Nat Allen. As a result, the ambience at ACG annual dinners was somewhat different from the Alpine Club, and almost invariably resulted in them being banned from returning to the same venue. In the 1960s the ACG also started producing English language guides to the Alps, which dramatically increased the number of British climbers going there in subsequent years.

In many ways, the Alpine Climbing Group is a testament to the survival instincts and adaptability of the Alpine Club. Like the British aristocracy, the Alpine Club, with its essentially nineteenth-century attitudes, should have perished by the mid-twentieth century, but somehow it succeeded in making just enough concessions to modernity to survive, while retaining sufficient of its essential character to be recognisably the same institution that was founded in 1857. While the Rock and Ice and many other working-class clubs have long since disappeared, the Alpine Club celebrated its 150th anniversary in 2007. The formation of the ACG, and its gradual merger back into the Alpine Club between 1967 and 1972, largely accounts for the Club's survival during the 1960s and beyond.

Tom Bourdillon went on to become a member of the 1951 Everest and 1952 Cho Oyu expeditions led by Eric Shipton and, with Charles Evans, made the first summit attempt during the 1953 Everest expedition. He was killed on the Jägihorn in the Oberland in 1956 with Dick Viney, another talented young climber from the Cambridge University Mountaineering Club.

Bourdillon was an academic physicist, and so enjoyed long holidays, but in the 1950s most ordinary workers still had only two weeks' paid leave a year. The post-war generation of working-class climbers now felt ready to take on the Alps, but they faced very considerable challenges. Before the days of fast autoroutes and cheap air travel, getting to and from the Alps took four days, leaving just 10 days for climbing in a typical holiday. Many had to curtail their climbing activities in Britain in order to save money for the trip, so that by the time they arrived they were often less than fully fit and were certainly not acclimatised. After fitting in a training climb or two, and allowing time for the uncertain alpine weather, it is not surprising that many British parties achieved relatively little. Several things changed in the 1950s and 60s that radically increased the standards achieved by British climbers in the Alps. Better information and higher standards of climbing back home in Britain gave top climbers the confidence to embark upon the hardest routes (particularly if they were mainly on rock) immediately after arrival, even in suspect conditions. Furthermore, full employment and higher rates of pay allowed determined climbers to give up their jobs and spend the whole summer in the Alps, in the expectation that they would be able to find work when they returned. The growth of tertiary education in the 1960s also vastly increased the number of young people with long summer holidays. The annual migration to the Alps often went via the fruit and vegetable farms of Kent, where seasonal work could be obtained that provided sufficient money for an extended, albeit frugal, stay in the Alps. For many climbers, it was a matter of pride to avoid paying for a single night's sleep. Half-built houses, bus shelters, private verandas and large boulders all provided shelter. Two climbers once spent a night in a roadside grit container with a swing lid. They were rudely awakened in the morning when a bucket of ashes was dumped on them.

British climbers congregated at the Biolay campsite and later Snell's Field near Chamonix. When the weather was bad, they mooched around town, drank at the Bar National and started fights with the local youths to relieve the monotony. While Camp 4, the equally legendary climbers' camp in Yosemite, is now on the United States National Register of Historic Places, after numerous raids by the French police Snell's Field was closed down and the entrance blocked with huge boulders to keep the British out.

The post-war generation took their inspiration from foreign climbers, especially Hermann Buhl and Gaston Rebuffat, and avidly read *Nanga Parbat Pilgrimage* and *Starlight and Storm*, with their tales of desperate struggles on the icy north faces of the Alps and in the Himalaya. But they also looked back to British climbing in the nineteenth century and recognised a kindred spirit in Fred Mummery: 'Though Mummery had been dead for over fifty years, he was the man to whom [Yorkshire climbers in the early 1950s] felt akin; he was in line with the spirit of the new age which exulted in the sheer freedom to be found in climbing.'[80]

In 1954 Joe Brown and Don Whillans completed the first British ascent (third overall) of the West Face of the Petit Dru (TD+), then considered the hardest rock climb in the Alps, in a very fast time. By doing so, they became the first British climbers to compete with continental climbers on an equal footing since the First World War. After the climb, several well-known French guides came up to them to shake their hands. The Brown–Whillans route on the Aiguille de Blaitière (ED2), in the same year, was by far the hardest new route put up by the British in the Alps at that time. Brown and Whillans' success gave confidence to other young British climbers and encouraged them to take on bigger challenges. Hamish MacInnes unsuccessfully attempted both the Eiger and the Grandes Jorasses with Chris Bonington in 1957 during Bonington's first season in the Alps. The following year they climbed the Bonatti Pillar on the Dru (TD+) with Don Whillans, Paul Ross and two Austrian climbers, Walter Phillip and Richard Blach. The route was first climbed solo by the Italian Walter Bonatti in 1955 and had the reputation of being very difficult. MacInnes was injured by rockfall at the first bivouac, but the party successfully completed the route after some fine leads by Whillans.

In 1959 Robin Smith and Gunn Clark made the first British ascent of one of the three great north faces when they climbed the Walker Spur. Two years later the first British ascent of the North Face of the Matterhorn (ED1) was made by Tom Carruthers from Glasgow and Brian Nally, a house painter from London. It was Carruthers' first year in the Alps. Both went on to make attempts on the North Face of the Eiger (ED2) in 1962: Nally was helped to safety by Whillans and Bonington after his partner Barry Brewster, a student from Bangor, was killed by stonefall; Carruthers fell to his death while Bonington and Ian Clough were making the first successful British ascent later in the season.

The North Face of the Eiger was by far the most famous climb in the Alps, and Bonington's success brought him to the attention of the British public for the first time. He went on to become, with Whymper and Mallory, one of the best-known British mountaineers and a pivotal figure in the development of British climbing in the Himalaya. Bonington was born in Hampstead and educated at public school and

Sandhurst. A Creagh Dhu climber meeting him for the first time in the early 1950s observed that 'the poor lad looked as though he'd been raised in a fucking doll's house'.[81] As a boy he was a rather lonely figure, brought up by his divorced mother and his grandmother. By his own admission he sought a family in the armed services, but did not really fit in. After being rejected by the airforce, Bonington spent time in the army and was briefly a margarine salesman for Unilever, before becoming a professional climber.

Bonington first rose to prominence in the climbing world after the winter ascent of Raven's Gully with Hamish MacInnes in 1953 and some hard routes in the Avon Gorge in the late 1950s. MacInnes continued to mentor him through his early alpine career, and the ascent of the Bonatti Pillar on the Dru with MacInnes in 1958 brought him into contact with Don Whillans. In 1959 he completed a long artificial route on the North Face of the Cima Grande (now E3 5c, without aid) with Gunn Clark, and the following year, through his army connections, he went on his first Himalayan expedition, led by ex-Gurkha Colonel Jimmy Roberts, reaching the summit of Annapurna II (7,937m/26,040ft).

In 1961 he was invited to join a small and famously acrimonious expedition to Nuptse (7,861m/25,790ft) together with Les Brown, Trevor Jones, John Streetly and others, which featured a high-altitude punch-up and bitter recriminations when the climbers returned to Britain. When he met Whillans in the Alps immediately after the expedition, having travelled directly from Kathmandu, Bonington was physically and mentally drained, but Whillans insisted on going for the Eiger: 'You can do your training on the Face. By the time you get to the top you'll be fit – or dead!'[82] Forced back from the Eiger by bad weather, Bonington and Whillans joined up with Ian Clough and the Polish climber Dlugosz for an attempt on the Central Pillar of Frêney (ED1), scene of a recent disaster in which four climbers had died when a team led by Walter Bonatti had been forced to retreat in a storm after pioneering much of the route. The Central Pillar of Frêney was one of the best new routes by a British team since the war. Bonington was never a polished climber

('He's a clumsy bugger, Chris',[83] was Joe Brown's verdict), but he was highly effective, and surmounting the crux pitch on the Frêney, after Whillans had fallen 15m/50ft, was the lead of his life. In 1962 Bonington teamed up with Ian Clough, and after a fine ascent of the Walker Spur on the Grandes Jorasses they went on to make the first British ascent of the Eigerwand together. It was then that Bonington discovered the other part of his vocation: 'I realised the potential value of the story of the first British ascent and intended to make the most of it.'[84]

Throughout the 1970s Bonington was criticised by parts of the climbing community for his commercial approach to climbing. Members of the general public, if they thought about it at all, probably assumed that this was because of the threat that he posed to the sport's great amateur tradition. The reality is more prosaic: Bonington was simply better than other leading climbers at gaining recognition and reward for his climbing, and they resented it. The gentlemanly amateur tradition belonged to the aesthetic school that had long since lost its influence in a rapidly professionalising world. The sport was now firmly in the hands of the heroic school, and fierce competition, jealousy and resentment had free rein.

The new breed of professional climbers sought to make a living from the sport in four main ways. As demand for outdoor education expanded, many acted as instructors and, in later years, a few became guides, an occupation that can become as routine and repetitive as any other job, except on the rare occasions when the client has the same ability and aspirations as the guide. A smaller number earned a living from designing or manufacturing climbing equipment. The third group consisted of the journalists, photographers and film-makers who fed the publicity machine that grew up around the sport as it progressively turned into a mass activity. The best of these were highly competent climbers in their own right. John Cleare, perhaps the most famous mountain photographer of the era, had numerous new routes to his credit as well as filming Clint Eastwood in *The Eiger Sanction*. The fourth, elite group consisted of those who earned a living by trading on their celebrity status as climbers. This enabled them to sell stories to the press, write books, charge for lectures and earn fees for endorsing equipment. This was perceived by many to be the most glamorous part of the business, and Bonington established an almost unassailable first-mover advantage by recognising the potential of the market at a time when there were few competitors and a number of unclimbed objectives that were sufficiently well known to be marketable to the general public. More than any other figure since Albert Smith in the 1850s, Bonington turned climbing into entertainment. He taught himself to be a competent photographer and writer, and introduced the sport to the wider public through a tireless succession of televised climbs, books, articles and public lectures. By doing so, he accelerated climbing's transition from a minority sport into a mainstream leisure activity.

Of course, in a sport with an instinctively irreverent attitude to any figure of authority, Bonington's business acumen and professionalism inevitably attracted both criticism and ridicule. As his fame grew, Bonington-baiting became one of the leitmotifs of the climbing world, perhaps most elegantly expressed in Tom Patey's song:

> *Onward, Christian Bonington, of the ACG,*
> *Write another page of alpine history.*
> *He has climbed the Eigerwand; he has climbed the Dru –*
> *For a mere ten thousand francs, he will climb for you:*
> *Onward, Christian Bonington of the ACG,*
> *If you name the mountain, he will name the fee.*[85]

But even Patey, the great Scottish amateur, had instigated and taken part in the Old Man of Hoy TV spectacular which attracted an audience of 15 million and was, presumably, not wholly unremunerative. Bonington simply ignored the criticism and carried on doing what he did best.

One year before Bonington and Clough's summer repeat of the 1938 route on the Eiger, four Austrians had made the first winter ascent of the route. Technical winter climbing on the smaller mountains of Scotland had been undertaken since the 1930s, but until the Austrian team made their audacious ascent of the Eiger in 1961, there had been relatively little interest in hard winter climbs in the Alps because the Himalayan climbing equipment needed to combat the extreme cold was too cumbersome and heavy for technical climbing. During the 1960s, new lightweight warm and windproof clothing began to appear, and the challenge of hard, technical winter routes was taken up. Soon, the North Face of the Matterhorn and the Walker Spur on the Grandes Jorasses were also climbed in winter.

Amongst British climbers, Dougal Haston, more than any other, was enthused by this new form of mountain masochism. The lack of crowds, the purity of the winter landscape, the technical difficulties of the climbing and probably the sheer suffering involved all appealed to this solitary and austere man. Haston, like many others of his generation, was attracted to the high standards and commitment of German and Austrian climbers, particularly Hermann Buhl. But as a former philosophy student at Edinburgh, Haston also acknowledged, somewhat self-consciously, the influence of Nietzsche: 'I still feel the urge to fight with the forces of unknown walls. It has become a necessary part of life for me. I am searching into self, and must undertake these tests in order to reach a degree of happiness – temporary though this may be – before the next test...A great hardness is setting in, and I am increasingly able to treat the petty and mundane with utter contempt. I have a few friends in the true sense of the word, but no one will complete this path with me...One as an individual must think of self...I will do many things for people I respect, and for fools nothing. They deserve to be trampled on. One has freedom at birth. Why should one submerge or lose this freedom in attempting to help others who also had this, but lost it?... This is the freedom I pursue. Thus spake DH.'[86]

Haston was a romantic, but in the Germanic rather than English tradition, steeped in the cult of the hero, contemptuous of weakness and suffering. He made the second British ascent of the North Face of the Eiger with Rusty Baillie, one year after Bonington, in the summer of 1963. In 1966 he was persuaded by the American climber John Harlin to join a team attempting a new direct route on the North Face in winter. Harlin, Bonington and Baillie had inspected the line the previous summer, but the weather was poor. Harlin believed that the 10 days of good weather needed to complete the climb were more likely to occur in winter. Cold conditions would also reduce the risk of rockfall on the face. However, 10 days of continuous good weather is almost unheard of in the Bernese Oberland in summer or winter, and putting up a new route on the North Face in winter conditions was inevitably going to be a gruelling challenge. For Harlin, the reward was fame. The 'Blond God' was a statuesque figure: college football hero, former fighter pilot in the US Air Force and a strong, but not outstanding, climber. Harlin was also a relentless self-publicist with a sometimes tenuous grip on the truth. Bonington took the decision to drop out of the climbing team and chose instead to cover the ascent for the *Daily Telegraph*: 'I never felt totally committed to the climbing; whether because of the strength of my own interest in the photographic coverage of the climb, or an awareness of the risk-level still involved in that final push, I am not at all sure.'[87] Mick Burke joined him as cameraman. Harlin next approached Whillans, who declined because he thought the route too risky and doubted Harlin's ability. Finally Harlin recruited Dougal Haston. Haston's relationship with Harlin was ambiguous, but perhaps he too recognised the need for publicity if he was to fulfil his ambition to climb full-time.

In the end the team consisted of Harlin, Haston and the American aid specialist Layton Kor. Competition soon emerged in the form of a strong German team led by Jörg Lehne and Peter Haag. The North Face of the Eiger lends itself to media coverage because the route is easily seen from the comfort and safety of the hotel terraces at Kleine Scheidegg, and the promise of an international race to the top sparked immense media interest. Inevitably, the desired weather window never opened and both teams were soon reduced to using siege tactics, with fixed ropes to allow the lead climbers to be rotated. As Whillans observed: 'If it's a race, it's the slowest race in the world.' Eventually the two teams combined, then tragedy struck when one of the fixed ropes broke as John Harlin was jumaring up, and he fell to his death. The remaining climbers decided to push on, and Haston and four Germans made the final push for the summit, arriving in a virtual white-out. Haston's lead of a section of 60 degree ice near the summit, without an ice axe or hammer, showed immense will power and self-control. Meanwhile Bonington got frostbite waiting on the summit to photograph the party's arrival.

Success on the Eiger Direct (subsequently named the Harlin Route) propelled Haston to instant stardom. Though the climbing community criticised the siege tactics, no-one doubted the difficulty of the route, which is now graded ED3/4. Haston had his teeth capped and straightened and spoke in public for the first time. He began to dress with an 'almost foppish elegance, in a very mod style...a strange mixture of sensual and ascetic'.[88] He also took over the International School of Mountaineering that John Harlin had established at Leysin. Mick Burke, Davie Agnew (of the Creagh Dhu), Don Whillans and others acted as instructors from time to time, and there was a constant stream of young male and female students passing through. Whillans was made proctor of the school for a time, in charge of maintaining morals.

Haston held court in the Club Vagabond in Leysin, drinking until the early hours of the morning night after night, before heading off to climb the most difficult routes, including the fourth winter ascent of the North Face of the Matterhorn with Mick Burke in 1967. Like Che Guevara or Jimi Hendrix, part of the appeal of Haston was that he seemed destined for an early grave. As time went on, he became even more introverted, treating close friends as if they were strangers from a distant past. As Don Whillans said: 'It's as though he were behind glass. You can see him, but you can't touch him.'[89]

THE GREATER RANGES

The 1950 ascent of Annapurna by Maurice Herzog and Louis Lachenal caused a sensation in the climbing world. It was the first 8,000m peak to be climbed, and the account of the expedition demonstrated a level of commitment, suffering and self-sacrifice that inspired the post-war generation. New equipment certainly played a role, but the French team included many outstanding climbers, including Lachenal and Lionel Terray, who together made the second ascent of the North Face of the Eiger, and Rebuffat who made the second ascent of the Walker Spur. In terms of technical ability, they were way ahead of the British, who were struggling to climb their first modern *grandes courses* in the Alps at the time.

The British climbing establishment may have been critical of the nationalism of German climbers in the 1930s, but they were equally capable of confusing sport and national prestige when it came to Everest. With the French success on Annapurna they also realised that after seven failures over 30 years, time was running out. The Chinese invasion of Tibet in 1950 had sealed off the northern route to Everest, and the end of the Raj in 1947 had significantly reduced Britain's influence to the south. Everest was no longer a British monopoly, and the idea that it might be climbed by another nation (especially the French) was too awful to contemplate.

In 1951 a reconnaissance expedition under the leadership of Eric Shipton was despatched to Nepal, newly opened to foreigners, to determine the practicality of an approach from the south through the imposing Khumbu Icefall. The team consisted of Tom Bourdillon, Bill Murray and Michael Ward and was later joined by two New Zealanders, Ed Hillary and Earle Riddiford. Hillary described their meeting: 'Feeling not a little like a couple of errant schoolboys going to visit the headmaster, we followed our Sherpa into a dark doorway and up some stairs into the upper room of a large building. As we came into the room, four figures rose to meet us. My first feeling was one of relief. I have rarely seen a more disreputable bunch, and my visions of changing for dinner faded away forever.'[90] As usual Shipton had adopted an abstemious approach to food, and the other British climbers eagerly fell upon the tins that the New Zealanders had brought with them. Tom Bourdillon later informed the BBC that 'the main thing about expedition food is that there should be some'.[91]

The Khumbu Icefall and Western Cwm clearly provided a feasible route to the South Col, but Shipton had qualms about repeatedly exposing porters to the unavoidable risk of icefall. Hillary, on the other hand, had no doubts: 'The only way to attempt this mountain was to modify the old standards of safety and justifiable risk...The competitive standards of Alpine mountaineering were coming to the Himalaya, and we might as well compete or pull out.'[92] During the 1930s the British public had lost interest in Everest after so many failures but, following the success of the French on Annapurna, the 1951 expedition rekindled public enthusiasm. *The Times* published a series of articles and a special supplement and, perhaps as a reaction to post-war austerity and travel restrictions, a new audience read the pre-war mountaineering books by Smythe, Tilman and Shipton, the latter becoming something of a folk hero, not least because, to the British public, he had found the way to 'the roof of the world'.

In 1952 the British were shocked to discover that the Nepalese authorities had granted permission for a Swiss expedition. They watched with bated breath, and not a few ungenerous thoughts, as the Swiss very nearly succeeded in climbing Mount Everest at their first attempt. Prevented from going to Everest, Shipton led a rather unsatisfactory training expedition to Cho Oyu (8,201m/26,906ft), which failed to reach the summit. The French were lined up for 1954 and the Swiss had booked again for 1955. It was clear to the British climbing establishment that the 1953 expedition was their last chance. Their first step to ensure success was to sack the romantic, individualistic Shipton and replace him with Colonel John Hunt, a military leader who had won the sword of honour at Sandhurst.

Shipton was shattered by the decision, but he could not have been entirely surprised. He simply failed to recognise the importance of what had become a nationalistic project: 'Everest had become the focus of greatly inflated publicity and of keen international competition, and there were many who regarded success in the coming attempt to be of high national importance. My well known dislike of large expeditions and my abhorrence of a competitive element in mountaineering might well seem out of place in the present situation.'[93] Many climbers, particularly those who still saw climbing primarily as an aesthetic activity, were deeply sympathetic. As Charles Evans observed: 'It was said that Shipton lacked the killer instinct – not a bad thing to lack in my view.'[94] Chris Bonington, writing some years later in language reminiscent of a management text book, disagreed: '[Shipton] was essentially a mountain traveller and in his restless urge to explore would never have the single-minded drive of the goal-oriented climber to solve a major mountaineering problem.'[95] Shipton's marriage broke up, and Geoffrey Winthrop Young had the unenviable task of removing him from his post as warden of the Outward Bound School in Eskdale when, after an unfortunate affair with the bursar's wife, he was chased round the school grounds by the outraged husband brandishing a carving knife and shouting, 'You're a shit Shipton.'[96] For a while Shipton retreated to rural Shropshire where he worked as a forestry labourer. He made a final trip to the Karakoram in 1957 before rediscovering the joy of true exploration among the remote and stormy mountains of Patagonia.

John Hunt was born into a military family in India. His father was killed in France in 1914 when John was four. Educated at Marlborough and Sandhurst, he was an earnest, hardworking man who sometimes worried that he lacked 'the means to off-set the pressures of work and worry with a little light relief'.[97] He climbed in the Alps as a child and in the Himalaya following his army posting to India in 1931, taking part in James Waller's spirited attack on Saltoro Kangri in the Karakoram in 1935. He was shortlisted for the 1936 Everest expedition but failed to pass the medical. In 1937 he explored the approaches to Kangchenjunga and climbed the South West summit of Nepal Peak (7,145m/23,440ft). When war broke out he was posted back to Britain and became chief instructor at the Commando Mountain and Snow Warfare School in Braemar, corresponding with Geoffrey Winthrop Young and Kurt Hahn about the benefits of outdoor education. After the war the Duke of Edinburgh, who had been educated at Gordonstoun where Hahn was headmaster, took up the cause and established the Duke of Edinburgh Awards. Hunt became the first director of the scheme in 1956 and held the post for 10 years, becoming a life peer in 1966. The scheme was originally designed for boys only and was intended to bridge the gap between leaving school at 15 and national service at 18 with a combination of outdoor pursuits, physical fitness and community service. A parallel scheme for girls was set up in 1958 which included make-up, hair-styling, dress design and flower arranging.

Hunt brought a level of professionalism to the organisation of the 1953 expedition that had certainly been lacking in previous attempts on the mountain. But in other respects it was still an old-fashioned, class-conscious, imperial project. None of the younger generation of climbers, such as Brown, Whillans or Patey, was included in the team. Instead, Hunt selected a team drawn from the military and the older universities. He treated the Sherpas in a high-handed manner, in marked contrast to the democratic Swiss, billeting them in the embassy garage in Kathmandu (a converted stable with no toilets) while the white climbers stayed in the residence. The Sherpas duly urinated in the road in front of the embassy, earning a dressing down from Hunt which did little to improve relations.

George Band, ex-president of the Cambridge University Mountaineering Club and the youngest member of the team, recorded the public school atmosphere that pervaded the expedition in his diary: 'At 5:30 listened to the boat race. Cambridge won by 19 lengths in 19 minutes 54.5 seconds. Hurray! Tom [Bourdillon] set off a magnesium fuse during supper...I set up the short wave radio and aerial at Camp III on the lip of the Western Cwm and had the most marvellous reception from the Free Trade Hall, Manchester. John Barbirolli was conducting the Hallé Orchestra playing Beethoven's Leonora Overture No. 3.'[98] They were certainly good climbers by British standards, but they were not in the front rank of the sport, and they knew it. Band described the team as 'club players – like the London Irish – rather than internationals'[99] and few did any real training. Dr Roger Bannister, the first man to run a mile in less than four minutes, tested the fitness of some of the participants at his laboratory and was shocked by the poor results. Griff Pugh, a member of the Joint Himalayan Committee wrote: 'It was clear that having regard to the lower level of fitness and mountaineering experience of any British party, that only the very best oxygen equipment could enable us to put up a better performance than the Swiss.'

In the end, the 1953 expedition was a triumph of planning and technology. As well as much improved oxygen equipment and windproof garments, which were tested in the wind tunnel at the Royal Aircraft Establishment at Farnborough, 30 different firms were involved in the manufacture of the specially designed boots. There were also advances in high-altitude physiology, particularly the recognition of the critical role of rehydration in effective acclimatisation.

George Lowe and Wilfrid Noyce made the breakthrough by reaching the South Col despite heavy snowfall. From there Tom Bourdillon and Charles Evans (the deputy leader) made the first summit attempt, turning back at the South Summit when it was clear that they could not reach the top and return in the time remaining. Hillary and Tenzing tried again from a higher camp and finally reached the summit. As Hillary so concisely expressed it: 'We knocked the bastard off.' News of their success was sent in code to London where it was published by *The Times* in time for the coronation of Queen Elizabeth II on 2 June 1953. It seemed a fitting start to the New Elizabethan Age, but acrimony soon followed. The white members of the team were appalled when the popular press in India and Nepal claimed that Tenzing had reached the summit before Hillary. A banner in Kathmandu showed Tenzing dragging a semi-conscious Hillary towards the summit. John Hunt insisted that it had been a team effort, but the British establishment showed that they were equally capable of petty bigotry: while Hunt and Hillary both received knighthoods, a George Cross was deemed sufficient reward for Sherpa Tenzing. In their celebration of this national triumph they also conveniently overlooked the fact that neither of the summiteers was British. British attempts to climb Everest, which had begun in earnest in 1921, finally reached fruition more than half a century later when Dougal Haston and Doug Scott reached the summit by way of the South-West Face in 1975. Hunt called his account of the 1953 climb *The Ascent of Everest,* with the clear implication that there would be only one of any significance. When Bonington finally put two Britons onto the summit in 1975 the book was titled *Everest the Hard Way*, with the equally clear implication that Hunt had chosen the easy way. Today the line pioneered by the 1953 expedition is disparagingly called the 'Yak Route' by the Sherpas and is certainly not technically difficult in good weather conditions. But in 1953 it was a major psychological breakthrough.

Following the expedition, Hillary and Hunt were invited to give a talk at the Supreme Headquarters, Allied Powers in Europe, hosted by Field Marshal Montgomery. After the lecture, Monty addressed the assembled staff. 'Well', he said, 'you have now heard the story and I want you to all buy a copy of Hunt's book. Turn to Appendix III, and you will see the basis on which the whole operation was planned. Brigadier Hunt served as GSO (Ops and Plans) on my staff at Fontainebleau before taking charge of the Everest expedition.'[100] The inference was clear: Monty had planned the expedition.

The ascent of Everest was certainly magnificent, but was it mountaineering? As Bill Tilman noted in 1937, 'I have always admired those people who before ever reaching a mountain, perhaps even before seeing it, will draw up a sort of itinerary of the journey from base camp to summit...It reminds me of the battle plans an omniscient staff used to arrange for us in France.'[101] The appeal of climbing, for most people, lies in the liberating sense of personal freedom that it gives, and the very last thing they would wish to do is take part in a military operation, no matter how good the General Staff Officer (Operations and Plans) might be as a leader of men. While the general public celebrated the success on Everest, most climbers probably agreed with Shipton when he said: 'Thank goodness. Now we can get on with some real climbing.' Unfortunately, the very success of the Everest expedition meant that it formed the model on which future expeditions to the major Himalayan peaks were based for the next two decades. But it also gave a great spur to British mountaineering generally, both through the public interest that it generated and the profit from the sale of Hunt's expedition book and the expedition film, which were used to set up the Mount Everest Foundation, a charity that continues to sponsor climbing expeditions to this day.

The 1955 Kangchenjunga (8,586m/28,169ft) expedition led by Charles Evans was broadly based on the Everest model of a military-style siege, but with one notable exception. For the first time, 'other ranks' were allowed to join the team. On Everest, only Alf Gregory, the expedition photographer, came from a working-class background. On Kangchenjunga, Joe Brown – the 'Manchester plumber' – was invited to join the team. As always, Tom Patey celebrated the event in song:

> *Customs change and so alas*
> *We now include the working-class,*
> *So we invited Good Old Joe*
> *To come along and join the show.*
> *He played his part, he fitted in,*
> *He justified our faith in him;*
> *We want the climbing world to know –*
> *That the chaps all got on well with Joe...*[102]

When Joe Brown reached the summit of Kangchenjunga in 1955, it marked the culmination of 100 years of social 'trickle down' in the sport. As it happened, it was also the first and only 8,000m peak where British climbers made the first ascent. During the 1960s and 70s, as class distinctions gradually faded, the sport progressively became a true meritocracy, with climbers earning the opportunity to climb the highest mountains based on ability rather than social background. A surprisingly high proportion have continued to come from Oxford, Cambridge and the red brick universities that stand on either side of the Pennines. This may be because climbing 'is a sport that...appeals mainly to the cultivated intellect', as Charles Mathews suggested in 1897, but it seems more likely that long holidays are the root cause. Climbers on the dole are also well represented in the leading ranks of the sport.

As well as being deputy leader of the 1953 Everest expedition, Charles Evans had been with Tilman on his Nepal journey in 1950, reaching 24,000ft on Annapurna IV (7,524m/24,688ft), and was with Shipton on Cho Oyu in 1952. Like so many of his generation, Evans' father was killed in the First World War. He was brought up in rural Wales and spoke Welsh as his first language. After studying medicine at Oxford, he became a brain surgeon and later principal of University College of North Wales (now called Bangor University). He was by all accounts one of the best expedition leaders British climbing has ever produced, with an 'uncanny knack of encouraging people willingly to do their best'.[103] He married Denise Morin (daughter of Nea), who was herself a noted climber. Charles became president of the Alpine Club in 1967 and Denise became the first female president in 1986.

Although conceived largely as a reconnaissance expedition, Joe Brown and George Band succeeded in reaching the summit of Kangchenjunga via a tough jamming crack led by Brown. The next day, Tony Streather and Norman Hardie discovered an easy way round which allowed them to walk to the summit. Captain Streather had already shown himself to be a strong high-altitude climber by reaching the summit of Tirich Mir (7,700m/25,263 ft) after being recruited as transport officer for the 1950 Norwegian expedition.

The 1956 British expedition to the Muztagh Tower (7,273m/ 23,862ft) adopted a very different approach. Discovered and named by Martin Conway during his 1892 Karakoram expedition, the Muztagh

Tower appeared to be completely impregnable, and its ascent had obsessed John Hartog ever since he had seen a photograph of the peak at the age of 17. When he was 34, Hartog persuaded Ian McNaught-Davis to join him on an expedition, and the two of them then set out to recruit Joe Brown and Tom Patey. McNaught-Davis turned up on Joe Brown's doorstep and said: 'We are going to the Muztagh Tower in a fortnight...would you like to join us?'[104] Remarkably, both Brown and Patey agreed. Even more remarkably, all four climbers reached the summit. The expedition cost less than £4,000. Its purity of style pointed the way for future climbs focused on the technical difficulty and beauty of the line, rather than altitude and national pride. However, as with Everest, competition from a French team attempting to climb the same mountain by a different route added spice to the venture.

Another notable climb was the 1961 ascent of Ama Dablam (6,812m/22,349ft) by Michael Ward and others. Ama Dablam is a beautiful pyramid of rock and ice in a stunning position not far from Everest. Today it is a popular destination for commercial expeditions, and both its beauty and aura of difficulty have been tainted by a proliferation of fixed ropes, but its ascent in 1961 was a fine achievement.

In 1963, a year after his success on the North Face of the Eiger, Chris Bonington travelled to Chile to attempt the Central Tower of Paine (2,460m/8,070ft), a spectacular rocky spire in Patagonia, with a team including Don Whillans, Ian Clough, John Streetly and Barrie Page. The team was tested by appalling weather and the unprecedented presence of two wives. Bonington had done a deal with the *Daily Express* to cover the climb, but probably did not expect an article to appear on the Women's Page about his wife, Wendy, Barrie Paige's wife, Elaine, and their son, Martin 'the base camp baby': 'Elaine...is turning the wilderness itself into home', the article gushed. '"I can cook very good bread and cakes in a hole in the ground...[and] I have made myself an efficient hairdresser with only cold water and a few rollers..."' Sadly, Bonington failed to record Whillans' comments on this article in his account of the climb.

After a long period when the expedition appeared to be drifting towards failure, they were spurred into action by the appearance of an Italian team intent on claiming the prize, with the added advantage of a permit to climb the peak, which the British expedition lacked. The competitive threat was sufficient inducement for Bonington and Whillans to make a sprint for the summit during a brief break in the bad weather. On the descent Bonington had a potentially fatal fall but survived with a fractured ankle. 'I was on the point of breakdown from fatigue and shock', Bonington recorded, 'yet still felt compelled to write a report for the *Daily Express*, of the successful climb and my near-accident.' With the report written and safely despatched with John Streetly, Bonington thought that he could finally relax, but Whillans had other ideas: 'You'd better do the cooking, Chris. I'm no good at it.'[105]

Subsequent British expeditions to Patagonia in the 1960s faced equally challenging conditions. In 1967, an expedition to Cerro Torre (3,102m/10,177ft), a slender spire capped by a mushroom of ice, including Martin Boysen, Mick Burke, Peter Crew and Dougal Haston, was defeated by bad weather. During 37 days trapped in base camp by storms, while the others swore and cursed, Haston simply switched off, displaying no outward signs of boredom or frustration. Yet it was Haston who almost invariably led when conditions allowed.

By 1970, mountaineering in the Himalaya had reached a similar stage of development as the Alps a century earlier. All the 8,000m peaks had been climbed by their easiest routes and the highest and most famous had been climbed several times. With better information, better equipment and better planning, success on the biggest peaks was not guaranteed, but the uncertainty of the outcome had certainly been reduced, and ambitious climbers were looking for new challenges. Just as their Victorian predecessors had done in the 1870s, climbers started to examine the possibility of climbing the highest peaks by different and more difficult routes. The success of expeditions such as the Muztagh Tower showed that technical climbing was possible on 7,000m peaks. The question now was whether such climbing was possible on one of the 8,000m peaks, with the added complexity of altitude and logistics. This was the challenge that Bonington decided to take on after a break from major climbing expeditions lasting almost seven years, during which time he had undertaken a variety of assignments as an adventure journalist. The mountain he chose was the South Face of Annapurna (8,075m/26,493 ft), a steep 3,000m/10,000ft wall of rock and ice.

Based on his experience reporting the ascent of the Harlin Route on the Eiger, Bonington was convinced that only siege tactics would work on a face of this size and difficulty. He therefore needed a large team of lead climbers who could be regularly rotated as they tired, and set about recruiting the best British mountaineers of the time: Don Whillans, Dougal Haston, Ian Clough, Martin Boysen, Mick Burke and Nick Estcourt. Nearly all of them had climbed together and knew each other's abilities. Bonington was probably closest to Ian Clough, who had shared his triumph on the Eiger, and Nick Estcourt, a wild, excitable computer programmer and former president of the Cambridge University Mountaineering Club.

Worried that Whillans might not be fit enough to join the expedition, Bonington agreed to meet at Whillans' house near Manchester on a Friday night and drive to Scotland for the weekend. Whillans eventually returned from the pub at 2:30 on Saturday morning having sunk 11 pints. They drove to Scotland overnight ('I kept the wheel most of the way, afraid that Don had had too much to drink'[106]) and reached Glencoe in the morning. They then made the first ascent of the Great Gully of Ardour with Tom Patey. Whillans led the final, difficult pitch in magnificent style and Bonington offered him the Deputy Leadership of the expedition. Bonington's agent told him that the inclusion of an American climber would help to sell the book rights in the United States, so Tom Frost was drafted in. Frost was both an outstanding climber and a practising Mormon, a faith that forbids strong drink, gambling, smoking, bad language, tea and coffee. As Bonington observed: 'Tom turned out to be not only a good Mormon but also a splendidly tolerant one.'[107]

Although the climbing objective and the climbing team were distinctly modern, the organisation resembled a pre-war Everest expedition. There was an organising committee consisting of Sir Douglas Busk, ex-ambassador, former leader of the Young Shavers and current vice-president of the Alpine Club; Pat Pirie-Gordon, a director of Glyn, Mills & Co., the bankers; Anthony Rawlinson, a senior Treasury official and future president of the Alpine Club; Colonel Charles Wylie; and Tom Blakeney, the secretary of the Mount Everest Foundation. Lord Hunt, Lord Tangley and Sir Charles Evans were patrons. Bonington noted, almost with regret, that 'leading a siege-style expedition in 1970 was a different matter from doing so in the 'fifties and 'sixties. The habit of obeying a leader, inculcated by war service or National Service, was no longer there and the climbers themselves were becoming more skilled, competitive, individually ambitious and deserving of their chance to succeed.'[108] The increasing professionalisation of the sport placed significant additional pressures on leading climbers, who constantly needed to refresh their record of achievement in order to maintain their income from book sales, lecturing and equipment endorsements, and, in the eyes of the public, success meant reaching the summit. Playing a supporting role, no matter how crucial, did not provide the celebrity status that had become the life-blood of the professional climber.

Whillans and Haston, for different reasons, were perhaps the hungriest for success. Despite past achievements, Whillans knew that his climbing career, particularly in the greater ranges, had been less illustrious than his erstwhile partner Joe Brown, who had reached the summit of Kangchenjunga and the Muztagh Tower. He also knew that at the age of 37 and with a lifestyle that was not exactly conducive to maintaining the highest levels of physical fitness, time was running out. For Haston, this was his first season in the Himalaya and he saw in Whillans an older, wiser climber from whom he could learn the tricks of the trade. The two formed an unlikely partnership, with Haston calling Whillans 'Dad', just as during his early days in Scotland he had called Jimmy Marshall the 'Old Man'.

During the expedition Whillans carefully husbanded his strength, leaving most of the hard work to Haston. Haston knew that he was serving his apprenticeship, but he still begrudged Whillans his laziness. 'It's a case of one leg after the other, what a senseless existence. W behind me, but unable or unwilling to go to the front. It's too much to hope, I suppose, that he will ever actually get his fucking finger out, and make a brew.'[109] While Whillans and Haston were resting at base camp, Burke and Frost, supported by Estcourt and Boysen, pushed the route to within reach of Camp IV, making an assault on the summit feasible; but time was running out with the approach of the monsoon. Until then Bonington had more or less rotated the lead climbers, but with so much at stake he took a decision to push Whillans and Haston to the front. Boysen, Estcourt and Burke were furious. Nevertheless Bonington stuck to his decision, and a few days later Whillans and Haston stood on the summit. For Whillans, it was the high point of his climbing career after many previous disappointments in the Himalaya and the Andes. During the descent, when the whole team was almost within reach of base camp, Ian Clough was killed in an avalanche. Clough had been with Bonington on the Central Pillar of Frêney, the North Face of the Eiger and the Central Tower of Paine. His was the first of many deaths as Bonington's Himalayan circus gathered pace in the ensuing years.

Success on Annapurna re-launched Bonington's career as a climbing leader, rather than a leading climber. Britain once more stood at the forefront of high-altitude mountaineering and there was a suggestion that Bonington should receive an honour in recognition of the achievement. The convention established by the 1953 Everest expedition was that the leader of the expedition and the climbers reaching the summit should be honoured. It was a sign of the times that on Annapurna one summiteer had spent time in jail while the other had been extremely lucky to avoid doing so after several run-ins with the police. Both were therefore considered unworthy of such recognition, and Bonington had to wait another five years before he received his CBE.

7

AFTER 1970:

REINVENTING THE IMPOSSIBLE

In the increasingly international world of climbing, three major new routes in 1970 raised questions about the future direction of the sport: Bonington's Annapurna expedition to Nepal; the Wall of the Early Morning Light in the United States; and the South-East Ridge of Cerro Torre in Argentina. The South Face of Annapurna was probably the hardest climb attempted in the Himalaya at that time and helped to reinforce Britain's reputation as a leading climbing nation, but for many climbers it represented a dead end. It demonstrated that with enough time, money, manpower and equipment almost anything was climbable. There were fears that the true spirit of climbing – the feeling of individual liberty, self-reliance and adventure – was being lost in the business of fund-raising, planning and logistics. Similar concerns were arising in Europe and the United States where the new *direttissimas* in the Alps and big wall climbs in Yosemite required ever increasing amounts of artificial aid and manpower. Warren Harding's Wall of the Early Morning Light on El Capitan in Yosemite took 27 days to equip and climb. Meanwhile, the leading Italian climber Cesare Maestri bludgeoned his way up the graceful granite spire of Cerro Torre in Patagonia using a mobile compressor to power a mechanical drill.

The mood of many members of the international climbing community was captured by Reinhold Messner, also an Italian, when he talked about 'the murder of the impossible'[1] in 1971 and advocated placing less reliance on equipment and organisation and more on personal courage and skill. In the United States, Yvon Chouinard identified two possible futures for the sport: 'We are entering a new

261

era of climbing, an era that may well be characterised by incredible advances in equipment, by the overcoming of great difficulties, with even greater technological wizardry, and by the rendering of the mountains to a low, though democratic, mean. Or it could be the start of more spiritual climbing, where we assault the mountains with less equipment and with more awareness, more experience and more courage.'[2] What actually happened was that the sport fragmented, and both futures became a reality.

A highly influential article appeared in the first issue of the American journal *Ascent* in 1967 entitled 'The Games Climbers Play'. Its author, Lito Tejada-Flores, divided climbing into a hierarchy of 'games' from the least to the most risky, ranging from bouldering, through crag, big wall and alpine climbing, to expeditions in the greater ranges. He suggested that the informal conventions and 'rules' that govern the conduct of each game are, in effect, a handicap system designed to maintain the uncertainty of the outcome and therefore the challenge of the sport. Those games that have the lowest level of intrinsic risk necessarily have the greatest number of restrictive rules to maintain the challenge, while the riskiest games have the fewest restrictions because the outcome is inherently uncertain. Hence the rules of the expedition game permit the use of a ladder to bridge a crevasse on the Khumbu Icefall because a single ladder will not make success on Everest a foregone conclusion. Using a ladder to climb a boulder problem in the Peak District would be pointless.

In bouldering the rules of the game prohibit all technical aids, including a rope, and the climber simply ascends the rock solo. In crag climbing, certain defined forms of protection are permitted but the aim is to climb without using direct aid. In big wall climbing, some direct aid is allowed and each member of the team need not climb every pitch; the second may jumar up the rope, hauling up food, water and equipment. In alpine climbing the rules are relaxed to reflect the increase in objective dangers, but the party must move as a self-contained unit in one continuous push from the bottom to the top, without the benefit of a series of pre-placed camps or fixed ropes. The expedition game is the least restrictive, allowing 'siege tactics', whereby a series of camps are pushed up the mountain, often connected by fixed ropes and supplied by Sherpas, until a summit attempt can be made from the highest camp. As Alan Rouse noted, success on Annapurna in 1970 demonstrated that 'anything was possible, if everything was allowed'.[3]

Tejada-Flores' thesis was that 'ethical' climbing and 'good style' simply mean respecting the rules applicable to the climbing game being played. Conversely, 'unethical' climbing is the adoption of rules applicable to a riskier game, such as using siege tactics on an alpine peak, as happened on the Eiger Direct (Harlin Route) one year before the article appeared. He postulated that success in climbing, and the progress of the sport, can be seen in terms of elite climbers using the restrictive rules applicable to safer games in increasingly risky situations. Hence elite climbers will attempt to climb a mountain crag solo, or eliminate all direct aid on a big wall climb. It followed that as increasingly restrictive ethical rules became the norm, the least restrictive game – the expedition game – would gradually disappear, and that is exactly what has happened. From 1970 onwards, big expeditions were progressively rejected by leading climbers in favour of what came to be called alpine-style ascents – the application of alpine rules in a setting where expedition rules had previously applied. Harking back to a philosophy first advocated by climbers in the nineteenth century, the ambition was to adopt a lightweight approach, eliminating all unnecessary artificial aids that stand between the climber and the mountain.

There was very little that was completely new in Tejada-Flores' article – it may even have been written slightly tongue-in-cheek – but his simple codification of the sport and definition of the 'rules' of climbing brought a new clarity to the ethical debates that had been swirling around on the use of bolts and other artificial aids, as well as focusing the ambitions of climbers at the leading edge of the sport. Ken Wilson, the hyperactive editor of *Mountain*, used the article 'to provide a firm ideological base for the magazine'[4] which he took over in 1968. Wilson launched a crusade against the use of aid which, on occasions, became faintly ludicrous. *Crags* magazine, a rival rock climbing 'lads' mag' in the 1970s, parodied *Mountain* magazine's obsession with the subject by running a self-assessment quiz, in the style of *Cosmopolitan*, entitled 'Ow's Yer Effics?' but, through his sheer energy as a controversialist, Wilson has had a major influence on the development of the sport in Britain.

Alongside the ethical debates of the 1970s and early 1980s an extraordinary leap in climbing standards was taking place in Britain as a result of better training, technology and mass unemployment. The Brown–Whillans routes in the 1950s were typically around E1 or E2. During the 1960s numerous climbers reached this standard and a number of harder climbs started to appear, particularly on gritstone and limestone outcrops. By the end of the 1970s the highest grade had risen to E7. Thereafter the rate of progress slowed. By the end of the 1980s, the hardest climbs were E9. During the 1990s the first E10 appeared. The first E11 was claimed in 2005.

Training played a major role in the step change that occurred during the 1970s. Writing in 1970, Dennis Gray probably spoke for the majority of climbers when he said that 'most would feel, on the present basis of mountain ethics, that actually to train for climbing...is the antithesis of what the sport is all about'.[5] Even in 1979 Peter Boardman and Joe Tasker, two of the best mountaineers that Britain has ever produced, were stunned by the rigorous fitness routine described by the leading Italian climber Reinhold Messner: 'In the morning I have a cold shower, run up 1,000m on my toes within thirty minutes and then chew garlic to dilate my vascular walls...My personal physician advises me on everything I eat, everything I do. He tells me I am a superman.'[6] In contrast, when Boardman went for a training run it was sufficiently novel to warrant a mention in his book, while Tasker noted that Georges Bettembourg's 'Gallic enthusiasm for "training" mesmerised us indolent British, who were unwilling to subscribe to any dogmas about climbing mountains'.[7]

Don Whillans, who summited Annapurna South Face in 1970, personified the traditional British approach to climbing. Someone asked him when he stopped drinking before going on an expedition: 'When I reach the last pub,' he replied. Asked why he drank so much, he replied: 'Aye, well I've got this morbid fear of dehydration.' At the end of a pre-expedition meeting at Bonington's house in Manchester, some of the climbers decided to go for a training run. 'Is there a bus strike?' asked Whillans. In public, most leading climbers subscribed to Whillans' point of view – that was how hard men were supposed to behave – but a lot of training was going on in private. Rowland Edwards had to own up when he broke his neck doing pull-ups in his kitchen.

In reality, by the late 1960s climbing standards had more or less reached the limit of what was possible applying the traditional British technique of training in the pub. To push standards further demanded a systematic approach to training, as athletes in every other 'amateur' sport were discovering. Two developments accelerated this trend. The first was the invention of artificial climbing walls – at first, little more than brick walls with a few protruding bricks – and the second was the spread of gyms and weight rooms. Climbing walls allowed climbers to repeat difficult moves over and over again in complete safety, improving balance, finger strength and confidence. Many climbers found that they could improve their standard of climbing by as much as two grades this way. Weight training allowed climbers to build arm strength and stamina. By the 1980s, competition for new routes was so intense that some climbers started to use drugs to suppress the body's natural warning systems, and many suffered serious shoulder injuries and acute tendonitis.

The huge advance in the standard of climbing in the 1970s cannot be explained by training alone, however. Systematic training has been applied in athletics for far longer than in climbing, but over the last century the world record time for the men's 100m sprint improved by just eight per cent and the world record distance for the long jump increased by 18 per cent. This probably gives a fair indication of how much the physical performance of the human body can be improved through better training, improved nutrition and competition alone. Although climbing is a far less exact sport than athletics, almost all climbers would agree that standards have increased by far more than 8–18 per cent since 1900, and most would acknowledge that they increased by more than this during the 1970s alone.

Better training certainly played a major role, but the real break-through was psychological rather than physical: during the late 1960s and early 1970s climbers ceased to be afraid of falling off. Alan Blackshaw's *Mountaineering*, the climbers' 'bible' published in the mid-1960s, reflected the orthodoxy that had prevailed since the invention of the sport by emphasising that 'it is a basic principle of all climbing that *the leader never falls*, and everything must be subordinated to this'.[8] By the 1970s, improvements in technology made it possible for climbers to ignore this principle with relative impunity.

Specially designed nuts, chocks, wedges and hexes that would fit into cracks of different shapes and sizes started to appear on the market in the 1960s. Climbers of a certain age will fondly remember their first MOAC, a metal wedge first cast in Manchester in 1962, but like so much of British industry, leadership soon passed to the USA. In 1976 mechanical camming devices called 'friends' were invented, which jammed into parallel-sided spaces transforming the protection on climbs with cracks or bedding planes. Belay devices and dynamic ropes stopped a leader fall gradually, reducing the strain on belays and the second. Sit harnesses, which cushion the impact of falls on the leader and have convenient slings for racking gear, became ubiquitous. In the 1950s climbers tended to use a maximum of two or three running belays per pitch. By the 1970s, safety-conscious leaders could reach above their heads on many climbs and put in a runner every two or three metres, effectively giving themselves a top-rope for much of the climb. The psychological benefit of protection cannot be overstated. Bill Peascod, who started climbing in the Lake District in the late 1930s, emigrated to Australia after the war and returned to Britain when he was in his sixties. He repeated a number of his old routes and in many cases found them easier. Since his physical fitness and strength had clearly diminished he put the difference down to the psychological support of better protection: 'When the going got hot I popped another nut into the crack and ran the rope through the krab. Immediately I felt relaxed. I could savour the situation and search for the most appealing sequence of moves.'[9]

Many climbers discovered that the limit of their ability was defined more by the psychological barrier caused by fear of falling than by the physical barrier of strength or stamina. Those willing to accept the risk of repeated falls were able to push their grade. Moreover, as they became habituated to higher technical standards of difficulty, and fitter, the bolder ones felt able to climb at the higher standard even without the technical and psychological support of top-ropes and protection. Peter Livesey was one of the first to make the breakthrough: 'That's what I could do and most climbers can't. Their perception of difficulty changes with height. They look at a pitch high up and say "I can't climb that", when in fact they *can* climb it or rather, they could climb it if it were only five feet from the ground.'[10]

If technological improvements in rock climbing equipment were important, those in ice climbing were revolutionary. On steep snow and ice the climber now relies directly on technology to maintain contact with the mountain. Prior to the 1970s the technique of ice climbing had hardly changed since Victorian times. Axes had a straight pick, designed for cutting steps, which prevented climbers from pulling up directly on the axe because the pick tended to slip out of the ice. This problem was solved almost simultaneously in the USA and Scotland when Yvon Chouinard produced the dropped pick 'Climax' and Hamish MacInnes produced the 'Terrordactyl'. The curved Chouinard design is now the basis for nearly all conventional ice axes used for alpine climbing, while the Terrordactyl design, with its steeply inclined pick, is the model for most modern technical ice climbing tools. The new designs rendered years of hard-won step-cutting technique and experience redundant overnight. Rigid boots and 12 point crampons allowed climbers to move up steep or even vertical ice using just the front points of their crampons and two short ice axes. Powerful head torches with long-life batteries allowed alpinists to climb at night, when ice couloirs are relatively free from the objective risk of rockfall, and protection also improved with the invention of hollow tubular ice screws. As a result of these technical innovations, ice routes which had previously taken days could now be climbed in a matter of hours.

Technology was also changing the way big mountains were climbed. Lightweight, warm and windproof clothing and better boots reduced the risk of frostbite. Big wall techniques from the USA were transferred to Europe where they were tried out in the Alps and then applied in the Himalaya, Baffin Island, Patagonia and anywhere else where there are huge vertical expanses of rock. Unlike most other parts of the world, where climbing had followed the European alpine tradition, climbing in the USA evolved in isolation, resulting in different techniques and approaches. Hard steel pitons, hauling systems, sleeping hammocks and portaledges for bivouacking on vertical rock, and crash pads for bouldering were all invented in the USA.

The technological developments that drove these breakthroughs reflected the fact that climbing was becoming a mass activity, and the size of the potential market for new products justified a greater investment in research and development, marketing and retailing. A whole new cluster of cottage industries sprang up to supply the rapidly growing outdoor market. Small manufacturing firms designed and produced climbing equipment, rucksacks, tents, sleeping bags, footwear and clothes. Specialist outdoor sports shops opened in almost every major town, and clothing originally conceived for the outdoor market, such as fleeces, even became fashionable on the High Street for a time.

Perhaps the most controversial technological breakthrough initially had nothing to do with climbing. In the early 1980s, the invention of long-life, lightweight rechargeable batteries enabled the development of the cordless powerdrill. Prior to that time, inserting bolts was a labour-intensive activity requiring the climber to hand-drill each hole or carry a portable generator or compressor to the rock face. Cordless drills made it possible to equip any climb with expansion bolts with minimal effort, and therefore posed perhaps the greatest ever threat to traditional climbing ethics on British crags. It also represented the culmination of a process that had been going on for a number of years, whereby technical difficulty and risk had progressively become de-coupled.

In the earliest days of climbing, increased technical difficulty necessarily involved increased risk. As climbs became more difficult the risk of falling off rose and, in the absence of protection, all falls were serious. In tackling harder routes, climbers therefore had to overcome two barriers: the athletic challenge of climbing steeper rock using smaller holds; and the psychological challenge of increasing exposure and risk. This relationship started to break down with the development of better protection. Certain routes, especially crack climbs, allow the leader to place protection at regular intervals. Others, particularly steep slabs, can be devoid of natural protection. The distinction was acknowledged in the creation of two grading systems: a technical grade which measures the hardest move or series of moves on the climb; and an adjectival grade, which takes into account the overall seriousness of the climb, including the availability of protection. Some modern guide books even have a separate symbol for climbs where the absence of protection or a bad landing make a fall potentially fatal. This approach enabled climbers to decide for themselves how much technical difficulty and how much risk they were prepared to accept.

The cordless powerdrill enabled the development of 'sport-climbs' that are pre-equipped with bolts at regular intervals of two to three metres. To all intents and purposes, sport-climbing is a risk-free activity; statistically it is safer than many everyday activities such as driving. It allows the climber to concentrate solely on the technical difficulty of the route without worrying about the consequences of a fall. Throughout much of Europe, where the use of pitons was widely accepted, 'plaisir-climbing' was welcomed. In many cases existing routes that had been climbed using traditional protection were 'retro-bolted' to improve safety or reduce the damage done to the rock by repeated pegging. In some countries local authorities even paid for cliffs to be equipped with bolts in the hope of attracting climbing tourism to the area. During the 1980s, British rock climbers started to holiday in the south of France, the Costa Blanca or Majorca specifically to enjoy sport-climbing in a warm, safe and controlled environment, free from the vagaries of the British weather, the stresses of placing protection and the problems of route-finding (on a sport-climb you simply follow the bolts). However, many traditional British climbers were dismissive: '*Plaisir* crags...have many of the elements of urban life: repetitive monotony and uniformity, making the crags in France, Spain, Switzerland...safe, predictable and totally unadventurous. It's the same bland pap in the USA, Russia, Britain or wherever.'[11]

Perhaps the increasing demand for sport-climbs was the inevitable consequence of introducing young people to climbing in the risk-free environment of an outdoor education course or an artificial climbing wall. Many people enjoy the frisson that exposure gives, but a much smaller number want to risk death or serious injury if they fall. Sport-climbs give the frisson of fear without the risk of harm. They are an artificially created 'sublime' experience; the perfect example of Burke's doctrine that terror 'always produces delight when it does not press too close'. The purely athletic focus of sport-climbing also encouraged the development of competitions, usually held on artificial walls. Competitions were a feature of climbing in the former Soviet Union, often involving speed ascents on a top-rope, and became popular in France and Italy in the early 1980s. Initially the British opposed the idea, particularly when it involved using a natural crag – a proposal by the BBC to televise a competition at Malham Cove was vigorously opposed by the British Mountaineering Council – but competition climbing on artificial walls is now an accepted part of the sport. A British climber, Simon Nadin, became the first world indoor climbing champion in 1989.

In large parts of western Europe, the tradition of free climbing barely exists and, in any event, it is possible for sport-climbers and traditional climbers to co-exist because of the vast expanses of rock that are available. The same does not apply to Britain, with its more limited supply of natural rock faces and long tradition of free climbing. The result has been an uneasy truce, whereby bolting is banned, by common consent, from high mountain crags and other traditional climbing venues, but tolerated on certain quarries, outcrops and sea cliffs, particularly on limestone and slate where natural protection is poor. As Leo Houlding said at the Kendal Mountain Festival in 2005: 'With so little to work with, we have to be ethical to ensure that we can always do more with less.'

Amongst elite climbers there has been a clear move back to traditional, adventurous rock climbing during the 1990s and 2000s, but the new, danger-lite varieties of climbing appeal to a far broader cross section of society than traditional climbing. The social atmosphere at many climbing walls today is more akin to a leisure centre than it is to the climbing clubs and pubs of the past. The number of men and women climbing on walls is fairly evenly balanced, and during the day there are often large numbers of children. The American female climber Lynn Hill came third overall at the Grand Prix climbing championships held at Lyon in 1989, demonstrating that women have the physical capacity to climb at the highest standards of technical difficulty. The much smaller number of women climbing the hardest traditional rock climbs may be a reflection of differing attitudes to risk or may simply reflect the fact that women find the puerile, macho posturing that often accompanies extreme climbing unappealing.

In the 1930s, Alf Bridge invented the 'five year rule for hardmen', after which they retired, partly because their physical powers diminished but mainly because they lost their nerve. Today, the five year rule may still apply to those competing at the absolute pinnacle of the sport, but the lower-risk alternatives now available allow many climbers, both male and female, to continue to climb at a high technical standard well into middle age. During the 1950s most climbing club members were in their early twenties. Today, outside the university clubs, the average is probably around 40, and for many younger climbers the wall and the gym have replaced the club as the social focus of the sport. As the membership continues to age, many traditional clubs will probably disappear.

In addition to training and technology, social and economic changes were the other key factor driving climbing standards higher. By the 1970s climbing had become a truly democratic sport, equally accessible to Cambridge undergraduates and Manchester plumbers. A few institutions, such as the Alpine Club and the Climbers' Club where, even then, the average age of the membership was higher than the sport as a whole, retained some vestigial snobbery, but they were neither representative nor particularly relevant. The expansion of tertiary education produced a new generation of 'classless' climbers brought up in the university clubs. Leeds University alumni during this period included Roger Baxter Jones, Brian Hall, Alex MacIntyre, John Porter and John Syrett, while across the Pennines, Manchester University climbers included Joe Tasker, Dick Renshaw and Johnny Dawes. Universities were early adopters of purpose-built indoor climbing walls. The walls, and the social scene that surrounded them, even attracted non-student climbers to the university towns. Steve Bancroft moved to Leeds in the early 1970s to take advantage of the innovative Leeds University climbing wall, and post-industrial Sheffield, with its cheap housing, large student community and proximity to the Peaks, became home to many climbers from the mid-1970s onwards. The increasing concentration of climbers gave rise to fierce competition. One leading Sheffield-based climber noted wryly that he was only the fifth best climber on his street. Rab Carrington, former member of the Creagh Dhu and temperamentally very much part of the traditional climbing scene, was less than enamoured of the new approach: 'As soon as you get to the outskirts of Sheffield you can hear the popping and snapping of tendons and the straining of ligaments. The young kids drink only orange juice – in half pints, just in case even orange juice might be bad for them.'[12]

The 1970s was also a time when Britain appeared to be heading towards economic collapse. The oil price shock, continuous balance of payment crises, devaluation, stagflation and appalling industrial relations turned Britain into the poor man of Europe. In 1979 Margaret Thatcher was elected prime minister and adopted monetarist economic policies to try to control inflation. Unemployment jumped from 1 million to 3 million, and heavy industry in south Wales, the north of England and Scotland was decimated. North Sea oil and the growth of the service sector, particularly in the City of London, saved the economy, but long-term unemployment, especially among the young in the industrial north, became endemic. In the 1930s being on the dole had been a shameful thing. In the late 1970s and early 1980s it became standard practice, almost a form of political protest. One of the unintended consequences of high unemployment was that many young people turned their energy and enthusiasm to other activities, and the Thatcher generation produced many outstanding sportsmen and women, not least climbers, as well as a tidal wave of petty crime, from disaffected youth.

The 'Government climbing grant', as the dole came to be known, was hardly generous, but rock climbing is a relatively cheap activity. Unemployed climbers acquired the fitness and self-confidence that comes from doing something every day, and the commitment that arises from having very few alternatives for self-fulfilment. During the Great Depression of the 1930s a Swiss journalist, appalled by the rising death toll on the North Face of the Eiger, wrote: 'What is to become of a generation to which society offers no social existence and which has only one thing left to look to, a single day's glory? To be a bit of a hero...a gladiator, victorious one day, defeated the next.'[13] That same single-minded intensity applied to many British climbers in the 1970s and 80s, and as their ambitions extended from Britain to the Alps and the greater ranges they became the generation that 'nearly climbed itself into extinction'.[14]

The growth of outdoor education continued in the 1970s and 80s, as did mainstream media interest in the sport. In 1974 BBC Television ran a series called *Rock Face* on Sunday lunchtimes, immediately after *Thunderbirds*, which was designed to introduce young people to the techniques of rock climbing, and millions of readers and viewers followed Chris Bonington's well-publicised exploits in the Himalaya. There was also an explosion of specialist climbing media, including magazines, literature, guidebooks, videos and films. The Kendal Mountain Festival was established to showcase mountain films and videos, while the Boardman Tasker Prize celebrated the best of mountain literature. Joe Simpson's *Touching the Void* was an early prize winner that crossed over to the mainstream, winning a number of literary awards and being made into a highly acclaimed film documentary. *Touching the Void* is a vivid and harrowing account of a climbing accident in the Peruvian Andes and Simpson's solitary crawl back to camp. Its wide appeal had much in common with the public taste for polar exploration in the nineteenth century, with its moving combination of suffering and fortitude.

As a result of this dramatic growth in publicity, climbing became one of the fastest growing leisure activities in the UK, with ever increasing numbers competing to establish a reputation at the leading edge of the sport. The climbing media whipped up rivalries and controversies, and new routes were publicised within a few weeks of their first ascent, rather than the years that it had previously taken to produce a new guidebook. In order to retain their position and status in the sport, top climbers had to discover new routes or debunk old ones on a regular basis. All of this resulted in a trend towards practices that might loosely be described as 'cheating', recognising that in climbing there are no formal rules to break.

Over the years climbers have adopted a variety of techniques to make first ascents easier. In 1897 Owen Glynne Jones practised Kern Knotts Crack with a top rope before committing himself to leading it; in 1914 Siegfried Herford pre-inspected the Great Flake on Central Buttress from almost every angle, and then used combined tactics to overcome the crucial pitch; in the 1920s Harry Kelly frequently downclimbed routes before leading them; and in the 1950s Arthur Dolphin top-roped many routes using rubbers before he led them in nailed boots. But in each case, the climbers who followed knew roughly what techniques had been used on the first ascent. In the 1970s, some top climbers became more economical with the truth. Jim Perrin noted in the *Climbers' Club Journal* in 1978 that 'you cannot trust the route descriptions of many of our pioneers because they provide an account which is conceptual rather than actual; they describe the route not as they have done it, but as they would like it to have been done'.[15] For new routes of E4 and above, traditional 'on sight' leads, from the bottom to the top without pre-inspection or preparation, became increasingly rare. Top-rope or abseil inspections became routine and often involved extensive 'gardening' to remove loose rock and vegetation and 'brushing' to remove slippery lichen. Some routes received particularly vigorous brushing which revealed new holds on previously blank faces. Many climbers rehearsed difficult sections of the climb with a top-rope to work out the sequence of moves. Like gymnasts, they used magnesium carbonate chalk on their hands, which improves the grip but also marks the holds, making subsequent attempts easier. With the plethora of new protection available which could be inserted and removed without marking the rock, there were suspicions that many climbers were using direct aid or resting between moves by taking tension from the rope. None of these techniques are illegitimate. However, because of widespread memory lapses about the amount of aid actually used to create new routes, climbers making subsequent attempts in pure style frequently faced a more difficult challenge than the party making the first ascent.

The demanding training now required to remain competitive in the upper echelons of the sport inevitably led to growing specialisation and professionalism. The number of professional jobs for climbers rose with the expansion of outdoor education, but typically these involved the individual giving up the very thing that probably attracted them to the sport in the first place. In an increasingly litigious and regulated world, professional climbers are now trained to lead others in an environment that is as close to being risk-free as possible, whilst retaining some semblance of climbing. A very small number of elite climbers succeeded in making money from *real* climbing by writing, lecturing and sponsorship, but it was always a precarious existence. By virtue of their great deeds and unusual longevity, Chris Bonington and Doug Scott established a virtual duopoly in the mountaineering arena in the 1970s and 80s, although younger climbers such as Peter Boardman, Joe Tasker, Alex MacIntyre and Al Rouse were breaking into the market when they died. Bonington, in particular, has been extraordinarily successful in keeping his name in the public eye and obtaining money from unexpected sources. When he succeeded in raising the unprecedented sum of £100,000 of sponsorship from Barclays Bank for the 1975 Everest South-West Face expedition there were questions in parliament. An expedition to K2 three years later was sponsored by the manufacturers of Durex. Even so, the total amount of sponsorship money raised by climbers throughout the 150 year history of the sport would probably be insufficient to pay the wage bill of Manchester United for a month.

Despite the very modest amounts of money flowing into climbing compared to other professional sports, many climbers, including some at the leading edge, believe that increasing commercialisation has corroded the moral value of the activity and regret the decline of the amateur tradition. But there have been climbing professionals since the very beginnings of the sport. Albert Smith accumulated a small fortune based upon a single ascent of Mont Blanc in 1851 by creating a level of public interest that is inconceivable in today's more savvy and cynical world. Smith was certainly the most incompetent climber ever to make a living from the sport, but he was an outstanding entertainer. Today, with a few brilliant exceptions, the skills and personality required to have a climbing story worth telling appear to be incompatible with the ability to tell it well.

The growth of the mass market for climbing equipment and clothing opened up new commercial opportunities for professional climbers and established an increasingly symbiotic relationship between climbers, media and manufacturers. The media soon realised that, for the majority of readers, climbers are more interesting than climbs, resulting in 'the embarrassing candour'[16] of much recent expedition reporting.

30. Peter Crew, 1965.
After dropping out of Oxford, Crew became rock climbing's first pop icon: 'Loud, arrogant, confident, brash, dismissive...He'd psyche himself up...and blast off.'
(John Cleare)

31. Ed Drummond and Dave Pearce on the first ascent of A Dream of White Horses, Anglesey, October 1968. Climber, poet and magnet for controversy, Drummond created perhaps the most evocative name for a rock climb in Britain with this route.
(Leo Dickinson)

32. Rusty Baillie on the first
ascent of the Old Man of Hoy,
18 June 1966.
Britain's most inaccessible
summit was the scene of an
extraordinary TV rock climbing
spectacular in 1967 which
attracted an audience of 15
million viewers.

(Chris Bonington)

33. Doug Scott on the
first ascent of The Scoop,
Sron Ulladale, June 1969.
Overhanging rock and wind
created 'a unique experience in
fear and fascination'. Originally
climbed by Scott using artificial
aid, it was climbed free in 1987 by
Johnny Dawes and Paul Pritchard.

(Ken Wilson)

34. Peter Livesey, 1974. Thin, wiry and bespectacled, Livesey adopted an almost obsessive training regime to become the best British rock climber in the 1970s. When he was no longer able to compete at the highest level he gave up the sport.

(*John Cleare*)

35. Ron Fawcett, 1984. Fawcett replaced Livesey as the best rock climber in Britain. 'I knew when I first climbed with Ron that he was better than me,' recalled Livesey. 'The thing was, not to let Ron know that.'

(*John Beatty*)

36. (Left to right) Al Rouse, Dave Wilkinson, Brian Hall, Jim Curran and Al Burgess packing for the 1986 K2 expedition.

'It became imperative that expeditions like K2 should exist and, almost as important, be seen to exist, so that somehow [Rouse] could still use his name and reputation to carry him through the next season of trade fairs, lectures, magazine articles.'

(Alpine Club)

37. Mick Fowler on the summit of Taulliraju, 1982.
The secret life of a taxman: voted 'the mountaineers' mountaineer' by his peers, Fowler has maintained the amateur tradition by combining extremely adventurous climbing with a job at the Inland Revenue.

(Mick Fowler)

38. A climber on Left Wall, Dinas Cromlech, in the Llanberis Pass with Snowdon in the background. First climbed by Ron Moseley in 1956, Left Wall was typical of the hard new climbs produced by the Manchester-based Rock and Ice Club in the post-war years.

(John Cleare)

39. Tom Patey tests the strength of Chris Bonington's new continental climbing helmet, using a MacInnes North Wall hammer, 1964. Patey was a satirist whose humorous writing and songs captured the changing social dynamics of the sport in the 1950s and 60s. Bonington became Britain's most famous mountaineer and the undisputed impresario of Himalayan climbing in the 1970s.

(Chris Bonington)

40. (Opposite) Ian Clough on the South Face of Annapurna, May 1970.
A triumph of money, manpower and planning, Annapurna showed that 'anything was possible, if everything was allowed', but Clough still died on the expedition.

(Chris Bonington)

41. Doug Scott, 1975.
Britain's greatest living high-altitude mountaineer. Tall and powerful, with straggly hair and John Lennon glasses, he was 'a man designed to fell mountains'.

(Doug Scott)

42. Dougal Haston arriving on the summit of Everest at dusk on 24 September 1975.
Over half a century after the first attempt, Haston and Scott were the first British climbers to reach the summit of Everest in 1975. Peter Boardman described the expedition as 'one of the last great Imperial experiences'.

(Doug Scott)

43. Leeds University Union Climbing Club in Snell's Field, Chamonix, 1973.
From left to right: Bernard Newman (president), John Powell, John Porter, Alex
MacIntyre, John Eames. Climbers from the university clubs on either side of the
Pennines led the lightweight, alpine-style revolution in the mid-1970s.

(Bernard Newman Collection)

44. Joe Tasker (left) and Peter Boardman below the West Face of Changabang, 1976.
The disappearance of Boardman and Tasker on the North-East Ridge of Everest in 1982 inevitably
brought back echoes of Mallory and Irvine. They were leading members of the brilliant generation
that 'nearly climbed itself into extinction' in the 1970s and 80s.

(Photo: Peter Boardman, Chris Bonington Picture Library)

Climbing magazines needed recognisable personalities to sell copy as well as advertising revenue from equipment manufacturers to pay the rent. Manufacturers in turn needed recognisable climbers to endorse and recommend their products. The increasing commercialisation of the sport resulted in some bizarre experiments. In 1981 the first sponsored rock climb appeared: *Asolo* (a manufacturer of rock boots) is a fine E3 in the Lake District put up by Bill Birkett, the son of Jim Birkett, a leading Lakeland climber in the 1930s and 40s, but its name inevitably invited controversy. Competition climbing also provided a convenient forum for both the media and the manufacturers to promote their wares. The iconography of the sport increasingly reflected the new commercial priorities, with the mountains disappearing even further into the background while the camera focused on the well-honed muscles of the latest climbing hero and the branded equipment that he or she was using. Naturally, the heroes retained their commercial value only for as long as they remained in the public eye by winning competitions or completing hard new climbs.

During the 1960s, the regional differences that had characterised so much of British climbing history were progressively eroded by greater mobility and the growth of the national climbing media. By the 1970s such differences in England and Wales had virtually disappeared, and the development of the motorway network even made it possible for dedicated London climbers to go to Scotland for the weekend. However, the Scottish climbing community retained a distinctive character and, especially in winter, the more remote regions of Scotland had a pioneering atmosphere reminiscent of the Lake District a century earlier. Mick Fowler, a London-based climber, made 11 weekend visits to the north-west of Scotland during the winter of 1986 and did not once meet a climber there that he did not know. These weekend trips provided an interesting contrast to his working life as a tax inspector: 'Chris [Watts], Victor [Saunders] and I groped blindly in the worsening blizzard, remembering to be revelling in the contrast between weekday deskbound dreariness and character-building weekend excitement...

Fourteen hours later I was back in the tax office listening to how colleagues had spent the weekends going shopping or catching up on a few odd jobs.'[17]

Rising living standards and cheaper travel made summer visits to the Alps almost routine and progressively opened up the Himalaya and the Andes, as well as more exotic locations such as Patagonia, Greenland and Baffin Island. As the numbers travelling to these once remote locations increased, so too did the amount of information available in English. The early pioneers tended to concentrate on one area because they needed time to build up their knowledge of local bureaucracy, food supplies, camp sites, approach routes and descents. Most expeditions now follow well-worn paths. The battles with bureaucracy and haggles with porters still happen, but everybody knows that it will work out in the end. It is possible to fly into a new country, climb a new route, and fly back, all within the four or five weeks of paid holiday granted by most employers. Some climbers continue to delude themselves that they are pioneers, breaking new ground and exploring unknown territory, but the best have recognised the truth: 'The mountaineer observes himself as part of an industry', wrote Alex MacIntyre, 'and, incongruously, it is the tourist industry he is part of.'[18]

Mountain guides, whose profession was once thought to be in terminal decline, have reappeared in the greater ranges. Like their Victorian antecedents, they take busy urban professionals with more money than time to the tops of the highest mountains. Commercial climbing expeditions have become an experiential consumer product, prepared, packaged and sold with very little involvement by the 'climbers'. It is now possible to reach the summits of the highest peaks on each continent, including Everest, in seven back-to-back packaged holidays. 'Doing Everest' became possible for people with limited climbing ability but ample disposable income in the 1990s, when a number of experienced climbers started offering guided ascents. The professional climbers and Sherpas outfit the mountain with camps, oxygen and fixed ropes and haul the punters up the hill. 'Everest is the ultimate feather in the pseudo-mountaineer's hat',[19] according to one of the organisers of these commercial expeditions. Rebecca Stephens was awarded an MBE after becoming the first British woman to reach the summit of Everest in 1993 with a commercial expedition. Her website[20] states that her achievement was 'recognised around the world'. It is a good choice of words. The Everest brand is immediately recognisable, and becoming the first British woman to climb it provided instant fame to a journalist who knew how to work the system. But the reality of climbing Everest with a commercial expedition could hardly be more different from the experience of the pioneers. On a fine day, during the short climbing season, the summit is more crowded than a Scottish Munro, and queues form to move up or down the difficult sections. Over a four day period in October 1990, 31 people reached the summit via the South Col route, more than the total number that had climbed the mountain prior to 1970. If the weather turns bad the death toll can be appalling, because many of the 'climbers' do not have the requisite toughness and experience to be there.

Everest attracts obsessives who will stop at nothing to achieve their ambition. Theft is endemic, with porters, Sherpas and yak herders liberating tents and sleeping bags, and climbers stealing oxygen, food and equipment, particularly at the higher camps. Foul smells drift from crevasses where waste has been dumped by generations of climbers. The South Col is a rubbish dump of abandoned oxygen cylinders, tents, garbage, faeces, even dead bodies. On Everest the romance of climbing – beauty, solitude and an escape from the dirt and overcrowding of the city – is a distant memory. What remains is the achievement of reaching the summit – an achievement 'recognised around the world'. Based on her celebrity status as the first British woman to climb the mountain, Stephens has become a motivational speaker, employed by companies to talk to their employees about 'personal development – defining one's passions and goals, self-belief, growth through management of fear, calculated risk, tenacity and commitment'. In the world of commercial climbing, reaching the summit has become a clichéd metaphor for success.

While the photogenic Rebecca Stephens received plaudits from the mainstream media, Ginette Harrison, arguably Britain's best high-altitude female mountaineer, was largely ignored. Harrison was a doctor who succeeded in climbing Everest (shortly after Stephens); Mount Logan (5,959m/19,551ft) in Canada in a continuous 28 day alpine-style push; Cho Oyu (8,201m/26, 906ft) and Ama Dablam (6,812m/22,349ft) in quick succession; Kangchenjunga (8,586m/28,169ft) without oxygen, where she was the only member of the expedition to reach the summit; Shishapangma (8,046m/26,398ft); and Makalu (8,463m/27,266ft). She died in an avalanche while attempting to climb Dhaulagiri (8,167m/26,795ft) in 1999.

Prior to the 1970s there were regional differences and some class snobbery, but in many respects the climbing community in Britain was remarkably homogenous in its outlook and ambitions. It was dominated by men, who started climbing on outcrops, graduated to the mountain crags, did some winter climbing in Scotland and then went to the Alps. The chosen few were invited to go to the Himalaya. It was a sport where technical difficulty and risk went hand in hand and a certain amount of suffering was taken for granted. Although rock climbing in Britain has always been a relatively safe activity, in the Alps, and particularly the Himalaya, the death toll was considerable as the graveyards in so many alpine villages testify.

With the vast influx of new participants in the 1970s and 80s, climbing has simultaneously become a mass movement and fragmented into a myriad of sub-activities where people mix and match technical difficulty, risk and suffering to suit their personal taste. Some climbers never touch natural rock, preferring the safety and convenience of a warm and dry climbing wall. Some graduate to sport-climbing, often travelling abroad to warmer climes where they can practise the sport wearing shorts and a T-shirt, just like in a gym. There are specialists in bouldering, who have achieved extraordinary levels of difficulty in this uniquely gymnastic, but relatively low risk, aspect of the sport. Deep-water soloing is a spectacular variant that involves climbing without ropes on overhanging sea cliffs.

There are legions of low to middle grade rock climbers ticking off the traditional classic routes, a smaller number doing the same thing on the harder routes, and a tiny elite developing hard new routes in Britain and abroad. Scottish snow and ice attracts climbers who like a bit of suffering with their pleasure. The Alps are no longer the teleological extension of climbing in Britain, but thousands of British climbers still go there each summer, and here too the sport has fragmented. There are *via ferrata* and plaisir-climbs on which it is possible to walk or climb in spectacular situations but in perfect safety. There are crowded *grandes courses* and remote climbs on lesser peaks where you would be unlucky to see another soul. Winter climbing and ski-mountaineering still create the illusion of exploration, when a fresh fall of snow makes the mountains look as pristine as they did in the Golden Age, provided you avoid the ski resorts. The search for novelty has created bizarre combinations of climbing and other adrenaline sports, including slack line (tightrope) walking thousands of feet above the ground, base jumping from the top of big wall climbs and extreme skiing. In the Himalaya there are commercial expeditions that will take hill walkers to the summit of an 8,000m peak by a well-worn route, but there are also thousands of unclimbed ridges and faces awaiting the adventurous climber. Climbing may have become a sub-division of the leisure and tourist industry, but at the heart of the sport there is still a small, single-minded elite willing to take 'unjustifiable' risks.

Lytton Strachey observed that 'the history of the Victorian age will never be written: we know too much about it'.[21] The same could be said of climbing since 1970. There is an overwhelming amount of information, and increasingly media-savvy professionalism has distorted the record, obscuring the achievements of equally accomplished but less celebrated climbers in what still remains overwhelmingly an amateur sport. In such an overcrowded field, individual climbers inevitably lose definition and, unlike in the past, the very best have little time for any activities or interests other than climbing.

The mythical aura of difficulty enjoyed by Brown–Whillans routes during the decade of the 1950s owed much to lack of information. Today, when information is updated in real time on the web, the reputation of individual routes can be won and lost in days, and the task of identifying significant achievements inevitably becomes more difficult when they have not withstood the test of time. Nevertheless it is possible to distinguish some important trends within the two principal branches of the sport – rock climbing and mountaineering – and a few of the individuals who have made an outstanding contribution to the development of climbing over the past 40 years.

ROCK CLIMBING

As so often in the history of the sport, the major advances in rock climbing during the 1970s started on gritstone. In 1968 John Syrett, a Leeds University student who was an outstanding gymnast at school but had hardly climbed before, became obsessed by training on the university's then state-of-the-art climbing wall. For the first 12 months he hardly ventured outside, but in 1970 he emerged onto the real crags where he proceeded to set new standards of difficulty on Yorkshire grit. Syrett demonstrated that by obsessively repeating extremely difficult moves a few feet above the floor on a climbing wall, it was possible to build up sufficient strength and self-confidence to climb the hardest routes on the crags without aid and often solo.

Syrett was 'a wild party animal, and yet a total purist, a stylistic puritan on rock'.[22] He had a profound influence on a generation of Leeds University climbers who carried the purist ethic to the greater ranges. However, as time went by, drink, drugs and depression began to take their toll, particularly after an accident prevented him from climbing at the highest standard. Peter Livesey recalled that '[Syrett] walked through my door in Malham...carrying a rucksack containing only whisky. We drank it together and the following morning he said goodbye. That night he spent sat on top of Malham Cove and at first light he jumped to his death.' Shortly before his suicide he had written an article in *Extreme Rock* describing his student days, climbing on Yorkshire grit: 'Oh those halcyon days! On the crags with barrels of beer, parties in Leeds, the Stones, rasping and grasping at Brimham – it all seems a thousand years ago.'[23]

The rejection of aid and a willingness to solo even the hardest routes became two of the defining themes of climbing in the 1970s, but neither was entirely new. In 1927 Ivan Waller, an engineering undergraduate at Cambridge, soloed Belle Vue Bastion (VS 4b) on Tryfan, one of the hardest routes in Wales at that time. The climbing establishment did not know whether to be shocked or amazed. Some 40 years later, Alan Rouse, a mathematics undergraduate at Cambridge, soloed Peter Crew's 1960s test piece The Boldest (now graded E4 5c) on Clogwyn Du'r Arddu. Rouse also led the first E4 in Wales, Positron (now graded E5 6a, 1971), while his second played pop music full blast on a transistor radio, just as Waller's ascent of Belle Vue Bastion had been accompanied by a gramophone. Rouse and his peers marked the cross-over point between the old and the new: firmly part of the new generation in their obsession with style, but still keenly interested in the more debauched aspects of the climbing scene. Pat Littlejohn described Positron as the 'ultimate expression of sixties climbing...when top climbers were dare-devils rather than athletes, more interested in mind-games than muscles'.[24]

Rouse made a series of hard solos in Wales, including Chris Preston's Suicide Wall (E2 5c) and Joe Brown's Vector (E2 5c). In the Alps he soloed the North-East Spur of the Droites (TD+) and was given a rousing reception at an Alpine Club symposium in 1974 when he gave a speech entitled 'Two's a Crowd', extolling the virtues of his approach while his leg was in plaster as a result of a soloing accident the previous weekend. With Al Harris, Rab Carrington, Adrian and Alan Burgess (the Burgess twins) and others, Rouse was part of the informal Piranha Club (motto: 'More than enough is not sufficient'), whose spiritual homes were The Moon at Stoney Middleton and Al Harris' house near Llanberis. All the members of this group had a reputation for hard climbing and hard living, but the Burgess twins became particularly notorious. 'Of Viking descent, [they] have inherited their forebear's predilection for rape and pillage',[25] according to Joe Tasker, while American author Jon Krakauer observed that 'in a sub-culture that has come to be dominated by clean-living, hard-training, high-profile Frenchmen and Germans and Austrians…the twins remain low-lying pub-crawlers and brawlers, forever staying just one step ahead of the authorities. They are among the last of a breed of working-class British climbers for whom how much one drinks and with whom one fights have always been as important as what mountains one climbs.'[26] Rouse, Carrington and the Burgess twins soon transferred their very considerable climbing talents to the Alps, South America and the Himalaya.

In contrast, Pete Livesey had no ambition to become a high-altitude mountaineer. A highly competitive all-round athlete, successful at running, canoeing and caving as well as rock climbing, he followed Syrett's lead by adopting an obsessive training regime. As a result, he climbed almost two grades harder than everybody else for the first part of the 1970s. Thin, wiry and bespectacled, with hair that resembled a clown's wig, he preferred to climb in the sunny south of France or Yosemite rather than snow-covered mountains. When he wrote an English language guidebook to rock climbing in the south of France, hundreds of British climbers breathed a sigh of relief and abandoned the long tradition of wet summers in the Alps. Livesey's big breakthrough came in 1974. In April he climbed Footless Crow on Goat Crag in Borrowdale (E5 6b), and in June Right Wall on Dinas Cromlech in the Llanberis Pass (E5 6a). The two climbs were the first of their grade in the country and both had a lack of protection that deterred would-be followers. The main 6b pitch on Footless Crow is 50m/165ft, one of the longest extreme pitches in the country and 15ft longer than the standard length of a climbing rope at that time. On the first ascent Livesey climbed the last 15ft solo. Right Wall follows a line of weaknesses up the apparently blank wall next to Cenotaph Corner, which Joe Brown had climbed 22 years earlier. Both routes had a dramatic impact, but the jump in standards was probably most pronounced in the Lakes, where the first major E3 route, Richard McHardy's The Viking on Tophet Wall, Great Gable, had been climbed just five years earlier. Members of the Fell and Rock Climbing Club were apparently so stunned that they simply failed to mention the climb in the 'Climbs Old and New' section of their *Journal*. Two years later, Livesey pushed Lake District standards even higher with Das Kapital (E6 6b, 1977) on Raven Crag in Thirlmere.

In 1985, Chris Bonington persuaded Livesey to make a televised ascent of Footless Crow. With his usual professionalism, Bonington practised the route, which was well above his normal standard of climbing, and succeeded in seconding it with the help of a tight top-rope. On the televised ascent, Livesey led the route with apparent ease, but when Bonington tried to follow, the gamesmanship started. As Bonington struggled with the crucial moves, Livesey taunted him: 'Come on, Chris. You'd get up fast enough if I dangled a fiver over the edge.' Meanwhile, every time Bonington screamed 'tight', 'the rope would give a couple of inches and at the same time, for the benefit of the microphone...Livesey would croon, "I'm pulling as hard as I can. Do you want me to call for a winch?"'[27] Eventually the inevitable happened and Bonington fell off. Bonington's ascent was apparently filmed the day after Livesey's, and there is a story – almost certainly apocryphal – that some Carlisle-based climbers abseiled down the route overnight and smeared lard onto the crucial holds.

Livesey started climbing relatively late in life and was never a member of a club, rising to the top of the sport through personal drive and an absolute determination to be the best. Competition soon emerged in the form of Ron Fawcett, an exceptionally talented young rock climber, also from Yorkshire, who put up his first new route, Mulatto Wall (E3 5c), at the age of 15. 'I knew when I first climbed with Ron that he was better than me', recalled Livesey. 'The thing was, not to let Ron know that.' When Livesey found that he was unable to compete at the highest level, climbing held no further attraction for him and he gave up the sport.

Unlike Livesey, who was an outstanding climber but not exactly photogenic, Ron Fawcett was a handsome man, and it is probably no coincidence that he became one of the first pure rock climbers to earn a modest living from the sport, as well as being one of the first to appear in a series of 'rock' videos. Fawcett made the second ascents of both Right Wall and Footless Crow in 1976. Such was the pace of change that Phil Davidson soloed Right Wall in 1982 and Jill Lawrence became the first woman to lead the route in 1984. Lawrence was perhaps the most accomplished of a group of women climbers including Gill Kent, Bonny Masson and Gill Price who started to set high standards on rock after a relatively fallow period for women's climbing in the 1950s and 60s. Lawrence, Masson and Price were all students at Bingley Teacher Training College, where Livesey was a physical education lecturer.

Fawcett remained at the top of the sport for a decade, creating hard new routes across the country, including The Lord of the Flies (E6 6b, 1979) on Dinas Cromlech, Strawberries (E6 7a, 1980) on Tremadog, which he succeeded in climbing after numerous falls (a technique called yo-yoing), and Hell's Wall (E6 6c, 1979) in Borrowdale, regarded as the hardest climb in the Lakes for many years. He was also active on the Yorkshire and Derbyshire outcrops, producing Master's Edge on Millstone Edge (E7 6c, 1983) and The Prow (E7 6c, 1982) on Raven Tor. In a climbing world still accustomed to training in the pub, his fitness was legendary. In one day he climbed 100 gritstone extremes, up to and including E5. Following his second ascents of Footless Crow and Right Wall in 1976, *Crags* magazine interrogated him on his training routine:

Crags: I feel certain that some of the best climbers around are exercising like mad behind closed doors. So come on, cough up and let us know what you do.

Fawcett: Press ups.

Crags: How many?

Fawcett: One or two.

Crags: This is like robbing the crown jewels.

Fawcett: Well, 200 straight off before I get tired.

Crags: So, here you are, a 21-year-old star, and you've never been a plumber or a margarine salesman – amazing. Do you really bath in rubber gloves to keep your hands from going soft?

Fawcett: You can't publish that.

Crags: It's all right, the tape's switched off.

Both 1975 and 1976 were exceptionally hot summers, which gave rise to the great chalk controversy. When John Allen made the first free ascent of Peter Crew's Great Wall (E3 6a, 1976) on Clogwyn Du'r Arddu, Ken Wilson, the editor of *Mountain,* was not impressed: 'Allen...climbed the route with the help of chalk, and this was very controversial at the time as some climbers felt that this was another form of aid. The first chalk-free ascent was made two years later by Ed Hart – one of the sternest anti-chalk critics.'[28] Allen has often been compared with John Streetly for his dramatic rise to prominence and equally rapid departure from the British climbing scene. He started climbing at 14, and by the age of 17, when he moved to Australia, had repeated all the hard routes in the country and put up many of his own, including London Wall on Millstone Edge (E5 6a, 1975), originally an aid route climbed by Peter Biven in 1956.

Steve Bancroft was another leading gritstone specialist in the mid-1970s. One of the first full-time 'dole-climbers', he was responsible for a series of new routes in the Peaks, including Strapidictomy

(E5 6a, 1976) and Narcissus (E6 6b, 1978), which he soloed, on Froggatt Edge. Mick Fowler also rose to prominence for the first time in the mid-1970s with the first free ascent of Linden (E6 6b, 1976) on Curbar Edge. The route had originally been climbed by Ed Drummond in controversial style using two small drilled holes and a sky hook for aid. Fowler inspected and cleaned the route by abseil, practised the hard moves, and finally led it, but he found the experience dissatisfying: 'I *knew* that I could do it before I started climbing. I had effectively destroyed the sense of adventure.'[29] Instead he turned his attention to climbing at a slightly lower technical standard, but with a strong element of uncertainty, specialising in crumbling cliffs and sea stacks. His description of climbing a 120m/400ft overhanging cliff composed of disintegrating shale in north Devon gives some idea of his new approach: 'It was becoming obvious that a particularly fine epic was imminent; a sea mist had now engulfed the crag, daylight was fading fast and the rain increased. Simon [Fenwick] was about twenty-five metres below and ten metres to one side. Looking closely at the belays I was uncomfortably aware that they were not going to permit care-free, bouncing abseils. However, there seemed no option but an abseil of some sort – I vaguely wondered what Blackshaw's *Mountaineering Manual* would suggest in such circumstances.'[30] Fowler also exchanged an increasingly listless and decadent lifestyle on the dole in Sheffield for a job in the Harrow Collection Office of the Inland Revenue, a decision which resulted in him becoming the most respected amateur mountaineer of his generation.

Pat Littlejohn also began his long and prolific career at around this time, initially specialising in the coastal cliffs of south west England and Wales. He started climbing in Devon with Peter Biven, but soon overtook his mentor in terms of technical ability and commitment. 'A new concept of what constitutes bad rock enabled young Pat Littlejohn to power his way up incredible new lines, often of very unusual character.'[31] Routes such as Il Duce (E5 6b, 1972) on Tintagel involved long run-outs with very little protection, often on suspect rock. Ten years later, in 1982, Jim Perrin wrote an article about Littlejohn in which he observed that 'not many people who have stuck their necks out in this fashion are either still alive or still pioneering at a high standard'.[32] He also became the fourth director of the International School of Mountaineering in Leysin (following John Harlin, Dougal Haston and Peter Boardman, each of whom died in office), but Littlejohn has proved to be one of the great survivors, pioneering over 1,000 routes and continuing to perform at the highest level on both rock climbs and in the mountains. Recent routes include Misión Improbable (XS 6a, 2003), which follows a 460m/1,500ft line up some of the highest and loosest sea cliffs in the world on Tenerife.

In the Lake District, the Carlisle-based scaffolder Peter Whillance narrowed the gap created by Livesey with Take it to the Limit (E5 6b, 1978) on Deer Bield Crag. In Wales he put up an even harder route with his lead of A Midsummer Night's Dream on the Great Wall of Clogwyn Du'r Arddu (E6 6b, 1978), where Ed Drummond had caused widespread outrage when he climbed the first pitch using four pitons and a bolt. Climbing with Dave Armstrong and others, Whillance, whose understated, graceful climbing style earned him the nickname 'Captain Cool', stayed at the forefront of Lake District climbing until the mid-1980s, maintaining the regional tradition of adventurous free climbing as well as adding some hard and very committing routes in Scotland and elsewhere.

In the early 1970s standards of rock climbing in Scotland generally were somewhat lower than in England and Wales, reflecting the smaller number of active climbers and the less frequent occurrence of dry rock. Dave Cuthbertson put up the first E5 north of the border with Wild Country (E5 6b, 1976) on the Cobbler, and Mick Fowler added a number of hard routes, including Stairway to Heaven (E4 6a, 1976) on Skye. Cuthbertson later achieved a major breakthrough in Scottish standards with Requiem (E7 7a, 1983), on Dumbarton Rocks near Glasgow, which he succeeded in climbing after numerous falls. Cuthbertson was also an accomplished winter climber, repeating John

Cunningham's summer route Guerdon Grooves (HVS 5b) in 1984 under winter conditions at grade IX.

John Redhead, a 'Byronic figure with flowing black hair',[33] was Ron Fawcett's main rival for the position of best climber in Wales in the late 1970s and early 1980s. 'Fawcett is the great ape, all free-swinging elasticity; ...Redhead is the big cat...poised elegant, relaxed, grinning, where there is nothing.'[34] An artist who lived in Llanberis, Redhead was never entirely comfortable with the climbing scene: 'A lot of unstable characters play out their visions and anarchy here...exuding their dangerous misery.'[35] On rainy days, Pete's Eats was the centre of activity: 'The climbing royalty used to sit at a round table...all dressed like tramps, penniless and on the dole. At the weekends all the "nobodies" – climbers with good jobs, careers and families – would sit around them, gazing in awe.'[36]

Redhead specialised in desperate, unprotected lines, including The Bells! The Bells! (E7 6b, 1980) on Anglesey, and prepared for each new climb like a 'priest about to carry out a sacrifice'.[37] After the first ascent he wrote: 'My abstracted involvement in leading a route like The Bells! The Bells! never ceased to amaze me...I could rarely analyse a climb afterwards move by move, even just after the ascent.'[38] Inevitably, Great Wall on Clogwyn Du'r Arddu attracted his attention. Peter Crew's first ascent in 1962 used five points of aid. John Allen freed the route in 1976. To the right there is a faint line of weakness involving a 45m/150ft pitch, the last 12m/40ft of which are the hardest and totally unprotected. Redhead made numerous attempts, abseiling, inspecting, psyching himself up: 'It's possible...It'll go. But it's death...there's nothing!'[39] His attempts ended with a 24m/80ft ground-scraping fall from a pre-placed bolt. While he was nursing his injuries, Jerry Moffatt abseiled down the face and removed the bolt, soloed Curving Arête (E4 5c) and the original Great Wall (E4 6a) to warm up, then he set off on Redhead's route, but when he reached the position of Redhead's bolt he traversed right onto Mick Fowler's route, Spread Eagle. Moffatt's ascent was helped by one of the first pairs of Boreal Firé rock boots with high friction 'sticky' soles. He named the new route Master's Wall (E7 6b, 1983), as Great Wall had been known in the 1950s in acknowledgement of Joe Brown's numerous attempts to climb it. It was perhaps Moffatt's finest lead of a traditional rock climb. The following day, still riding a wave of adrenaline and feeling 'the most incredible euphoria...in control... and fully relaxed',[40] he soloed seven extreme routes on Dinas Cromlech, including Pete Livesey's Right Wall (E5 6a, 1976). In later years he more or less abandoned traditional routes in favour of sport-climbs, competition climbing (where he won a round of the World Cup in front of a home crowd at Leeds in 1989) and the esoteric art of bouldering.

Redhead consoled himself with a second ascent of Master's Wall and climbed Margins of the Mind (E7 6c, 1984) nearby, but the challenge of a direct finish remained. Johnny Dawes finally made the long awaited first ascent in 1986 calling the line The Indian Face (E9 6c, 1986). Like Brown and Whillans before him, many of Dawes' routes had an aura of difficulty that deterred would-be followers. It was eight years before The Indian Face was repeated by Nick Dixon and, just a few days later, Neil Gresham. Dixon helpfully described it as 'like an HVS only with smaller holds'.[41] Trained on grit, Johnny Dawes had a profound impact on the development of the sport in the mid- to late 1980s, establishing two new grades of difficulty with End of the Affair (E8 6c, 1986) on Curbar Edge in the Peaks and The Indian Face. He had a distinctive sense of style which he applied to his climbing and to the production of rock climbing videos: 'I was like an autistic wild boy. There's no way you could climb as well if you're not.'[42] Like many great climbers, Dawes has extraordinary balance and the ability to move smoothly and apparently effortlessly on steep rock. But he also developed an extremely dynamic style of climbing: 'Small but powerfully built...he stood on non-existent footholds and jumped...for a pathetically small pebble...What he possessed more than anyone I had ever met was balance. He really was dancing on rock.'[43]

All previous attempts on Master's Wall and The Indian Face had involved pre-inspection by abseil and top-rope. In 1997 the 17-year-old

Leo Houlding led Master's Wall on sight, wearing a pair of borrowed rock boots a size and a half too big for him, thereby instantly establishing a reputation as a leading adventure climber. He also climbed Ron Fawcett's classic Lord of the Flies (E6 6a) at night using a head torch, before applying his skills and idiosyncratic enthusiasm to rock faces around the world, including the 500m/1,640ft Passage to Freedom (E8 7a, 1999) on El Capitan in Yosemite, whose crux involves a 2.5m/8ft sideways leap from small holds on an almost vertical face, some 150m/500ft above the ground. Houlding later shattered his foot in a fall while trying to free climb the Maestri–Egger route on Cerro Torre in Patagonia, but has since returned to climbing. As Chris Bonington observed: 'I think life is for living. I think Leo thinks this and hopefully, Leo will carry on living.'[44]

One of the major developments in Wales in the 1980s was the recognition of the climbing potential of the old slate mines near Llanberis where Stevie Haston put up several fine routes, including Comes the Dervish (E5 6a, 1981). A distant relative of Dougal Haston, Stevie Haston has been one of the most successful British climbers on both rock and ice over the past three decades. During the 1980s, he put up numerous E6s and E7s in Britain and the first grade VII ice route in the world. In the Alps he has completed over 60 solo routes up to ED, including the first British solo ascent of the North Face of Les Droites. Obsessive training sessions involving thousands of pull-ups and press-ups ultimately resulted in chronic tendonitis, but after moving to Chamonix in the 1990s (where, as an unwelcome British import, he was called *La Vache Folle*) his climbing recovered with on-sight leads of French grade 8a (roughly equivalent to a British technical grade of 7b), Scottish grade X ice climbs in Colorado and the first free winter solo of the Walker Spur (ED1) in eight hours. Ironically, he failed to qualify as a mountain guide because of his attitude, underlining the growing gulf between the small, obsessive, difficult climbing elite and the ever-growing, safety-conscious mainstream climbing profession. Haston was typically unrepentant: 'They say you're not a master until you've become a good teacher. And I'm teaching the world to fucking ice climb at the moment.'[45] Now in his fifties, Haston is still climbing as hard as ever. As he says: 'I'm not going to be 60 and wonder "What if?"'[46]

Development of Welsh slate accelerated with the discovery of the Rainbow Slab by John Redhead in 1984. Raped by Affection (E7 6c, 1984) was one of several Redhead test pieces that emerged. The new-route bonanza soon attracted other climbers: 'It was a friendly scene in Llanberis at the beginning of the slate boom. But now the jackals from the Peak have arrived with their put-downs...and niggling competitiveness. Things have changed.'[47] Johnny Dawes made the second ascent of Raped by Affection, but at just over five foot tall he was unable to reach the vital bolt at 24m/80ft on the near vertical and blank face. Despite the prospect of a huge fall, he decided to jump for it and clip the karabiner in mid-flight. It was an extraordinary confirmation of his physical balance and mental control that he succeeded. Paul Pritchard also put up some new routes on slate, before turning his attention to the steep and loose cliffs of Gogarth. In 1987, attracted by Ken Wilson's photograph of the crag in Hard Rock, Pritchard teamed up with Johnny Dawes to try to free Doug Scott's classic aid route The Scoop (originally A4, now E6 6b) on Harris in the Outer Hebrides. His description gives a taste of hard modern climbing: 'There appeared to be no protection but there was a smattering of pinches and small edges...In a situation like this, lonely and homesick and faced with a terrifying lead, Johnny could be counted on to dispense with caution and just be downright irresponsible...[He] lurched across the overhang, pinching and struggling to keep his feet in contact with the lichenous rock. On the lip, pumping, he fiddled a slider into a little slot and slowly, quietly sat on it...As he fiddled with the gear on his harness the slider shifted. "Aaaah, don't rip, don't rip." Then, as he was futilely trying to place a blade in a blank seam, the piece stripped and Johnny plummeted. He disappeared under a band of overhangs and began a long pendulum. I held the ropes tight and watched with horror as they slid along the sharp lip, spraying a cloud of nylon fluff into the air. As one rope snapped, the blade tinkled on the rocks 700 feet below. Johnny prusiked up and, silent and worried, we did the space abseil and tried to get our heads together. After a solemn discussion we both agreed things were getting a little out of hand.'[48] Pritchard suffered a devastating head injury while climbing a Tasmanian sea stack in 1997 but has fought back with characteristic courage.

The mid-1980s marked the arrival of the first bolt-protected sports-climbs in Britain, including Ben Moon's Statement of Youth (1984) at Pen Trwyn on the Great Orme near Llandudno and Jerry Moffatt's Revelations (1984) at Raven Tor in the Peaks. Both were graded F8a, using the French grading system commonly used for sport-climbs, roughly equivalent to a British technical grade of 7b. When Ben Moon climbed Hubble (F8c+), also on Raven Tor, in 1990, it was probably the hardest sport-route in the world. It was repeated two years later by Malcolm Smith, who has taken obsessive training and weight loss to new heights. Always rather thin, during the weeks before attempting Hubble he went on a crash diet and lost 10kg/21lb. 'I could happily have given up climbing and just continued to train,' he confided. 'I gave up drink and food and became very intense.'[49] After mammoth sessions at the notorious training venue called The School in Sheffield ('mythical home of lost youth and strong fingers'[50]), Smith reputedly treated his hands with 'Bag Balm', an American product used by farmers to stop cows' udders from chapping. In 2003 he suffered the ultimate repetitive stress injury when the metacarpal bones snapped in one of his hands.

Ruth Jenkins became the first British woman to climb F8b with Zeke the Freak at Water-cum-Jolly in the Peak District in 1995. She subsequently became a stuntwoman who specialised in doubling for small boys in dangerous places. Lucy Creamer climbed an F8b soon after and has also demonstrated a willingness to undertake hard traditional routes, including an on-sight lead of Ghost Train (E7 6b) at Stennis in Pembrokeshire and the 15-pitch Venus Envy (E4 6a, 2001) in Greenland, which she climbed with Airlie Anderson, who had the memorable beer-fuelled argument with Al Burgess and punched one of the 'sad bunch of Sheffield armchair critics'[51] after he criticised one of her routes.

The standard of climbing on grit continued to advance with Andy Pollitt's Knockin' on Heaven's Door (E9 6c, 1988) on Curbar, using a pre-placed piton. The route was soloed a year later. John Dunne produced The New Statesman at Ilkley (E8 7a, 1987), followed by Parthian Shot (E9 6c, 1989) on Burbage. Dunne withdrew from serious climbing for a few years with a severe shoulder injury brought about by over-training, but returned in the 1990s, claiming the first E10, Divided Years (E10 7a, 1995), in the Mountains of Mourne in Ireland and Breathless (E10 7a, 2000) on Great Gable, both of which were repeated by Dave Birkett. Dunne also climbed Total Eclipse on Malham Cove, the first F9a sport-climb in Britain. Born in Bradford, Dunne played rugby as a teenager and his physique appears better suited to that sport than to rock climbing, which perhaps explains the incredulity that greeted some of his first ascents. As Dunne commented philosophically: 'I'd rather be called a fat bastard than a liar.'[52]

Meanwhile, Ben Heason has shown that adventurous climbing is alive and well with numerous solo ascents up to E8, including Johnny Dawes' End of the Affair (E8 6c, 1988), as well as traditional first ascents such as Ozbound (E9 7a, 2003) at Froggatt. In Greenland he freed an old aid route, A Wonderful Life, on-sight over two days, at a US grade of 5.12 (roughly equivalent to E6), and in 2005 he made the first ascent of Venezuela's Angel Falls in 31 pitches, of which nine were E7 or harder.

In 2005 Dave MacLeod claimed Britain's first E11 with Rhapsody (E11 7a) on Dumbarton Rocks near Glasgow. He succeeded in completing the 10 minute climb after 70 days of practice spread over a two year period. His latest route is called Echo Wall, a massive prow at the top of Tower Ridge on Ben Nevis. 'I first tried Echo Wall in 2006 and I knew then I wasn't good enough to climb it. I'd need to go away and train. And not bother it again until I really was ready. That took the best part of two years. I returned...in May 2008, much stronger and half a stone lighter.'[53] The route remains unrepeated.

MOUNTAINEERING

After the conquest of Annapurna's South Face in 1970, the South-West Face of Everest was duly anointed 'the last great problem'. Unlike Annapurna, the South-West Face of Everest is not a beautiful route. It consists of a steep snow slope leading up to a prominent rock band starting at about 8,230m/27,000ft, followed by further snow slopes leading to the summit ridge. There are few natural features to capture the eye or the imagination, but it has the unique advantage of being on Everest, the most marketable name in mountaineering. The 'last great problem' was mainly one of logistics and finance. The vertical supply chain required to enable the lead climbers to overcome the anticipated difficulties of the rock band demanded large numbers of porters, Sherpas and support climbers, and therefore huge amounts of money.

After an unsuccessful Japanese attempt, Norman Dyhrenfurth, leader of the successful 1963 American Everest expedition, and Jimmy Roberts, ex-Gurkha colonel and founder of Mountain Travel, the original Nepalese trekking agency, organised an expedition in 1971. Following Bonington's example of including the American climber Tom Frost in the Annapurna team in order to sell the book rights in the US, Dyhrenfurth decided to up the ante by organising an international expedition consisting of 33 members drawn from 13 different countries. Dougal Haston and Don Whillans, who summited Annapurna, made up the British contingent. The French team included Pierre Mazeaud, who had been with Walter Bonatti during the ill-fated 1961 attempt on the Central Pillar of Frêney during which four climbers died. Mazeaud had never forgiven Whillans for subsequently 'stealing' the route. The international brotherhood of the mountains soon dissolved into jealousy and factional fighting. The Austrian-made crampons did not fit the German-made boots. The food packages were selected by an Austrian vegetarian and health food fanatic, which found little favour with the French or the British and presumably appalled the Japanese. Every one of the cast of climbing stars wanted to reach the summit but no-one was prepared to do the grunt work. Shocked by the idea that he might be required to carry a load up the mountain, Mazeaud gave vent to a magnificent outpouring of Gallic pride: 'They expect me, Pierre Mazeaud, Member of the French Assembly, aged 42, to work as a Sherpa for Anglo-Saxons and Japanese. Never! This is not me, but France they have insulted!'[54] The expedition collapsed before getting to grips with the crucial rock band.

Within 12 months the international ideal was resurrected by the famously argumentative Dr Karl Herrligkoffer with his 1972 European expedition. Herrligkoffer was a controversial figure responsible for organising a series of expeditions, including Nanga Parbat in 1953 and 1970, which had ended in personal disputes and legal battles. Like Dyhrenfurth, Herrligkoffer realised that to raise the finance for a serious attempt on the South-West Face he would need to recruit climbers and sponsors from several nations. He met Bonington and his agent to negotiate a split of the media rights, but they were unable to cut a deal, and Herrligkoffer tried to go it alone. Bonington and Haston withdrew, but Whillans, Hamish MacInnes and Doug Scott signed up, only to leave early as the expedition once again fell apart with bitter recriminations all round.

It was Doug Scott's first introduction to big expedition climbing. Born in Nottingham, Scott started climbing at 12 after a visit to the White Hall Outdoor Centre near Buxton, established by Jack Longland. He forged his way to the top of the sport outside the mainstream, undertaking a series of imaginative and adventurous low cost expeditions with friends during the long holidays allowed by his profession as a school teacher. Big expeditions did not suit Scott's temperament, but in common with other young and ambitious climbers, he saw them as a means of establishing his reputation in the sport.

Like Dougal Haston before him, he also watched and learnt from Whillans, observing his remarkable ability to pace himself: 'I spent a week in a tent with him, cooking all his meals. I finally told him "Don, I'm not your mother." He just sat there and said "You're not one of those types that moans about a bit of cookin', are you?"'[55] It is a measure of the force of Whillans' personality that he got away with it. In later years Scott built up a reputation for being quite forceful himself. Tall and powerful, with huge nicotine-stained hands, straggly shoulder-length hair, John Lennon glasses and a thick beard, the French climber Georges Bettembourg described him as a man 'designed to fell mountains'.[56] According to Joe Tasker, 'his relaxed manner belied the strength of his personality and weight of his opinions. Physically he dominated us all.'[57] During one expedition, Scott found himself in a minority of one on a particular issue but refused to back down. Someone suggested that they put the matter to a vote. 'You know, youth,' Scott observed, 'democracy is a bit of a failure if you end up having to vote on it.' He also had a passion for popular philosophy and mysticism. Many found his constant soul-searching wearing, but others treated it with wry amusement. As Peter Boardman observed: 'He's either undergoing a second adolescence or he's in touch with something beyond the range of all of the rest of us.'[58]

After the failure of the European expedition, Bonington obtained permission for a post-monsoon attempt that same year. He recruited Jimmy Roberts as deputy leader and Mick Burke, Nick Estcourt and Dougal Haston from the Annapurna team. Doug Scott and Hamish MacInnes, with their recent experience on the face, also joined the team, but Whillans was left out. The decision followed a team vote in which only Scott and MacInnes voted in favour. The consensus amongst the other lead climbers, particularly those who still bore a grudge from Annapurna, was that Whillans was too old, too fat, too bolshie and too lazy. But the climbing community saw it differently, and Whillans felt personally betrayed by Bonington. The decision to try the South-West Face in the post-monsoon season was always a gamble, and bad weather prevented the climbers from getting higher than 8,300m, roughly the same height as the previous four failed attempts.

In 1974 Bonington, Haston, Scott and Boysen were together again on an Indo-British expedition to Changabang (6,864m/22,519ft). It was a relatively small, relaxed team and all four reached the summit, together with Indian climbers Tandi and Sashu. The next year, the assault on Everest was resumed.

By the time that the 1975 Everest South-West Face expedition set off, Bonington was the undisputed impresario of British mountaineering, but the climbing community was increasingly sceptical about both the objective and the means of climbing it. In a satirical article in *Mountain*, a fictitious expedition leader Cassius Bonafide [Chris Bonington] explained the rationale of his new expedition to bloated climbing commentator Mac the Belly [Ian McNaught-Davis]: 'Nobody is interested in cheap, trashy peaks...In the professional climbing world we call it creative mountaineering marketing. You find the mountain, create the image, sell like hell and then go out and climb it...This year's hardest climb in the world is the South Face of Everest. Great box office.'[59] Bonington raised an unprecedented £100,000 in sponsorship from Barclays Bank in the depths of the worst post-war recession. He made mountaineering history by using a computer to plan the logistics on the mountain. There were 18 climbers, a four-man TV crew, a *Sunday Times* reporter, an army of Sherpas and porters, camp managers, liaison officers, secretaries and media specialists. 'Perhaps I am a frustrated Field Marshal,'[60] Bonington mused at one stage. The newly designed tents included a compact 'assault box' for the final camp, and the lower camps had specially designed bullet-proof mesh to deflect stonefall.

After a near perfect approach, Nick Estcourt and Tut Braithwaite broke through the rock band, and Dougal Haston and Doug Scott reached the summit of Everest, the first Britons to do so. Two days later Peter Boardman and Sherpa Pertemba also reached the summit. Martin Boysen and Mick Burke followed, but Boysen had to turn back when his oxygen system failed and he lost a crampon. Burke pressed on and probably reached the summit, but disappeared in a storm on his return. Small, tough, outspoken and gregarious, Mick Burke came from a working-class background in Wigan. He made the first British ascent of El Capitan in Yosemite in 1968 and was with Bonington on Annapurna and Everest in 1972.

The publicity surrounding the ascent turned the members of the expedition, particularly Haston, Scott and Boardman, into household names. Bonington was awarded a CBE and some years later received a knighthood for services to mountaineering. But for most leading climbers the focus had long since moved on to small, lightweight alpine-style ascents, and the 1975 expedition looked like an extravagant throwback to a bygone era. Jim Perrin wrote of 'the increasingly desolate and dispiriting moveable caravanserai of Second Lieutenant Christian Bonington, camping out under the latest last great problem with its corporate sponsorship, contracts, career structure and increasing death toll'.[61] Even Peter Boardman, who was on the expedition, observed that 'for a mountaineer, surely a Bonington Everest expedition is one of the last great Imperial experiences life can offer'. [62]

Boardman was 16 years younger than Bonington, and his inclusion in the team was a response to the increasing clamour in the climbing press, and from Ken Wilson in particular, about perceived cronyism. Bonington described Boardman as 'our token representative of the new generation of climbers'.[63] Born in Bramhall, a rich suburb of Manchester, Boardman studied English at Nottingham, where he became president of the University Mountaineering Club, and completed a teaching diploma at the University of North Wales, Bangor. He joined the staff of Glenmore Lodge in 1973 and moved to the British Mountaineering Council as National Officer in 1975. As well as accumulating a long list of hard alpine routes, Boardman had climbed in the Hindu Kush, Alaska and the Caucasus before Everest, but he was still relatively unknown in the climbing world. His rise to stardom inevitably attracted the disrespectful attention of the climbing community, but Boardman was smart enough to deflect the criticism. Soon after his return from Everest he was interviewed by *Crags* magazine:

> *Crags:* Have you managed to shake off your snow plodding image?

> *Boardman:* Alas no. A week later I had steeled myself to grapple with Quietus at Stanage. As I moved around the lip one of my runners fell out, the rope jammed, and a group of "the new breed" peered coldly from around the corner. "Help me" I squeaked, in a fragile, pathetic voice. Now if I had been in the company of the Altrincham Allstars [several members of the Everest expedition lived near the south Manchester suburb] they, being of a nobler previous generation, would have formed a human chain suspended from a summit hand jam, to link fates in a desperate pull to survival. But I was left alone to find my own existential destiny. The "new breed" just smiled grimly.[64]

In contrast, Bonington was never entirely comfortable with the irreverent attitude of the climbing community. He was a great admirer of John Hunt and the way that he had organised the 1953 Everest expedition: 'It was Hunt who ran the expedition, chose the team, allocated responsibilities to the right people and left them to get on with it. The principles of running a brigade and laying siege to a mountain are very similar and Colonel Hunt was to demonstrate that he was good at both.'[65] Unlike Hunt, however, Bonington lived in an age when authority was invariably questioned and usually criticised. Mike Thompson's classic account 'Out with the Boys Again' was an example of the more good-humoured variety of criticism: '[Bonington] had now entered his Mad Mahdi phase, running out drums of fixed rope in the wrong direction, ranting on at Ang Phurba about "really good Sherpa food", working out logistics on his porridge encrusted electronic calculator, and communicating with the outside world on a broken walkie-talkie that had been persuaded to work again by jamming a ballpoint pen into its circuitry...One needs a leader who changes his mind a lot and has difficulty in remembering from one day to the next what he has decided. We were very fortunate to have such a leader.'[66] Many of Bonington's critics no doubt realised that without his organisational and commercial skills, they might never have had the opportunity to climb in the Himalaya. But they chose to keep this knowledge to themselves.

The South-West Face expedition represented the apotheosis of the big, military-style expeditions started by Martin Conway in 1892 and converted to establishment orthodoxy by the death of Fred Mummery on a small expedition in 1895. There were attempts to challenge the orthodoxy during the 1930s, notably by Eric Shipton and Bill Tilman, but climbing the highest Himalayan peaks was expensive and difficult to organise without the support of the British authorities in India, the Royal Geographical Society and the Alpine Club. After the Second World War the success of the 1953 Everest expedition, after so many failures, appeared to underline the merits of military leadership, but by the mid-1970s a conjunction of events resulted in an emphatic shift to smaller, alpine-style expeditions.

The ethical debates of the early 1970s encouraged a leaner, purer approach in all aspects of the sport, and many top climbers were unwilling to submit to the discipline of a big expedition. During the 1970s, cheap air travel, a developing tourist infrastructure within the Himalayan countries and dramatic improvements in lightweight equipment and clothing made small, low cost expeditions a realistic alternative. The final hurdle that stood in the way of small teams tackling the highest peaks in alpine-style was oxygen. During the 1920s there had been a lively debate about the merits of using oxygen on Everest, both from an ethical and a practical standpoint. The practical argument against oxygen was that the additional weight of the oxygen equipment offset the physiological benefits. The ethical argument revolved around the question of whether the use of supplemental oxygen represented 'legitimate means' of climbing a mountain. Arthur Hinks, the universally despised honorary secretary of the Everest Committee in the 1920s, believed that anyone who used oxygen was 'a rotter', but in the end the practical objections were overcome by the development of lighter weight and more reliable oxygen equipment, while any ethical scruples were cast aside in the scramble to reach the summit before someone else did.

In the post-war years, the use of oxygen on the highest peaks became standard practice, and there were apparently well-founded medical concerns that failure to do so might result in permanent brain damage. All of this overlooked the fact that several climbers had reached well over 8,000m on Everest in the 1920s and 30s with apparently little damage to their long-term health, despite much more primitive clothing and equipment and a poorer diet. Lawrence Wager and Percy Wyn Harris both reached 8,580m/28,150ft on Everest in 1933. Wyn Harris was later knighted for services as the Governor of Gambia while Wager went on to become a distinguished Professor of Geology at Oxford. Neither man appeared to suffer any mental impairment, although one undergraduate rather unkindly observed that Wager 'often [gave] the impression of having to stop and think what he was talking about'[67] during lectures.

The problem with using supplementary oxygen is logistics. In order to get sufficient oxygen tanks up to the highest camp to support a summit bid, a huge pyramid of Sherpas, high-altitude porters and normal porters is required. A porter typically carries a 27kg/60lb load, less at high altitude, and consumes about 0.9kg/2lb of food per day, so 30 porters will consume one porter's load each day. Assuming a 10 day walk to base camp and roughly half that time to get back (going downhill, without a load), the porters will have eaten roughly half the total load before the climbing even begins. Put another way, a single porter is capable of carrying food for himself plus sufficient oxygen for one climber for one day. The oxygen then has to be transported up the mountain to the lead climbers, which may take many days, depending upon the weather. Regardless of progress on the mountain, the climbers and Sherpas will also need food, tents, sleeping bags, ropes and climbing equipment. On large expeditions several porters are employed just to carry the small denomination notes and coins needed to pay the other porters.

On their return from the summit of Everest in 1975, Doug Scott and Dougal Haston bivouacked at 8,760m/28,740ft without oxygen and both survived, without frostbite and with no apparent long-term harm. In terms of the future development of the sport, the bivouac without oxygen probably represented a more important breakthrough than reaching the summit with oxygen. By demonstrating that oxygen was not required, it opened the way for small and, above all, cheap expeditions to the highest peaks. The description applied to this new style of climbing – 'lightweight, alpine-style' – was grossly misleading, however, since it often involved the individual lead climbers carrying packs of truly staggering dimensions and weight.

While the public eye was focused on the Himalaya, lower profile revolutions were taking place elsewhere in big wall climbing and winter mountaineering. Big wall climbing first developed on the warm granite of Yosemite in the USA. Initially, huge amounts of aid were used to overcome the technical difficulties, often using a siege approach with fixed ropes. The first ascent of The Nose of El Capitan was completed in 1958 after 45 days of climbing spread over several years. The climbers used 600 pegs and 125 bolts. Increasingly during the 1970s climbers adopted a purer approach using less aid and aiming to reach the top in a single push. The current record time for an ascent of El Capitan is two hours and 45 minutes. Big wall techniques were transferred to the Alps and then to the steep, glaciated walls of the sub-Arctic and Antarctic regions, including Norway, Baffin Island, Greenland and Patagonia. In 1972, Ed Drummond, the poet mountaineer, teamed up with Hugh Drummond (no relation) to climb Arch Wall (E2/A4+), a new route on the steepest part of Troll Wall, the highest in Norway. Hauling 12 days of rations, they were pinned down by storms for days at a time, resting in frail hammocks or on tiny ledges while water cascaded down the face. After 20 days of difficult climbing, the last three with no food, they finally reached the summit. Although at relatively low altitude, the climb demonstrated that a two-man team could undertake hard climbing over many days carrying all their gear in a single alpine-style push.

Meanwhile, legend has it that modern Scottish winter climbing was invented in February 1970 when Hamish MacInnes, John Cunningham and the American climber Yvon Chouinard met up at the Clachaig Inn in Glencoe. Using revolutionary short ice axes and the front points of their crampons, MacInnes and Cunningham made extremely fast ascents of some classic Scottish ice climbs. They were soon followed by Al Rouse and Mike Geddes from Cambridge University, who made the second ascents of Marshall and Haston's Minus Two Gully and Marshall and Smith's Orion Face Direct in 1971, and Ian Nicholson, who soloed both Point Five and Zero Gully in a single morning in 1973. The new technology rapidly turned Scotland into a testing ground for ever more strenuous and technical ice and mixed rock and ice climbing.

In the 1960s the hardest ice climbs were Scottish grade V, a standard of difficulty first achieved in the nineteenth century. The hardest grade today is grade XI, reflecting further advances in ice climbing technology and the development of 'dry-tooling' and 'torqueing' techniques, where ice axes are twisted into cracks in order to climb steep mixed ground of rock and ice. Major advances were made by Mick Fowler and Victor Saunders (who was educated at Gordonstoun School) with routes such as The Shield Direct (VII, 1979) on Ben Nevis, and Andy Nisbet and Colin MacLean with The Needle (VIII, 1985) on Shelter Stone Crags in the Cairngorms. Dave MacLeod's 2005 ascent of The Hurting (XI) in Coire an t-Sneachda in the Cairngorms represents the current state of the art. The Hurting was ascended after an abseil inspection, but on-sight leads are still the norm, and Scottish winter climbing remains at the forefront of clean, ethical winter climbing worldwide.

Winter climbing techniques developed in Scotland were soon transferred to the Alps. In 1975 Al Rouse and Rab Carrington made the first ascent of the North Face of the Pélerins (ED2), and the following year Alex MacIntyre and Nick Colton ascended their eponymous route on the right flank of the Walker Spur on the Grandes Jorasses (ED3), probably the hardest ice route in the Alps at that time. Four years earlier, Bonington had spent 17 days laying siege to the route before admitting defeat. MacIntyre and Colton climbed it alpine-style in 20 hours.

Also in 1975, after a succession of first British ascents of hard routes in the Alps, Joe Tasker and Dick Renshaw made a winter ascent of the North Face of the Eiger (the first British and fourth overall). On their way to the foot of the climb they bought one-way rail tickets. As Tasker observed: 'I had a certain reserve about planning beyond the next climb when so much depended on fate.' Born in Hull into a poor family of 10 children, Joe Tasker attended Ushaw Seminary in County Durham between the ages of 13 and 20, training to be a Jesuit priest. With his beard and ascetic manner, a liaison officer in India once commented that he should audition for a role in *Jesus Christ Superstar,* and Tasker acknowledged the influence of his religious upbringing on his climbing career: 'It had been absorbed into my subconscious many years before that physical discomfort was a valuable penance.'[68] After leaving the seminary, Tasker studied sociology at Manchester University and started climbing with Dick Renshaw who was, if anything, even more ascetic and obsessive than Tasker: 'Motivated by a blind drive to climb and climb, without stopping to wonder about the purpose of it all.'[69]

Both Tasker and Renshaw were drawn to hardship and suffering: 'We began to prefer the shadowy north faces...thinking we should climb these precipices of ice-coated rocks while we were young and save the more pleasant walls of sun-warmed granite and limestone for later years.'[70] In 1975 they bought a second-hand white Escort van for £170 and set off to attempt the first ascent of the South-East Ridge of Dunagiri (7,066m/23,182ft) in the Indian Garhwal. To help pay for the trip they applied for a grant from the Mount Everest Foundation.

During the interview at the Royal Geographical Society a frail-looking, white-haired gentleman, who seemed to have been asleep, opened his eyes and asked why they did not try to climb a nearby mountain called Kalanka instead. 'It looks too easy,' Renshaw replied. Only later did he find out that the old man was Eric Shipton.

During the drive to India they ate bread and sandwich spread. When they could no longer get bread, they ate chapatti and sandwich spread. 'I felt [Renshaw] looked askance at my self-indulgence if I bought a glass of beer, as if I was recklessly squandering valuable resources, but never a word passed.'[71] The climb took two days longer than planned and they had to descend with no food and no fuel to thaw snow for water. After 11 days on the mountain, near the point of collapse, they separated during the descent but were reunited at base camp. Renshaw suffered severe frostbite and had to fly back for treatment. Tasker drove back, but ran out of money part way and sold the van and a pint of blood to raise enough cash to buy a bus ticket home from Kabul. The whole expedition, which took place in the same year as Bonington's blockbuster £100,000 Everest South-West Face, cost £1,600.

During his lectures on the climb, Tasker showed a slide of Renshaw lying semi-conscious in the snow near the summit. There is a famous photograph of Mohammed Ali, taken from a low angle, looming menacingly over his prostrate opponent. It is one of the great images of boxing, but many climbers found Tasker's photograph deeply disturbing in a sport that still tried to maintain the pretence of teamwork, not rivalry, even at the highest level.

While they were climbing Dunagiri, Tasker had seen the steep and beautiful West Face of Changabang (6,864m/22,520ft), and gradually the idea of climbing it began to obsess him. Many years before, Bill Murray, the Scottish climber and mountain mystic, had been equally entranced: 'Seemingly as fragile as an icicle; a product of earth and sky rare and fantastic, and of liveliness unparalleled, so that unawares one's pulse leapt and the heart gave thanks that this mountain should be as it is.'[72] The ascent of its West Face would clearly involve some of the hardest climbing yet attempted in the Himalaya. With Renshaw still recovering from frostbite, Tasker hesitantly approached Peter Boardman, recently returned from Everest, to join him. The timing was perfect. Boardman was searching for 'something...that would bring my self-respect into line with the public recognition I had received for Everest'.[73] It was the start of an extraordinary partnership.

In preparation for the climb Boardman and Tasker slept in a deep freeze in Manchester to test the hammocks they intended to use on the steep face. 'We stumbled and thrashed around getting inside the hammocks, standing on crates of cheesecakes and holding onto pallets of ice-lollies.'[74] Eventually the time for departure came and the climbing community watched with bated breath. Most experienced climbers gave them little chance of success. 'Just the two of you? Sounds like cruelty to me',[75] was Joe Brown's verdict. Doug Scott thought it was beyond the bounds of possibility, but he wanted to join them anyway. Boardman and Tasker turned him down, preferring to go alone rather than with the more experienced Scott. Remarkably, they made it to the summit and back in safety, putting up a route of great beauty and technical difficulty with many pitches of VI/A2 standard.

One year earlier Joe Brown, then aged 45, had set out with Mo Anthoine, Martin Boysen and Martin Howell to attempt the Trango Tower (6,286m) in the Karakoram, another spectacular and apparently impregnable rocky spire. Just 250m from the summit, Boysen got his knee jammed and spent a desperate three hours trying to cut himself free from the 'Fissure Boysen'. They returned in 1976 to complete the route, which involved 20 pitches of grade VI rock climbing and was not repeated for 14 years.

Meanwhile, the Italian and Austrian team of Reinhold Messner and Peter Habeler set the pace for climbers worldwide by climbing Gasherbrum I (8,068m), named Hidden Peak by Martin Conway, in a remarkable two-day dash. Marcus Schmuck, Fritz Wintersteller, Kurt Diemberger and Hermann Buhl had made a lightweight ascent of Broad Peak (8,047m/26,401ft) without oxygen in 1957, but Messner and

Habeler's ascent of Hidden Peak was the first true alpine-style ascent of an 8,000m peak and set a precedent that British climbers sought to follow.

During the winter of 1977 Dougal Haston was killed in an avalanche while skiing near his home in Leysin, Switzerland. His death almost exactly re-enacted events that he had created for the hero of his semi-autobiographical novel *Calculated Risk*, completed just before his death. The only difference was that in the book the hero survives the avalanche. At 36, Haston was still extremely strong and fit and had just completed an alpine-style ascent of a new route on Mount McKinley in Alaska with Doug Scott. However, it was clear that his time as Britain's leading mountaineer was reaching its natural end. Improvements in ice climbing techniques meant that young climbers were completing routes in the Alps in half the time that it had taken Haston and his generation, while on rock his standard never exceeded about E2. His death, while absolutely at the top of the game, sealed his reputation: an enigmatic mixture of self-indulgence and impenetrable asceticism.

Haston had been due to join Chris Bonington, Doug Scott, Mo Anthoine, Clive Rowland and Tut Braithwaite on an expedition to the Ogre (7,285m/23,901ft) in the Karakoram. Nick Estcourt took his place. Scott and Bonington reached the summit, but during the descent Scott broke both of his legs at the ankle. It took eight days to crawl back to base camp, five of them in a storm, four without food. Bonington broke two ribs while abseiling and thought that he was getting pneumonia. Anthoine and Rowland broke trail, fixed abseils and navigated through the storm. By the fifth day, Bonington's voice had been reduced to a sandpaper whisper. According to Anthoine, he rolled over in his sleeping bag and croaked: 'We're going to make a fortune out of this.' 'How come?' Anthoine asked. 'The book!' said Bonington.[76] Whatever the truth of this story, Bonington did not in fact write an account of the climb until much later. But Anthoine did. His article in the *Alpine Journal* was written with sang-froid worthy of the Victorian founders of the Club: 'Strangely enough it was not a frightening experience and while not pleasurable, it certainly did not lack in excitement.'[77]

In 1978 Al Rouse, Rab Carrington, Brian Hall and Roger Baxter Jones climbed Jannu (7,710m/25,295ft) in pure alpine-style. Rouse had by this time developed very firm views on mountaineering ethics: 'Foremost among these was the rule that to claim a true alpine-style ascent one team should not benefit from the work of another team. That...meant ignoring the fixed ropes...[and] tents...even avoiding their footsteps!'[78] Rouse was pleased with the ascent but conceded that there had been little pleasure in it. 'Certainly there had been hard climbing but not of the enjoyable type. Hard work is the best description of Himalayan climbing...memory will dull the pain.'[79] 'A long, hard, exhausting climb and perhaps verging on the necky',[80] was Carrington's verdict. Shortly afterwards Carrington and Rouse argued, and their longstanding and highly successful partnership came to an end.

That same year Messner and Habeler once again raised the bar by climbing Everest without oxygen, finally confirming the instincts of William Graham in 1883 and the scientific predictions of Alexander Kellas in 1920.

Meanwhile Bonington led an attempt on the unclimbed West Ridge of K2 (8,611m/28,251ft), the second highest mountain in the world, which had not received a British ascent at that time. The team consisted of Doug Scott, Nick Estcourt, Tut Braithwaite and Peter Boardman from the Everest South-West Face expedition. Joe Tasker was drafted in to replace Dougal Haston and Martin Boysen was dropped. As a result, Boysen gave up his ambition to become a professional climber and returned to teaching and rock climbing. For Tasker, the K2 expedition marked 'the end of a naive attitude to climbing mountains'. A Bonington-led expedition involved 'the search for sponsorship on a scale undreamt of...and a courting of publicity in order to establish the importance and prestige of the venture...it took some adjusting to the need for organised meetings...the steady stream of expedition circulars that poured through the letter box, the minuting of discussions...

and the endless talk of money'.[81] Almost before the team was properly established on the mountain Nick Estcourt was killed in an avalanche. His many friends in the climbing community mourned him. 'Excitable, grinning Nick, with thinning curly hair and such big gaps between his teeth that Mo Anthoine had once accused him of cleaning them with a bath towel, Nick of innumerable pubs, parties, of long boozy evenings in The Moon in Derbyshire.'[82] The expedition was abandoned.

In 1979 Boardman, Tasker, Scott and the French climber Georges Bettembourg were back in the Himalaya to attempt a new route on Kangchenjunga, the third highest mountain in the world. Constant expeditioning was beginning to take its toll, with both Tasker and Boardman questioning their motives for climbing: 'Sometimes the life I was leading seemed empty and pointless...I wondered if it was only because I thought I would lose face amongst my peers that I kept on riding the merry-go-round that I stepped onto.'[83] The three Britons reached the top, becoming the first climbers to reach the summit of an 8,000m peak by a new route without oxygen or support. Later that same year, Boardman led a successful expedition to the West Ridge of Gauri Sankar (7,134m/23,405ft) in Nepal, a long, hard and committing climb along an intricate rock and ice ridge.

The following year Messner stunned the climbing world by climbing Everest solo, without oxygen.

Boardman, Tasker and Scott were joined by Dick Renshaw, now recovered from frostbite, for another attempt on the West Ridge of K2 that same year. Delayed by bad weather, and running out of time, Boardman, Tasker and Renshaw decided to change their objective to the established route on the Abruzzi Ridge, while Scott departed for other commitments. On their first attempt the three reached almost 8,000m when a storm struck, their tent was buried by an avalanche and they had to cut their way out. The retreat in white-out conditions took over three days with little food and water. Astonishingly, they decided to make another attempt, but once again were pushed back by bad weather.

Tasker then joined Al Rouse, the Burgess twins, Brian Hall, Paul Nunn, John Porter and Peter Thexton for an attempt on the West Ridge of Everest in winter. It was an unremitting struggle against strong winds and low temperatures. Returning, exhausted, Tasker wrote the expedition book, *Everest the Cruel Way*, which may have overstated his role and was critical of a 'leaderless' team. The criticism hurt Rouse badly. Nevertheless, just a few months later Rouse and Tasker joined Boardman on a Bonington expedition to climb Kongur (7,649m/25,095ft) in China. At a press conference arranged by Bonington to drum up media interest in the climb, Rouse was asked whether he foresaw any problems and suggested that, if there were any, they might have to use a rope. Don Whillans asked if it was some kind of dance and always referred to it as 'aye, aye, aye, aye Kongur'. Bonington was not impressed and relations became frosty. 'Al...was forever questioning the validity of traditional siege climbs such as Annapurna South Face and Everest South-West Face, seeing them almost as evidence of the Decline and Fall of Western Civilisation...Chris Bonington...as leader of both these highly successful ventures, understandably defended them with some vehemence.'[84] In the event both Rouse and Tasker performed less well than Bonington and Boardman, probably because they were still recovering from their winter attempt on Everest.

Rouse had permission to climb the North-East Ridge of Everest in 1982 which he passed to Bonington, knowing that Bonington would stand a better chance of raising the necessary finance. Bonington duly raised the money but omitted Rouse from the team, inviting Dick Renshaw instead. He had the full support of Boardman and Tasker, both of whom were fed up with Rouse's 'incessant bullshit'. Rouse was distraught and spent the remaining years of his life desperately trying to prove his ability to climb at high altitude. Whillans offered some consolation: 'Aye-aye, lad – welcome back t'uman race!'[85]

By this stage, Bonington had become a convert to the cult of alpine-style ascents and with missionary zeal sold the new message to the media. 'I thought of the times I had arrived at Heathrow to see Chris

Bonington unloading a Volvo Estate and watched awe-struck as a pile of rucksacks, kitbags, cameras, satellite phones and computers mounted. Invariably, all this would have occurred just after a press conference in which Chris had extolled the virtues of lightweight Alpine-style expeditions', Jim Curran remembered.[86] However, the unclimbed North-East Ridge of Everest was a huge undertaking for an expedition with just four lead climbers, and at 48 even Bonington was beginning to slow up and realised that he could not take part in a summit attempt. The team was further weakened when Dick Renshaw had a minor stroke. Nevertheless Boardman and Tasker pushed on. They were last seen passing the pinnacles high up on the North-East ridge.

For many British climbers the death of Boardman and Tasker had a particular poignancy. Inevitably, there were echoes of Mallory and Irvine, but both of them also wrote outstanding books that were unusually frank about their motives, ambitions and self-doubts. They seemed to sense the tragic inevitability of the path they had chosen and yet both felt compelled to carry on. Boardman talked about being 'on a conveyor belt, carrying me from one booked peak to another'.[87] Tasker openly wondered where it was all leading: 'For nearly two years I had been totally involved in climbing three mountains. Each one...the greatest test I could conceive. Each test had been passed and I was left bewildered. I was alarmed to have succeeded; in a way it would have been more reassuring to have failed. Instead success left me with an uneasy, unsettling question about where to go next...What had I gained from the last two years if all that was left to me was an indefinable dissatisfaction?'[88] Both felt a pressing need to prove themselves: 'We did not want to overcome a mountain with ease, we needed to struggle, needed to be at the edge of what was possible for us, needed an outcome that was uncertain...I wondered if the climbing had become an addiction, if the pleasure of this drug had gone and only the compulsion to take it in ever stronger doses remained.'[89]

In many ways they were contrasting characters. Boardman was well-spoken, slightly diffident, with an innocent romanticism – when he first saw the glacial valleys radiating from Concordia on the 1977 K2 expedition he wanted to play Bach or Beethoven on the tape recorder and was horrified when Nick Estcourt put on 'Bat out of Hell' instead – but there was also an iron will. He was fully aware of the dangers of his existence, and he chose to face them. Tasker was intense, iconoclastic, abrasive. According to Dick Renshaw: 'Behind his frail appearance, Joe concealed a determination and will-power which was almost frightening.'[90] Doug Scott gently mocked him after the Kangchenjunga expedition: 'I can just see him now in The Moon, hands out splayed in an earnest blue-eyed expression: "Well there we were at 28,000 feet, just three ordinary johns like us. Anyone could have done it. It all felt really normal."'[91] Tasker did try to jump off the merry-go-round, spending the summer of 1977 in Europe instead of the Himalaya, but the Alps felt 'too civilised and too accessible…There was none of the catharsis of total involvement.'[92] As a young man he had felt drawn to people living on the fringes of society – down-and-outs, alcoholics and gypsies. Towards the end of his life he too felt increasingly isolated: 'Of late, expeditions had gone on for a long time and on returning to England I found it took me quite a long while before I regained the habit of feeling and emotion. This was very difficult for anyone close to me.'[93] It probably also encouraged an early return to the mountains. Similarly, Boardman sought an escape from the anxieties of normal life: 'I almost dreaded letters, in case something had happened, in case they were not happy letters, in case something in them disturbed us from climbing.'[94]

There was intense competition between the pair. When Tasker photographed Boardman resting, exhausted, on Changabang, Boardman was furious, perhaps remembering Tasker's photographs of Renshaw semi-conscious on Dunagiri. 'The rivalry between them was often evident, both of them setting very high standards…which the other felt he had to attain or to better.'[95] But there was also great respect: 'I hoped [Joe] was not weakening, because I trusted his judgement implicitly, and felt that there could be something invincible about our combination.'[96] On the North-East Ridge of Everest, their invincibility finally ran out.

That same year, Doug Scott, Roger Baxter Jones and Alex MacIntyre put up a new route on Shishapangma (8,027m/26,335ft), the only 8,000m peak entirely within Tibet, which China had opened up to western climbers in 1979. The successful ascent of an 8,000m peak by a new route in a single push from base camp perhaps came closest to achieving Bill Tilman's 'unattainable ideal...two or three men carrying their food with them as in the Alps'. But it is hard to imagine Tilman engaging in a drunken brawl in a Beijing disco, as Scott and MacIntyre did in the aftermath of the climb.

Alex MacIntyre was educated at a Jesuit School near Sheffield and read law at Leeds. A 'doppelganger for Marc Bolan of T Rex',[97] he was aggressive and driven: he wanted to be as famous as Chris Bonington *now*, not when he was 40. The Burgess twins thought that he had 'a bit of the-smell-of-death about him'.[98] In 1977 he climbed Koh-y-Bandake, a 2,500m/8,200ft wall, in six days, alpine-style with Voytek Kurtyka as part of a joint Anglo-Polish expedition, described by John Porter as 'the first East/West alpine-style big-peak-bashing affair; five capitalist yahoos teamed up with six socialist aristocrats. The anarchistic approach we shared in common.'[99] On his return to Europe he made the first alpine-style ascent of the Harlin Route on the North Face of the Eiger (ED3) with Tobin Sorenson, describing it as 'easy – only three days'. MacIntyre, Porter, Kurtyka and Christof Zurek made an alpine-style ascent of the South Face of Changabang the following year, spending 11 days on the mountain, with five nights hanging in hammocks designed by MacIntyre. This was one of the first big walls to be climbed in the Himalaya without using siege tactics and remains unrepeated despite attempts by strong teams from America and Italy. The same team, plus Rene Ghilini (a Franco-Italian guide) and Ludwik Wilczynski (a Polish musician and classical philologist) climbed the East Face of Dhaulagiri (8,167m/26,795ft) in a single three day alpine-style push in 1979. Like many of his generation, MacIntyre was absolutely committed to small scale, alpine-style expeditions: 'The wall was the ambition; the style became the obsession,'[100] he wrote of the ascent of Shishapangma. He was killed just a few months later when a single stone bouncing down the South Face of Annapurna I broke his neck while he was attempting an alpine-style ascent of a new line with Ghilini and Porter. Shortly before MacIntyre's death, Messner described him as 'the purist exponent of the true style alive today'. In his obituary, Porter simply wrote: 'I had lost a friend...my link to the freedom of years gone by.'[101]

Roger Baxter Jones, a contemporary of MacIntyre and Porter at Leeds University, had a more relaxed manner and a plummy southern accent. After numerous major summer alpine routes in the early 1970s, he turned to winter alpinism, climbing the Super Couloir on Mont Blanc de Tacul (ED2) with Tut Braithwaite in 1972 and the Whymper Spur Direct on the Grandes Jorasses (ED3) with Nick Colton in 1975. In 1977 he made the first solo winter ascent of North Face of Grands Charmoz (TD). Following Shishapangma, Baxter Jones climbed Broad Peak (8,047m) alpine-style with Al Rouse, Andy Parkin and Jean Afanassieff in 1983, but became increasingly disillusioned with high-altitude climbing: 'I always had the quaint idea that climbing was something to do with pleasure.'[102] He moved to France, married a local girl, and became the first Briton to become a Chamonix guide. He died in an avalanche while guiding in the Alps in 1985.

Despite being dropped by Bonington from the Everest North-East Ridge, Al Rouse continued to pursue a career as a professional mountaineer. As the Burgess twins noted: 'In Britain there is room for only a few truly "professional" mountaineers. Bonington and Scott were the most prominent. The rest, like Rouse, were left to scrabble their way up the pile.'[103] In 1986 he led an expedition to attempt a new route on the North-West Ridge of K2 including the Burgess twins, Brian Hall, John Porter and Dave Wilkinson. After a long period of bad weather the others decided to call it a day, but Rouse stayed on to attempt the first British ascent of K2 by the 'normal route' on the Abruzzi Spur – a route that could only be called 'normal' for a climber of Rouse's ambition and ability. During a chaotic, multinational scramble for the summit a storm struck the mountain, lasting for five days. Six climbers died, including Rouse and Julie Tullis, another British climber who was attempting the peak with her climbing partner Kurt Diemberger. Both Rouse and Tullis made it to the summit, but were trapped by the storm and died during the descent. Jim Curran, who was making a film of the expedition, described Rouse's motives for making one last attempt: 'His precarious life-style of climber, writer, committeeman, vice president of the BMC, lecturer and gentleman of leisure was always something of a balancing act...it became imperative that expeditions like K2 should exist and, almost as important, be seen to exist, so that somehow he could still use his name and reputation to carry him through the next season of trade fairs, lectures, magazine articles.'[104]

At an Alpine Club symposium on Lightweight Expeditions to the Greater Ranges shortly before his death, Rouse described 'the best trip ever' in 1976–77: 'A nine months' climbing expedition covering most of South America, particularly Patagonia and Peru. We left in three climbing pairs, Rab Carrington and myself, Brian Hall and John Whittle, Alan and Adrian Burgess; accompanying us were various wives and girl friends...For all of us this was a highly successful expedition and we managed seventeen major first ascents between us. Each pair operated separately on the mountain but we offered each other moral assistance in Base Camps as well as the possibility of rescue if needed.'[105] He also retained a nostalgic affection for hard British rock climbing, but he regarded Himalayan climbing as an activity to be endured rather than enjoyed. He certainly did not 'die as he would wish to have died', as the climbers' cliché would have it.

Mick Fowler, the London-based taxman, has continued to amass a remarkable number of hard new climbs through to the present day on both rock and ice. In the greater ranges he has concentrated on 6,000m peaks where acclimatisation is possible within the constraints of a five week civil service holiday, putting up some outstandingly beautiful and technically demanding new routes including the 40-pitch, 1,100m/3,600ft ascent of the Golden Pillar of Spantik (7,027m/23,054ft) with Victor Saunders in 1987, Cerro Kishtwar North-West Face (6,200m/20,341ft) with Steve Sustad in 1993, a 45-pitch climb on the North-East Pillar of Taweche (6,542m/21,463ft) with Pat Littlejohn in 1995 and the North Face of Siguniang (6,250m/20,505ft) in 2002 with Paul Ramsden, for which they received the Piolet d'Or (the mountaineering 'Oscar') from the Groupe de Haute Montagne. Like Fowler, Ramsden has a job and a family to support, and therefore has relatively little time for climbing. But he did manage to snatch time for a winter ascent of the North Face of the Droites and the North Face of the Matterhorn one weekend. Meanwhile Fowler was voted the 'mountaineers' mountaineer' by his peers in a competition organised by the *Observer* magazine.

Stephen Venables[106] became the first British climber to reach the summit of Everest without oxygen as a member of the 1988 American expedition, with a new route up the Kangshung (East) Face. He reached the summit alone and bivouacked at 8,500m, losing four toes to frostbite. As he observed: 'To climb unsupported on one of the very highest peaks, treading close to the edge of what is physiologically possible, will always be exciting, but not necessarily enjoyable.'[107] His success won him an interview with Terry Wogan and an appearance on *Blue Peter*. Educated at Charterhouse and Oxford, Venables had already established a reputation for alpine-style climbing with the first ascent of Kishtwar-Shivling (6,000m/19,685ft) with Dick Renshaw in 1983 and an attempt to climb Rimo I (7,385m/24,229ft) with Victor Saunders in 1985, which they had to abandon within 400m/1,300ft of the summit when Venables dropped his rucksack. The climbing expedition to Rimo, on the disputed border between India and Pakistan, was one of the first to visit the Siachen Glacier region since Eric Shipton in 1957.

Following the disintegration of the former Soviet Union, new areas for exploration also opened up in the Pamirs and Tien Shan mountains that had previously been off-limits to western climbers.

In 1991 a large British team went to the Tien Shan, including Allen Fyffe, Simon Yates and the husband and wife team of Roger Payne and Julie-Ann Clyma. Members of the team climbed the beautiful Khan Tengri (7,010m/22,999ft) and Victory Peak (7,439m/24,406ft). Clyma has built a reputation as one of the most accomplished female mountaineers based in Britain (she was born in New Zealand), with numerous expeditions to the greater ranges, including the first alpine-style ascent of Nanda Devi East (7,434m/24,390ft) in 1995, a new route on Changabang (6,864m/22,520ft) in 1996 and the first ascent of Mount Grosvenor (6,376m/20,919ft) in China in 2003.

In 1993 Jonathan Pratt finally succeeded in making the first British ascent of the West Ridge of K2, which had been attempted by Bonington in 1978 and Scott in 1980, and was finally climbed siege-style by the Japanese in 1981. Pratt reached the summit with American Dan Mazur in a single push, without oxygen, from 8,200m/26,900ft. His ascent was initially greeted with a degree of scepticism by the British climbing community who had never heard of Pratt, but he has gone on to climb the five highest mountains in the world, including the first British ascent of Gasherbrum I (8,035m/26,362ft).

The wet summer of 1993 was also a season of super-peak bagging in the Alps. Martin Moran and Simon Jenkins made a non-stop traverse of all 75 alpine peaks over 4,000m in 52 days, while Alison Hargreaves[108] soloed six north faces including the Piz Badile, Cima Grande, the Dru, the Eiger via the Lauper Route, the Grandes Jorasses via the Shroud, and the Matterhorn. In November of the same year she made the first female solo ascent of the Croz Spur on the Grandes Jorasses, being dropped by helicopter at the *bergschrund* and picked up from the summit. The hyperbole of her husband, Jim Ballard, a former climbing shop owner, diminished the scale of her achievement in many climbers' eyes, and the mass media was more interested in journalist Rebecca Stephens being guided to the summit of Everest. In May 1995, Hargreaves became the first woman to climb Everest without the aid of Sherpas or oxygen. She died returning from the summit of K2 in a storm in August the same year, attempting the same thing. Her death unleashed a debate in the mainstream press about the unjustifiable risk of high-altitude climbing that was uncannily similar to the Matterhorn disaster of 1865, but this time directed at women and, in particular, mothers, since Hargreaves had two young children. Nigella Lawson, writing in *The Times*, the same paper that had condemned the Matterhorn accident 130 years earlier, wrote: 'If the Alison Hargreaves' of this world really value life so little maybe we should not worry on their behalf if they lose it...it is the disparity between the essential futility of the deed and the breast-swelling brouhaha that greets the achievement that makes this sort of me-first mountaineering so contemptible.' Even Polly Toynbee, normally a liberal commentator, was appalled: '[Hargreaves] behaved like a man...She put danger first and her family a poor second.'[109]

Hargreaves became an icon of sexual stereotyping to be venerated or vilified according to taste, but beneath the very public debate there was certainly a private tragedy. Emotionally distant, ambitious parents, a decision to live with a man 16 years her senior who tried to live his frustrated climbing ambitions vicariously through her, fragile self-confidence and a desperate need for approval all contributed to her death. When Jim Ballard's climbing shop went bankrupt the financial burden of supporting their two young children fell on Hargreaves and her uncertain income as a professional mountaineer. At the suggestion of George Band, the Everest veteran, she decided to try to climb Everest, K2 and Kangchenjunga without oxygen in a single year. The events on K2 had all the tragedy of a death foretold.

Meanwhile, big wall climbing continued in Patagonia, Baffin Island and Greenland. In 1994 Paul Pritchard, famous for his adventurous routes on Gogarth, teamed up with Noel Craine and others to climb Hyperboria on the remarkable flat-topped column of granite called Mount Asgard in Greenland, scene of James Bond's ski jump, complete with Union Jack parachute, in *The Spy Who Loved Me*. The route took 11 days to climb and consisted of 19 pitches graded E4 6a/A4+. At the top, 'Noel led through, pulled an overhang and clasped the summit with both hands. There are no soul-destroying false summits on Asgard – you just slap the top and mantelshelf.'[110]

In 1996 Andy Parkin, Brendan Murphy, Roger Payne and Julie-Ann Clyma put up a new route on the North Face of Changabang, using a series of static camps, before making a final dash for the summit, as Boardman and Tasker had done on the West Face in 1976. The following year Payne, Clyma and Murphy were back with Andy Cave, Mick Fowler and Steve Sustad, climbing alpine-style in three independent pairs. Payne and Clyma retreated after 12 days on the face. The other four reached the summit in a single push despite a potentially fatal fall by Sustad. On the descent Brendan Murphy was swept away by an avalanche, and the three survivors made an exhausting retreat after spending a total of 16 nights on the mountain. Jules Cartwright and Rich Cross made a stylish lightweight first ascent of the North-West ridge of Ama Dablam over 11 days in 2001. The route consisted of over 4,000m of steep, sinuous ridge and had rebuffed a dozen previous attempts, including a bolt-assisted siege by an eight man team. Cartwright was killed in the Alps just two years later.

The extraordinary Italian climber Reinhold Messner became the first man to climb all 14 peaks over 8,000m in 1986. Alan Hinkes from Yorkshire became the first British climber, and the 13th overall, to accomplish the ultimate peak-bagger's dream, starting with Shishapangma in 1987 and ending with a very fast ascent of Kangchenjunga in 2005. His 18 year campaign included three attempts on K2, Nanga Parbat and Kangchenjunga, and four attempts on Makalu. He suffered a series of accidents, including the bizarre 'chapatti incident' on Nanga Parbat when he slipped a disc as a result of a violent fit of sneezing induced by inhaling chapatti flour. Hinkes was initially sponsored by Bull Computers of France, as part of their 'Esprit d'Équipe – Challenge 8000' advertising campaign, which came to an abrupt halt when the company suffered heavy financial losses and French workers protested at the extravagance of the sponsorship programme. He accomplished the remaining climbs by raising sponsorship wherever possible and tagging along with other expeditions that had already booked the peaks. He was awarded an OBE in the 2006 New Year's Honours List for his labours. After completing the last climb, at the age of 51, he sat down in base camp and thought: 'Now I am free – finished with near death experiences. Free just to enjoy the hills.'[111]

8

BECAUSE IT'S THERE?

As people have grown richer, healthier and better educated, as they have acquired greater comfort, security, leisure and mobility, as knowledge has increased and technology has improved, so ever increasing numbers have deliberately undertaken ever more dangerous climbs in order to expose themselves to risks that are clearly unjustifiable by any normal moral or rational standard. And so the perennial question: why do people climb?

Mallory had no recollection of ever having said 'because it's there'. He believed that to those familiar with the mountains, the answer to the inevitable question would be obvious. As a young reporter for *The Times* attached to the 1953 Everest expedition, James Morris, had several months to consider the question. He identified five reasons: pride; ambition; aestheticism; mysticism; and masochism. He found the last the most convincing.[1] These five motives clearly play a role, but they are not the whole story. Throughout the rich and diverse literature of mountaineering, climbers have tied themselves in verbal knots trying to explain the fascination of their sport, which clearly involves a complex interplay between social, cultural, economic and very personal influences. Insofar as it is possible to draw any general conclusions about a sport that prides itself on being individualistic, it is that climbing is first and foremost an escape: from the familiar to the unknown; from noise and crowds to peace and beauty; from comfort and convenience to discretionary danger; from compliance and conformity to freedom and self-reliance; from complexity to simplicity. Climbing is an escape from an existence that is useful but purposeless to one that is useless but purposeful.

That the British urban, professional middle classes were the first to express this need to escape through climbing mountains reflects the fact that they were the first to feel it most acutely *and* to have the means to do something about it. As more people have felt the same need and acquired the same means, so the sport has expanded across national and class boundaries. And while the motivations of ordinary and elite climbers clearly differ in degree, they do not appear to differ in kind. The 4 million hill walkers and climbers in Britain today seek to escape from normal life for exactly the same reasons as the small community of elite climbers. But they know the escape is only temporary. They seek the *contrast* of the mountains in order to refresh and revitalise their ordinary lives. Many elite climbers, on the other hand, seem to wonder whether they really want to come back.

James Morris placed the heroic instinct – pride and ambition – ahead of the aesthetic and the mystical, but he was observing a group of experienced climbers attempting to 'conquer' the highest mountain on earth. The initial impulse that takes young people into the hills has more to do with exploration, freedom, friendship and adventure than pride and ambition. A dawning recognition of beauty usually follows. So too does a sense of achievement, the personal satisfaction that comes from doing something that is certainly hard work and possibly dangerous.

A recent article in *The Economist* entitled 'Happiness and Economics'[2] reported on research carried out by highly paid management consultants that has shown that people are at their happiest when undertaking tasks that meet three criteria: the task must be stretching without defeating them; there must be a clear goal and unambiguous feedback on progress towards that goal; and the person undertaking the task must have a sense of control. The fact that the consultants needed to conduct research to reach these conclusions shows that none of them were climbers.

Alfred Wainwright, the misanthropic writer of guide books for hill walkers, hated the Pennine Way, but he took pride in the achievement: 'The Pennine Way...is a tough bruising walk and the compensations are few. You do it because you want to prove to yourself that you are man enough to do it. You do it to get it off your conscience. You do it because you count it a personal achievement.'[3] Despite the lack of compensations, hundreds of hill walkers choose to follow in Wainwright's footsteps each year, spending two or three weeks of their lives completing the 270-mile walk in order to feel that sense of personal achievement when they finish. Many more spend days staggering through the peat hags and heather of Scotland ticking off the 283 mountains that exceed the magical height of 3,000 feet (914m). On many Munros the most direct and quickest route to the summit is not the best. With an extra hour or two of walking it is often possible to visit remote, hidden lochans or scramble up narrow rocky ridges. But the direct route to the summit is almost invariably the most eroded, and the marks left by generations of passing boots act as a silent poll of the motives of the ascensionists: most people who climb Munros do so primarily for the sense of achievement when they reach the summit. They are not interested in beauty or adventure, if it involves an extra hour or two of effort.

It is the nature of human affairs that a personal sense of achievement is not enough for most people. They also seek the recognition and admiration of their peer group, and when such recognition is granted it inevitably invites competition. For many years the British climbing establishment was in denial about the central role of pride, ambition and competition in climbing, maintaining that it undermined the aesthetic and spiritual elements of the sport and threatened the fundamentally uncompetitive relationship between man and mountain. But John Tyndall, the pioneering alpinist, was surely motivated by pride when he 'pressed the very highest snowflake of the mountain and the prestige of the Weisshorn was forever lost',[4] and when Haskett Smith, the father of British rock climbing, noted that 'when A makes a climb...B, C, and D are...anxious to say that they followed the exact line that Mr A found so difficult, and thought it perfectly easy',[5] it was surely competition that he was describing. The pioneers were ambitious professional men, struggling to enhance their position in a hierarchical and status-conscious society. Competition, pride and ambition transformed Victorian ramblers into peak-baggers, bog-trotters, fell-runners and scramblers, and scrambling soon evolved into the elaborate and competitive game of 'chicken' called climbing. Initially competition took the form of rivalry between 'friends'. Writing before the First World War, Arnold Lunn observed: 'Theoretically we all climb just for the love of the sport. There are, of course, a number of mountaineers who are...as indifferent as mortal man can be to the credit of achievement. But I have often thought that...some recognised rivalry in competition would be better than the bitter jealousies that divide the alpine world.'[6] As the sport expanded, publicity promoted competition between individuals who had never met, between people from different regions, different nations, even different generations. As Tom Patey observed: 'The qualification "perhaps unjustifiable" had, of course, the unintended effect of securing for the climb the attention of successive generations of young aspirant V.S. men who may be relied upon to accept any open invitation to deride their elders.'[7] R. L. G. Irving, Mallory's teacher at Winchester, noted with regret that 'mountaineering has certainly not escaped the baneful effects of human rivalry',[8] and even Mallory, the staunch defender of the aesthetic creed, recognised the role of pride and ambition: 'Mountaineering, like the greater part of man's activities, is not as a rule wholly independent of praise. "Fame" we call it for those with whose motives we are apt to sympathise; and for the others – "Advertisement" or "Low Competitive Spirit".'[9]

But why should people choose to satisfy their craving for achievement and recognition through climbing? Wilfrid Noyce observed in 1947 that 'those who have been unsuccessful at games...find that by pushing their abilities they can win the casual repute of the climbing world',[10] and it does seem to be the case that throughout history climbing has attracted a high proportion of young men (and a smaller number of young women) who suffer from myopia, lack of co-ordination or are otherwise poorly adapted to succeed in more conventional sports. For those that are strong, and crave the status that success in sport can bring, but lack the attributes necessary to excel in more popular games, climbing provides the perfect outlet. Everyone suffers from a fear of heights – a fact that is remorselessly exploited by Outward Bound and management team-building courses – so while the subtleties of climbing may be lost on the general public it is obvious to all that it demands a mastery of fear. Climbers are therefore granted a level of public esteem that participants in many other minority sports are denied. The climber who discusses his weekend activities with work colleagues is generally met with the gratifying response: 'Oh, I could never do that!' This creates the conceit that climbers are different: more courageous, more heroic than ordinary people. The reality, of course, is somewhat different. Most young people who 'graduate' from hill walking to climbing do so with a sense of relief. Unlike hard hill walking, which demands stamina and determination, rock climbing involves short bursts of intense activity and fear interspersed by extended periods of doing nothing. Provided the fear is mastered, it is possible to feel pleasantly superior to hill walkers with remarkably little effort. As Ruskin noted in 1866: 'The real ground for reprehension of ... climbing is that with less cause, it excites more vanity than any other athletic skill.'[11]

But the feeling of fear is very real. Like all adrenaline sports, climbing provides an intensity of experience that fortunately is absent from most ordinary lives in the developed world. Intense physical effort and mental control banish all other distractions, and the climber exists in a simple world where all thoughts apart from survival are temporarily suspended. Young people attracted to the sport are, of necessity, risk-takers, and many may feel a sense of moral cowardice in their ordinary lives as they pursue the safety and security of qualifications, a job, a house, a spouse and a pension. Climbing provides a heroic interlude, an opportunity to test personal courage and resolve. There is also an 'otherworldly' quality about climbing that is lacking in most other sports. A muddy inner-city football pitch or leafy suburban golf course is still palpably part of the urban, corporatist world of rules, regulations, responsibilities and obligations. In contrast, climbing is a quest that takes the climber outside the boundaries of normal 'civilised' life.

Elite climbers, like all elite sportsmen, are obsessed by their sport. But unlike most other games or sports that may demand a few hours of intense activity each day while still permitting a relatively normal existence, climbing can easily take over your whole life. Challenging climbing, by its very nature, takes place in remote places far removed from normal society and involves spending many months in the company of those who are equally obsessed. Moreover, while they are engaged in their chosen activity, elite climbers resent the encroachment of 'normal' people, such as trekkers, who undermine the heroic personal landscape they create as they grapple with their icy peaks. In Alex MacIntyre's account of the ascent of Shishapangma you can feel the sense of triumph and relief amongst the 'experienced climbers' when Nick Prescott, the least experienced member of the party (who had organised the expedition), demonstrates his weakness: '[He] had not logged enough hours slogging through the Scottish bogs in winter blizzards, lumbering through the frantic, non-stop twenty-four hour exhaustion of the Alps...Like a pack of pursued wolves with a badly wounded mate, the experienced climbers smelt the inevitable. "Nick's had it".'[12] In the small, competitive, hot-house world of the elite, it is easy to see how ambitious young climbers with fragile self-esteem, craving the approval of their peer group, can create the conditions for their own personal tragedy. As education, career, non-climbing friends and relations are progressively sacrificed, alternative opportunities for self-fulfilment are abandoned, and they feel obliged to undertake ever harder climbs to maintain both their standing with their peers and their own heroic self-image. Of course, most climbers break out of this cycle and enjoy perfectly well-balanced, happy and fulfilling lives in which climbing may or may not play a role. But a small number play the game to its logical conclusion.

Artificial climbing walls, sports-climbs and even well-protected traditional routes involve low levels of risk, and that is exactly the way most climbers want it. But hard soloing or routes in the high mountains with significant objective risk represent a deliberate dicing with death.

By their own admission, climbers who habitually take these risks exhibit symptoms akin to post traumatic stress disorder. Joe Tasker described being 'so conditioned to the sounds experienced during a climb that we found ourselves ducking for shelter if a plane droned overhead, thinking that it was the sound of an avalanche'.[13] In soldiers the symptoms include flashbacks, insomnia, anger and impaired personal relationships. Not surprisingly, the adjustment back to ordinary life after a hard and extended climb is not straightforward: 'We had pushed ourselves to the limit mentally and physically and stayed at that limit so long that we scarcely had the strength left to drag ourselves back to normal life.'[14] When confronted, once again, with the problems, complexities and ambiguities of real life, the temptation to return to the simplicity and purposefulness of climbing a mountain must be almost overwhelming: 'We returned to the mountain with relief', Peter Boardman wrote, 'fleeing from the moral problems of another planet, a different reality.'[15] Some elite climbers appear to become almost institutionalised to expedition life, like soldiers, or prisoners. When Alan Burgess, a committed exponent of alpine-style climbing, considered joining a later aborted Bonington expedition to Everest, his brother explained the reasoning behind his decision: 'Basically, going to Everest means three free meals a day and a place to call 'ome for three months.'[16]

Inevitably, comparisons have been drawn between climbing and war. Geoffrey Winthrop Young talked of 'a hollowness of mood, a physical catch in the breath, in part the excitement, in part the anxiety, in part the impatience which precedes momentous action. No custom quite banished this. In war-time the sensation even became commonplace, the "night-before-attack" feeling; and we confessed to it more readily.'[17] But Young was at pains to point out the difference between war and climbing: 'How could anyone who has lived through even a week of bombardment in Ypres and a day of action and sight upon the Matterhorn continue to compare the jangling monotone of death with the deep resonant chords of life...' Young went climbing during relatively infrequent holidays in an otherwise busy life. For the overwhelming majority of climbers, it is the *contrast* with normal life, the brief but intense flirtation with fear, which attracts them to the sport. Elite climbers pursue that sensation relentlessly, obsessively, and while most do not want to die, there is certainly an acceptance of death.

During one of his periodic bouts of despondency about climbing, Jim Perrin wrote: 'There is an element of the mystical about climbing, but the climbers are not lost in God but in themselves...The ego and the will are the driving forces in climbing, the philosophy behind it is one of despair...Ego and will by no means bring happiness, the times when I have been best at my climbing have been the least happy times of my life...The toying with death (any arguments that this is not so are utterly spurious) that represents so strong a part of climbing adds yet another facet to the negativity of the sport. Each new death is a reiteration of the question "Is it worth it"...Is it worth it? Yes, for those who are weak, aimless, discontent, strong and directionless, childless, unhappily married, unresolved or in despair.'[18]

When elite climbers head to the hills, many of them appear to leave behind them unhappy or unfulfilling personal relationships. There is even a theory that the absence of sex may have been one of the factors that led to the birth of climbing as a sport in the nineteenth century.[19] Noting that the Golden Age of British mountaineering coincided with the new ethic of sexual inhibition that followed the accession of Victoria to the throne, this theory holds that whereas men were content to pursue their wives and mistresses during the Regency, in the Victorian era they sublimated their sex urge into other sporting pursuits, including the conquest of proud and icy 'virgin' peaks, not infrequently 'draped with bridal lace'. Sexual imagery is certainly quite common in the accounts of the pioneers, perhaps reflecting the popularity of children's books of the era such as *The Snow Queen* by Hans Christian Andersen (1844), itself an allegory for Andersen's unreciprocated love of an unattainable woman. Whymper described his frustration at finding the Aiguille de Trélatête shrouded in clouds: 'Our mountain, like a beautiful coquette, sometimes unveiled herself for a moment, and looked charming above, although very mysterious below.'[20] But while mountains were often seen as objects of desire, they were by no means always seen as female. To R. L. G. Irving, a Winchester schoolmaster, the mountains were definitely male: 'There is an overwhelming sense of personality about a peak when we feel its broad snowy chest almost touching our own, when his great rocky shoulders rub against ours and our hands clutch at his hard, rough skin to get a hold.'[21]

The sport of climbing developed at a time when interest in social and economic Darwinism was at its peak and when the British defined themselves partly in contradistinction to the peoples that they conquered. The British regarded themselves as frugal, courageous and manly, whereas foreigners were luxurious, lazy and effeminate. In the Victorian and Edwardian era the ascent of an alpine peak was an emphatically masculine activity, conferring a social and moral status on the climber. Since it was also overwhelmingly a pastime of the upper middle classes, alpine resorts, like English tennis and golf clubs, provided a convenient place for vigorous young men to meet eligible young women. So many engagements were announced in the romantic atmosphere of Zermatt, Chamonix or Grindelwald that Sir Edward Davidson, the 'King of the Riffel' and a well-known socialite and snob, accused women climbers of being more interested in husbandeering than mountaineering. From the start of the Golden Age, the Alps were also a favourite destination for honeymoons, where desk-bound professional men could display their physical prowess. Skiing holidays in the Alps continued to provide useful opportunities for upper-middle-class mating until the late twentieth century, but as climbing became increasingly democratic it lost much of its social cachet.

Some modest achievement in climbing, as in any other sport, is probably useful in attracting a mate, provided the desired status can be obtained without excessive risk. The typical Victorian climber who returned 'brandishing his ice axe in everybody's face'[22] after ascending an alpine peak had usually been dragged up an easy route by an experienced guide, and even today few people know the difference between a Very Difficult climb and a very difficult climb. Throughout the history of the sport, effective self-publicists have typically enjoyed a higher social status than the best climbers, and from a purely Darwinian perspective extreme climbing, unlike the lower-risk alternatives, is not an obviously successful strategy. As Fred Mummery, the founder of modern mountaineering, noted in his description of climbing the Aiguille Verte: 'It is open to the objection that at almost every step the texture of one's skull is likely to be tested by the impact of a falling stone. Though this lends much interest and excitement to the climb, it is of a sort that altogether loses its power of pleasing, so soon as the mountaineer has passed the first flush of youth.'[23] Since people in the first flush of youth tend not to have reproduced themselves, natural selection imposes a heavy toll upon those that undertake such climbs, suggesting that the root cause of *extreme* climbing is nurture, rather than nature. Moreover, it often seems to be the case that extreme climbers are far more concerned with impressing each other, rather than any potential mate.

One of the striking omissions from the five motives for climbing identified by James Morris is friendship. For the vast majority of ordinary climbers, the friendships formed through the shared experience of hardship and danger are amongst the most enduring and valuable aspects of the sport. But Morris was an outsider observing an elite group of mountaineers seeking to reach the summit of the world's highest peak, and aspiring heroes are more inclined to see fellow climbers as rivals than as friends. The romantic reticence of the past may contrast with the current fashion for embarrassing candour, but it does not disguise the fact that throughout the history of the sport there have been many strong partnerships between equally outstanding climbers, but very few friendships. Ordinary British climbers tend to adopt a squaddy group mentality, where shared humour and vulgarity, coupled with a certain bloody-minded determination, help to alleviate the discomfort and inevitable squalor of life in the mountains. In contrast, the climbing hero is essentially selfish and solitary, and relationships with rival climbers are edgy, mistrustful and competitive, with the hero constantly seeking to establish a psychological or physical advantage.

For most people, climbing starts as a youthful obsession but develops into one of many interests competing for the scarce resource of adult spare time. Elite climbers, like people who excel in many other specialised walks of life, remain obsessed and seem to suffer from a form of arrested development. Their 'teenage' self-absorption and selfishness may make them charismatic figures in later life, but it does not make them the easiest of friends or spouses. On one of the many occasions when Don Whillans crashed his motorbike, his long-suffering wife Audrey had the misfortune to be riding on the back. She broke her femur and had to spend three months in hospital. Rather than make the journey to visit her, Whillans wrote a letter: 'I'm always doing something...working, washing pots, sweeping, buying food...I'm really tired when I get home, falling asleep in the chair before I even get my tea... Well sweetheart, mend up quick – I'm missing you more than I ever thought I could.'[24] Years later, when Whillans died of a heart attack, a crowd of climbers was about to enter the crematorium when a piercing Brummy voice floated over the assembled company: 'Well, Audrey got her revenge – she fed him to death!'[25]

Some leading climbers do appear to succeed in finding partners who are prepared to shoulder the twin burdens of home-maker and hero-worshipper without complaint, but there is something childishly poignant about the number of top male climbers (some of them middle-aged) who write with sad incomprehension about the wives and girlfriends that have deserted them, as they head off for another three month expedition to the Himalaya. Ed Drummond, the climber and poet, speculated that the emotional control so vital in hard climbing actually inhibits a climber's ability to form close, personal relationships: 'I...used to think that the pursuit of calmness, that vital need to suppress anxiety in the high risk situations of climbing, would help me to become a better, steadier, person. It no longer seems so simple. Can't the capacity not to feel threatened become a tranquilliser, debilitating our awareness of what is actually happening, in just those situations where we most need to know, that is, in personal relationships with others, situations in which it is vital to express, not to suppress, feeling?'[26] Inevitably, it is hard to disentangle cause and effect, but for many elite climbers the need to escape *from* ordinary life seems to be at least as powerful as the need to escape *to* the mountains. When Jim Perrin said 'the times when I have been best at my climbing have been the least happy times of my life', he expressed a sentiment that is the exact opposite of the experience of most ordinary climbers. But ordinary climbers do not put up the extremely difficult and dangerous new routes that Perrin created when he was climbing at his best.

In addition to pride and ambition, James Morris also identified aestheticism and mysticism as motives for climbing. There have been climbers, such as Edward Whymper, Owen Glynne Jones or Peter Livesey, who were apparently indifferent to the grandeur, beauty and purity of the mountain landscape, but for the majority of climbers a visit to the mountains is both an aesthetic and a spiritual experience. John Ruskin was an aesthetic-extremist who believed that 'the true beauty of the Alps is to be seen *only* where all may see it – the child, the cripple, the man of grey hairs'. But Ruskin was wrong: not all may enjoy the full beauty of the mountain landscape, because mountain beauty is inextricably linked with movement. A static observer of a magnificent mountain view, like a visitor to an art gallery, feels a sense of detachment, whereas climbers are part of the environment, experiencing it with every sense as they move through the landscape from the known to the unknown. Every climber and hill walker recognises the sense of anticipation expressed by Bill Tilman as he set off one morning: 'I felt I could go on like this for ever, that life had little better to offer than to march day after day in unknown country to an unattainable goal.'[27] Moving on steep ground, there is an added sense of balance and rhythm. The polished holds and scratches on a popular climb are like steps in a dance, and perhaps only other climbers can fully appreciate the poise and grace of great climbers on a hard route.

Most people who take up climbing do so at an impressionable age, and most have felt the 'spontaneous overflow of powerful feelings' that mountain beauty can induce, even if they may be reluctant to say so. There has always been a tension between the search for beauty and spiritual renewal and the desire for adventure, self-fulfilment and achievement. Under the influence of Ruskin, many Victorian and Edwardian alpinists felt obliged to conceal their heroic instincts behind a veil of aesthetic appreciation, in much the same way that an earlier generation had hidden behind scientific respectability. After the Second World War, as the influence of the romantic poets and writers declined, a reaction set in. All thoughts of beauty were banished behind the macho posturing of the climbing hero. But even Adrian Burgess, unquestionably a hard man, as famous for drinking and fighting as for climbing, admitted that 'as we shuffled along through pristine snow I became aware of how beautiful and wild were our surroundings. Of course it was forbidden to voice such thoughts.'[28] Nearly all climbers recognise that there is more to mountaineering than the fleeting feeling of conquest or the grudging admiration of their peers. People go to the mountains in search of solace, an experience that will uplift and revitalise the body *and* the spirit. Aesthetics is a dismal branch of philosophy – there is no rational explanation for beauty – but the intense emotional response to the landscape that many climbers feel does appear to be tied up with the profound sense of physical well-being that hard exercise and danger can induce. And in middle age, when youthful vigour has declined somewhat, memories of wild and reckless adventures suffuse the now familiar mountain landscape with the soft glow of nostalgia.

Ruskin wrote an entire book trying to capture the essence of mountain beauty, and failed.[29] Lesser writers have liberally sprinkled their books with mildly embarrassing passages of purple prose. Sir Leslie Stephen wisely counselled authors to 'pass by with a simple confession of wonder and awe'.[30] But that sense of wonder and awe is, and always has been, one of the prime motives for climbing. As Kenneth Clark observed: 'Apart from love, there is perhaps nothing else by which people of all kinds are more united than by their pleasure in a good view.'[31]

But Ruskin was right in recognising that after a long, hard climb, aesthetic appreciation may become a little dulled, and that climbers bent on 'conquest' can be surprisingly blind to the beauty of the mountain environment. After the first crossing of the Eigerjoch, even Leslie Stephen recorded that 'it was a beautiful day, and before us... rose one of the loveliest of Alpine views. I looked at it with complete indifference, and thought what I should order for breakfast.'[32] In the Karakoram near K2, surrounded by some of the most magnificent mountain scenery in the world, Greg Child recalled seeing 'glacial pools polluted by the waste of past expeditions. During the heat of the day a rank stench rises from behind the camp...Out of the shimmering noon we come across a scene that looks like a plane crash, with the survivors living amongst the wreckage...Tents float in puddles of slush that freeze solid at night. Heaps of rotting garbage and excrement lie everywhere.'[33]

Climbers have always polluted the mountain landscape. When James Eccles reached the summit of Mont Blanc after climbing the Peuterey Ridge in 1877 he was disgusted by the amount of litter left behind by climbers and their guides. Geoffrey Winthrop Young recounted how he 'cleared off all the tins and bottles within reach of a sluggard's arm'[34] after reaching the summit of the Grépon in 1907. For the pioneers, the wilderness seemed limitless, and such attitudes might be forgiven. Today, with every corner of this crowded world accessible, when all climbing is a 'credit card adventure', to use Joe Simpson's expression, it is self-delusion for climbers to think of themselves as pioneers. They are simply tourists, passing through a very beautiful and very fragile environment. It is possible that some climbers really are so self-absorbed and anti-social that they do not care about the damage they cause, but for the majority it is simply a reflection of the age-old tension between the aesthetic and the heroic instincts. On the way up the mountain, everything is subordinated to the sense of fulfilment that they hope they will feel when they reach the summit. On the way down, cold, hungry and physically drained, it is all too easy to leave the fixed ropes in place, throw the rubbish into a crevasse, and hurry back to the fleshpots of civilisation. As Sir Alfred Wills, whose ascent of the Wetterhorn started the Golden Age of climbing, admitted: 'You cannot – at least I never could – appreciate the picturesque while the teeth are chattering with cold and the inner man loudly proclaims its detestation of that which nature also abhors.'[35]

The final motive identified by James Morris (and, to him, most convincing) was masochism, and the one aspect of mountaineering that both aesthetes and heroes appear to have in common is a love of suffering. Climbing and the industrial revolution share a common root in Protestantism. Most of the major religions of the world incorporate the idea of a period of fasting or abstinence as a means of spiritual renewal or redemption, but it was northern European Protestantism, with its emphasis on hard work, self-reliance and self-restraint, which refined the concept to the point where the ideal holiday became one that involved significant suffering. There are some degenerate rock climbers who seek the instant gratification of warm rock on roadside crags, but real climbers like their gratification deferred, and in its more extreme forms it is hard to escape the conclusion that many mountaineers have a pronounced streak of masochism. Andy Cave, an ex-coal miner accustomed to tough conditions, recorded that after 16 days climbing the North Face of Changabang alpine-style, the last few without food, including an epic descent during which his partner, Brendan Murphy, was killed in an avalanche, 'Steve [Sustad] and Mick [Fowler] were insistent that we should pose with our tops off...and get some shots of our emaciated bodies; I didn't fancy it much, but couldn't particularly explain why.'[36] This may seem like odd behaviour, but many perfectly normal climbers and hill walkers would probably admit, reluctantly, to admiring their waistlines after a week or two in the hills, and Mo Anthoine spoke for many when he said: 'Every year you need to flush out your system and do a bit of suffering.'[37]

The aesthete emerges from a period of suffering and danger with the senses heightened and a greater awareness of beauty. The aspiring hero finds strength through will, the ability to withstand hardship reinforcing their personal sense of identity. For both, climbing is a form of redemption for the idleness and indulgence of urban life. Just the right amount of suffering enables even the ordinary hill walker to be pleasantly preoccupied with immediate concerns about survival rather than longer term worries, such as whether they enjoy their work, and the meaning of life. 'Such struggles with nature produce a moral invigoration of enduring value,' according to Lord Conway. 'They wash the mind free of sentimental cobwebs and foolish imaginings. They bring a man in contact with cold stony reality and call forth all that is best in his nature. They act as moral tonics.'[38] Better still, both the aesthete and the hero can enjoy the piquancy of pleasures resumed after a period of abstention. Bill Murray talked of the 'wild ecstasy' of chill water after being severely dehydrated in the Cuillins of Skye. Norman Collie – climber, academic and connoisseur of good food, wine and cigars – observed that 'hunger, exposure, and exhaustion are hard taskmasters, and the relief brought by rest, comfort and plenty of food is a pleasure never to be forgotten. It is certainly one of the keenest enjoyments I have ever experienced.'[39] Mike Thompson, in his account of the food arrangements for Chris Bonington's lavishly supplied expedition to the South Face of Annapurna, acknowledged that 'food was the consuming passion and obsession of the expedition, and if members were not actually engaged in eating it or getting rid of it, from one end or the other, they would be talking of it or dreaming of it...At Base Camp recipes and tips were continually being swapped as if it were some remote branch of the Women's Institute.'[40]

Peter Boardman described surviving a devastating storm at about 8,000m/26,000ft during his alpine-style ascent of Kangchenjunga as 'a rich experience...perhaps I needed, almost enjoyed it, for this feeling... Out of one of the worst experiences of my life, I've learned again how precious life is.'[41] There is, of course, a difference between building up a good appetite during a long country walk and a near-death experience in the icy winds of Kangchenjunga, but all climbers and hill walkers lack, to some extent, the ability to distinguish what they enjoy doing from what they enjoy having done.

It is not surprising that James Morris failed to identify peace and solitude as motives, during a huge expedition involving hundreds of porters, Sherpas and mountaineers, but most climbers would probably list both as reasons for climbing. It is not necessary to be completely alone, although that is the ultimate escape, but there is certainly a strong appeal in being surrounded by a landscape where there is little evidence of recent human activity. Since the eighteenth century, the idea of mountains has been inextricably linked with the idea of solitude, but the increasing popularity of the sport and the desire, even on the part of those responsible for conserving the landscape, to make access easy for all, makes solitude an increasingly rare and precious experience. In Britain there is no such thing as 'wilderness'; almost every part of the country is a cultural landscape that looks the way it does because of the activities of man. But in a land that has become so tamed and domesticated, it is perhaps not surprising that climbers and hill walkers should seek out the few remaining enclaves where a feeling of wildness and solitude can still be found.

Morris also failed to identify one further attraction of climbing, and that is the feeling of liberty. Under the military leadership of Colonel Hunt, and with the eyes of the nation upon them, perhaps this feeling was missing on Everest in 1953. But in general, when climbers go to the mountains, they leave rules, regulations and obligations behind them, and enter a world of unrestrained freedom. The professional men who invented the sport must have felt this more keenly than most when they left behind the suffocating social conventions of the Victorian drawing room and entered the 'companionable chaos' of the Wasdale Head Inn. In a more tolerant and emancipated world, it is perhaps inevitable that climbers have felt compelled to act in more anti-social ways in order to experience the same intoxicating sense of liberation that their forebears must have felt as they played billiard fives. The Cambridge-educated climber who stole a chicken from a pavement rotisserie, only to discover to his astonishment that a roasting chicken is extremely hot, and who then ran through the streets of Chamonix, pursued by the shopkeeper, juggling the chicken in the air and laughing hysterically, was not primarily motivated by hunger or by criminal instincts. He was motivated by the wild, wanton, spontaneous joy of freedom which forms such an important part of the overall climbing experience. Of course, for the French shopkeeper and the gendarme, the distinction was irrelevant.

Why do people climb mountains? Every climber has a slightly different reply to the inevitable question. There is no definitive answer, and perhaps we should not seek one. After all, it's just a game: a beautiful, humbling, absurdly funny and, occasionally, deadly serious game.

NOTES

CHAPTER 1 INTRODUCTION

1. Quoted in W. Unsworth, *Hold the Heights: The Foundations of Mountaineering* (London: Hodder & Stoughton, 1993), p. 312

2. A. F. Mummery, *My Climbs in the Alps and Caucasus*, 2004 Ripping Yarns ed. (London: Fisher Unwin, 1895), p. 213

CHAPTER 2 BEFORE 1854: IN SEARCH OF THE SUBLIME

1. See P. Coates, *Nature: Western Attitudes Since Ancient Times* (Cambridge: Polity Press, 1998)

2. See K. Thomas, *Man and the Natural World: Changing Attitudes in England 1500–1800* (London: Penguin, 1983), pp. 254–69

3. J. S. Mill, *Principles of Political Economy*, 2008 Oxford University ed. (1848), p. 129

4. See M. H. Nicolson, *Mountain Gloom and Mountain Glory*, 1997 Washington University ed. (Cornell University Press, 1959), pp. 34–5

5. See Nicolson, *Mountain Gloom and Mountain Glory*, p. 40 and S. Schama, *Landscape and Memory* (New York: Alfred A. Knopf, 1995), pp. 478–90

6. J-J. Rousseau, *Emile*, 2004 Kessinger ed. (1762), p. 360

7. J-J. Rousseau, *The Confessions*, 1996 Wordsworth ed. (1792), p. 167

8. See Schama, *Landscape and Memory*, pp. 447–9

9. E. Burke, *A Philosophical Enquiry*, 2008 Oxford University ed. (1757), p. 60

10. Ibid., p. 40

11. Mill, *Principles of Political Economy*, p. 129

12. See Introduction to P. Bicknell, *Beauty, Horror and Immensity: Picturesque Landscape in Britain, 1750–1850* (Cambridge University Press, 1981)

13. Quoted in ibid., p. ix

14. S. Johnson, *A Journey to the Western Islands of Scotland*, 1984 Penguin Classic ed. (1775), p. 60

15. See P. Bicknell, 'The Picturesque, the Sublime and the Beautiful', *Alpine Journal* 85 (1980)

16. J. Ruskin, *Modern Painters Volume IV: Of Mountain Beauty*, 1897 George Allen ed. (London: Smith Elder, 1856)

17. See Schama, *Landscape and Memory*, p. 459

18. See D. Craig, *Native Stones* (London: Pimlico, 1995), pp. 131–5

19. W. C. Slingsby, *Norway: The Northern Playground*, 2003 Ripping Yarns ed. (Edinburgh: David Douglas, 1904), p. 43

20. Quoted in B. Willey, *The Eighteenth Century Background: Studies on the Idea of Nature in the Thought of the Period*, 1972 Pelican ed. (London: Penguin, 1940), p. 276

21. See B. Russell, *History of Western Philosophy,* 1996 Routledge ed. (London: George Allen & Unwin, 1946), p. 656

22. Quoted in ibid., p. 663

23. A. Hankinson, *The First Tigers* (London: J. M. Dent, 1972), p. 110

24. Windham, *An Account of the Glaciers Or Ice Alps in Savoy*, AC Tracts 388 ed. (London: Peter Martel, 1741), p. 11

25. Quoted in Schama, *Landscape and Memory*, p. 494

26. Quoted in R. L. G. Irving, *The Romance of Mountaineering* (London: J. M. Dent, 1935), p. 42

27. Quoted in C. E. Engel, *A History of Mountaineering in the Alps* (London: George Allen & Unwin, 1950), p. 59

28. J. D. Forbes, *Travels Through the Alps of Savoy*, 2nd ed. (Edinburgh: Adam and Charles Black, 1845), p. 14

29. Quoted in J. Hunt, 'Mountaineering and Risk', *Alpine Journal* 86 (1981), p. 3

30. Quoted in C. Gamble, 'John Ruskin, Eugene Viollet-Le-Duc and the Alps', *Alpine Journal* 104 (1999), p. 188

31. J. Ruskin, *Sesame and Lilies*, preface to 1866 ed., pp. vi and xiii

32. Quoted in A. Lunn, *A Century of Mountaineering 1857–1957* (London: George Allen & Unwin, 1957), p. 23

33. F. Nietzsche, *Beyond Good and Evil*, 2004 1st World ed. (1886), p. 149

34. See A. N. Wilson, *The Victorians* (London: Hutchinson, 2002), p. 409

35. Quoted in Coates, *Nature: Western Attitudes Since Ancient Times*, p. 158

36. P. H. Hansen, 'British Mountaineering 1850–1914' (PhD, Harvard, 1991), p. 53

37. Ruskin, *Sesame and Lilies*, p. 46

38. Ruskin, *Sesame and Lilies*, p. 46

39. Quoted in F. S. Smythe, *British Mountaineers* (London: Collins, 1942), p. 10

40. Quoted in R. W. Clark, *The Victorian Mountaineers* (London: B. T. Batsford, 1953), p. 54

CHAPTER 3   1854–65: A CONSCIOUS DIVINITY

1. See T. Braham, *When the Alps Cast Their Spell* (Glasgow: The In Pinn, 2004), pp. 279–301

2. Quoted in Clark, *The Victorian Mountaineers*, p.65

3. Quoted in Lunn, *A Century of Mountaineering*, p. 54

4. Obituary of Thomas Stuart Kennedy, *Alpine Journal* 17 (1895), p. 332

5. C. Barrington, *Alpine Journal* 11 (1883), p. 174

6. Quoted in Unsworth, *Hold the Heights*, p. 66

7. F. C. Grove, 'The Comparative Skill of Travellers and Guides', *Alpine Journal* 5 (1870), p. 90

8. C. T. Dent, 'The History of an Ascent of the Aiguille Du Dru', *Alpine Journal* 9 (1878), p. 189

9. L. Stephen, *The Playground of Europe*, 1936 Blackwell ed. (London: Longmans, Green, 1871), p. 13

10. Ibid., p. 46

11. Mummery, *My Climbs in the Alps and Caucasus*, p. 100

12. See Lunn, *A Century of Mountaineering*, p. 44

13. Unsworth, *Hold the Heights*, p. 69

14. A. Trollope, *Travelling Sketches* (London: Chapman & Hall, 1866), p. 93

15. Quoted in Braham, *When the Alps Cast Their Spell*, p. 75

16.   K. T. Hoppen, *The Mid-Victorian Generation 1846–1886* (Oxford University Press, 1998), p. 488

17.   Quoted in Braham, *When the Alps Cast Their Spell*, p. 59

18.   Quoted in ibid., p. 52

19.   Stephen, *The Playground of Europe*, p. 39

20.   L. Stephen, *Some Early Impressions* (London: Hogarth, 1924), p. 189

21.   J. F. Hardy, 'The Ascent of the Lyskamm', *Peaks, Passes and Glaciers* 1, 2nd Series (1862), p. 392

22.   A. Lunn, 'The Playground of Europe 1871 to 1971: A Centenary Tribute to Leslie Stephen', *Alpine Journal* 77 (1972), p. 4

23.   Stephen, *The Playground of Europe*, p. 108

24.   A commentary on George Frederic Watts' portrait of Stephen, on display in the National Portrait Gallery in 2008

25.   Stephen, *The Playground of Europe*, p. 28

26.   Ibid., p. 53

27.   Quoted in Braham, *When the Alps Cast Their Spell*, p. 95

28.   Stephen, *The Playground of Europe*, p. 40

29.   L. Stephen, 'Review of Scrambles Amongst the Alps', *Alpine Journal* 5 (1872), p. 237

30.   Quoted in Unsworth, *Hold the Heights*, p. 79

31.   E. Whymper, *Scrambles Amongst the Alps*, 1985 Century ed. (London: John Murray, 1871), p. 9

32.   Ibid., p. 239

33.   F. S. Smythe, *Edward Whymper* (London: Hodder & Stoughton, 1940), p. 236

34.   Quoted in Irving, *The Romance of Mountaineering*, p. 71

35.   Smythe, *Edward Whymper*, p. 77

36.   Whymper, *Scrambles Amongst the Alps*, p. 332

37.   C. Bonington, *The Climbers* (London: BBC Books/Hodder & Stoughton, 1992), p. 44

38.   Quoted in Smythe, *Edward Whymper*, p. 230

39.   T. S. Blakeney, 'Whymper and Mummery', *Alpine Journal* 57 (1950), p. 339

40.   J. Simpson, *Dark Shadows Falling* (London: Jonathan Cape, 1997), p. 48

41.   Quoted in Braham, *When the Alps Cast Their Spell*, p. 223

42.   Quoted in K. Reynolds, 'Because It's There – and All That', *Alpine Journal* 83 (1978), p. 18

43.   Letter from A. Wills to E. Whymper, 6 August 1865, quoted in Hansen, 'British Mountaineering 1850–1914', p. 194

44.   Quoted in Unsworth, *Hold the Heights*, p. 89

CHAPTER 4   1865–1914: GENTLEMEN AND GYMNASTS

1.   Quoted in J. Morris, *Pax Britannica: The Climax of an Empire*, 1998 ed. (London: Faber & Faber, 1968), p. 119

2.   Mummery, *My Climbs in the Alps and Caucasus*, p. 213

3.   Hoppen, *The Mid-Victorian Generation*, p. 41

4. C. T. Dent, 'Two Attempts on the Aiguille du Dru', *Alpine Journal* 7 (1876), p. 79

5. H. G. Willink, 'Clinton Thomas Dent', *Alpine Journal* 27 (1913), p. 63

6. Dent, 'The History of an Ascent of the Aiguille du Dru', p. 199

7. See Lunn, *A Century of Mountaineering*, pp. 82–3

8. Dent, 'The History of an Ascent of the Aiguille du Dru', p. 198

9. M. Conway, 'Some Reminiscences and Reflections of an Old Stager', *Alpine Journal* 31 (1917), p. 151

10. Quoted in Clark, *The Victorian Mountaineers*, p. 187

11. Braham, *When the Alps Cast Their Spell*, p. 93

12. Quoted in Hankinson, *The First Tigers*, p. 8

13. Slingsby, *Norway: The Northern Playground*, p. 199

14. Irving, *The Romance of Mountaineering*, p. 109

15. Lunn, *A Century of Mountaineering*, p. 105

16. Quoted in Unsworth, *Hold the Heights*, p. 97

17. Quoted in Clark, *The Victorian Mountaineers*, p. 167

18. Quoted in Braham, *When the Alps Cast Their Spell*, p. 186

19. Quoted in ibid., p. 189

20. Mummery, *My Climbs in the Alps and Caucasus*, p. 79

21. Ibid., p. 65

22. W. Unsworth, *Because It Is There* (London: Victor Gollancz, 1968), p. 72

23. M. Conway, *Mountain Memories: A Pilgrimage of Romance* (London: Cassell, 1920), p. 127

24. Mummery, *My Climbs in the Alps and Caucasus*, p. 232

25. Ibid., p. 213

26. Ibid., p. 89

27. Conway, *Mountain Memories*, p. 126

28. Mummery, *My Climbs in the Alps and Caucasus*, p. 106

29. Ibid., p. 216

30. Quoted in Hankinson, *The First Tigers*, p. 69

31. C. Mill, *Norman Collie: A Life in Two Worlds* (Aberdeen University Press, 1987), p. 12

32. Hankinson, *The First Tigers*, p. 81

33. G. W. Young et al., 'John Norman Collie', *Himalayan Journal* XIII (1946), p. 116

34. R. Hillary, *The Last Enemy* (1942), quoted in the epilogue of J. N. Collie, *From the Himalaya to Skye*, 2003 Ripping Yarns ed. (Edinburgh: David Douglas, 1902), p. 174

35. Quoted in A. Hankinson, *Geoffrey Winthrop Young* (London: Hodder & Stoughton, 1995), p. 60

36. D. Pilley, *Climbing Days*, 1989 Hogarth Press ed. (London: G. Bell and Sons Ltd, 1935), p. 120

37. Mummery, *My Climbs in the Alps and Caucasus*, p. 65

38. *Daily Graphic*, 4 May 1910, quoted in Hansen, 'British Mountaineering 1850–1914', p. 318

39. Quoted in Clark, *The Victorian Mountaineers*, p. 184

41. C. Wells, *Who's Who in British Climbing* (Buxton: The Climbing Company, 2008), p. 391

42. R. W. Clark, *Men, Myths and Mountains* (London: Weidenfeld & Nicolson, 1976), p. 83

43. Lunn, *A Century of Mountaineering*, p. 135

44. Quoted in Wells, *Who's Who in British Climbing*, p. 401

45. A. Hankinson, *The Mountain Men* (London: Heinemann, 1977), p. 104

46. G. W. Young, *On High Hills*, 1947 5th ed. (London: Methuen, 1927), p. 23

47. Ibid., p. 28

48. Quoted in Hankinson, *Geoffrey Winthrop Young*, p. 141

49. Quoted in Hankinson, *The Mountain Men*, p. 181

50. G. W. Young, 'I have not lost the magic of long days', *April and Rain* (London: Sidgwick & Jackson, 1923), p. 44

51. See G. S. Sanson, *Climbing at Wasdale Before the First World War* (Somerset: Castle Cary Press, 1982)

52. Hankinson, *The First Tigers*, p. 40

53. Ibid., p. 108

54. Quoted in R. W. Clark and E. C. Pyatt, *Mountaineering in Britain* (London: Phoenix House, 1957), p. 35

55. Quoted in Clark and Pyatt, *Mountaineering in Britain*, p. 39

56. Young, *On High Hills*, p. 25

57. Quoted in A. Hankinson, *A Century on the Crags* (London: J. M. Dent, 1988), p. 38

58. Quoted in ibid., p. 52

59. H. M. Kelly, J. H. Doughty et al., '100 Years of Rock-Climbing in the Lake District', *Fell and Rock Climbing Club Journal* XXIV(2), 70 (1986)

60. K. Chorley, *Manchester Made Them* (London: Faber and Faber Ltd, 1950), pp. 16 and 53

61. Quoted in Hankinson, *A Century on the Crags*, p. 24

62. W. P. Haskett Smith, *Climbing in the British Isles*, 1986 Ernest Press ed. (London: Longmans, Green, 1895), p. 6

63. C. E. Benson, *British Mountaineering* (London: George Routledge & Sons Ltd, 1909), p. 9

64. Hankinson, *The Mountain Men*, p. 61

65. Hankinson, *The First Tigers*, p. 157

66. Ibid., p. 99

67. H. C. Bowen, 'Obituary of O. G. Jones', *Alpine Journal* 19 (1899), p. 584

68. A. Crowley, *The Confessions of Aleister Crowley* (London: Mandrake Press, 1929), p. 99

69. Quoted in Hankinson, *A Century on the Crags*, p. 38

70. See L. J. Oppenheimer, 'Wastdale Head at Easter', *Climbers' Club Journal* II, 5 (1899)

71. Pilley, *Climbing Days*, p. 79

72. Quoted in Hankinson, *The Mountain Men*, p. 80

73. H. V. Reade, 'Unjustifiable Climbs', *Climbers' Club Journal* VI, 21 (1903)

74. T. Jones and G. Milburn, *Cumbrian Rock: 100 Years of Climbing in the Lake District* (Glossop: Pic Publication, 1988), p. 40

75. Quoted in T. Jones and G. Milburn, *Welsh Rock: 100 Years of Climbing in North Wales* (Glossop: Pic Publications, 1986), p. 10

76. G. B. Bryant, 'The Formation of the Climbers' Club', *Climbers' Club Journal* I, 1 (1898), p. 1

77. Hankinson, *The Mountain Men*, p. 94

78. H. B. George and F. Morshead, 'Obituary of Charles Edward Mathews', *Alpine Journal* 22 (1905), p. 599

79. G. W. Young, G. Sutton and W. Noyce, *Snowdon Biography* (London: J. M. Dent, 1957), p. 28

80. Quoted in Clark and Pyatt, *Mountaineering in Britain*, p. 86

81. Orton, 'In Memoriam: J. M. Archer Thomson', *Climbers' Club Journal* I, 2 (1913), p. 70

82. Young, Sutton and Noyce, *Snowdon Biography*, pp. 31 and 36

83. Quoted in Hankinson, *The Mountain Men*, p. 163

84. Young, Sutton and Noyce, *Snowdon Biography*, p. 30

85. Ibid., p. 31

86. Crowley, *The Confessions of Aleister Crowley*, pp. 204 and 208

87. W. H. Murray, *The Evidence of Things Not Seen* (London: Bâton Wicks, 2002), p. 145

88. H. R. C. Carr and G. A. Lister (eds.), *The Mountains of Snowdonia*, 1948 Crosby Lockwood ed. (London: Bodley Head, 1925), p. 78

89. Clark and Pyatt, *Mountaineering in Britain*, p. 99

90. Quoted in Jones and Milburn, *Welsh Rock*, p. 14

91. R. Graves, *Goodbye to All That*, 1960 Penguin ed. (London: Jonathan Cape, 1929), p. 67

92. Hankinson, *Geoffrey Winthrop Young*, p. 120

93. Carr and Lister (eds.), *The Mountains of Snowdonia*, p. 79

94. Clark and Pyatt, *Mountaineering in Britain*, p. 33

95. Ibid., p. 61

96. Preface to *SMCJ* Vol. 1, quoted in W. D. Brooker (ed.), *A Century of Scottish Mountaineering* (Edinburgh: Scottish Mountaineering Trust, 1988), p. 6

97. Quoted in D. J. Bennet (ed.), *The Munros*, 1991 ed. (Edinburgh: Scottish Mountaineering Trust, 1985), p. 1

98. Letter to Mrs Thrale, 21 Sept 1773, in *Dr. Johnson's Works: Life, Poems and Tales*, p. 342

99. J. Dow, 'Munros, Beards and Weather', *SMCJ* Vol XX (1935), in Brooker (ed.), *A Century of Scottish Mountaineering*, p. 270

100. W. Inglis Clark, 'The Motor in Mountaineering', *Scottish Mountaineering Club Journal* VII (1903), p. 314

101. W. R. Lester, 'The Black Shoot', *SMCJ* Vol II (1892), in Brooker (ed.), *A Century of Scottish Mountaineering*, p. 163

102. W. W. Naismith, 'Buachaille Etive Mor – The Crowberry Ridge', *SMCJ* Vol IV (1896), in ibid., p. 170

103. Clark and Pyatt, *Mountaineering in Britain*, p. 27

104. J. Laycock, *Some Gritstone Climbs in Derbyshire and Elsewhere* (Manchester: 1913), p. vii

105. J. P. Farrar, 'Obituary of William Edward Davidson', *Alpine Journal* 35 (1923), p. 266

106. M. Conway, *The Alps From End to End* (London: Constable, 1905), p. 2

107. M. Conway, 'Centrists and Excentrists', *Alpine Journal* 15 (1891)

108. Unsworth, *Hold the Heights*, p. 141

109. Quoted in Lunn, *A Century of Mountaineering*, p. 92

110. G. W. Young, 'Mountain Prophets', *Alpine Journal* 54 (1949), p. 107

111. *The Times*, 6 October 1888, quoted in Hansen, 'British Mountaineering 1850–1914', p. 396

112. C. Phillips-Woolley, writing in *The Field*, 15 December 1888, quoted in Hansen, 'British Moutaineering 1850–1914', p. 397

113. B. Russell, *Autobiography*, 1998 Routledge ed. (London: George Allen & Unwin, 1967), p. 38

114. Quoted in Mill, *Norman Collie: A Life in Two Worlds*, p. 132

115. W. Weston, 'Mountaineering in the Southern Alps of Japan', *Alpine Journal* 23 (1907), p. 8

116. Quoted in Clark, *Men, Myths and Mountains*, p. 109

117. J. N. Collie, *From the Himalaya to Skye*, 2003 Ripping Yarns ed. (Edinburgh: David Douglas, 1902), p. 17

118. K. Mason, *Abode of Snow*, 1987 Diadem ed. (London: Rupert Hart Davis, 1955), p. 75

119. Quoted in W. Unsworth (ed.), *Encyclopedia of Mountaineering* (London: Penguin, 1977), p. 154

120. Quoted in Unsworth, *Hold the Heights*, p. 233

121. C. E. Mathews, 'The Growth of Mountaineering', *Alpine Journal* 10 (1882), p. 262

122. See J. Evans, *The Conways* (London: Museum Press, 1966)

123. Letter from C. G. Bruce to W. M. Conway, quoted in Hansen, 'British Mountaineering 1850–1914', p. 410

124. Conway, *Mountain Memories*, p. 3

125. Quoted in Clark, *The Victorian Mountaineers*, p. 216

126. Conway, 'Some Reminiscences and Reflections of an Old Stager', p. 157

127. Quoted in F. Fleming, *Killing Dragons: The Conquest of the Alps*, 2001 ed. (London: Granta Books, 2000), p. 331

128. Collie, *From the Himalaya to Skye*, p. 40

129. Crowley, *The Confessions of Aleister Crowley*, p. 70

130. Ibid., p. 129

131. Ibid., p. 128

132. Letter from Crowley to the Indian newspaper *Pioneer*, 11 September 1905, quoted in Unsworth, *Hold the Heights*, p. 243

133. T. Longstaff, *This My Voyage* (London: John Murray, 1950), p. 69

134. Ibid., p. 154

135. Quoted in J. B. West, 'A. M. Kellas: Pioneer Himalayan Physiologist and Mountaineer', *Alpine Journal* 94 (1989), p. 211

136. W. Unsworth, *Everest* (London: Allen Lane, 1981), p. 38

CHAPTER 5 1914–39: ORGANISED COWARDICE

1. Young, Sutton and Noyce, *Snowdon Biography*, p. 43

2. J. Longland, 'Between the Wars, 1919–39', *Alpine Journal* 62 (1957)

3. Hankinson, *The Mountain Men*, p. 150

4. Pilley, *Climbing Days*, pp. 26 and 41

5. K. Treacher, *Siegfried Herford: An Edwardian Rock-Climber* (Glasgow: Ernest Press, 2000), p. 116

6. Pilley, *Climbing Days*, p. 41

7. H. R. C. Carr, '1919 – C. F. Holland's Year', *Climbers' Club Journal* 102 (1981), p. 79

8. Quoted in Jones and Milburn, *Cumbrian Rock*, p. 60

9. Pilley, *Climbing Days*, pp. 88–9

10. David Kirkwood quoted in D. Thomson, *England in the Twentieth Century*, 1983 Pelican ed. (London: Penguin, 1965), p. 92

11. A. Borthwick, *Always a Little Further* (Glasgow: Faber & Faber, 1939), p. 133

12. Quoted in Jones and Milburn, *Cumbrian Rock*, p. 71

13. E. A. M. Wedderburn, 'A Short History of Scottish Climbing from 1918 to the Present Day', *Scottish Mountaineering Club Journal* XXII (1939), p. 314

14. J. Perrin, *Menlove: The Life of John Menlove Edwards* (London: Victor Gollancz, 1985), p. 57

15. Douglas Milner in K. Wilson (ed.), *Classic Rock* (St Albans: Granada Publishing, 1978), pp. 143, 144

16. D. Cox, 'Early Years', *Alpine Journal* 85 (1980), p. 91

17. Quoted in the Prologue to B. Rothman, *The 1932 Kinder Trespass* (Altrincham: Willow Publishing, 1982)

18. Ibid., p. 41

19. J. Perrin, *The Climbing Essays* (Glasgow: Neil Wilson Publishing, 2006), p. 117

20. Quoted by Douglas Milner in Wilson (ed.), *Classic Rock*, p. 144

21. S. Dean, *Hands of a Climber: A Life of Colin Kirkus* (Glasgow: Ernest Press, 1993), p. 28

22. Quoted in K. Smith, 'Who Was J. I. Roper?', *Climber & Rambler* 17, 6 (1978), p. 30

23. Clark and Pyatt, *Mountaineering in Britain*, p. 162

24. See D. Cook, 'The Mountaineer and Society', *Mountain* 34 (1974), p. 38

25. Jones and Milburn, *Cumbrian Rock*, p. 108

26. W. Birkett, 'Talking With Jim Birkett', *Climber & Rambler* 21, 8 (1982), p. 27

27. Hankinson, *A Century on the Crags*, p. 120

28. M. Guinness quoted in G. Milburn, *Helyg* (Climbers' Club, 1985), p. 28

29. See ibid.

30. J. Morris, *Coronation Everest* (London: Faber & Faber, 1958), p. 39

31. Hankinson, *Geoffrey Winthrop Young*, p. 243

32. See J. Soper, K. Wilson and P. Crew, *The Black Cliff: The History of Climbing on Clogwyn Du'r Arddu* (London: Kaye & Ward Ltd, 1971)

33. H. Hartley, 'Obituary of A. S. Pigott', *Alpine Journal* 85 (1980), p. 262

34. Irving, *The Romance of Mountaineering*, p. 121

35. Jones and Milburn, *Welsh Rock*, p. 39

36. J. Longland, 'Hugh Ruttledge', *Alpine Journal* 67 (1962), p. 365

37. P. Nunn, 'Obituary of Jack Longland', *High* 135 (1994), p. 61

38. Ibid., p. 78

39. A. B. Hargreaves and J. Longland, 'Obituary of Colin Kirkus', *Climbers' Club Journal* VII 2, 69 (1943), p. 168

40. See A. B. Hargreaves, 'Alfred William Bridge', *Climbers' Club Journal* XVI, 96 (1974)

41. A. W. Bridge, 'Prelude', *Climbers' Club Journal* IX, 74 (1949), p. 88

42. C. Kirkus, *Let's Go Climbing!* (London: Thomas Nelson, 1941), p. 90

43. Quoted in Dean, *Hands of a Climber*, p. 80

44. Quoted in A. B. Hargreaves and K. Smith, 'Maurice Linnell', *Climber & Rambler* 20,12 (1981), p. 41

45. Quoted in Clark, *Men, Myths and Mountains*, p. 147

46. Hargreaves and Longland, 'Obituary of Colin Kirkus', p. 170

47. Quoted in Dean, *Hands of a Climber*, p. 117

48. Perrin, *Menlove*, p. 47

49. W. Noyce, *Mountains and Men* (London: Geoffrey Bles, 1947), p. 50

50. Perrin, *Menlove*, p. 126

51. Ibid., p. 176

52. N. Morin, *A Woman's Reach* (London: Eyre & Spottiswoode, 1968), p. 170

53. Murray, *The Evidence of Things Not Seen*, p. 25

54. E. MacAskill, 'Portrait of Jock Nimlin', *Climber & Rambler* 22, 9 (1983), p. 26

55. Wedderburn, 'Scottish Climbing 1918–1939', p. 107

56. W. H. Murray, 'Scotland: The 1930s', *Mountain* 98 (1984), p. 19

57. W. H. Murray, *Mountaineering in Scotland* (London: J. M. Dent, 1947), p. 122

58. Ibid., p. 127

59. Borthwick, *Always a Little Further*, p. 141

60. W. H. Murray, *Highland Landscape* (National Trust for Scotland, 1962), p. 9

61. Murray, *The Evidence of Things Not Seen*, p. 320

62. E. Byne and G. Sutton, *High Peak* (London: Secker and Warburg, 1966)

63. Foreword to C. Bonington, *I Chose to Climb*, 2001 Weidenfeld & Nicolson ed. (London: Victor Gollancz, 1966), p. 1

64. P. French, *Younghusband*, 1995 Flamingo ed. (London: Harper Collins, 1994), p. 384

65. R. Greene, *Moments of Being* (London: Heinemann, 1974)

66. E. Shipton, *That Untravelled World* (London: Hodder & Stoughton, 1969), p. 73

67. Quoted in Unsworth, *Hold the Heights*, p. 308

68. Unsworth, *Hold the Heights*, p. 270

69. Conway, *The Alps From End to End*, p. 208

70. See Unsworth, *Hold the Heights*, pp. 104–5

71. Quoted in Clark, *Men, Myths and Mountains*, p. 177

72. Quoted in ibid., p. 150

73. Shih Chan-Chun, 'The Conquest of Mount Everest by the Chinese Mountaineering Team', *Alpine Journal* 66 (1961), p. 35

74. Unsworth, *Hold the Heights*, p. 276

75. Unsworth, *Everest*, p. 33

76. Clark, *Men, Myths and Mountains*, p. 153

77. E. L. Strutt, 'Presidential Valedictory Address', *Alpine Journal* 50 (1938), p. 9

78. Lunn, *A Century of Mountaineering*, p. 186

79. Longland, 'Between the Wars, 1919–39', p. 88

80. D. Busk, 'The Young Shavers', *Mountain* 54 (1977), p. 43

81. French, *Younghusband*, p. 329

82. P. Gillman and L. Gillman, *The Wildest Dream* (London: Headline, 2000), p. 186

83. Quoted in Unsworth, *Everest*, p. 22

84. Unsworth, *Because It Is There*, p. 96

85. T. S. Blakeney, 'Obituary of Charles Kenneth Howard-Bury', *Alpine Journal* 69 (1964), p. 171

86. Quoted in C. Wells, *A Brief History of British Mountaineering* (The Mountain Heritage Trust, 2001), p. 36

87. Letter to Vanessa Bell (daughter of Leslie Stephen) quoted in Gillman and Gillman, *The Wildest Dream*, p. 53

88. Wells, *Who's Who in British Climbing*, p. 452

89. J. B. L. Noel, *Through Tibet to Everest* (1927), quoted in M. Isserman and S. Weaver, *Fallen Giants: A History of Himalayan Mountaineering from the Age of Empire to the Age of Extremes* (New Haven: Yale University Press, 2008), p. 112

90. Quoted in Hankinson, *Geoffrey Winthrop Young*, p. 239

91. Unsworth, *Everest*, p. 72

92. Found in George Finch's papers when he died and probably composed by Howard Somervell. Quoted in S. Russell's introduction to G. Finch, *The Making of a Mountaineer* (Bristol: J. W. Arrowsmith Ltd, 1924), p. 59

93. E. F. Norton, *The Fight for Everest: 1924* (London: Edward Arnold & Co., 1925), p. 138

94. Unsworth, *Everest*, p. 125

95. Quoted in B. Blessed, *The Turquoise Mountain* (London: Bloomsbury Publishing, 1991), p. 20

96. Quoted in Hankinson, *The Mountain Men*, p. 190

97. F. S. Smythe, *Kamet Conquered*, 2000 Bâton Wicks ed. (London: Victor Gollancz, 1932), p. 368

98. Shipton, *That Untravelled World*, p. 76

99. See J. R. L. Anderson, *High Mountains and Cold Seas: A Biography of H. W. Tilman* (London: Victor Gollancz, 1980), pp. 189–96

100. H. W. Tilman, *Two Mountains and a River*, 1997 Diadem ed. (Cambridge University Press, 1949), p. 517

101. Perrin, *The Climbing Essays*, pp. 190 and 193

102. H. W. Tilman, *Snow on the Equator*, 1997 Diadem ed. (London: G. Bell & Sons, 1937), p. 108

103. Shipton, *That Untravelled World*, p. 85

104. Ibid., p. 95

105. Ibid., p. 95

106. *Morning Post*, 17 October 1936, quoted in Unsworth, *Everest*, p. 209

107. H. W. Tilman, *The Ascent of Nanda Devi*, 1997 Diadem ed. (Cambridge University Press, 1937), p. 248

108. Isserman and Weaver, *Fallen Giants*, p. 195

109. H. W. Tilman, *Everest 1938*, 1997 Diadem ed. (Cambridge University Press, 1948), p. 438

110. Unsworth, *Everest*, p. 215

111. Tilman, *Everest 1938*, p. 441

112. H. W. Tilman, *When Men and Mountains Meet*, 1997 Diadem ed. (Cambridge University Press, 1946), p. 277

113. Shipton, *That Untravelled World*, p. 54

114. Tilman, *Everest 1938*, p. 431

115. Ibid., p. 432

CHAPTER 6 1939–70: HARD MEN IN AN AFFLUENT SOCIETY

1. Milburn, *Helyg*, p. 126

2. Hoppen, *The Mid-Victorian Generation*, p. 85

3. Wilson (ed.), *Classic Rock*, p. 212

4. D. Haston, *In High Places*, 1974 Arrow ed. (London: Cassell, 1972), p. 174

5. D. Gray, *Rope Boy* (London: Victor Gollancz, 1970), p. 53

6. J. Cleare and A. Smythe, *Rock Climbers in Action in Snowdonia* (London: Secker & Warburg, 1966), p. 79

7. Gray, *Rope Boy*, p. 36

8. P. Nunn, *At the Sharp End* (London: Unwin Hyman, 1988), p. 31

9. Cleare and Smythe, *Rock Climbers in Action in Snowdonia*, p. 77

10. D. Brown and I. Mitchell, *Mountain Days & Bothy Nights* (Edinburgh: Luath Press, 1987), p. 71

11. H. Drasdo, *The Ordinary Route* (Glasgow: Ernest Press, 1997), p. 9

12. A. Burgess and A. Burgess, *The Burgess Book of Lies* (Seattle: Cloudcap, 1994), p. 40

13. D. Roberts, 'Hanging Around', *Mountain Gazette* 19 (1974), in J. Perrin (ed.), *Mirrors in the Cliffs* (London: Diadem Books, 1983), p. 643

14. Perrin, *The Climbing Essays*, p. 29

15. Nunn, *At the Sharp End*, p. 44

16. Burgess and Burgess, *The Burgess Book of Lies*, p. 68

17. Quoted in Engel, *A History of Mountaineering in the Alps*, p. 189

18. Clark and Pyatt, *Mountaineering in Britain*, p. 238

19. K. Wilson (ed.), *Hard Rock* (London: Hart-Davis, MacGibbon, 1975), p. 187

20. J. Brown, *The Hard Years*, 1975 Penguin ed. (London: Victor Gollancz, 1967), p. 73

21. Letter from E. C. Pyatt to J. R. Allen quoted in T. Gifford (ed.), *The Climbers' Club Centenary Journal* (Climbers' Club, 1997), p. 205

22. Wells, *A Brief History of British Mountaineering*, p. 71

23. Peter Crew in Wilson (ed.), *Hard Rock*, p. 139

24. Jim Perrin in ibid., p. 169

25. Gray, *Rope Boy*, p. 305

26. Perrin, *The Climbing Essays*, p. 116

27. Jones and Milburn, *Welsh Rock*, p. 120

28. D. Gray, *Tight Rope* (Glasgow: Ernest Press, 1993), p. 63

29. Quoted in G. Child, *Thin Air* (Seattle: The Mountaineers Books, 1988), p. 220

30. C. Bonington, *Annapurna South Face*, 1973 Penguin ed. (London: Cassell, 1971), pp. 21 and 22

31. D. Whillans and A. Ormerod, *Don Whillans: Portrait of a Mountaineer* (London: Heinemann, 1971), p. 25

32. Jones and Milburn, *Welsh Rock*, p. 128

33. Perrin, *The Climbing Essays*, p. 114

34. Cleare and Smythe, *Rock Climbers in Action in Snowdonia*, p. 108

35. Soper, Wilson and Crew, *The Black Cliff: The History of Climbing on Clogwyn Du'r Arddu*, p. 129

36. Perrin, *The Climbing Essays*, pp. 13, 171 and 172

37. K. Wilson, 'Obituary of Al Harris', *Climber and Rambler* 20, 12 (1981), p. 18

38. J. Cleare and R. Collomb, *Sea Cliff Climbing in Britain* (1973), quoted in Perrin (ed.), *Mirrors in the Cliffs*, p. 419

39. G. Birtles, *Alan Rouse: A Mountaineer's Life* (London: Unwin Hyman, 1987), p. 62

40. Young, Sutton and Noyce, *Snowdon Biography*, p. 55

41. Gray, *Tight Rope*, p. 14

42. Jones and Milburn, *Cumbrian Rock*, p. 139

43. P. Bartlett, *The Undiscovered Country: The Reason We Climb* (Glasgow: Ernest Press, 1993), p. 89

44. Drasdo, *The Ordinary Route*, p. 47

45. Ibid., p. 53

46. Ibid., p. 114

47. P. Livesey quoted in Kelly, Doughty, et al., '100 Years of Rock-Climbing in the Lake District', p. 76

48. E. Douglas, 'The Vertical Century', *Climber* 39, 1 (2000), p. 48

49. Nunn, *At the Sharp End*, p. 71

50. Kelly, Doughty, et al., '100 Years of Rock-Climbing in the Lake District', p. 73

51. Wilson (ed.), *Hard Rock*, p. xv

52. D. Brown and I. Mitchell, *A View From the Ridge* (Glasgow: Ernest Press, 1991), p. 1

53. J. Connor, *Creagh Dhu Climber: The Life and Times of John Cunningham* (Glasgow: Ernest Press, 1999), p. 56

54. T. Patey, *One Man's Mountains*, 1997 Canongate ed. (London: Victor Gollancz, 1971), p. 30

55. See Interview With John Cunningham, *Mountain* 14 (1971), p. 24

56. Connor, *Creagh Dhu Climber*, p. 48

57. Ibid., p. 122

58.   Haston, *In High Places*, p. 31

59.   J. Cruickshank, *High Endeavours: The Life and Legend of Robin Smith* (Edinburgh: Canongate, 2005), p. 82

60.   Cruickshank, *High Endeavours*, p. 70

61.   J. Marshall, 'Dougal Haston – a Tribute', *Alpine Journal* 83 (1978), p. 132

62.   A. Austin in Wilson (ed.), *Classic Rock*, pp. 34–8

63.   See Cruickshank, *High Endeavours*, p. 336

64.   M. Boysen in Wilson (ed.), *Hard Rock*, p. 22

65.   Marshall, 'Dougal Haston – a Tribute', p. 133

66.   Cruickshank, *High Endeavours*, p. 113

67.   Ibid., p. 125

68.   Ibid., p. 197

69.   Noyce, *Mountains and Men*, p. 19

70.   Perrin, *Menlove*, p. 137

71.   Introduction to Patey, *One Man's Mountains*, p. 11

72.   Foreword to ibid., p. 9

73.   T. Weir in W. D. Brooker et al., 'The Incomparable Dr. Patey', *Climber* 26, 5 (1987), p. 30

74.   Bonington, *I Chose to Climb*, p. 17

75.   Cruickshank, *High Endeavours*, p. 148

76.   J. Cleare, 'Obituary of Peter Biven', *Alpine Journal* 82 (1977), p. 267

77.   E. Douglas, 'Cafe Society', *Climber* 40, 11 (2001), p. 37

78.   Shipton, *That Untravelled World*, p. 212

79.   D. Gray, 'Confessions of a Parvenu', *Alpine Journal* 107 (2002), p. 189

80.   Gray, *Rope Boy*, p. 18

81.   See J. Curran, *High Achiever: The Life and Climbs of Chris Bonington* (London: Constable & Robinson Ltd, 1999), p. 40

82.   Bonington, *I Chose to Climb*, p. 117

83.   J. Perrin, *The Villain: The Life of Don Whillans* (London: Random House, 2005), footnote p. 220

84.   Bonington, *I Chose to Climb*, p. 144

85.   Patey, *One Man's Mountains*, p. 274

86.   J. Connor, *Dougal Haston: The Philosophy of Risk* (Edinburgh: Canongate, 2002), p. 102

87.   C. Bonington, *The Next Horizon*, 2001 Weidenfeld & Nicolson ed. (London: Victor Gollancz, 1973), p. 135

88.   Ibid., p. 131

89.   Perrin, *The Villain: The Life of Don Whillans*, p. 263

90.   Quoted in Unsworth, *Everest*, p. 271

91.   E. Hillary, *View From the Summit*, 2000 ed. (London: Doubleday, 1999), p. 111

92.   Quoted in G. Band, *Everest Exposed* (London: Harper Collins, 2003), p. 102

93.   Shipton, *That Untravelled World*, p. 212

94. Quoted in J. Perrin, 'Sir Charles Evans', *Climber* 35, 2 (1996), p. 45

95. Bonington, *The Climbers*, p. 192

96. P. Steele, *Eric Shipton: Everest and Beyond* (London: Constable, 1998), p. 208

97. J. Hunt, *Life Is Meeting* (London: Hodder & Stoughton, 1978), p. 106

98. Band, *Everest Exposed*, pp. 135 and 147

99. Ibid., p. 195

100. Hunt, *Life Is Meeting*, p. 110

101. Tilman, *The Ascent of Nanda Devi*, p. 222

102. Patey, *One Man's Mountains*, p. 263

103. J. Clegg, 'Obituary of Sir Charles Evans', *Alpine Journal* 102 (1997), p. 336

104. Brown, *The Hard Years*, p. 115

105. Bonington, *The Next Horizon*, p. 39

106. Bonington, *Annapurna South Face*, p. 22

107. Ibid., p. 24

108. Bonington, *The Climbers*, p. 216

109. Connor, *Dougal Haston: The Philosophy of Risk*, p. 154

CHAPTER 7   AFTER 1970: REINVENTING THE IMPOSSIBLE

1. R. Messner, 'Murder of the Impossible', *Mountain* 15 (1971)

2. Y. Chouinard, 'Coonyard Mouths Off' (1972) in K. Wilson (ed.), *The Games Climbers Play*, 1996 Bâton Wicks ed. (London: Diadem Books, 1978), p. 309

3. A. Rouse, 'Changing Values', *Alpine Journal* 90 (1985), p. 116

4. Wilson (ed.), *The Games Climbers Play*, p. 13

5. Gray, *Rope Boy*, p. 308

6. Quoted in P. Boardman, *Sacred Summits*, 1996 Bâton Wicks ed. (London: Hodder & Stoughton, 1982), p. 87

7. J. Tasker, 'Kangchenjunga North Ridge 1979', *Alpine Journal* 85 (1980), p. 50

8. A. Blackshaw, *Mountaineering* (Harmondsworth: Penguin, 1965), p. 149. The emphasis is in the original text.

9. W. Peascod, *Journey After Dawn* (London: Butler & Tanner, 1985), p. 155

10. Hankinson, *A Century on the Crags*, p. 192

11. D. Scott, 'Resisting the Appeasers', *Alpine Journal* 112 (2007), p. 78

12. Quoted in Burgess and Burgess, *The Burgess Book of Lies*, p. 326

13. Quoted in E. Douglas, 'The Morality of Risk', *Alpine Journal* 104 (1999), p. 149

14. John Porter, during a speech at the Kendal Mountain Film Festival in 2004

15. Quoted in Jones and Milburn, *Welsh Rock*, p. 238

16. Audrey Salkeld quoted in Wells, *Who's Who in British Climbing*, p. 412

17. M. Fowler, *Vertical Pleasure*, 2006 Bâton Wicks ed. (London: Hodder & Stoughton, 1995), p. 96

18. D. Scott and A. MacIntyre, *Shisha Pangma: The Alpine-Style First Ascent of the South-West Face* (London: Bâton Wicks, 2000), p. 22

19. G. Child, 'How I (Almost) Didn't Climb Everest', in C. Willis (ed.), *Climb* (New York: Thunder's Mouth Press, 1999), p. 37

20. www.rebeccastephens.com

21. Quoted in R. J. Evans, *In Defence of History* (London: Granta, 1997), p. 22

22. J. Stainforth quoted in S. Dean, 'John Syrett', *Climber* 35, 8 (1996), p. 35

23. K. Wilson and B. Newman (eds.), *Extreme Rock* (London: Diadem Books Ltd, 1987), p. 173

24. Ibid., p. 116

25. J. Tasker, *Everest the Cruel Way*, 1996 Bâton Wicks ed. (London: Methuen, 1981), p. 8

26. J. Krakauer, *Eiger Dreams*, 1998 Pan Books ed. (London: Macmillan, 1997), p. 131

27. Hankinson, *A Century on the Crags*, p. 191

28. Wilson (ed.), *Hard Rock*, p. 149

29. Fowler, *Vertical Pleasure*, p. 60

30. Ibid., p. 69

31. R. Collomb quoted in J. Perrin, 'Pat Littlejohn', *Climber & Rambler* 21, 3 (1982), p. 30

32. Ibid., p. 32

33. M. Campbell, 'A Profile of John Redhead', *Climber* 25, 11 (1986), p. 50

34. Perrin, *The Climbing Essays*, p. 149

35. J. Redhead, 'Alternative Slate', *Climber* 25, 11 (1986), p. 54

36. George Smith quoted in N. Grimes, 'That's Me: George Smith', *Summit* 53 (2009), p. 17

37. P. Twomey, 'John Redhead', *On The Edge* 78 (1998), p. 36

38. Quoted in Jones and Milburn, *Welsh Rock*, p. 259

39. Quoted in Perrin, *The Climbing Essays*, p. 149

40. J. Moffatt and N. Grimes, *Revelations* (Sheffield: Vertebrate Publishing, 2009), p. 3

41. Quoted in Wells, *Who's Who in British Climbing*, p. 138

42. Ibid., p. 134

43. A. Cave, *Learning to Breathe* (London: Hutchinson, 2005), p. 100

44. Quoted in Wells, *Who's Who in British Climbing*, p. 236

45. E. Douglas, 'Fast Burn Fuse', *Climber* 37, 2 (1998), p. 27

46. Quoted in Wells, *Who's Who in British Climbing*, p. 216

47. Campbell, 'A Profile of John Redhead', p. 52

48. P. Pritchard, *Deep Play* (London: Bâton Wicks, 1997), p. 56

49. Wells, *Who's Who in British Climbing*, p. 442

50. E. Douglas, 'The Art of Strong: Malcolm Smith', *Climber* 42, 2 (2003), p. 34

51. Wells, *Who's Who in British Climbing*, p. 7

52. Interview with John Dunne, *Summit* 41 (2006), p. 41

53. D. MacLeod, *John Muir Trust Journal* 46 (2009), p. 5

54. Unsworth, *Everest*, p. 418

55. Child, *Thin Air*, p. 35

56. Ibid., p. 18

57. J. Tasker, *Savage Arena*, 1996 Bâton Wicks ed. (London: Methuen, 1982), p. 130

58. Boardman, *Sacred Summits*, p. 96

59. 'Mac the Belly Talks to Cassius Bonafide', *Mountain*, 15 (1971), p. 33

60. Unsworth, *Everest*, p. 448

61. Perrin, *The Climbing Essays*, p. 228

62. C. Bonington, *Everest the Hard Way* (London: Hodder & Stoughton, 1976), p. 48

63. C. Bonington, *The Everest Years*, 2001 Weidenfeld & Nicolson ed. (London: Hodder & Stoughton, 1986), p. 23

64. P. Boardman, 'Peter the Pooh', *Crags* 4 (1976), p. 9

65. Bonington, *The Climbers*, p. 193

66. M. Thompson, 'Out With the Boys Again', *Mountain*, 50 (1976)

67. C. Hughes, *A Worm's-Eye View of the Department 1949–52,* www.earth.ox.ac.uk (2008)

68. Tasker, *Savage Arena*, p. 104

69. Ibid., p. 14

70. Ibid., p. 14

71. Ibid., p. 17

72. Murray, *The Evidence of Things Not Seen*, p. 167

73. P. Boardman, *The Shining Mountain*, 1996 Bâton Wicks ed. (London: Hodder & Stoughton, 1978), p. 17

74. Ibid., p. 22

75. Ibid., p. 20

76. A. Alvarez, *Feeding the Rat* (London: Bloomsbury, 2003), p. 72

77. J. V. Anthoine, 'The British Ogre Expedition', *Alpine Journal* 83 (1978), p. 7

78. Child, *Thin Air*, p. 111

79. A. Rouse, 'Jannu', *Alpine Journal* 85 (1980), p. 83

80. R. Carrington, 'Obituary of Alan Rouse', *Alpine Journal* 92 (1987), p. 305

81. Tasker, *Savage Arena*, p. 127

82. J. Curran, *The Middle-Aged Mountaineer* (London: Constable & Robinson Ltd, 2001), p. 179

83. Tasker, *Savage Arena*, p. 94

84. J. Curran, *K2, Triumph and Tragedy* (London: Hodder & Stoughton, 1987), p. 21

85. Curran, *High Achiever: The Life and Climbs of Chris Bonington*, p. 198

86. Curran, *The Middle-Aged Mountaineer*, p. 35

87. Boardman, *Sacred Summits*, p. 15

88. Tasker, *Savage Arena*, p. 125

89. Ibid., p. 20

90. R. Renshaw, 'Obituary: Joseph Thomas Tasker (1948–82)', *Climber & Rambler* 21, 8 (1982), p. 20

91. Boardman, *The Shining Mountain*, p. 166

92. Tasker, *Savage Arena*, p. 127

93. Tasker, *Everest the Cruel Way*, p. 100

94. Boardman, *Sacred Summits*, p. 142

95. R. Renshaw, 'Obituary of Joe Tasker', *Alpine Journal* 88 (1983), p. 273

96. Boardman, *Sacred Summits*, p. 153

97. D. Gray, *Slack* (Glasgow: Ernest Press, 1996), p. 12

98. Burgess and Burgess, *The Burgess Book of Lies*, p. 265

99. J. Porter, 'Reverse Polish', *Mountain* 60 (1978), p. 24

100. Scott and MacIntyre, *Shisha Pangma: The Alpine-Style First Ascent of the South-West Face*, p. 21

101. J. Porter, 'Obituary of Alex MacIntyre', *Alpine Journal* 88 (1983), p. 279

102. B. Hall, 'Obituary of Roger Baxter Jones', *Climber and Rambler* 24, 11 (1985), p. 15

103. Burgess and Burgess, *The Burgess Book of Lies*, p. 328

104. Curran, *K2, Triumph and Tragedy*, p. 22

105. G. Band, *Summit: 150 Years of the Alpine Club* (London: HarperCollins, 2006), p. 194

106. See S. Venables, *Higher Than the Eagle Soars* (London: Arrow Books, 2007)

107. S. Venables in A. Fanshawe and S. Venables, *Himalaya Alpine Style* (London: Hodder & Stoughton, 1995), p. 8

108. See D. Rose and E. Douglas, *Regions of the Heart: The Triumph and Tragedy of Alison Hargreaves* (London: Penguin, 1999)

109. Quoted in Douglas, 'The Morality of Risk', pp. 152 and 154

110. P. Pritchard, 'Hammering the Anvil', *Alpine Journal* 100 (1995), p. 50

111. Band, *Summit: 150 Years of the Alpine Club*, p. 217

CHAPTER 8 BECAUSE IT'S THERE?

1.   Morris, *Coronation Everest*, p. 60

2.   'Happiness and Economics', *The Economist*, 19 December 2006

3.   A. Wainwright, *Pennine Way Companion* (Kendal: Westmorland Gazette, 1968), p. xiii

4.   *Illustrated London News*, 7 September 1861, quoted in Hansen, 'British Mountaineering 1850–1914', p. 149

5.   Hankinson, *A Century on the Crags*, p. 38

6.   A. Lunn, 'In Defence of Popular Writing', *Climbers' Club Journal* 2 (1913), p. 83

7.   Patey, *One Man's Mountains*, p. 68

8.   R. L. G. Irving, *A History of British Mountaineering* (London: B. T. Batsford, 1955), p. 222

9.   Quoted in Clark, *Men, Myths and Mountains*, p. 270

10. Noyce, *Mountains and Men*, p. 27

11. Ruskin, *Sesame and Lilies*, preface to the 1866 ed, p. vi

12. Scott and MacIntyre, *Shisha Pangma: The Alpine-Style First Ascent of the South-West Face*, p. 107

13. Tasker, *Savage Arena*, p. 15

14. Ibid., p. 259

15. Boardman, *Sacred Summits*, p. 214

16. Krakauer, *Eiger Dreams*, p. 148

17. Young, *On High Hills*, p. 46

18. Perrin, *The Climbing Essays*, p. 257

19. See Clark, *Men, Myths and Mountains*, p. 48

20. Whymper, *Scrambles Amongst the Alps*, p. 197

21. R. L. G. Irving, 'Five Years With Recruits', *Alpine Journal* 24 (1909), p. 380

22. Ruskin, *Sesame and Lilies*, preface to the 1866 ed, p. viii

23. Mummery, *My Climbs in the Alps and Caucasus*, p. 154

24. Perrin, *The Villain: The Life of Don Whillans*, p. 216

25. Ibid., p. 290

26. E. Drummond, *A Dream of White Horses* (London: Bâton Wicks, 1997), p. 196

27. Tilman, *Two Mountains and a River*, p. 536

28. Birtles, *Alan Rouse: A Mountaineer's Life*, p. 185

29. Ruskin, *Modern Painters Volume IV: Of Mountain Beauty*

30. Stephen, *The Playground of Europe*, p. 213

31. K. Clark, *Landscape Into Art* (London: John Murray, 1949), p. 74

32. Stephen, *The Playground of Europe*, p. 62

33. Child, *Thin Air*, pp. 112 and 114

34. Young, *On High Hills*, p. 158

35. A. Wills, 'The Passage of the Fenêtre de Salena', *Peaks, Passes and Glaciers* 1 (1859), p. 30

36. Cave, *Learning to Breathe*, p. 263

37. Alvarez, *Feeding the Rat*, p. 152

38. Conway, *The Alps From End to End*, p. 170

39. Collie, *From the Himalaya to Skye*, p. 53

40. Bonington, *Annapurna South Face*, p. 324

41. Boardman, *Sacred Summits*, p. 141

APPENDIX I

A NOTE ON GRADES

The table below sets out the grading systems used for British rock climbs, Scottish winter climbs and alpine climbs.

British Rock Climbs		Scottish Winter Climbs	Alpine Climbs	
Adjectival	Technical		Adjectival	Technical
Moderate (M)		I	Facile (F)	I, II
Difficult (Diff)		II	Peu Difficile (PD)	II, III
Very Difficult (VD)		III	Assez Difficile (AD)	III, IV
Severe (S)		IV	Difficile (D)	IV, V-
Very Severe (VS)	4a, 4b, 4c	V	Très Difficile (TD)	IV+, V
Hard Very Severe (HVS)	4c, 5a, 5b	VI etc	Extrêmement Difficile (ED1)	V+, VI
Extremely Severe (E1)	5a, 5b, 5c			VI, VI+
(E2)	5b, 5c, 6a		(ED2)	VI+, VII
(E3)	5c, 6a		(ED3)	VII
(E4) etc	6a, 6b		(ED4) etc	VII+, VIII

Throughout the book UK adjectival grades have been used for British rock climbs. These describe the overall difficulty and seriousness of the climb, taking into account how sustained it is, the exposure and the availability of protection (see Appendix II for a Glossary of Climbing Terms). In addition, on harder climbs, an alphanumeric technical grade has been added, which attempts to rate the hardest single move or sequence of moves on the climb. Hence a climb with a 5b move at the start, close to the ground, might be HVS. If the same move was 25m above the ground and protection was scarce, it might be graded E1 or even E2.

Scottish winter climbs use a numeric grade intended to represent the overall difficulty of the route. However, because snow and ice conditions are much more variable than rock, winter grades are necessarily more approximate.

On alpine climbs the adjectival grade takes into account additional factors such as the approach, the descent, the aspect of the climb, the quality of the rock, exposure to rockfall and difficulty of retreat in bad weather. The numeric technical grades refer to the hardest section of the climb. Given the far greater length and complexity of alpine routes, comparisons with British rock climbing grades and Scottish winter grades are very approximate.

Artificial climbs, where the climber pulls directly on pitons, slings or other artificial aids rather than climbing the rock, are graded A1, A2, A3 etc, reflecting the difficulty of placement and security of the aid.

In most cases, the grades quoted in this book are those given for the route in a recent guidebook or on a website such as UKClimbing.com or Rockfax.com. These grades are not necessarily the same as those that were assigned when the route was first climbed. Until the 1950s, VS was the hardest grade in Britain. As standards increased a new grade, Extremely Severe (XS) was added. During the 1970s it became clear that the range of difficulty within the XS grade was becoming as great as all the other grades put together, and therefore new sub divisions (E1, E2, E3 etc) were created. Established routes also change over time. Loose rock and vegetation are progressively removed, generally making the climbs easier, while increasing traffic makes holds polished and slippery, adding to the difficulty. On the harder climbs, the first ascents often involved some direct aid. As this is progressively eliminated the grade of the climb usually increases.

Like most things in climbing, all grades are highly subjective.

APPENDIX II

GLOSSARY OF CLIMBING TERMS

Abseil A controlled slide down a doubled rope. The rope is retrieved, sometimes with difficulty, by pulling one end.

Aid, Artificial Aid, Artificial Climbing Where the climber pulls directly on a *Bolt, Chock, Ice Screw, Piton* or *Sling* rather than climbing the rock.

Belay Tying the *Leader* or the *Second* to the rock face while the other climbs a *Pitch*.

Bolt Expansion bolt with a hole into which a *Karabiner* can be clipped, inserted into bare rock by drilling a small hole.

Chock Wedge or hexagonal-shaped piece of metal, with a wire or rope loop to which a *Karabiner* can be attached. Inserted into a crack to provide a *Belay* or *Running Belay*. Chocks are removed by the *Second* and do not damage the rock.

Combined Tactics Where the *Leader* uses the *Second* for aid, typically using his knee, shoulder or head as a foothold.

Free Climbing Climbing the rock without direct aid from a *Bolt, Chock, Ice Screw, Piton* or *Sling*, although all of these may be used to provide *Running Belays*. See *Aid*.

Exposure The increasing sense of height as a climb is ascended. More pronounced on steep and open rock faces. The feeling of exposure can be very debilitating.

Ice Screw A hollow cylinder of metal which is screwed into ice to provide a *Belay* or *Running Belay*.

Jumar A mechanical device for climbing up fixed ropes.

Karabiner Metal snap link which allows the climbing rope to be attached to a *Belay* or *Running Belay*. Abbreviated to krab.

Leader The first person to climb a *Pitch*. The leader is potentially exposed to a significant fall unless able to find *Running Belays*.

On Sight A route led without pre-inspection by *Abseil* or *Top-Rope*.

Pegging The use of *Pitons*.

Pitch The stretch of rock or snow/ice between *Belays*. Limited by the length of the rope (typically 50m). The length of a pitch is sometimes referred to as a *Run-Out* [of rope].

Piton Metal peg with a hole to accommodate a *Karabiner*. Inserted into a crack using a hammer to provide a *Belay, Running Belay* or *Aid*. Pitons tend to damage the rock with repeated use.

Protection The availability of *Running Belays*.

Run-Out See *Pitch*.

Runner See *Running Belay.*

Running Belay A *Bolt, Chock, Ice Screw, Piton* or *Sling* to which a *Karabiner* is attached. The climbing rope is clipped into the karabiner, but not attached with a knot, so that it runs freely. A running belay limits the distance that a *Leader* may fall by acting as a pulley. If the *Leader* falls when he is 5m above a running belay the distance he will fall, provided his *Second* is alert and holds the rope, is 10m plus the stretch in the rope.

Second The second person to climb a *Pitch*. On a vertical *Pitch*, the second is protected by a rope from above and so is much safer than the *Leader*. On a traverse, both climbers are exposed to a potential fall.

Sling A loop of rope or tape with a *Karabiner* attached which can be put over a flake of rock or threaded behind a natural chockstone to provide a *Belay* or *Running Belay.*

Sport-Climbing Specially prepared routes with *Bolts* pre-placed every few metres. Relatively rare in Britain but common on the continent.

Top-Rope Climbing with a rope from above.

SELECTED BIBLIOGRAPHY

GENERAL MOUNTAINEERING AND CLIMBING

G. D. Abraham, *British Mountain Climbs*, 1923 ed. (London: Mills & Boon, 1909)

S. Angell, *Pinnacle Club: A History of Women Climbing* (The Pinnacle Club, 1988)

G. Band, *Summit: 150 Years of the Alpine Club* (London: HarperCollins, 2006)

A. Blackshaw, *Mountaineering* (Harmondsworth: Penguin, 1965)

C. E. Benson, *British Mountaineering* (London: George Routledge & Sons, 1909)

C. Bonington, *The Climbers* (London: BBC Books/Hodder & Stoughton, 1992)

R. W. Clark, *The Victorian Mountaineers* (London: B. T. Batsford, 1953)

R. W. Clark, *Six Great Mountaineers* (London: Hamish Hamilton, 1956)

R. W. Clark and E. C. Pyatt, *Mountaineering in Britain* (London: Phoenix House, 1957)

R. W. Clark, *Men, Myths and Mountains* (London: Weidenfeld & Nicolson, 1976)

W. P. Haskett Smith, *Climbing in the British Isles*, 1986 Ernest Press ed. (London: Longmans, Green, 1895)

R. L. G. Irving, *A History of British Mountaineering* (London: B. T. Batsford, 1955)

R. James, *Rock Face* (London: BBC Books, 1974)

D. Jones, *Rock Climbing in Britain* (London: Collins, 1984)

F. Keenlyside, *Peaks and Pioneers: The Story of Mountaineering* (London: Paul Elek, 1975)

J. Krakauer, *Eiger Dreams*, 1998 Pan Books ed. (London: Macmillan, 1997)

J. Lowe, *Ice World: Techniques and Experiences of Modern Ice Climbing* (Seattle: The Mountaineers Books, 1996)

A. Lunn, *A Century of Mountaineering 1857–1957* (London: George Allen & Unwin, 1957)

E. Newby, *Great Ascents* (Newton Abbot: David & Charles, 1977)

W. Noyce, *Mountains and Men* (London: Geoffrey Bles, 1947)

W. Noyce, *Scholar Mountaineers* (London: Dennis Dobson, 1950)

N. O'Connell, *Beyond Risk* (Seattle: The Mountaineers Books, 1993)

J. Perrin (ed.), *Mirrors in the Cliffs* (London: Diadem Books, 1983)

L. Peter, *Rock Climbing – Essential Skills and Techniques* (Capel Curig: Mountain Leader Training UK, 2004)

E. C. Pyatt and W. Noyce, *British Crags and Climbers* (London: Dennis Dobson, 1952)

A. Salkeld (ed.), *World Mountaineering* (London: Mitchell Beazley, 1998)

F. S. Smythe, *British Mountaineers* (London: Collins, 1942)

W. Unsworth, *Because It Is There* (London: Victor Gollancz, 1968)

W. Unsworth (ed.), *Encyclopedia of Mountaineering* (Harmondsworth: Penguin, 1977)

W. Unsworth, *Hold the Heights: The Foundations of Mountaineering* (London: Hodder & Stoughton, 1993)

C. Wells, *A Brief History of British Mountaineering* (Penrith: The Mountain Heritage Trust, 2001)

C. Wells, *Who's Who in British Climbing* (Buxton: The Climbing Company, 2008)

C. Willis (ed.), *Climb* (New York: Thunder's Mouth Press, 1999)

K. Wilson (ed.), *Classic Rock* (St Albans: Granada Publishing, 1978)

K. Wilson (ed.), *Hard Rock,* 1981 Granada Publishing ed. (London, Hart-Davis, MacGibbon Ltd, 1975)

K. Wilson (ed.), *The Games Climbers Play*, 1996 Bâton Wicks ed. (London: Diadem Books, 1978)

K. Wilson and B. Newman (eds.), *Extreme Rock* (London: Diadem Books, 1987)

G. W. Young, *Mountain Craft*, 1949 7th revised ed. (London: Methuen, 1920)

THE LAKE DISTRICT

A. Hankinson, *The First Tigers* (London: J. M. Dent, 1972)

A. Hankinson, *A Century on the Crags* (London: J. M. Dent, 1988)

T. Jones and G. Milburn, *Cumbrian Rock: 100 Years of Climbing in the Lake District* (Glossop: Pic Publication, 1988)

G. S. Sanson, *Climbing at Wasdale Before the First World War* (Somerset: Castle Cary Press, 1982)

W. Unsworth, *The High Fells of Lakeland* (London: Robert Hale, 1972)

W. Wordsworth, *Guide to the Lakes*, 2004 Frances Lincoln ed. (London: 1810)

SELECTED BIBLIOGRAPHY

WALES

H. R. C. Carr and G. A. Lister (eds.), *The Mountains of Snowdonia*, 1948 Crosby Lockwood ed. (London: Bodley Head, 1925)

J. Cleare and A. Smythe, *Rock Climbers in Action in Snowdonia* (London: Secker & Warburg, 1966)

T. Gifford (ed.), *The Climbers' Club Centenary Journal* (Climbers' Club, 1997)

A. Hankinson, *The Mountain Men* (London: William Heinemann, 1977)

T. Jones and G. Milburn, *Welsh Rock: 100 Years of Climbing in North Wales* (Glossop: Pic Publications, 1986)

G. Milburn, *Helyg* (Climbers' Club, 1985)

J. Soper, K. Wilson and P. Crew, *The Black Cliff: The History of Climbing on Clogwyn Du'r Arddu* (London: Kaye & Ward, 1971)

G. W. Young, G. Sutton and W. Noyce, *Snowdon Biography* (London: J. M. Dent, 1957)

SCOTLAND

D. J. Bennet (ed.), *The Munros*, 1991 ed. (Edinburgh: Scottish Mountaineering Trust, 1985)

W. D. Brooker (ed.), *A Century of Scottish Mountaineering* (Edinburgh: Scottish Mountaineering Trust, www.smc.org.uk/Publications, 1988)

W. H. Murray, *Highland Landscape* (Edinburgh: National Trust for Scotland, 1962)

OUTCROPS

E. Byne and G. Sutton, *High Peak* (London: Secker & Warburg, 1966)

J. Laycock, *Some Gritstone Climbs in Derbyshire and Elsewhere* (Manchester: 1913)

W. Unsworth, *The English Outcrops* (London: Victor Gollancz, 1964)

THE ALPS

T. Braham, *When the Alps Cast Their Spell* (Glasgow: The In Pinn, 2004)

C. E. Engel, *A History of Mountaineering in the Alps* (London: George Allen & Unwin, 1950)

F. Fleming, *Killing Dragons: The Conquest of the Alps*, 2001 ed. (London: Granta Books, 2000)

W. Unsworth, *North Face* (London: Hutchinson, 1969)

W. Unsworth, *Savage Snows: The Story of Mont Blanc* (London: Hodder & Stoughton, 1986)

W. Unsworth (ed.), *Peaks, Passes and Glaciers* (London: Allen Lane, 1981)

THE GREATER RANGES

J. Curran, *K2, Triumph and Tragedy* (London: Hodder & Stoughton, 1987)

A. Fanshawe and S. Venables, *Himalaya Alpine Style* (London: Hodder & Stoughton, 1995)

M. Isserman and S. Weaver, *Fallen Giants: A History of Himalayan Mountaineering From the Age of Empire to the Age of Extremes* (New Haven: Yale University Press, 2008)

K. Mason, *Abode of Snow*, 1987 Diadem ed. (London: Rupert Hart-Davis, 1955)

J. Morris, *Coronation Everest*, 1993 Boxtree ed. (London: Faber & Faber, 1958)

W. Unsworth, *Everest* (London: Allen Lane, 1981)

AUTOBIOGRAPHIES AND BIOGRAPHIES

A. Alvarez, *Feeding the Rat* (London: Bloomsbury, 2003)

J. R. L. Anderson, *High Mountains and Cold Seas: A Biography of H. W. Tilman* (London: Victor Gollancz, 1980)

G. Band, *Everest Exposed* (London: HarperCollins, 2003)

G. Birtles, *Alan Rouse: A Mountaineer's Life* (London: Unwin Hyman, 1987)

B. Blessed, *The Turquoise Mountain* (London: Bloomsbury, 1991)

P. Boardman, *The Shining Mountain*, 1996 Bâton Wicks ed. (London: Hodder & Stoughton, 1978)

P. Boardman, *Sacred Summits*, 1996 Bâton Wicks ed. (London: Hodder & Stoughton, 1982)

W. Bonatti, *The Mountains of My Life*, 2001 Modern Library ed. (New York: Random House, 1998)

C. Bonington, *I Chose to Climb*, 2001 Weidenfeld & Nicolson ed. (London: Victor Gollancz, 1966)

C. Bonington, *Annapurna South Face*, 1973 Penguin ed. (London: Cassell, 1971)

C. Bonington, *The Next Horizon*, 2001 Weidenfeld & Nicolson ed. (London: Victor Gollancz, 1973)

C. Bonington, *Everest the Hard Way* (London: Hodder & Stoughton, 1976)

C. Bonington, *The Everest Years*, 2001 Weidenfeld & Nicolson ed. (London: Hodder & Stoughton, 1986)

C. Bonington, *Mountaineer* (London: Diadem Books, 1989)

A. Borthwick, *Always a Little Further* (London: Faber & Faber, 1939)

D. Brown and I. Mitchell, *Mountain Days & Bothy Nights* (Edinburgh: Luath Press, 1987)

D. Brown and I. Mitchell, *A View From the Ridge* (Glasgow: Ernest Press, 1991)

J. Brown, *The Hard Years*, 1975 Penguin ed. (London: Victor Gollancz, 1967)

H. Buhl, *Nanga Parbat Pilgrimage: The Lonely Challenge*, 1998 Bâton Wicks ed. (London: Hodder & Stoughton, 1956)

A. Burgess and A. Burgess, *The Burgess Book of Lies* (Seattle: Cloudcap, 1994)

H. Calvert, *Smythe's Mountains: the Climbs of F. S. Smythe* (London: Victor Gollancz, 1985)

A. Cave, *Learning to Breathe* (London: Hutchinson, 2005)

F. S. Chapman, *Memoirs of a Mountaineer*, 1945 ed. (London: The Reprint Society, 1940)

G. Child, *Thin Air: Encounters in the Himalayas* (Seattle: The Mountaineers Books, 1988)

K. Chorley, *Manchester Made Them* (London: Faber & Faber, 1950)

J. N. Collie, *From the Himalaya to Skye*, 2003 Ripping Yarns ed. (Edinburgh: David Douglas, 1902)

J. Connor, *Creagh Dhu Climber: The Life and Times of John Cunningham* (Glasgow: Ernest Press, 1999)

J. Connor, *Dougal Haston: The Philosophy of Risk* (Edinburgh: Canongate, 2002)

M. Conway, *The Alps From End to End* (London: Constable, 1905)

M. Conway, *Mountain Memories: A Pilgrimage of Romance* (London: Cassell, 1920)

M. Conway, *Episodes in a Varied Life* (London: Country Life, 1932)

A. Crowley, *The Confessions of Aleister Crowley* (London: Mandrake Press, 1929)

J. Cruickshank, *High Endeavours: The Life and Legend of Robin Smith* (Edinburgh: Canongate, 2005)

J. Curran, *High Achiever: The Life and Climbs of Chris Bonington* (London: Constable & Robinson Ltd, 1999)

J. Curran, *The Middle-Aged Mountaineer* (London: Constable & Robinson Ltd, 2001)

S. Dean, *Hands of a Climber: A Life of Colin Kirkus* (Glasgow: Ernest Press, 1993)

M. Dickinson, *The Death Zone* (London: Hutchinson, 1997)

H. Drasdo, *The Ordinary Route* (Glasgow: Ernest Press, 1997)

E. Drummond, *A Dream of White Horses* (London: Bâton Wicks, 1997)

J. Evans, *The Conways* (London: Museum Press, 1966)

A. S. Eve and C. H. Creasey, *Life and Work of John Tyndall* (London: Macmillan, 1945)

G. I. Finch, *The Making of a Mountaineer*, 1988 ed. (Bristol: J. W. Arrowsmith, 1924)

J. D. Forbes, *Travels Through the Alps of Savoy*, 2nd ed. (Edinburgh: Adam and Charles Black, 1845)

M. Fowler, *Vertical Pleasure,* 2006 Bâton Wicks ed. (London: Hodder & Stoughton, 1995)

M. Fowler, *On Thin Ice* (London: Bâton Wicks, 2005)

P. French, *Younghusband*, 1995 Flamingo ed. (London: HarperCollins, 1994)

P. Gillman and L. Gillman, *The Wildest Dream* (London: Headline, 2000)

R. Graves, *Goodbye to All That*, 1960 Penguin ed. (London: Jonathan Cape, 1929)

D. Gray, *Rope Boy* (London: Victor Gollancz, 1970)

D. Gray, *Tight Rope* (Glasgow: Ernest Press, 1993)

D. Gray, *Slack* (Glasgow: Ernest Press, 1996)

R. Greene, *Moments of Being* (London: William Heinemann, 1974)

N. Gresham and T. Emmett, *Preposterous Tales* (Twickenham: Sam & Neil, 2005)

A. Hankinson, *Geoffrey Winthrop Young* (London: Hodder & Stoughton, 1995)

H. Harrer, *The White Spider*, 1995 Flamingo ed. (London: Rupert Hart-Davis, 1959)

D. Haston, *In High Places*, 1974 Arrow ed. (London: Cassell, 1972)

A. Heckmair, *Anderl Heckmair: My Life* (Seattle: The Mountaineers Books, 2002)

M. Herzog, *Annapurna*, 1997 Pimlico ed. (London: Jonathan Cape, 1952)

E. Hillary, *View From the Summit*, 2000 Corgi ed. (London: Doubleday, 1999)

J. Hunt, *The Ascent of Everest* (London: Hodder & Stoughton, 1953)

SELECTED BIBLIOGRAPHY

J. Hunt, *Life Is Meeting* (London: Hodder & Stoughton, 1978)

R. L. G. Irving, *The Romance of Mountaineering* (London: J. M. Dent, 1935)

S. Johnson, *A Journey to the Western Islands of Scotland*, 1984 Penguin Classic ed. (1775)

O. G. Jones, *Rock-Climbing in the English Lake District*, 1973 facsimile of 2nd ed. (Keswick: G. P. Abraham & Sons, 1900)

A. Kirkpatrick, *Psychovertical* (London: Hutchinson, 2008)

C. Kirkus, *Let's Go Climbing!* (London: Thomas Nelson, 1941)

J. Krakauer, *Into Thin Air*, 1998 Pan Books ed. (London: Macmillan, 1997)

T. Longstaff, *This My Voyage* (London: John Murray, 1950)

H. MacInnes, *Climb to the Lost World*, 1976 Penguin ed. (London: Hodder & Stoughton, 1974)

C. Mill, *Norman Collie: A Life in Two Worlds* (Aberdeen: Aberdeen University Press, 1987)

G. Moffat, *Space Below My Feet*, 1976 Penguin ed. (London: Hodder & Stoughton, 1961)

J. Moffat and N. Grimes, *Revelations* (Sheffield: Vertebrate Publishing, 2009)

M. Moran, *Alps 4000: 75 Peaks in 52 Days* (Newton Abbot: David & Charles, 1994)

N. Morin, *A Woman's Reach* (London: Eyre & Spottiswoode, 1968)

A. F. Mummery, *My Climbs in the Alps and Caucasus*, 2004 Ripping Yarns ed. (London: Fisher Unwin, 1895)

W. H. Murray, *Mountaineering in Scotland* (London: J. M. Dent, 1947)

W. H. Murray, *The Evidence of Things Not Seen* (London: Bâton Wicks, 2002)

E. Newby, *A Short Walk in the Hindu Kush*, 1981 Picador ed. (London: Secker & Warburg, 1958)

E. F. Norton, *The Fight for Everest: 1924* (London: Edward Arnold, 1925)

P. Nunn, *At the Sharp End* (London: Unwin Hyman, 1988)

T. Patey, *One Man's Mountains*, 1997 Canongate ed. (London: Victor Gollancz, 1971)

W. Peascod, *Journey After Dawn* (London: Butler & Tanner, 1985)

J. Perrin, *Menlove: The Life of John Menlove Edwards* (London: Victor Gollancz, 1985)

J. Perrin, *The Villain: The Life of Don Whillans* (London: Random House, 2005)

J. Perrin, *The Climbing Essays* (Glasgow: The In Pinn, 2006)

D. Pilley, *Climbing Days*, 1989 Hogarth Press ed. (London: G. Bell & Sons, 1935)

P. Pritchard, *Deep Play* (London: Bâton Wicks, 1997)

P. Pritchard, *The Totem Pole* (London: Constable & Robinson Ltd, 1999)

G. Rebuffat, *Starlight and Storm* (London: J. M. Dent, 1956)

D. Rose and E. Douglas, *Regions of the Heart: The Triumph and Tragedy of Alison Hargreaves* (London: Penguin, 1999)

V. Saunders, *No Place to Fall* (London: Hodder & Stoughton, 1994)

D. Scott, *Himalayan Climber* (London: Diadem, 1992)

D. Scott and A. MacIntyre, *Shisha Pangma: The Alpine-Style First Ascent of the South-West Face* (London: Bâton Wicks, 2000)

E. Shipton, *Nanda Devi*, 1997 Diadem ed. (London: Hodder & Stoughton, 1936)

E. Shipton, *Blank on the Map*, 1997 Diadem ed. (London: Hodder & Stoughton, 1938)

E. Shipton, *Upon That Mountain*, 1997 Diadem ed. (London: Hodder & Stoughton, 1943)

E. Shipton, *Mountains of Tartary*, 1997 Diadem ed. (London: Hodder & Stoughton, 1950)

E. Shipton, *The Mount Everest Reconnaissance Expedition 1951*, 1997 Diadem ed. (London: Hodder & Stoughton, 1951)

E. Shipton, *Land of Tempest,* 1997 Diadem ed. (London: Hodder & Stoughton, 1963)

E. Shipton, *That Untravelled World* (London: Hodder & Stoughton, 1969)

J. Simpson, *Touching the Void* (London: Jonathan Cape, 1988)

J. Simpson, *This Game of Ghosts* (London: Jonathan Cape, 1993)

J. Simpson, *Storms of Silence* (London: Jonathan Cape, 1996)

J. Simpson, *Dark Shadows Falling* (London: Jonathan Cape, 1997)

M. Slesser, *Red Peak* (London: Hodder & Stoughton, 1964)

M. Slesser, *With Friends in High Places* (Edinburgh: Mainstream Publishing, 2004)

W. C. Slingsby, *Norway: The Northern Playground*, 2003 Ripping Yarns ed. (Edinburgh: David Douglas, 1904)

F. S. Smythe, *Climbs and Ski Runs*, 2000 Bâton Wicks ed. (Edinburgh: Blackwood, 1929)

SELECTED BIBLIOGRAPHY

F. S. Smythe, *The Kangchenjunga Adventure*, 2000 Bâton Wicks ed. (London: Victor Gollancz, 1930)

F. S. Smythe, *Kamet Conquered*, 2000 Bâton Wicks ed. (London: Victor Gollancz, 1932)

F. S. Smythe, *Camp Six*, 2000 Baton Wicks ed. (London: Hodder & Stoughton, 1937)

F. S. Smythe, *The Valley of Flowers*, 2000 Bâton Wicks ed. (London: Hodder & Stoughton, 1938)

F. S. Smythe, *Mountaineering Holiday*, 2000 Bâton Wicks ed. (London: Hodder & Stoughton, 1940)

F. S. Smythe, *Edward Whymper* (London: Hodder & Stoughton, 1940)

P. Steele, *Eric Shipton: Everest and Beyond* (London: Constable, 1998)

L. Stephen, *The Playground of Europe*, 1936 Blackwell ed. (London: Longmans, Green, 1871)

L. Stephen, *Some Early Impressions* (London: Hogarth, 1924)

J. Tasker, *Everest the Cruel Way*, 1996 Bâton Wicks ed. (London: Methuen, 1981)

J. Tasker, *Savage Arena*, 1996 Bâton Wicks ed. (London: Methuen, 1982)

H. W. Tilman, *Snow on the Equator*, 1997 Diadem ed. (London: G. Bell & Sons, 1937)

H. W. Tilman, *The Ascent of Nanda Devi*, 1997 Diadem ed. (Cambridge University Press, 1937)

H. W. Tilman, *When Men and Mountains Meet*, 1997 Diadem ed. (Cambridge University Press, 1946)

H. W. Tilman, *Everest 1938*, 1997 Diadem ed. (Cambridge University Press, 1948)

H. W. Tilman, *Two Mountains and a River*, 1997 Diadem ed. (Cambridge University Press, 1949)

H. W. Tilman, *China to Chitral*, 1997 Diadem ed. (Cambridge University Press, 1951)

H. W. Tilman, *Nepal Himalaya*, 1997 Diadem ed. (Cambridge University Press, 1952)

K. Treacher, *Siegfried Herford: An Edwardian Rock-Climber* (Glasgow: Ernest Press, 2000)

S. Venables, *A Slender Thread* (London: Hutchinson, 2000)

S. Venables, *Higher Than the Eagle Soars* (London: Arrow Books, 2007)

D. Whillans and A. Ormerod, *Don Whillans: Portrait of a Mountaineer* (London: William Heinemann, 1971)

E. Whymper, *Scrambles Amongst the Alps*, 1985 Century ed. (London: John Murray, 1871)

A. Wills, *Wanderings Amongst the High Alps*, 1937 Blackwell ed. (London: R. Bentley, 1856)

W. Windham, *An Account of the Glaciers or Ice Alps in Savoy*, AC Tracts 388 ed. (London: Peter Martel, 1741)

S. Yates, *Against the Wall* (London: Vintage, 1998)

S. Yates, *The Flame of Adventure* (London: Vintage, 2002)

G. W. Young, *On High Hills*, 1947 5th ed. (London: Methuen, 1927)

SELECTED ARTICLES

J. V. Anthoine, 'The British Ogre Expedition', *Alpine Journal* 83 (1978)

S. Ashton, 'Guide Books in British Climbing', *High* 40 (1986)

C. Barrington, 'The First Ascent of the Eiger', *Alpine Journal* 11 (1883)

P. Bicknell, 'The Picturesque, the Sublime and the Beautiful', *Alpine Journal* 85 (1980)

W. Birkett, 'Talking With Jim Birkett', *Climber & Rambler* 21, 8 (1982)

W. Birkett, 'Pete Whillance', *Climber & Rambler* 22, 5 (1983)

T. S. Blakeney, 'Whymper and Mummery', *Alpine Journal* 57 (1950)

T. S. Blakeney, 'The Alpine Journal and its Editors: 1927–53', *Alpine Journal* 81 (1976)

A. W. Bridge, 'Prelude', *Climbers' Club Journal* IX, 74 (1949)

W. D. Brooker et al., 'The Incomparable Dr. Patey', *Climber* 26, 5 (1987)

G. B. Bryant, 'The Formation of the Climbers' Club', *Climbers' Club Journal* I, 1 (1898)

D. Busk, 'The Young Shavers', *Mountain* 54 (1977)

M. Campbell, 'A Profile of John Redhead', *Climber* 25, 11 (1986)

H. R. C. Carr, '1919 – C. F. Holland's Year', *Climbers' Club Journal*, 102 (1981)

J. Cartwright, 'Ama Dablam', *Alpine Journal* 107 (2002)

M. Conway, 'Centrists and Excentrists', *Alpine Journal* 15 (1891)

M. Conway, 'Some Reminiscences and Reflections of an Old Stager', *Alpine Journal* 31 (1917)

D. Cook, 'The Mountaineer and Society', *Mountain* 34 (1974)

D. Cox, 'The Life and Times of Geoffrey Winthrop Young', *Mountain* 47 (1976)

D. Cox, 'Early Years', *Alpine Journal* 85 (1980)

S. H. Cross, 'Climbing Memories', *Rucksack Club Journal* XIV 2, 54 (1961)

D. F. O. Dangar and T. S. Blakeney, 'The Rise of Modern Mountaineering 1854–65', *Alpine Journal* 62 (1957)

S. Dean, 'John Syrett', *Climber* 35, 8 (1996)

C. T. Dent, 'Two Attempts on the Aiguille du Dru', *Alpine Journal* 7 (1876)

C. T. Dent, 'The History of an Ascent of the Aiguille du Dru', *Alpine Journal* 9 (1878)

C. T. Dent, 'Alpine Climbs – Past, Present and Future', *Alpine Journal* 9 (1880)

E. Douglas, 'Fast Burn Fuse', *Climber* 37, 2 (1998)

E. Douglas, 'The Morality of Risk', *Alpine Journal* 104 (1999)

E. Douglas, 'The Vertical Century', *Climber* 39, 1 (2000)

E. Douglas, 'Cafe Society', *Climber* 40, 11 (2001)

E. Douglas, 'The Art of Strong: Malcolm Smith', *Climber* 42, 2 (2003)

C. Gamble, 'John Ruskin, Eugene Viollet-Le-Duc and the Alps', *Alpine Journal* 104 (1999)

D. Gray, 'Confessions of a Parvenu', *Alpine Journal* 107 (2002)

N. Grimes, 'That's Me: George Smith', *Summit* 53 (2009)

F. C. Grove, 'The Comparative Skill of Travellers and Guides', *Alpine Journal* 5 (1870)

A. Hankinson, 'Aleister Crowley: How Beastly Was He Really?' *Climber & Rambler* 18, 11 (1979)

P. Harding, 'A Rock Climbing Apprenticeship', *Rucksack Club Journal* XIV 2, 54 (1961)

A. B. Hargreaves and K. Smith, 'Maurice Linnell', *Climber & Rambler* 20, 12 (1981)

J. Hunt, 'Mountaineering and Risk', *Alpine Journal* 86 (1981)

W. Inglis Clark, 'The Motor in Mountaineering', *Scottish Mountaineering Club Journal* VII (1903)

R. L. G. Irving, 'Five Years With Recruits', *Alpine Journal* 24 (1909)

R. L. G. Irving, 'Unclouded Days, 1901–1914', *Alpine Journal* 62 (1957)

C. T. Jones, 'The Late Fifties: A Personal Account', *Climbers' Club Journal* XV, 96 (1973)

H. M. Kelly, J. H. Doughty et al., '100 Years of Rock-Climbing in the Lake District', *Fell and Rock Climbing Club Journal* XXIV(2), 70 (1986)

J. Longland, 'Between the Wars, 1919–39', *Alpine Journal* 62 (1957)

J. Longland, 'The Once-Upon-A-Time Pen y Pass', *Mountain* 123 (1988)

A. Lunn, 'In Defence of Popular Writing', *Climbers' Club Journal* 2 (1913)

A. Lunn, 'Whymper Again', *Alpine Journal* 17 (1966)

A. Lunn, 'The Playground of Europe 1871 to 1971: A Centenary Tribute to Leslie Stephen', *Alpine Journal* 77 (1972)

E. MacAskill, 'Creagh Dhu', *Climber & Rambler* 17, 3 and 4 (1978)

E. MacAskill, 'Portrait of Jock Nimlin', *Climber & Rambler* 22, 9 (1983)

D. MacLeod, 'Echo Wall', *John Muir Trust Journal* 46 (2009)

G. Mallory, 'Mont Blanc from the Col du Géant by the Eastern Buttress of Mont Maudit', *Alpine Journal* 32 (1918)

C. E. Mathews, 'The Growth of Mountaineering', *Alpine Journal* 10 (1882)

C. M. Mathews, 'On Climbing Books', *Climbers' Club Journal* I, 1 (1912)

R. Messner, 'Murder of the Impossible', *Mountain* 15 (1971)

J. Millar, 'Hard Days, Easy Days', *Climber* 30, 9 (1991)

W. H. Murray, 'Scotland: The 1930s', *Mountain* 98 (1984)

L. J. Oppenheimer, 'Wastdale Head at Easter', *Climbers' Club Journal* II, 5 (1899)

J. Perrin, 'Pat Littlejohn', *Climber & Rambler* 21, 3 (1982)

J. Perrin, 'The Essential Jack Longland', *Mountain* 123 (1988)

J. Perrin, 'In the Big Holes', *Climber* 29, 10 (1990)

H. E. L. Porter, 'After the Matterhorn, 1865–80', *Alpine Journal* 62 (1957)

J. Porter, 'Reverse Polish', *Mountain* 60 (1978)

P. Pritchard, 'Hammering the Anvil', *Alpine Journal* 100 (1995)

A. K. Rawlinson, 'Crescendo, 1939–1956', *Alpine Journal* 62 (1957)

H. V. Reade, 'Unjustifiable Climbs', *Climbers' Club Journal* VI, 21 (1903)

J. Redhead, 'Alternative Slate', *Climber* 25, 11 (1986)

K. Reynolds, 'Because It's There – and All That', *Alpine Journal* 83 (1978)

A. Rouse, 'Jannu', *Alpine Journal* 85 (1980)

A. Rouse, 'Changing Values', *Alpine Journal* 90 (1985)

C. Rowland, J. Perrin and C. Bonington, 'Remembering Mo', *Climber* 28, 10 (1989)

S. Richardson, 'Scottish Winter Climbing: The Last 50 Years', *Alpine Journal* 112 (2007)

D. Scott, 'Resisting the Appeasers', *Alpine Journal* 112 (2007)

Shih Chan-Chun, 'The Conquest of Mount Everest By the Chinese Mountaineering Team', *Alpine Journal* 66 (1961)

K. Smith, 'Epitaph to a Cragsman: A Profile of Claude Deane Frankland', *Climber & Rambler* 17, 2 (1978)

K. Smith, 'Who Was J. I. Roper?' *Climber & Rambler* 17, 6 (1978)

K. Smith, 'A Portrait of A. T. Hargreaves', *Climber & Rambler* 18, 6 (1979)

K. Smith, 'The Improbable Leader: The Tragic Career of Bert Gross', *Climber & Rambler* 20, 5 (1981)

K. Smith, 'J. Menlove Edwards', *Climber & Rambler* 22, 11 (1983)

L. Stephen, 'Review of Scrambles Amongst the Alps', *Alpine Journal* 5 (1872)

E. L. Strutt, 'Presidential Valedictory Address', *Alpine Journal* 50 (1938)

J. Tasker, 'Kangchenjunga North Ridge 1979', *Alpine Journal* 85 (1980)

M. Thompson, 'Out With the Boys Again', *Mountain* 50 (1976)

P. Twomey, 'John Redhead', *On The Edge* 78 (1998)

T. Waghorn and C. Bonington, 'A Tribute to Don', *Climber and Rambler* 24, 10 (1985)

D. Walker, 'The Evolution of Climbing Clubs in Britain', *Alpine Journal* 109 (2004)

M. Ward, 'Rab', *Climber* 35, 6 (1996)

E. A. M. Wedderburn, 'A Short History of Scottish Climbing From 1918 to the Present Day', *Scottish Mountaineering Club Journal* XXII (1939)

J. B. West, 'A. M. Kellas: Pioneer Himalayan Physiologist and Mountaineer', *Alpine Journal* 94 (1989)

W. Weston, 'Mountaineering in the Southern Alps of Japan', *Alpine Journal* 23 (1907)

A. Wills, 'The Passage of the Fenêtre de Salena', *Peaks, Passes and Glaciers* 1 (1859)

G. W. Young, 'Mountain Prophets', *Alpine Journal* 54 (1949)

G. W. Young, 'Club and Climbers 1880–1900', *Alpine Journal* 62 (1957)

SOCIAL AND CULTURAL HISTORY

P. Bartlett, *The Undiscovered Country: The Reason We Climb* (Glasgow: Ernest Press, 1993)

P. Bicknell, *Beauty, Horror and Immensity: Picturesque Landscape in Britain, 1750–1850* (Cambridge University Press, 1981)

E. Burke, *A Philosophical Enquiry*, 2008 Oxford University Press ed. (1757)

K. Clark, *Landscape Into Art* (London: John Murray, 1949)

P. Coates, *Nature: Western Attitudes Since Ancient Times* (Cambridge: Polity Press, 1998)

D. Craig, *Native Stones* (London: Pimlico, 1995)

D. W. Crawford, 'The Aesthetics of Nature and the Environment', in P. Kivy (ed.), *Aesthetics* (Oxford: Blackwell, 2005)

R. Graves and A. Hodge, *The Long Weekend: A Social History of Great Britain 1918–1939*, 1971 Penguin ed. (London: Faber & Faber, 1940)

P. H. Hansen, 'British Mountaineering 1850–1914' (PhD, Harvard, 1991)

R. Macfarlane, *Mountains of the Mind* (London: Granta Books, 2003)

M. H. Nicolson, *Mountain Gloom and Mountain Glory*, 1997 Washington University ed. (Cornell University Press, 1959)

B. Rothman, *The 1932 Kinder Trespass* (Altrincham: Willow Publishing, 1982)

J. Ruskin, *Modern Painters Volume IV: Of Mountain Beauty*, 1897 George Allen ed. (London: Smith Elder, 1856)

J. Ruskin, *Sesame and Lilies*, 2008 Arc Manor ed. (1865)

S. Schama, *Landscape and Memory* (New York: Alfred A. Knopf, Inc., 1995)

F. Spufford, *I May Be Some Time*, 2003 ed. (London: Faber & Faber, 1996)

K. Thomas, *Man and the Natural World: Changing Attitudes in England 1500–1800* (London: Penguin, 1983)

A. Trollope, *Travelling Sketches* (London: Chapman & Hall, 1866)

B. Willey, *The Eighteenth Century Background: Studies on the Idea of Nature in the Thought of the Period*, 1972 Pelican ed. (London: Penguin, 1940)

REPORTED INTERVIEWS

P. Boardman, *Crags* 4 (1976)

John Cunningham, *Mountain* 14 (1971)

John Dunne, *Summit* 41 (2006)

Ron Fawcett, *Crags* 3 (1976)

OBITUARIES

The Late Principal Forbes, *Alpine Journal* 4 (1870)

Thomas Woodbine Hinchcliff, *Alpine Journal* 11 (1884)

A. W. Moore, *Alpine Journal* 13 (1888)

John Ball, *Alpine Journal* 14 (1889)

Thomas Stuart Kennedy, *Alpine Journal* 17 (1895)

A. F. Mummery, *Alpine Journal* 17 (1895)

John Tyndall, *Alpine Journal* 17 (1895)

John Hopkinson, *Alpine Journal* 19 (1899)

O. G. Jones, *Alpine Journal* 19 (1899)

E. S. Kennedy, *Alpine Journal* 19 (1899)

J. Oakley Maund, *Alpine Journal* 21 (1903)

Richard Pendlebury, *Alpine Journal* 21 (1903)

Charles Edward Mathews, *Alpine Journal* 22 (1905)

C. E. Mathews, *Climbers' Club Journal* VIII, 30 (1905)

Sir Leslie Stephen, *Alpine Journal* 22 (1905)

Horace Walker, *Alpine Journal* 24 (1909)

Edward Whymper, *Alpine Journal* 26 (1912)

Clinton Thomas Dent, *Alpine Journal* 27 (1913)

J. M. Archer Thomson, *Climbers' Club Journal* I, 2 (1913)

Rt. Hon. Sir Alfred Wills, *Alpine Journal* 27 (1913)

William Edward Davidson, *Alpine Journal* 35 (1923)

Thomas Middlemore, *Alpine Journal* 35 (1923)

G. D. Abraham, *Climbers' Club Journal* VI 3, 67 (1941)

Colin Kirkus, *Climbers' Club Journal* VII 2, 69 (1943)

Charles Granville Bruce, *Himalayan Journal* XIII (1946)

John Norman Collie, *Himalayan Journal* XIII (1946)

Sir Francis Younghusband, *Himalayan Journal* XIII (1946)

C. W. F. Noyce, *Alpine Journal* 67 (1962)

Hugh Ruttledge, *Alpine Journal* 67 (1962)

Charles Kenneth Howard-Bury, *Alpine Journal* 69 (1964)

Tom Longstaff, *Alpine Journal* 69 (1964)

C. F. Holland, *Fell & Rock Climbing Club Journal* 21, 60 (1968)

Thomas Walton Patey, *Scottish Mountaineering Club Journal* XXIX, 162 (1971)

Alfred William Bridge, *Climbers' Club Journal* XVI, 96 (1974)

Peter Biven, *Alpine Journal* 82 (1977)

Dougal Haston, *Alpine Journal* 83 (1978)

Sir Percy Wyn Harris, *Climber & Rambler* 18, 11 (1979)

H. W. Tilman, *Mountain* 66 (1979)

H. M. Kelly, *Climber and Rambler* 19, 5 (1980)

A. S. Pigott, *Alpine Journal* 85 (1980)

Al Harris, *Climber & Rambler* 20, 12 (1981)

Joseph Thomas Tasker, *Climber & Rambler* 21, 8 (1982)

Alex MacIntyre, *Climber & Rambler* 21, 12 (1982)

Alex MacIntyre, *Alpine Journal* 88 (1983)

Joe Tasker, *Alpine Journal* 88 (1983)

John Syrett, *Climber & Rambler* 24, 8 (1985)

Roger Baxter Jones, *Climber & Rambler* 24, 11 (1985)

Nea Morin, *Alpine Journal* 92 (1987)

Alan Rouse, *Alpine Journal* 92 (1987)

Captain John Baptist Lucius Noel, *Mountain* 128 (1989)

J. B. L. Noel, *Climber* 28, 5 (1989)

Jack Longland, *High* 135 (1994)

Nat Allen, *High* 153 (1995)

Sir Charles Evans, *Climber* 35, 2 (1996)

Paul Nunn, *Alpine Journal* 101 (1996)

Sir Charles Evans, *Alpine Journal* 102 (1997)

Alan Bennet Hargreaves, *Alpine Journal* 102 (1997)

Ivan Waller, *Alpine Journal* 102 (1997)

Peter Livesey, *Climber* 37, 5 (1998)

FICTION

W. E. Bowman, *The Ascent of Rum Doodle* (London: Max Parrish, 1956)

E. Coxhead, *One Green Bottle* (London: Faber & Faber, 1950)

D. Haston, *Calculated Risk* (London: Diadem, 1979)

L. Rees and A. Harris, *Take It to the Limit* (London: Diadem, 1981)

INDEX